Historical
Geography
of the
Holy Land

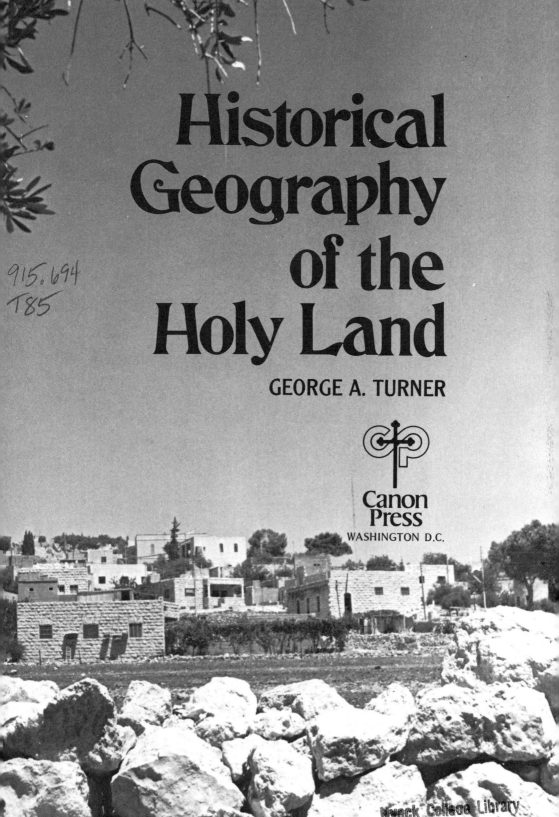

Historical Geography of the Holy Land

GEORGE A. TURNER

Canon Press
WASHINGTON D.C.

#5393772

Contents

List of Maps

List of Illustrations

Illustration Credits

Preface

The Holy Land—the narrow land bridge linking Africa, Europe, and Asia—remains a focal point of global significance. It has several names. "Land of Canaan" commemorates its inhabitants prior to the coming of the Israelites. The term "Palestine" honors the Philistines, who migrated from the Greek islands to the southeast coastal area of Palestine during the twelfth century B.C. It also was called the "Land of Israel" since the establishment of the kingdom there under King Saul and King David. From the Roman period until modern times, it was known as a part of "Syria." But to Abraham and his descendants it remains "The Promised Land." "Palestine" is the name still most widely used, although there are voices today that say this name is no longer applicable—given the choice neither the Arab nor the Jew would choose this name.

Palestine is the most coveted real estate on the globe. It is desirable not so much for its intrinsic wealth as for its historical associations and strategic location. But the importance of this area from the standpoint of history, politics, and religion is not self-evident. Visitors today are often disappointed in this aspect, as was Hiram of Tyre three millennia ago (1 Kings 9:11-13). From time immemorial Palestine has been the scene of constant struggle for occupancy by its neighbors. The first invaders known to history were the Sumerians from Mesopotamia. Then the Egyptians were its masters from the Pyramid Age (2800-2600 B.C.) until the time of the patriarchs, roughly a millennium. Amorites from the north were dominant after this (Gen. 15:16). The Hyksos from the north were in the ascendency thereafter. Pharaohs of the New Kingdom reasserted their claim to the Land of Canaan after this. Hebrews (from the east) and Philistines (from the west) contended for dominance for two centuries (c. 1200-1000 B.C.). After 331 B.C., Western influence was in the ascendancy, first by the Greeks and followed by the Romans and Byzantines. This period lasted until the Moslem invasion in the seventh century A.D. Moslem influence from the east prevailed until the second decade of the twentieth century, when the British and the

x

French came from the west followed by the Zionists. The exception to this was the two-century period (A.D. 1090-1290) when Islam was challenged by the Knights of the Cross. Therefore Palestine has been a "bone of contention" from the south, the north, the west, and the east—and now the west again—through the millennia of its turbulent history. Today the issue remains joined: the Orient (Arabs) and the Occident (Jews) both demand the dominant role in the Holy Land.

Linked with this military history is the political history of Palestine. This area has always been a buffer zone. Seldom has Palestine enjoyed true independence. Its limited resources continually made it dependent upon the favor of one or more of its more powerful neighbors. Even during the "golden age" of David and Solomon, its wealth lay in its control of trade routes; and its building operations were dependent on Phoenician timber and craftsmen. This dependence is evident today in the rivalry between Russia from the north and America from the west, one championing Israel and the other supporting the Arabs. Whereas many areas of the globe have had their periods of strength and decline, such as Central America and Spain, Palestine has been a constant zone of tension and the focus of vast international ambitions and struggles. Two movements out of these centuries of turbulence emerged to influence the entire world: Judaism and Christianity.

The importance of Palestine from the standpoint of religion is obvious. No other portion of the globe can appropriately be called "The Holy Land." Jews look to it as their historic homeland. Christians are intrigued by it as the place where Jesus and His followers "wrought and taught" and the base from which the influence of the Christian religion spread to all parts of the globe. The Moslems regard it as holy—second only to Mecca and Medina in the Arabian peninsula, their national homeland. They consider their leader and founder the last and most important of a series of prophets shared in common by Jews and Christians. Thus the three monotheistic (and hence universal) faiths among all the religions of mankind claim the Holy Land as the focus of their origins and aspirations.

The transliteration of Hebrew and Arabic names is always a problem. Few sources spell these names alike. Often one place has several names or the same name with three or four ways to spell it. The map that has been followed with reference to spelling is *The Survey of Israel* (1961, 1967). For Biblical sites, usually the spelling of the Revised Standard Version has been decisive. Scripture quotations are those of the Revised Standard Version, 1946-52, unless otherwise indicated (e.g., JB—Jerusalem Bible). References to Josephus are from the Whiston edition because it is more widely accessible than the Loeb edition.

Not all of the Bible lands are included in this survey—only that portion commonly called the Holy Land or Palestine. It has seemed best to concentrate on the areas most relevant from the Biblical and historical point of view. Not all will agree with this decision. But the experience of ancient Israelites in the Sinai area receive greater stress in Biblical literature than their occupancy of the lands east of the Jordan. The areas excluded are not unimportant, but self-imposed limits of space permit a detailed study only of lands west of the Jordan.

In a work such as this, indebtedness to others is considerable. For their assistance in finding valuable resources, my gratitude extends to Leslie Hunt, Principal of Wycliffe College (Toronto), who made my month's residence there pleasant and profitable; to Joan Winearls, Map Librarian for the Department of Geography at the University of Toronto; to G. Douglas Tushingham, Chief Archaeologist at the Royal Ontario Museum (Toronto); and to the library staffs of Lexington Theological Seminary and Asbury Theological Seminary.

Asbury Theological Seminary provided the six-month sabbatical leave that permitted the time for concentrated research and writing. The American School of Oriental Research in Jerusalem welcomed me as an Honorary Associate for residence; their field trips and library faculties were exceedingly helpful. A summer workshop in Israel, sponsored by New York University and led by Abraham Katsh, proved invaluable. The invitation by Joseph Free to study and lecture at the Near East School of Archaeology in Jerusalem is appreciated.

Among those who have read the manuscript and offered helpful suggestions are my colleagues and former students, Professor G. Herbert Livingston and Loal Ames. The services of the typists, especially Sherrill Yardy, are remembered with gratitude. Joseph James spent a vacation period providing editorial assistance. Students and pilgrims who were my companions on ten study tours of the Holy Land since 1953 provided stimulus and many helpful insights. The encouragement and counsel of Cornelius Zylstra, of Baker Book House, has been invaluable from the time the project was presented to him several years ago.

Introduction

At the outset of a study of the history and geography of the Holy Land a survey of available material is appropriate. Today's student is fortunate in that he can pursue his interest in this subject from a wealth of competent sources. There is an abundance of pertinent information concerning present-day Israel with an appreciative look to its long past. The *Macmillan Bible Atlas* provides an excellent survey of Israel's history up to the second century A.D., giving particular attention to the military campaigns of the area. *The New Israel Atlas* by Zev Vilnay is another source of helpful information. Unexcelled for its pictures is the *Atlas* of Gröllenberg. Among the more useful is the Filson-Wright *Westminster Bible Atlas*, 1946 and 1956. In a somewhat different format with emphasis on pictures rather than maps is the *Zondervan Pictorial Bible Atlas*, edited by E. M. Blaiklock (1969). *The Oxford Bible Atlas* 1962), edited by H. G. May is among the best. Similar in treatment is the *Rand McNally Bible Atlas* with its briefer volume, *Atlas of the Holy Land*, dated 1956 and 1959 respectively, both edited by E. G. Kraeling. H. H. Rowley is editor of *New Atlas of the Bible* (Doubleday, 1969), a survey of Biblical history, profusely illustrated. The eastern Mediterranean world with text and superb photography is covered by Denis Baly, *Atlas of the Biblical World*, (New York: World Publishing Co., 1971).

Books dealing with the relationship between the land and the event include the *Wycliffe Historical Geography of Bible Lands*, edited by Pfeiffer and Vos (Moody Press, 1967). This is noteworthy for the wide extent of the Bible lands covered: from Iran to Italy. Especially valuable for its detailed scholarship is Y. Aharoni, *The Land of the Bible* (London, 1968), with detailed and ample documentation of the history of the land up to the Exile and the Persian period. M. Avi-Yonah, *The Holy Land* (Baker, 1966) tells the story from the Persian to the Arab conquest, sixth century B.C. to the seventh century A.D. Avi-Yonah also edits the copiously illustrated *History of the Holy Land* (Macmillan, 1969) from antiquity to 1968.

One that is deservedly popular is that by Denis Baly, *The Geography of the Bible* (Harper's, 1957). This treatment is especially effective from the standpoint of geology and meteorology together with the appropriate Scripture selections. Inspired by George Adam Smith's *Historical Geography*, J. H. Kitchen wrote *Holy Fields* (Eerdmans, 1955), reflecting his visit to the Holy Land and his longtime interest in that subject. Emphasis on the geography of the area is reflected in E. Orni and E. Efrav, *Geography of Israel* (Jerusalem, 1964, 1970). More detailed and still valuable is F. M. Abel, *Geographie de la Palestine* (Paris, 1938). For detail and perspective, this is excellent in its field.

The most influential single treatment of the subject was written by George Adam Smith. It has gone through several editions, and even now it is still available through Harper in paperback. The popularity of this treatment is due to its unsurpassed verbal pictures of the land together with a scholar's discrimination and erudition. Whereas most treatments of the subject pursue the matter in terms of history, particularly Bible history, Smith's volume takes the country section by section, and brings to bear upon each section the influence of events upon that place. Precedent for this may be found in Edward Robinson's *Biblical Researches*, growing out of two extended trips to the Holy Land, in 1838 and again in 1852. Both Robinson and Smith traversed the land by mule and horseback during the days of Ottoman rule. Though they covered less territory and did not have cameras as we have today, the area they did command, both by observation and a knowledge of the records of their predecessors, enabled them to recreate the scenes with great effectiveness, their powers of observation accentuated by the very lack of the cameras the modern tourist finds so indispensable. A continuing source of invaluable information is the *Survey of Western Palestine*, edited by C. R. Conder and H. H. Kitchener and published by the Palestine Exploration Fund (London: 1883) in eight large volumes plus maps.

Another fertile source of information concerning the land of the Bible is the plethora of pilgrims' itineraries. The value of these eye-witness reports is their aid in identifying sites, and their witness to existing situations at the time of their visits. These extend from the Pilgrim of Bordeaux in the fourth century, to such modern "pilgrims" as Harry Emerson Fosdick and Norman Vincent Peale in this century. Especially welcome is the republication in thirteen volumes of the Palestine Pilgrims' Text Society by AMS Press, New York, 1971, of the 1883-1897 London edition. Noteworthy is the attractive *Pilgrims to the Holy Land* by Kollek and Pearlman (Harper and Row, 1970) which surveys pilgrimages over three millennia of history.

The impressions made upon the visitor to the Holy Land are so powerful that he is normally impelled to report it either by travelog, picture, illustrated lectures, or publishing a book. This gives him an opportunity to share his inspirations, and it is often prized by those who like to participate in his experience vicariously, as compensation for their own lack of opportunity for a similar experience.

The question arises whether another venture is justified in view of the wealth of material available. Some of these volumes mentioned do not take the reader through the events up to the present time. One of the most valuable leaves the reader at the sixth century B.C. Another stresses geography at the expense of history, whereas others stress history at the expense of geography. Numerous guidebooks are helpful in spelling out the details of itineraries, but their treatment of necessity must be fragmentary. Some of the older geographies were written before the British Mandate or the founding of the state of Israel.

The present volume seeks a synthesis. The plan is not that of following Bible history as such, as is done in most historical atlases. Rather, the plan is to take the land section by section, as did George Adam Smith, and bring to bear upon that section the sequence and significance of historic events. It thus seeks a middle road between the traveler's detailed itinerary and a volume on Bible history.

As designed by the author and publisher, a fourfold purpose is envisioned: 1) It may be used as a reference work. The text itself is often concise, but the Scriptural references and the footnotes will assist the reader to pursue the sources cited for further information. (2) It is designed as a textbook for courses on the history and geography of the Holy Land in Bible schools, colleges, and seminaries. (3) It will be useful for tour agencies and their clients. Their "pilgrimage" in Bible lands will be more meaningful as they are helped to bring into focus the ancient, medieval, and modern events that are linked with a specific site. (4) Preachers, church school teachers, and other readers will find this a helpful companion in Bible study and exposition. In other words, it seeks to bring together in a composite whole or synthesis the place and the event, with special reference to its bearing upon the message of the Bible. The overall purpose is to illumine the pages of Scripture. Thus, it should serve to provide the Bible reader with a "third dimension" to his comprehension of the text. To illustrate: as a Bible student reads of Samuel's circuit from Mizpah to Ramah to Gilgal, it is helpful if he can have a mental picture of the terrain and of the events linked with these historic sites. Likewise, in Jesus' itinerary from Nazareth through Cana to Capernaum, the additional light thrown on the place by the events that occurred there before and since the Scriptural account does much to enrich the Biblical record. Travelers to the Holy Land report that the experience is like reading a fifth gospel. Whether to enrich such an experience or to serve in the place of one, it is hoped that this volume will be beneficial.

GEORGE ALLEN TURNER
Asbury Theological Seminary

The southern end of the Sea of Galilee (Lake Tiberias) where the Jordan River leaves the lake. The mountains of Syria are in the background.

1

Topographical Survey

The task is that of synchronizing history and geography, of correlating time, place, and event. History and geography is best learned in connection with the topography of the land, including the hills, the valleys, the waterways, and the highways. The Bible records two individuals who were granted a panoramic view of the entire area. From the vantage point of a hill between "Bethel on the west and Ai on the east," Abraham was invited to look over the whole land—north, south, east, and west. For the Lord said, "All the land which you see I will give to you and to your descendants for ever" (Gen. 13: 14, 15). Since there are hills to the north that were higher than Abraham's campsite, much of the patriarch's perspective was in his imagination. In a second episode, Moses from the top of Mount Nebo, east of the northern edge of the Dead Sea, is said to have viewed "all the land of Judah as far as the Western Sea, the Negeb, and the Plain, that is, the valley of Jericho the city of palm trees, as far as Zoar" (Deut. 34:1-3). It is hard for the spectator to grasp the full significance of this tiny land in its bearing upon the history of mankind. On perhaps no other section of the globe has there been concentrated so much of importance to human history as on this land bridge between Asia and Africa. It has been and continues to be a "zone of tension." Through the millennia the land has witnessed a succession of struggles for its mastery, and the Scriptures envision in this place the final struggle of mankind (Rev. 16:16; 20:8; cf. Ezek. 39:4).

The Promised Land

1

GEOLOGY

It is important to note not only what lies on the surface but also the structure below the surface. Millions of years ago most of this area was covered by an ocean, which the geologists called "Tethys." Gradually the land rose and the ocean subsided approximately to the present shore line of the Mediterranean.[1] For this reason many of the rocks of the area are marine sediments deposited over long geological periods. Marine fossils have been seen as far east as the edge of the Arabian Desert. The most characteristic surface rock of central Palestine is limestone. The "Gilead Dome" of limestone, for example, extends from Gilead in a southwesterly direction into the hill country of Samaria and Judah. In Jerusalem, hard limestone about thirty-five feet thick lies over an area of softer limestone. The latter was quarried extensively for building purposes and can be seen underneath the Old City in the place known as "Solomon's Quarries."

It is believed that the mountains, especially those in the Sinai and Arabian peninsulas, were formed in the distant past, called "Pre-Cambrian" by the geologists. During successive geological ages, the ocean alternately penetrated to the east and retreated to the west. On the bottom of the Tethys Sea, strata of limestone, dolomite, chalk, and marl were deposited. The marine deposits increased from south to north. Nubian sandstone was deposited in the Negev (or Negeb) and east of the Arabah in the vicinity of Petra. Granite appears in the Sinai Peninsula. The most characteristic rock of the area is limestone, of which there are two varieties. The harder, Cenomanian, is best seen in the hill country of Samaria and of Judah as far south as Hebron. The softer, Eocene limestone, is seen in the area of Gilboa-Gerizim and in the Shephelah, extending south of Beer-sheba.

Between these is an area of chalk that is easily eroded and is virtually useless for agriculture. But it serves as a kind of natural moat to divide the Shephelah from the hill country. Its relatively swift erosion has often facilitated the formation of roadbeds in valleys.[2] It is the outcropping of this chalk that

1. Efriam Orni and Elisha Efrat, *Geography of Israel* (Jerusalem: Israel Program for Scientific Translations, 1964), p. 8.
2. Denis Baly, *The Geography of the Bible* (New York: Harper and Bros., 1957), p. 20.

The Judean hills as seen from the Jordan Valley just north of Bethshan.

has made possible the valley of Aijalon as an access route to the hill country, and the same is true of the Megiddo Pass through the Carmel range.

Lacustrine sediments such as "Lissan marl," gypsum, and rock salt appear on the western shore of the Dead Sea and extend north in the Jordan Valley east of Jericho.[3] This marl is powdery when dry and most of the time appears as barren as a moonscape, not unlike the Badlands of South Dakota. During the period known as the Middle Pleistocene, volcanic activity—especially in the area north of the Sea of Galilee—formed the extensive basalt rocks, which constitute the main building stone of the area. Basalt, being hard and porous, was the ideal stone for flour mills. Volcanic activity also accounts for the hot springs on the shore of the Sea of Galilee in the vicinity of Tiberias, on the south bank of the Yarmuk, and on the eastern shores of the Dead Sea.

---

3. Orni and Efrat, *Geography*, p. 6.

The plain of Sharon is famous for its Mousterian red sand, which is very fertile and conducive to citrus crops. In the Beer-sheba area, loess soil, composed of windblown sand (as in China) is deep and fertile when irrigated.

Human habitation has adapted itself to these rock forma-tions. In central Palestine, the limestone has facilitated the ex-cavation of caves for residence and tombs. It has also encouraged the building of storage pits for water, grain, and other products. In the vicinity of Edom, the colorful sandstone has made possible the amazing city of Petra, carved out of the sandstone rock walls that surround this portion of the Wadi Musa.

THE WATER

The advantage of Palestine over Egypt, as the Israelites were told, is that the land "drinks water by the rain from heaven" (Deut. 11:11). Heaviest in the north, rainfall decreases as one moves south, and it becomes nonexistent near Elat. Prevailing winds from the west carry moisture-laden air up the slopes of

The Jordan Valley looking eastward toward Trans-Jordan.

the central ridge, where it condenses as dew or rain. Then as the air passes over the central ridge, the eastern slopes of this ridge remain arid and the Rift Valley receives little rainfall. When the moist air moves farther east to the mountains of Moab, however, at an elevation of 3,000 feet condensation occurs again in sufficient quantity to water small grain crops without irrigation. Still farther east, in the Arabian Desert, the land is dry again. The rainy season varies, but it normally lasts from December through March. Occasionally the early rains come in November and the latter rains as late as May. Even during the summer months the dew is often heavy along the coast and in the hill country. In Jerusalem in mid-summer, the Kidron Valley on some mornings is blanketed with dew so dense that it looks like an enormous snowbank. Tomatoes are grown easily in the hill country because the ample dew is absorbed through the leaves.

Rainfall and Seasons

Palestine has only two seasons, winter and summer. Usually no rain falls from June through October, and normally January is the wettest month. Occasionally during the summer months, a hot dry wind from the eastern desert sweeps into the Promised Land bringing discomfort to both man and beast. This wind, known locally as the "hamsin," contributes seriously to one's lassitude and irritability.

Varying greatly, the rainfall averages thirty inches in upper Galilee, twenty-one inches on the coastal plain near Tev Aviv, twenty inches in Jerusalem, eight in Beer-sheba, and only one inch at the head of the Gulf of Aqaba.[4] The number of rainy days during the year averages forty-five in Jerusalem, sixty in upper Galilee and twenty in Beer-sheba.[5] In Jerusalem, snow falls about once every three years, and the snow is eagerly welcomed by the residents both for the novelty and the moisture it provides.

There is less variation in the temperatures. The average temperature in Jerusalem in winter is 50° F. and in August, 75°. Temperatures as high as 104° F. have been recorded at Elat, 95° in Tiberias, and 75° in Mount Canaan in upper Galilee. Freezing temperatures do not occur in the Jordan Valley or on the coastal plain.

Temperatures

---

4. Misha Louvish, ed., *Facts About Israel, 1970* (Jerusalem: Keter Books, 1970), p. 42.
5. Zez Vilnay, *The New Israel Atlas: Bible to Present Day* (Jerusalem: Israel University Press, 1968), p. 7.

Terraced hillsides near Bethlehem, in the hill country of Judea.

In this semitropical climate, bananas can be grown in the Jordan Valley, in the Hula Valley, and along the coast. Date-palm groves are also found in these areas. This climate extends as far north as southern Lebanon. During most of the year the skies are unclouded and the sun is bright. Modern Israelis take advantage of the sun's rays to heat water and innumerable glass-enclosed water heaters are visible on the roofs of houses. Unlike in northern climes, the sun is not always regarded as beneficent, and the Scripture includes references to the sun as a source of danger ("The sun shall not smite you by day, nor the moon by night"—Ps. 121:6); the shade of a great rock "in a weary land" as a protection from the sun's rays is greatly appreciated (Isa. 32:2).

Palestine has always been a land predominantly based on agriculture. The interdependence between food and water, mentioned repeatedly in the Scriptures, has encouraged the inhabitants to rely upon divine providence. This is reflected in the Canaanites' agricultural festivals, upon which the incoming Hebrews based their religious calendar. The residents of Palestine, both Canaanites and Israelites, tended to perpetuate the local gods of the vegetation cycle. Among the Hebrews the temptation to Baal worship to insure a good harvest was strong. But Israel's God spoke in judgment to His people by withholding rain (cf. Amos 4:7) or by sending locusts (cf. Joel 1:4), designed to stimulate Israel to seek the Lord. The Hebrew prophets used these occasions to exhort to repentance.

THE TERRAIN

The physical contours of the Holy Land lie parallel, extending north and south. The four parallel zones are the maritime (coastal) plain, the low country (Shephelah), the hill country, and the valley of the Jordan.

The western zone, the coastal plain, stretches north to south from Lebanon to the Sinai Peninsula. Divided horizontally into four subdivisions, it extends from the "Ladder of Tyre" (Rosh Haniqra—"white cliffs") south through the plain of Acre, and continues south of the Carmel headland along the "coasts of Dor" to the plain of Sharon and on to Philistia.

The plain of Acre is about eight miles wide and twenty-five miles long. This was the region allotted to Asher (Josh. 19:24-31). Its northern border (the "Ladder of Tyre") is the present and historic boundary between Lebanon and Palestine; north is the plain of Tyre.

South of the Carmel range is the northern region of the plain of Sharon, known in Bible times as "the coasts of Dor." From the standpoint of topography, this area would seem linked to the southern section of the plain of Sharon as it is today. But in historical times it belonged to Phoenicia, probably because the Crocodile River (Nahr ez-Zerqa), south of Dor, effectively shut off communication between the vicinity of Dor and the portion south. The marshes of the Crocodile River extended from the mountains to the sea, so that the land access to this area was not from the south but rather through the mountain pass of Jokneam.[6] Dor itself, located between the Crocodile River and Mount Carmel (Josh. 17:11), was one of the twelve administrative districts of Solomon and later became a province of Assyria.

The plain of Sharon extends from the Crocodile River south to Joppa. It comprises an area of Mousterian red sand some

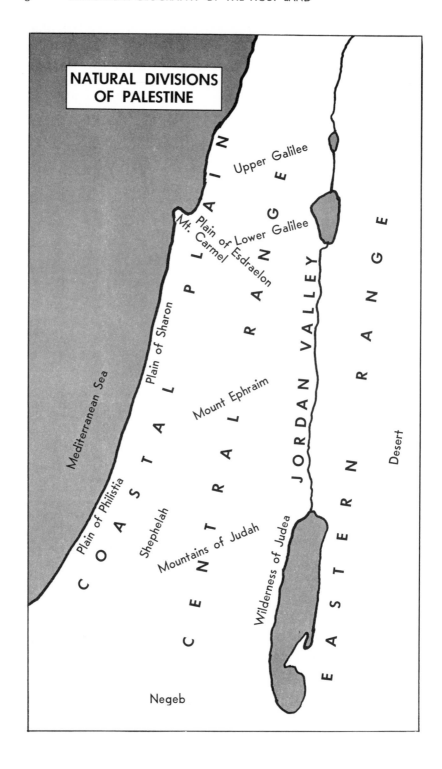

twenty miles in length and six to eight miles in width. Through this area flows the river Yarqon (Kanah), which in ancient times divided Ephraim from Manasseh. With the coming of the Zionists, this area has become the source of the best-tasting citrus fruit on the globe.

South of Joppa is the triangle known as the Philistine Plain with reminders of the five "lords" of the Philistines and their respective cities extending as far as Gaza, the traditional boundary between Palestine and Sinai. The Philistine Pentapolis included Ekron, Gath, Ashdod, Ashkelon and Gaza (1 Sam 6:17). Characteristic of this area are sand dunes created by the sand from the sea being blown up on the shore to form a dike between the coast itself and the inland. This contributed to the marshy conditions of times past. Historically, this meant that while the Phoenicians to the north were a sea-faring people, utilizing many natural harbors, the inhabitants of Palestine, limited by a regular coastline with no natural harbors, were a land-locked people. The seacoast extends from the Brook of Egypt to the Litani River in Lebanon, a distance of 210 miles, whereas Palestine itself extends from Gaza to the Ladder of Tyre, a distance of about 130 miles.

Between the maritime plain and the hill country of Judea and Samaria is a series of foothills known as the low country, or the Shephelah. It is separated from the hill country by a "moat" comprising a strata of Senonian chalk. The Shephelah was a scene of recurring conflicts between the Philistines and the Israelites and therefore figures prominently in Bible history. It is divided by three valleys: the valley of Aijalon on the north, from Beth-horon; the valley of Sorek in the middle, from Jerusalem; and the valley of Elah to the south, from Bethlehem. In the valley of Sorek Samson courted the Philistine woman, and in the valley of Elah, David and Goliath met. The Shephelah is excellent for growing fruit, and expansive fields of wheat may be seen today in the southern portion of this area.

To the east of the Shephelah a high ridgeline running north and south forms the hilly western boundary of the El-Ghor Rift (the Jordan Valley). This watershed extends from Hebron, at the southern end, to Mount Gilboa in the north. From a distance the ridge, about 2,500 feet above sea level, seems almost a straight line. A major highway extends along this ridge from

The Central Hill Country

Samaria. This highway also serves Bethel, Ramallah, Jerusalem, and Bethlehem.

The whole highland chain running north and south through Palestine is cut in three places: a shallow valley dividing upper and lower Galilee between the Sea of Galilee and the coast; another valley dividing lower Galilee from the mountains of Samaria between the harbor at Haifa and the Jezreel Valley; and still farther south, the east-west valley between Mount Ebal and Mount Gerizim.

The Rift Valley

From this ridgeline the land drops rapidly down into the El Ghor, as the Arabs call it, the deepest geological fault on the surface of the globe. It starts from the Lebanon Mountains to the north and extends to the south into central Africa. The fault includes the Sea of Galilee, the Jordan River, the Dead Sea, the Arabah, an arm of the Red Sea, and the Rift Valley in Central Africa. This enormous crevice reaches a maximum depth of 2,600 feet below sea level, at the bottom of the Dead Sea. It includes in northern Palestine the former Hula marshes, which have now been drained, and the Sea of Galilee, thirteen miles in length. From there the Jordan River runs in a zig-zag course, and although the actual distance is some sixty miles from the Sea of Galilee to the Dead Sea, the winding path of the Jordan covers two hundred miles. At the bottom of the Rift Valley the Jordan has carved a narrower channel called the Zor, a haven for wildlife. The Dead Sea itself is sixty-five miles in length and its surface lies 1,296 feet below the Mediterranean. In contrast, the Sea of Galilee is 696 feet below sea level.

The Arabah is the broad valley extending south from the Dead Sea to the Red Sea. It lies between the hills of southern Judea and the mountains of Edom that average 3,000 feet in height but farther south rise to nearly 6,000 feet. The Arabah itself is only 250 feet above sea level at its highest point, midway between the Dead Sea and the Gulf of Aqaba.

Trans-Jordan

East of the Jordan (Trans-Jordan) the land rises rather abruptly to a plateau averaging 3,000 feet above sea level. The area east of the Hula Valley and the Sea of Galilee is the Golan Heights, which is bounded on the south by the Yarmuk River draining the Hauran Plateau. South of the Yarmuk is Gilead, and south of the Jabbok River is Ammon. Moab is that portion east of the Dead Sea bounded on the north by the river Arnon and on the south by the river Zered. South of the Zered

Air view of the Jordan's torturous course (top), near the river's junction with the Jabbok. Below, is the ground view of the Jabbok at its confluence with the Jordan River.

lay Edom. The territory of the Ammonites was less clearly defined, but in general it lay east of the Moabite territory and on the rim of the Arabian Plateau.

Through history this varied topography required the major lines of communication to run north and south rather than east and west. It is noteworthy that when peoples from the west dominated Palestine they made their headquarters on the seacoast: the Philistines, for example; later the Roman; then the Crusaders; still later the British; and now the Israelis. When others such as the ancient Israelites and the Arabs dominated this land, their capitals were inland. Difficulty of access from east, west, or south helps explain the fact that the conquerors usually came from the north.

The Rivers

To the north (in modern Lebanon) is the Leontes, or the Litani River, which moving southward drains the valley between the Lebanon and Anti-Lebanon ranges and then turns

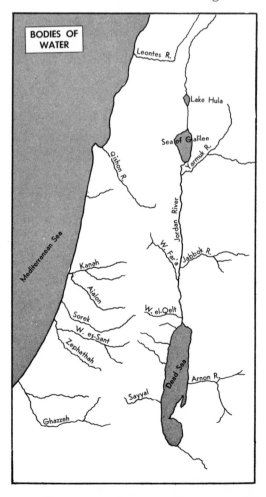

The Dead Sea, looking east from the cliffs of the Judean desert toward the low, white sandy Lisan peninsula and the mountains of Moab.

sharply to the west and enters the Mediterranean north of Tyre. This river and the city of Dan are the natural northern boundaries for upper Galilee. The river Qishon drains the valley of Esdraelon and lower Galilee into the Bay of Akko on the Mediterranean, while its companion stream flows through the valley of Jezreel to the Jordan. South of this, the Wadi Farah drains the east slope of the Samaritan hills and enters the Jordan south of Adam. From Jerusalem the Kidron Valley becomes the Valley of Fire before entering the Dead Sea below Qumran. The Crocodile River (Nahr ez-Zerqa) drains the west slope of the Carmel ridge and enters the Mediterranean near Dor. The western slope of the mountains of Samaria is drained by the Yarqon (Kanah) River, which enters the Mediterranean north of Jaffa. The Brook of Egypt (Wadi El-Arish) enters the Mediterranean near El Arish and formed the traditional boundary between Palestine and Egypt.

Few areas of the globe present in such a small area these striking contrasts of wet and dry climates, of heights and depths, and of varied flora and fauna. These features make Palestine a uniquely favorable site for divine revelation. Dwellers from many parts of the globe can find in Palestine a counterpart of their own homeland. In this sense Palestine can be called a microcosm.

Land of Contrasts

General view of the Old City of Jerusalem to the east. The temple area and the Mount of Olives are clearly seen at the top part of the photo.

2

Jerusalem Prior to the Moslem Conquest

Jerusalem may not be the "navel of the earth" as medieval geographers believed, but it does have a valid claim to be the "spiritual capital of the world." The Mount of Olives to the east of Jerusalem, especially from the Russian tower that dominates its summit, affords a spectacular panoramic view of the Holy City. The thoughtful viewer will see Jerusalem not only in terms of space but also of time. Jesus, when viewing Jerusalem from the Mount of Olives, saw the city in its past, present, and future: its stoning of past prophets; its murdering of the Messiah; and its coming destruction by the Romans (Luke 13:33-35; 19:41-44). Here, in an area of less than one square mile, lies neither forty nor four hundred but more than four thousand years of history, from Abraham to the present-day mayor, Ted Kollek.

In many historical sites of the Near East, archaeologists and historians can differentiate between various levels and ages of past occupancy because ancient civilizations left their deposits in horizontal layers. Some mounds, or tells, comprise nearly a score of successive civilizations, in levels one on top of the other. By digging a trench, an archaeologist can separate strata and reconstruct the long history of the site. But with Jerusalem it is different. Its long history is not buried in a mound, or tell, in which one civilization leveled off its predecessor and built upon it. Instead, Jerusalem is a sort of living fossil. Because it has been a holy city for at least four millennia, it has only rarely been leveled off and rebuilt. Consequently, a scan of the

15

city from the Mount of Olives simultaneously reveals the Bronze Age walls of Ophel; Hezekiah's tunnel of the seventh century B.C.; the remains of the Maccabean walls; the southeast corner-stones placed by Herod the Great; Justinian's Golden Gate; the splendid Dome of the Rock from the seventh century A.D.; structures of the Crusader Period such as Saint Anne's Church and the Church of the Holy Sepulchre; and structures of modern times including the Palestine Museum, the Church of the Dormition, the King David Hotel; and, on the horizon, buildings of the modern state of Israel including the Rabbinate Building. Few cities on the globe present data from the prehistoric, ancient, medieval, and modern periods in such close proximity.

Whereas Athens is honored for its contribution to art and philosophy, and Rome for its legal and administrative skill, Jerusalem remains the spiritual focus of the three great monotheistic religions. For the Moslem, it is second only to Mecca as a spiritual center, and for Jews and Christians it has often symbolized the ultimate blessings of God to His people.

During its long history, the "eternal city" has undergone many changes. The most pronounced periods of construction and reconstruction occurred at the time of Solomon; at the Exile and Restoration during the sixth century; at the time of Herod the Great; and at the time of Suleiman in the sixteenth century, when the present walls were built. The main periods of destruction occurred under Nebuchadnezzar in 587 B.C.; under the Romans Titus and Hadrian, in A.D. 70 and 134 respectively; at the time of Chosroes II in A.D. 614; and by "Mad" Hakim of Egypt in the eleventh century.

The periods of great political changes were from Jebusite to Hebrew under David's assault in the tenth century B.C.; in A.D. 134 when it changed from a Jewish to a Roman city; in 640 when it changed from a Christian to a Moslem city; in 1096 when it became a Christian commonwealth; in 1517 when the Ottoman Turks came and in 1917 when their domain ended; and in 1967 when it was reunited with west, or "new," Jerusalem.

No city in the world has experienced more of war than Jerusalem, the so-called city of peace. Toward the end of the nineteenth century, George Adam Smith already counted forty-six times when the city had known armed conflict.[1] This number

---

1. George Adam Smith, *Jerusalem . . . to A.D. 70* (New York: A. C. Armstrong & Son, 1908), vol. 2, p. 580.

Jerusalem from the Russian Tower on the Mount of Olives. The view is toward the southwest. In the foreground, the Pater Noster Church (lower left) and the Chapel of the Ascension (right) are visible.

can now be increased to forty-nine with the coming of the British in 1917, and with the wars between the Jews and Arabs in 1948 and again in 1967. Of the last three, the war of 1947-48 did by far the most damage to life and property. When the United Nations recently called once more for its internationalization, the Israeli government firmly refused to cease construction both within and without the ancient walls. As Aeschylus has noted, "Learning comes through suffering." Jerusalem has suffered much and has much to teach us.[2]

The prehistoric phase of Jerusalem goes back to the Old Stone Age. West of Jerusalem, early bifacial tools have been found, indicating settlements possibly as far back as 100,000 B.C.[3] Primitive flint artifacts testify to the presence of man in the Kidron Valley from about 12,000 B.C. Permanent settlement on the southeast hill can be dated from the debris left there as occurring at the end of the fourth millennium.[4] Early Bronze Age

2. Arnold Toynbee, ed., *The Crucible of Christianity* (London: Thames and Hudson, 1969), p. 37.
3. Emmanuel Anati, *Palestine Before the Hebrews* (New York: Alfred A. Knopf, 1963), pp. 56, 59.
4. John Gray, *A History of Jerusalem* (London: Robert Hale, 1969), pp. 74, 75.

(3150-2200 B.C.) tombs have been found on the slopes of Mount Olivet.[5] Nearly a thousand years later, Jerusalem appears in a written record. At this time (c. 2000 B.C.), the Execration Texts of Upper Egypt (Luxor) named *Urushamen* (Egyptian for Jerusalem) as a place under the control of Egypt.[6] The name itself is now believed to designate a city "founded by the God Salem,"[7] The fact that two persons linked with Jerusalem in the Bible, Melchizedek (Gen. 14:18) and Adonizedek (Josh. 10:1), contain the term *zedek* (righteousness) implies that the city was regarded as a holy city from antiquity. This would facilitate its transition to the holy city of Israel's God.

The mystery that surrounds Salem, or Jerusalem, of the days of Abraham and Melchizedek continues after the invasion of Palestine by the Hebrews. It is stated in Judges 1:7 that the Canaanite king, Adonibezek, was taken by the men of Judah to Jerusalem where he died. In the next verse, however, it says that the men of Judah fought against Jerusalem and set the city on fire. Apparently the invaders did not occupy it and the survivors reestablished themselves in the ruins, for later it is recorded that "the people of Benjamin did not drive out the Jebusites who dwelt in Jerusalem; so the Jebusites have dwelt with the people of Benjamin in Jerusalem to this day" (Judg 1:21). It is not stated that the Benjamites could not drive them out, but the implication is that the Benjamites and the Jebusites practiced a mutual coexistence.

Jerusalem, on the boundary between Benjamin and Judah, had few natural advantages. It is one of the few important cities of the world that does not lie on a seashore or along a navigable river. It was not on a major trade route nor was it adjacent to natural resources. Two factors account for its existence as a community. It had one of the few unfailing sources of water in the area. It could be relatively easily defended because of the steep valleys on the west, south, and east. It was accessible, however, from the north since the city lies on the high ridge that continues north as far as Shechem.

---

5. Kathleen M. Kenyon in *Palestine Exploration Quarterly* (1966): 74, 75.
6. Execration Texts were employed as "psychological warfare," a magic ritual in which breaking a vessel, on which was inscribed a name, brought a curse on the person of that name.
7. Teddy Kollek and Moshe Pearlman, *Jerusalem* (New York: Random House, 1968), p. 17.

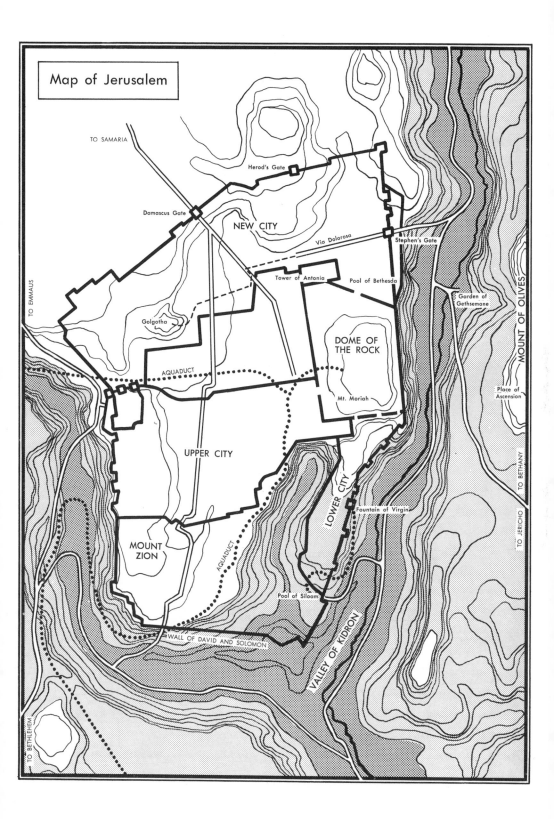

Map of Jerusalem

TO SAMARIA

Herod's Gate

Damascus Gate

NEW CITY

Via Dolorosa

Stephen's Gate

Tower of Antonia

Pool of Bethesda

Garden of Gethsemane

TO EMMAUS

Golgotha

DOME OF THE ROCK

MOUNT OF OLIVES

AQUADUCT

Place of Ascension

Mt. Moriah

UPPER CITY

TO BETHANY

LOWER CITY

Fountain of Virgin

TO JERICHO

MOUNT ZION

AQUADUCT

Pool of Siloam

VALLEY OF KIDRON

WALL OF DAVID AND SOLOMON

TO BETHLEHEM

THE "CITY OF DAVID"

Jerusalem remained an obscure village until by the stroke of genius the young King David, after reigning in Hebron for seven and a half years over his own tribe, made it his capital. When David saw the possibility of including in his reign the ten northern tribes that had been loyal to the sons of Saul, he recognized the need for changing the location of his capital. The move to Jerusalem was wiser perhaps than even David realized at the time. By a bold strategem, his troops under Joab entered the city, presumably by a water shaft, and overcame the overconfident and complacent Jebusite defenders (2 Sam. 5:6-10). It was a sagacious move politically, for Jerusalem lay in neutral territory as a Canaanite town on the border line between Judah and Benjamin, and therefore no one tribe would feel jealous. To its natural advantages David added buildings and fortifications that increased its strength.

The Jebusite village that David's men conquered consisted of a small, walled settlement on the crest of the hill south of and lower than the temple mount; it was bounded on the east,

The upper Tyropoeon Valley and a section of the city wall of Jerusalem.

south, and west by the Kidron, Hinnom, and Tyropoeon valleys. The source of water was the Gihon spring on the east slope. Access to the water was achieved by a channel cut in the rock above the spring, done perhaps a thousand years before David's time and similar to the channels discovered at Gezer, Megiddo, and Gibeon. This one consisted of a tunnel beginning at the pool of Gihon, running westward for sixty-seven feet, where a vertical shaft ascended for seventy feet and opened into a rock-cut passage leading to the surface. This permitted the inhabitants to have access to the water even in times of siege. Joab's men apparently gained access to the city in this manner. British officers, without the assistance of ladders, climbed the vertical shaft in 1910.[8]

David apparently strengthened but did not extend the Jebusite walls. The town that then became known as David's city consisted of a series of terraces on the steep slope above the Kidron extending down to the Late Bronze Age walls near the Gihon spring. These terraces and their retaining walls were vulnerable to earthquake and water erosion as well as to enemy attack, because the destruction of a lower terrace would invite the collapse of the retaining walls above it.[9] The shape of the Jebusite and Davidic city was oblong, like the shape of a human foot covering as it did the crown of the narrow peninsula (Ophel). The north wall, located near the 700 meter [2,296 feet] level, and traversing the ridge from east to west and northwest of the Gihon spring, served to protect the city from the north, the side most vulnerable to attack.[10]

When David decided to make Jerusalem the religious as well as the political center of his realm (2 Sam. 6:12), the city gained a prominence that it never lost. It was soon recognized by the Hebrew prophets and poets that this was uniquely Yahweh's city (2 Sam. 7:14-17). The building of the temple by Solomon dramatized this fact. Solomon's buildings were on the same ridge but to the north. On the summit of the ridge was the threshing floor of Araunah (2 Sam. 24:16), where the temple was erected. The place, referred to as The Tombs of the Kings, has never been positively identified. Recently, however, some

8. E. W. G. Masterman, "Jerusalem," *International Standard Bible Encyclopedia,* vol. 3, p. 1609.
9. Kathleen M. Kenyon, *Jerusalem: Excavating 3000 Years of History* (New York: McGraw-Hill Book Co., 1967), p. 49.
10. Ibid., pp. 26-29.

forty tombs—probably of nobles from the time of the monarchy—have been explored. They lie in and below the village of Silwan, east of the Kidron opposite Ophel. Some of these have gabled ceilings, others straight ceilings, and some are monolithic surface tombs.[11]

About three centuries later the sanctity of the city was dramatically impressed upon the nation and her neighbors. A succession of Assyrian invaders had devastated mighty city-states to the north and west, namely Accad, Gebal, Damascus, Samaria, and Lachish, all of them far larger and more important than Jerusalem. The crisis in 701 b.c., when Hezekiah in Jerusalem was confronted by the Assyrian army of Sennacherib, is one of the most dramatic episodes of Bible history.

Hezekiah's tunnel was dug at this time, which conducted water from the spring of Gihon through the Ophel ridge and into the Tyropoeon Valley to the Pool of Siloam ("Why should the kings of Assyria come and find much water"—2 Chron. 32: 4, 30, cf. Isa. 22:9-11). This remarkable tunnel, about two feet wide and from four to sixteen feet high, still conveys a copious stream of "living water" to Siloam and to what was formerly "the king's gardens."[12] Today a visitor can walk through this tunnel and see at firsthand the oldest of Jerusalem's antiquities, undisturbed since 700 b.c. except for the removal in 1890 of the Siloam Inscription (in ancient Hebrew), which is now seen in Istanbul.

As reported at length in Kings and Chronicles, and in Isaiah, the confrontation involved Sennacherib's challenge not only to Hezekiah but to Hezekiah's God (Isa. 26; 27). The proud hosts of the Assyrians, in the words of Lord Byron, "melted like frost at the glance of the Lord." The nations marveled at Jerusalem's survival, a unique phenomenon among the cities that experienced the horrors of an Assyrian siege. Judah's capital alone had survived (cf. Isa. 1:8), and the impression made upon the people was so profound that even more than a century later it was impossible for the prophet Jeremiah to convince his contemporaries that Jerusalem was in real danger from the Chaldeans (Jer. 7:11-20). As the "miracle of the Marne" during World War I made the French feel that Paris could not fall, so

11. David Ussushkin, "The Necropolis . . . at Silwan, Jerusalem," *Biblical Archaeologist* 33 (1970): 34-35.
12. L. H. Vincent, *Jerusalem de l' Ancient Testament* (Paris: Gabalda, 1954), pp. 260-278.

Absalom's tomb (left) and Zechariah's tomb (right) in the Kidron Valley. Immediately behind, on the slope of the Mount of Olives, is an old Jewish cemetery.

the people of Jerusalem felt that Jeremiah's warnings were not to be taken seriously and felt that "it can't happen here." But it did happen, and in 587 B.C., after an eighteen-month siege, even Jerusalem was crushed (2 Kings 25:1-21; Jer. 39:1-10). Its death throes receive eloquent expression in the Lamentations of Jeremiah, in marked contrast to the confident language of the Book of Kings.

POST-EXILIC JERUSALEM

But the faith that Jeremiah's prophecies inspired led to the city's reviving. In 536 B.C., following the emancipation decreed by the edict of Cyrus (2 Chron. 36:22-23; Ezra 1:2-4), the "ghost city" welcomed returnees from Babylonia. Foundations of the temple were laid immediately and then the people turned to constructing their own homes and wresting a livelihood out of the surrounding hillsides. Sixteen years later, the people were rebuked and exhorted by the prophets Haggai and Zechariah with the result that the superstructure of a new temple was

During
the
Persian
Empire

erected, and the second temple was dedicated in 516 B.C. Its dedication brought joy to the faithful mingled with the melancholy reflection that it was far inferior to the magnificent structure it replaced (Ezra 3:12-13). But this modest structure lasted almost twice as long as the temple of Solomon (i.e., 516 B.C.-A.D. 70). It is this "second temple" (including the Herodian structure) that most Jews today revere as the focus of their devotion and hopes.

The second chapter in this reborn Jerusalem occurred under the influence of two contemporaries whose work was mutually complementary. The traditional date for the return to Jerusalem of Ezra the scribe is 458 B.C. Regarded as the founder of modern Judaism, Ezra undertook the mission to make the Scriptures basic in the postexilic Hebrew commonwealth. Nehemiah, the sagacious and energetic layman, came twice to Jerusalem, first in 448 and again in 432 B.C. Under great difficulty he rallied the people, and the wall was rebuilt in only fifty-two days (Neh. 6:14), much to the dismay of hostile neighbors who professed

The hill of Ophel, looking south along Nehemiah's wall. The excavation was done by Kathleen Kenyon.

to see in this a new threat to the peace of the area (Neh. 2:20). The most complete description of Jerusalem is found in the account of Nehemiah's work, both in his preliminary investigation at night and later in the reconstruction of the walls. The walls and gates, described in some detail (Neh. 2:11-15; 3:1-32), are impossible to identify precisely today. Contrary to the conclusions of Bliss and Dickie in 1898, the walls of Nehemiah did not include the western section, or "Upper City," but were limited to the east, or Ophel Hill. In rebuilding the city walls, he left outside the portion of the city on the slope above the Gihon and placed the east wall along the crest of the hill on the approximate line of the modern houses. The city then did not need the extra space, and Hezekiah's tunnel made access to Gihon no longer essential.[13]

The importance of Jerusalem to the nation and the world was not to be measured so much in its buildings and in its walls but rather in its spiritual significance. To a greater extent than ever before, it symbolized hopes that far transcended the physical features of the city. Poets and song writers described it in glowing terms as "the joy of all the earth" (Ps. 48:2). The prophet comforted Jerusalem with the assurance that "her judgment is passed, her iniquities are pardoned" (Isa. 40: 1-5) and the reborn city continued to be the vehicle of divine revelation not only to the nation but to the world (Isa. 62:1-6). It was the faith of prophets and poets rather than the achievements of warriors and statesmen that gave Jerusalem the spiritual prestige it has enjoyed ever since. Jerusalem had now become the "city of God" in contrast to Babylon, the city of man opposed to God (cf. Gen. 11:1-9). The contrast is most dramatically displayed in the Christian apocalypse, in which Babylon is pictured as a harlot and Jerusalem as the bride of Christ (Rev. 17–19).

During much of the intertestamental period, Jerusalem and Judea were ruled by a government that allowed the separation between church and state. After the joint rule of Zerubbabel and Joshua (Zech. 4), and later between Ezra and Nehemiah (Neh. 8:9), the city was ruled jointly by a governor and a high priest. Later, however, under the Hasmoneans, the high priest possessed both secular and sacred authority.

The defeat of the Persians by the Greeks under Alexander

---

13. Kenyon, *Jerusalem,* p. 108.

in 333 B.C., at Issus, created no immediate change in Jerusalem. Jewish leaders transferred their allegiance from Persia to Alexander and gave the victorious Macedonian conqueror a royal welcome.[14] Jerusalem and Palestine enjoyed a great measure of local autonomy. But when the Seleucids of Syria became the dominant force in Palestine, after the victory of Antiochus III (223-187) over the Ptolemies in 198 B.C. near Banias, the Israelites were subject to increasingly hostile pressure to forsake the faith of their fathers and embrace Hellenistic culture. Antiochus III himself, however, showed favor to the Jews for their assistance against the Egyptians.[15] Jerusalem fell to the Seleucids under Antiochus IV Epiphanes) in 168 B.C. (1 Macc. 1:21); it remained desecrated and in disgrace until reoccupied by the victorious guerrilla forces of Judas Maccabeus (1 Macc. 4:36-58). The joyous occasion of the rededication of the temple is still commemorated in December in the Jewish festival Hannukah, the Feast of Lights.

When the Maccabees, under Jonathan, reoccupied the city and rededicated the temple in 164 B.C., a period of building was begun under the Hasmonean rulers that continued for over a century. The Akra (the fortress tower) of the Syrians had been built by Antiochus IV (Epiphanes) to keep the city subjugated; it remained for years a source of great irritation to the Jews (1 Macc. 1:33-40). Archaeologically, its location has been a matter of much dispute, and six sites have been proposed. Smith and Simons, on the evidence of 1 Maccabees and Josephus, concluded that it was located on the southeast hill, identified as "the city of David," south of the temple area and near Gihon. Access to water and to "the wilderness" supports their position (1 Macc. 13:21).[16] Kathleen Kenyon, while acknowledging that archaeology has not settled the question, believes that it lay on the western ridge near the Joppa Gate, where the former Turkish citadel now stands. This, she believes, was the first stage in the development of this hill and its eventual inclusion in Herodian Jerusalem.[17] This view is supported by the report that the Akra was separate from the city (1 Macc. 12:36) and yet close enough to harass the temple area (1 Macc. 1:36). Also

Under the Greeks

Jewish Independence

---

14. Josephus, *Antiquities* XI. 8, 5.
15. Ibid., XII. 3. 3.
16. Smith, *Jerusalem*, pp. 11, 444-452; J. Simons, *Jerusalem in the Old Testament* (Leiden: E. J. Brill, 1952), pp. 144-157.
17. Kenyon, *Jerusalem*, p. 113.

the term *Akra* is Greek for "high place," and the Citadel on the west wall is today about eighty feet higher than the temple mount. However, Abel and Vincent, supported by John Gray and contemporary Jewish scholars, locate the Akra "on the site of the Maccabean palace on the northeast spur of the southwest hill."[18]

The problem is the ambiguity of the two primary sources, 1 Maccabees and Josephus. It is not clear which distinction is made in these sources between the upper city, the lower city, Mount Zion, the Akra, the city of David, and the Citadel. Paradoxically, Josephus repeatedly refers to the Akra as the "Lower City."[19] His reference to the lowering of the citadel mount in three years by Simon is especially suspect for accuracy (Jos. *Antiq.* XIII, 6, 7). In spite of these difficulties, the most plausible solution appears to be the location on the "northeast spur of the southwest hill." This conclusion rests upon several considerations:

> "Agrippa built himself a very large dining-room in the royal palace at Jerusalem near to the portico. Now this palace had been erected of old by the children of Asamoneus, and was situated upon an elevation, and afforded a most delightful prospect to . . . the king; and there he could . . . observe what was done in the temple."[20]

The assumption is that the Hasmonean palace "of old" was erected on the site of the demolished Syrian Akra. Earlier it is reported that Simon starved the citadel into surrender and "strengthened the fortification of the temple alongside *[para]* the citadel" (1 Macc. 13:49-53), after the Citadel had been isolated from the rest of the city (1 Macc. 12:35-37).[21] These considerations argue for a location nearer to the temple than

18. Gray, *History of Jerusalem*, p. 48; F. M. Abel in *La Revue Biblique* 35 (1926): 520 ff.; L. H. Vincent, *Jerusalem*, pp. 17 ff.; see also Yohanan Aharoni and Michael Avi-Yonah, *The Macmillan Bible Atlas* (New York: Macmillan Co., 1968).

19. Judas attacked "the garrison that was in the city, . . . ejected them out of the upper city, and drove the soldiers into the lower, which part of the city was called the Citadel," (Jos. *Wars,* I, 1, 4). Also "But the other hill, which is called 'Acra' and sustains the lower city . . . a third hill, but naturally lower than the Acra," (Wars, I, 4.1).

20. Jos. *Antiq.* XX. 8. 11.

21. J. Simons objects, without justification, that the Greek term *para* "implies 'nearness' " but not " 'along' or 'parallel to,' " Simons, *Jerusalem in the Old Testament* (Leiden: E. J. Brill, 1952) p. 146.

a site on the south end of the eastern hill. They call for a site immediately west of the temple. A location on the spur that projected into the "Central Valley between the temple area ("Mount Zion") and the ridge of the western hill, where Herod the Great later built his sumptuous palace-fortress, best fulfills these conditions."[22] The latter site would have been too distant from the temple area for Agrippa to watch the proceedings from there. In short, the Hasmonean Palace appears to have been built on the site of the Citadel (cf. 1 Macc. 15:28) before the reign of Queen Alexandra, "no doubt at the western end of the Tyropoeon, facing the temple."[23] Here, Antipas taunted Jesus (Luke 23:6-21) before returning Him to Pilate.

Civil strife finally reduced the power and influence of the Hasmoneans, and foreign influence again became dominant in Judea. Victory of the patriots over the Syrians had brought independence, power, and affluence to Judea and her territories. But the Hasmonean rulers became increasingly worldly and self-serving. They usurped the power of the priesthood and consequently incurred the hostility of the Sadducees. Their worldliness also earned them the distrust of the Pharisees who insisted on conformity to the Covenant. Alexandra, however, widow of King Alexander and now queen (76-67 B.C.) followed her deceased husband's advice and made friends with the influential Pharisees. After her death, her sons Aristobulus II and Hyrcanus became rivals for the throne. The former claimed it as the right of the first-born, but the latter had the support of King Aretas of the Nabateans. Meanwhile, the Roman general Pompey, having conquered Asia Minor, Armenia, and Syria, received the two brothers in Damascus and listened to their complaints. Pompey decided against Aristobulus because of his obvious vacillation between submission and independence, and, instead, supported the claims of Hyrcanus.

Aristobulus fled from Damascus, and Pompey pursued him past Sythopolis to "a most beautiful fortress on the top of a mountain, called Alexandrium whither Aristobulus had fled."[24] The king surrendered to Pompey but later refused the Roman general permission to enter Jerusalem and collect the promised tribute money. The Hyrcanus faction, however, admitted the

Coming of the Romans

22. Gray, *History of Jerusalem,* pp. 46, 48; Michael Avi-Yonah, *Jerusalem* (New York: Arco Publishing Co., 1960), p. 64.
23. Michael Join-Lambert, *Jerusalem* (London: Elek Books, 1958), p. 67.
24. Jos. *Antiq.* XIV. 3. 4.

Romans into Jerusalem, while those loyal to Aristobulus stood siege in the temple-fortress. Moving his troops from Jericho to Jerusalem, Pompey camped within the city walls, north of the temple itself. During the next three months the Romans filled in a deep ditch, or moat, north of the temple, brought siege engines from Tyre, and at last overcame resistance, killing 12,000 Jews in the process. Pompey entered the temple, but was surprised to find the holy of holies empty in contrast to pagan temples. He did not, however, steal the temple treasure; this was done later by another Roman general, Crassus, during his ill-fated pursuit of the Parthians.

Here, as elsewhere, the Romans preferred to rule by remote control. In this case, it was through the Idumeans, Judea's neighbors to the south, who were descendants of Edomites, or Arabs. Their leader, Antipater (died 43 B.C.), had befriended Julius Caesar and was later confirmed as the procurator of Palestine. Antipater appointed his sons Phasael and Herod as governors of Jerusalem and Galilee respectively. Herod demonstrated his

The Mount of Olives as seen from the northeast corner of the Old City. The tower is that of the Russian church. The minaret to the right of it marks the "place" of the Ascension.

ability by eliminating robbers from Galilee. While being praised for this in Galilee, he was accused in Jerusalem for bypassing the Sanhedrin, who alone could try capital crimes. Herod was supported by the high priest Hyrcanus to the chagrin of the frustrated Sanhedrin.

The Parthians were Rome's greatest rival. Located south of the Caspian Sea, and of Hittite-Turkestan stock, they were "a vigorous race, patient in agriculture, skilled in handicraft, and unequalled in commercial acumen."[25] The Parthians watched the Roman world torn by civil war, especially the defeat of Pompey and Brutus near Philippi in 31 B.C. by Octavian and Antony. Aided by a Roman general, the Parthians planned to invade Roman-occupied territory while Antony dallied with Cleopatra. At this time Antigonus, the son of the slain Aristobulus, became the sole survivor of the Hasmonean dynasty. He made a league with the Parthians in which he agreed to resist Rome and kill Herod in exchange for their assistance in securing for him the throne. Meanwhile, Antony, bribed by Herod and counseled by Hyrcanus, appointed Herod as governor of Judea. The Parthians, with Jewish forces led by Antigonus, fought their way to Ptolemais (Acre), next defeated the army of Hyrcanus near Megiddo, and then advanced on Jerusalem. Jerusalem was defended by Herod and his brother Phasael and Hyrcanus the high priest. Phasael and Hyrcanus later responded to an invitation to make peace with the Parthian leader in Galilee, but were captured instead and turned over to Antigonus. Herod fled Jerusalem with his family, fought and defeated the pursuing Parthians near Herodium, east of Bethlehem, and escaped to Masada.[26] Three years later, after being named king by the Romans, Herod returned to Jerusalem and, after a four-month's siege, conquered it with the help of the Roman general Sosius, Anthony's appointee to the province of Syria.

UNDER ROMAN RULE

Herod the Great

Herod, a great builder as well as a warrior and administrator, transformed the topography of Jerusalem. First, he erected his sumptuous palace in the upper city west of the temple mount. It occupied the area in the southwest portion of the

25. Will Durant, *Caesar and Christ* (New York: Simon and Schuster, 1944), p. 528.
26. Jos. *Antiq.* XIV. 13. 9-11.

The Fortress of Antonia, as duplicated in the model of Herodian Jerusalem.

Old City known as the Armenian Gardens, and included three enormous towers named Phasael, Hippicus, and Mariamne—after his brother, friend, and wife. It served not only as the royal residence but also as a fortress; it was built so strongly that it held out in A.D. 70 even longer than either the Citadel or the temple. Farther north he erected the tower Psephimus; its foundations can still be seen under the building of the Brethren of the Christian Schools, and many archaeologists agree that this tower is the northwest corner of Agrippa's Third Wall of A.D. 41-44.[27] The city, enclosed with strong walls, now included the western hill, thus doubling its size. These structures transformed the western hill into the best part of Jerusalem, and thus the probable residence of the aristocracy, including the high priest. As a consequence of Herod's buildings,[28] the name *Zion* "migrated" north from the city of David (on Ophel), to the temple mount and then west to the southwest hill. The name Zion

27. Kolleck and Pearlman, *Jerusalem,* p. 98; Join-Lambert, *Jerusalem,* p. 64.
28. Smith, *Jerusalem,* vol. 2, p. 490.

Herodian Jerusalem including the temple area in the background.

"Solomon's porch" inside the court of the Herodian temple complex.

still clings to the southwest hill in spite of the testimony of history. The western hill city remained as the administrative center of the city until the British Mandate, thus testifying to Herod's foresight.

Herod then turned his attention to the temple mount, or lower city. On the northern summit he rebuilt the Hasmonean citadel, Baris, into the formidable castle which he named after his Roman patron Antony. The castle included four corner towers, a spacious stone-paved inner courtyard covering enormous cisterns, luxurious apartments, and barracks for the troops. (Troops from these barracks, thanks to their proximity to the temple, later saved Paul's life [Acts 21:30-39].)

The temple was the most ambitious of Herod's buildings in Jerusalem. The enormous platform surrounding the temple comprised Jerusalem's most impressive architectural masterpiece. Approximately 100 strong columns, some of them 150 feet in height, made possible the enlargement of the surface of the hill to a vast enclosure measuring 2,575 by 985 feet. The temple building was the size of Solomon's but twice its height, at 165 feet. The main construction of the temple building (naos) took only nineteen months, but the remaining construction took over eight years, and portions were still incomplete when Jesus walked its courts. Even today the viewer shares some of the admiration of Josephus who described it as "the most prodigious work that was ever heard of by man."[29] These were the structures that excited the admiration of the disciples and caused Jesus to warn of the temple's impending overthrow (Mark 13:1).

In addition, Herod provided for a double gate, leading from the south wall to the outer court of the temple, still to be seen under the Aqsa Mosque. Great bridges spanned the central valley and provided easy access to the western hill over "Robinson's Arch" and "Wilson's Arch." This and much more led the Talmudists to say of the dreaded monarch and his buildings, "He who has not set eyes upon the structure of Herod has not seen a structure of beauty in all his life."

What was the Jerusalem of Jesus' day? Most visitors to the Holy City eagerly try to envision the city as Jesus and His followers viewed it. The tourists are not likely to find it along the usual pilgrim itinerary, the Via Dolorosa, and the Holy Sepulchre. These mark the probable sites, but the area

Jerusalem in Jesus' Day

---

29. Jos. *Antiq.* XI. 11. 3.

has greatly changed in appearance because of the destruction and reconstruction over the intervening centuries.

Much, however, has remained essentially unchanged. This includes the Kidron Valley, especially the tombs of the Maccabean period—Absalom's tomb and those named after James and Zacharias. Hezekiah's Tunnel also remains unchanged (except for the removed Siloam Inscription, which now is in Istanbul). The recently uncovered Siloam steps, which lead from the Church of the Cock Crowing (Peter *Gallicanti*) down into the Tyropoeon Valley toward the Pool of Siloam, are steps that Jesus probably used just prior to His arrest in Gethsemane. The Mount of Olives retains much of its original profile so that Gethsemane and the summit are forceful reminders of Jesus' passion and triumphant ascension. The walls surrounding the temple area are Herodian and therefore were familiar to Jesus; the east, south, and west walls of the Haram area, now yellowed with age, retain their massiveness, and they elicit admiration now as when viewed by the disciples shortly before the crucifixion. The tombs that Jesus saw include the impressive monuments honoring Absalom and Zechariah. Opposite Ophel and below the village of Silwan, a cave necropolis of the kingdom of Judah recently has been explored. Many of these tombs, perhaps like that of Shebna (Isa. 22:16), are hewn in the rocky cliff and are relatively elaborate. Resemblances to Phoenician tombs of the preexilic period have been noted.[30]

Recent discoveries in the Kidron Valley vividly bring the first century to life. Archaeologists report the discovery of several bone boxes (ossuaries), including one from the first century that contains the skeleton of a man who had been crucified.

In June 1968, while excavating for a housing project northeast of the Old City (at *Giv'at ha Mivtar*), a vast necropolis was uncovered, probably extending from the lower slopes of the Mount of Olives north to Mount Scopus and west to the Sanhedriyan tombs northwest of the Old City.[31]

These tombs were hewn in the soft limestone of the area. Tomb Number 1, for example, contained an upper chamber with four *loculi* (burial chambers) and a lower chamber with eight *loculi*. Evidence from various data supports the conclusion

30. Ussishkin, "The Necropolis . . . ," p. 45.
31. V. Tzaferis, "Jewish Tombs at and near Giv'at ha-Mivtar, Jerusalem," *Israel Exploration Journal* 20 (1970): 30.

that this tomb was used after the Alexander Jannaeus revolt and before the revolt of A.D. 66-70. One ossuary (Number 4) in Tomb 1 contained words inscribed during the lifetime of the crucified man referred to above. The victim probably was "a rebel put to death at the time of the census revolt in A.D. 7 or the victim of some occasional crucifixion" since "individuals were also crucified occasionally by the Roman procurators."[32]

These bones, including the ankle bones pierced by an iron spike, are dated between A.D. 7 and 70. Now stored in the Rockefeller Museum of East Jerusalem, the bones "are the only extant remains from antiquity known to be evidence of a crucifixion."[33] Measurements of the skull were taken, and the sketch that resulted shows an asymetrical face of a man of average height and configuration. The experts conclude that this individual was marked by some defect from prenatal circumstances. "The portrait sketch of his visage is pleasing. . . . The chin contributes

32. Ibid., p. 31.
33. N. Haas, "Anthropological Observations on the Skeletal Remains from Giv'at ha Mivtar," *Israel Exploration Journal* 20 (1970): 51.

Closeup of the side of the monument called the "Tomb of Absalom," located in the Kidron Valley.

The Arch of Titus in Rome and a closeup of one of its panels (below), which records the destruction of Jerusalem in A.D. 70, showing the temple furniture being carried away by Roman soldiers.

to an energetic physiognomy; the cheek bones to a feminine appearance." The author continues, "The face was quite remarkable, but pleasant. . . . The body, being proportionate, was agreeable to sight, particularly in motion, because of the gracious, almost feminine allure; it reminds us of the Hellenistic ideal *ephebe*."[34]

Closer study reveals that the nail was about eighteen centimeters (about seven inches) in length, that it pierced both ankles, and that the knees had been so flexed that the body was in an awkward position. The arms had been fixed to the crossarm of the cross by a nail through each wrist. Evidence shows that when the corpse was removed from the cross, the nail through the ankle bones could not be removed because it had bent against a knot. Consequently the feet were severed by an axe blow, and the body was removed, and then interred together with the feet transfixed by the spike to the plaque of olive wood from which the spike had not been removed.[35]

Many besides Jesus of Nazareth had been crucified during these tumultuous decades. But these skeletal remains of a man who had been crucified roughly contemporaneous with Jesus are movingly evocative of the one who "gave His life as a ransom for many."

After Jesus' death, Herod Agrippa built the problematical third wall in A.D. 42.[36] In addition, he realigned the south wall along lines not sufficiently defined as yet.[37]

The siege of Jerusalem in the summer of A.D. 70 is described in graphic detail by Josephus. The proud but fanatical city was humiliated as thoroughly as it had been under Nebuchadnezzar. The walls were destroyed, and the temple was burned and pillaged; thousands were massacred, and other thousands were led into slavery. An inscription at a vast tunnel-aqueduct near Antioch of Syria states that it was constructed by Jewish survivors of the A.D. 70 siege. This engineering feat was designed to divert flood waters from Antioch's port city of Seleucia, from which Paul and Barnabas had departed for Cyprus (Acts 13:4).

Revolt of A.D. 70

The ruined site of Jerusalem then became the headquarters of the Roman Tenth Legion (Fretonius). Earthenware since

---

34. Ibid., p. 55.
35. Ibid., p. 59.
36. Jos. *Wars* V. 4. 2-3.
37. Kenyon, *Jerusalem,* pp. 155-162.

discovered there bears the Legion's distinctive insignia. Sacrifices apparently continued to be offered amid the ruins of the temple until the second revolt in 132-134. The surviving Jews, although subdued, "gradually resumed an existence of sullen normality under Roman rule."[38]

There is evidence that the Hasmoneans and the Zealots of Jesus' day had much in common, or were perhaps a continuum. The restiveness provoked by the repressive measures of the Seleucids and nurtured by the pious Hasadim for religious reasons, later became aggressive under the Hasmoneans and their successors for political reasons. Incipient revolution smoldered in many parts of the Diaspora and broke out into flame following the visit of the emperor Hadrian to Jerusalem in A.D. 129-30. His decisions to rebuild Jerusalem as a pagan city and to forbid circumcision were the "last straw."[39]

Hadrian's heavy hand inspired another suicidal revolt, led by Bar Kochba, the Jewish "Messiah" who was blessed by Rabbi Akiba. Preparations for this second revolt were extensive. The Romans suffered defeats and the garrison in Jerusalem withdrew to Caesarea. The insurrectionists held Jerusalem in defiance of the Romans for three years (A.D. 132-134), but they were finally dispersed. The Roman historian Dio Cassius called this a major war; he reported that the Romans had to capture fifty fortresses, destroy 985 villages, and kill one million persons before victory came. The patriots' last stand was taken at Beitar (or Battir), about six miles southwest of Jerusalem, although pockets of resistance held out in caves near the Dead Sea, as indicated by recently discovered scrolls and artifacts in the area.

Second Jewish Revolt

With enormous resources, the Romans were determined that Jerusalem would never again be a source of trouble. Jerusalem was demolished, the area plowed to symbolize its annihilation, and a pagan city named Aelia Capitolina was built, honoring the emperor and the Capitolina Jupiter. The lines of the present north and south walls are now believed to be those of Hadrian, the area thus compressed into a rough square in the fashion of a Roman army camp or barracks. As in a typical Roman

38. Kollek and Pearlman, *Jerusalem,* p. 137; also K. W. Clark (Duke University) in a paper read before the Society of Biblical Literature, New York City.
39. Abraham Schalit, "Palestine Under the Seleucids and Romans," *The Crucible of Christianity,* ed. Arnold Toynbee (London: Thames and Hudson, 1969), p. 76.

camp, there were two main streets at right angles to each other, one going from north to south, the other from east to west. The larger road, Cardo Maximus, ran from the Damascus Gate straight south to the Zion Gate, just as it does today. As the Madaba map indicates, this main street was lined on either side with columns.[40]

The east-west street called the Decumanus Maximus, now David Street, began at the Jaffa Gate and went due east to the temple area. The Forum (now the Muristan) was near the site of the Holy Sepulchre; the entrance to it is preserved in the arch seen today in the Russian convent. Hadrian had an ornamental gate of three doors erected upon the ridge of the eastern hill, where Dames de Zion now have their convent. The gate was built not for protection but for ornamentation, and is often called the "Ecco Homo" Arch. Similar tripartite gates honoring Hadrian are still to be seen in Jerash, in Athens, in Damascus, and in Antalya, Turkey.

The north wall is now widely believed to rest on the foundations of Herod Agrippa's "Third Wall" as defined by Josephus.[41] Israeli archaeologists, however, remain convinced that the "Third Wall" is represented by the line of huge stones between the American Consulate and the Albright Archaeological Institute.[42] The vast stone pavement now seen on the site of the Antonia fortress is believed by some to have been built at that time to cover the Herodian cisterns.[43] Others believe the pavement to be that of the fortress Antonia, thus built by Herod.[44]

Jews were forbidden to enter Aelia Capitolina for nearly two centuries thereafter except for annual pilgrimages. The few who returned did so only when the rule was relaxed.[45] The defenders had shown unity and fanatical zeal, but this time no poets or prophets were present to predict a resurrection from

40. Michael Avi-Yonah, *The Madaba Mosaic Map* (Jerusalem: Israel Exploration Society, 1954), p. 52.

41. Jos. *Wars* V. 4; Kenyon, *Jerusalem*, pp. 162-164, 190.

42. Kollek and Pearlman, *Jerusalem*, p. 140; E. L. Sukenick and L. A. Mayer, *The Third Wall of Jerusalem* (Jerusalem, 1930); Edward Robinson, *Biblical Researches in Palestine* (Boston: Crocker and Brewster, 1868), vol. 1, pp. 309, 310, 314, 315.

43. Clemens Kopp, *The Holy Places of the Gospels* (New York: Herder and Herder, 1963), pp. 370-373.

44. Marie Aline, *Forteresse Antonia* (Jerusalem, 1955), p. 74; L. H. Vincent, *Jerusalem*, pp. 114-170.

45. Kollek and Pearlman, *Jerusalem*, pp. 141, 142.

the ruins, as had been true in the sixth century B.C. Instead, "the Jewish people were reduced to a dispersed nation without a center in its own land, while Christianity launched a campaign of expansion probably unparalleled in the history of the world."[46]

CHRISTIAN JERUSALEM

Unlike Jews and Moslems, who place great importance on places, the early Christians mostly stressed the significance of persons. Therefore the zeal for pilgrimages and the veneration of holy sites has never been as strong in Christendom as in the other two monotheistic faiths (with the possible exception of the Crusaders). Nevertheless, holy places in Palestine are almost as important to some Christians as they are to Jews and Moslems. For Christians, Jerusalem is more important than the place of Jesus' birth or the scenes of His boyhood and early ministry, for Jerusalem is the site of Jesus' preaching, suffering, death, resurrection, and ascension. In one of the most provocative statements attributed to our Lord, He declared: "for it cannot be that a prophet should perish away from Jerusalem" (Luke 13:33). To Jesus, Jerusalem was not only the golden city, but it was also the focal point of sinful man's opposition to God's messengers. In detailed accounts, remarkable for their restraint, the four evangelists narrated the last week of Jesus' earthly sojourn. It was in Jerusalem that the church was "born" on the day of Pentecost and from Jerusalem that the witness went first into Judea, then Samaria, and ultimately to the "uttermost parts of the earth" (Acts 1:8–KJV). The New Testament portrays heaven as the "new Jerusalem," which is "as a bride adorned for her husband" where "the tabernacle of God is with men and he will dwell with them, and they shall be his people and God himself shall be with them, and be their God" (Rev. 21:2, 3–KJV). This city is both the symbol of defiance and death and the embodiment of hope and true life. Even more than Rome, Jerusalem merits the epithet "the eternal."

But the leadership of the Christian church soon passed from Jerusalem to Antioch, where the first Christian missions to the west were initiated. The Gentiles accepted the gospel more readily than did the Jews, and believers in Jerusalem and Judea were the subjects of donations from the more affluent Christian

---

46. Schalit, "Palestine . . . ," p. 98.

communities of Asia Minor and Europe. Prior to the first rebellion, Christians—mindful of Jesus' warning—had departed from
the city and sought refuge in the Jordanian city of Pella near
the scene of John's early ministry and Jesus' baptism. Here, at
this important Graeco-Roman city now called Tabaqat Fahl,
they found refuge from A.D. 68–135.[47] Although the first two centuries of our era witnessed little Christian curiosity about holy
places and pilgrimages, by the third century people began coming to Jerusalem eager to learn more about the sites mentioned
in the New Testament.

The location of the earliest sites are not known, but almost
certainly the first was in the southwest corner of the city, near
the traditional house of John Mark, the site of the Last Supper
and of the outpouring of the Spirit at Pentecost, under or near
the Armenian church there.[48] Later, the present Armenian church
marked the site. For two decades (1947-67) the church lay in
ruins in "no man's land." Today the buildings and the adjacent
cemetery are being reconstructed.

After A.D. 134, the bishopric was shifted to Caesarea co-
inciding with the political organization of the province. The
bishop of Jerusalem, therefore, was under the patriarch of
Antioch. Gradually, however, the bishop of Jerusalem increased
in stature and prestige. He was numbered among the patriarchs in A.D. 270 and again at Nicaea in 325. At the time of
the Council of Chalcedon (A.D. 451), the bishop of Jerusalem
was made a patriarch with authority over all the Holy Land.
Gradually Christians acquired an interest in the holy sites, and
men like Origen traveled there to understand better the land
of the Bible. Jerome, the leading scholar of the ancient church,
lived near Bethlehem and became an active participant in dis-
cussions and squabbles of the period. A native of Jerusalem
named Julius Africanus did extensive work in Christian origins.
His *Chronography*, a century earlier than Eusebius's *Onomasticon*, was "an enormous work of erudition, which attempted to
place the origins of Christianity on a precise basis."[49]

---

47. Nelson Glueck, *The River Jordan* (New York: McGraw-Hill Book
Co., 1968), pp. 142, 143.
48. According to Epiphonus (315-403) when Hadrian was in Jerusalem
in A.D. 130, he found all in ruins "except a few houses and the little church
of God upon the spot where the disciples went up into the upper room . . ."
Kopp, *Holy Places*, p. 323.
49. Join-Lambert, *Jerusalem*, p. 105.

Because of emphasis upon asceticism, monks became more important than bishops. Gradually the deserts around Jerusalem became occupied by monks. As many as 5,000 monks inhabited the deserts of Judea during the Byzantine period. Among the more famous monks was Mar Saba, the revered abbot of the monastery of the same name southeast of Jerusalem, one of the few monasteries still functioning in this area. Increasingly the Romans turned their wrath from the Jews to the Christians. Alexander, bishop of Jerusalem, was twice summoned to Caesarea during the Decian persecution of the mid-third century.

SYNOPTIC VIEW OF CHRISTIAN JERUSALEM

From the Christian perspective, the historian can stand on the Mount of Olives and visualize nineteen centuries of Christian history focused in the "Holy City" spread out before him in panorama. Many view Jerusalem from the tower of the Augustus Victoria Hospice on Mount Scopus to the northwest, or from the Latin Chapel of the Ascension where most tourists go. Others view the Old City from the roof of the Intercontinental Hotel or the Panorama Hotel, located on the Mount of Offense upon the east side of the Kidron over the village of Silwan. The best location from which to view Jerusalem is the Russian tower, the most conspicuous landmark on the crest of the Mount of Olives. Although open to tourists until

Panorama of Jerusalem from the Mount of Olives.

recently, access to the Russian tower is now forbidden to visitors.

Just below the Russian tower is the site of one of the earliest Christian churches, one of four founded by the mother of Constantine. The arrival of the emperor's mother, Helena, in Jerusalem marked the first time in history, after three centuries and ten great persecutions, that a representative of the imperial family showed personal concern for Christianity. The Christian church had finally won toleration in A.D. 313 and official recognition in 325 under Constantine. As emperor, Constantine presided at the Council of Nicaea in 325, where he met Marcarius, bishop of Jerusalem. Consistent with the emperor's command to restore Christian sanctuaries, as reported by Eusebius, Marcarius secured from Constantine the assurance of the emperor's moral and financial support for the excavation of Christian origins and the erection of churches.[50] The emperor authorized the cleansing in Jerusalem of the site that Marcarius was convinced was the sepulchre of Jesus. Marcarius wrote, "The discovery of the cavern, the new holy of holies, was a striking confirmation for the Savior's return to life."

The implementation of the emperor's decision was conveyed through Bishop Marcarius and the emperor's mother, Helena,

Under Constantine

---

50. Eusebius, *Ecclesiastical History*, X, v, 6-10 (New York: G. P. Putnam, 1932), vol. 2, pp. 449-451.

who had become a Christian at the age of sixty-five. Under Queen Helena's munificence, churches were erected on the presumed site of Jesus' sepulchre, on the site of the ascension on the Mount of Olives, on Mount Gerizim, and at Bethlehem. The main interest was in the site of the Church of the Resurrection (*anastasis*), as the Greeks called it, or of the Holy Sepulchre, as the more somber Latins termed it. The architects Zendbius and Eustathius built a vast basilica eastward with fine naves and an apse called the Martyry (witness). The zeal of Bishop Marcarius and the interest of Constantine and his mother in the Holy Sepulchre focused the attention of the Christian world upon Jerusalem, an emphasis that has remained to this day.

On the Mount of Olives are the sites of two ancient churches commemorating the ascension. The first, built by Helena, was supposedly above the cave in which Jesus announced to His disciples His coming departure and the ruin of Jerusalem.[51] This basilica of Helena was destroyed during the Persian invasion, and the site was almost forgotten. In 1868, however, adjacent to a grotto and on the site of the Constantinian church, the impressive church honoring the Lord's Prayer was built. It has been occupied since 1876 by the Carmelite order of France. Here the Lord's Prayer is pictured in mosaic on the portico walls in forty-six languages. The grotto itself is said to be the place where Jesus predicted the fall of Jerusalem and where He taught His disciples to pray the "model prayer" (Luke 11:1-7).

A few rods farther up the slope of the Mount of Olives and to the northeast lies the site of the other church commemorating the ascension, called the Imbomon, meaning the "higher one." The circular structure was built before A.D. 378 by a Roman matron named Pomenia.[52] This large structure, paved with mosaic and marble, was about 105 feet in diameter and consisted of three concentric circles of columns covered over to form two porticos. In the center, with the roof open to the sky, was claimed to be the rock showing the footprint of Jesus before His ascension. Facing west toward the Holy City itself was the street facade that included a large cross over a bronze door. It was reached by a stairs of twenty-five steps. Today, there remains on the site only the small rotunda built by the

---

51. P. B. Meistermann, *Guide de Terre Sainte* (Paris: Editions Franciscaines; Librarie Letouzey & Ane, 1936), p. 272.
52. Ibid., p. 272.

The Kidron Valley as seen from the Old City wall. This view includes the Church of all Nations and the Garden of Gethsemane.

Saracen conqueror, Saladin. A Moslem mosque adjoins the structure to the south.

Paganism revived after A.D. 361 under a new emperor, Julian. This did not, however, entirely stop the growth of the Christian community nor the building of churches. Still visible from the Mount of Olives is the "site of the Last Supper" upon the western hill, where once stood a church called "Holy Zion," the seat of the bishopric. This site is now dominated by the impressive Church of the Dormition of Mary, built in 1898 for the Roman Catholics under the sponsorship of Kaiser Wilhelm II. Slightly to the north is the church built over the traditional site of the house of Caiaphas, where Jesus was on trial. It is an Armenian structure, and for two decades (A.D. 1941-67) it was in "no man's land." Toward the bottom of the Kidron Valley is another church built during this Byzantine period, at the site of Gethsemane. The bare rock can still be seen within the modern church, called the Church of the Agony or the

Church of All Nations. Beyond this, also in the Kidron Valley, is the crypt over which once stood the church honoring the burial place of the Virgin Mary. Directly to the west, in what was the Tyropoeon Valley, is a small chapel commemorating the place of Peter's repentance following his threefold denial of Jesus. Still farther down the Tyropoeon Valley is the Pool of Siloam, which became the site of another Byzantine church that is no longer there, but it recalls the man born blind who found healing as he washed in this pool.

The Byzantine period (A.D. 350-636) marked the "golden age" of eastern Christianity and of the Mediterranean world.

Byzantine Period   Although pilgrimages were disparaged by Gregory of Nyssa, Christians from most nations flocked to Jerusalem to see the holy sites, to acquire merit, and to gather souvenirs. Nearly every Biblical site was commemorated by a church or a monastery or a chapel. The Mount of Olives alone had twenty-five churches.[53]

Among these churches on the Mount of Olives was one on the site commemorating Jesus' weeping over Jerusalem (Luke 19), and its Latin name was Dominus Flevit. Today a modern structure has preserved the site of the ancient one. The number of churches built during the Byzantine period throughout the whole land is amazing. Many times they are preserved only in fragments of mosaic or small cubes of stone tessera lying under the debris of the centuries.

While Rome was being ravaged by the barbarians in the West, the East still had relative peace in which to engage in theological disputes, to build churches, and to establish monasteries. Jerusalem was the recipient of great benefactions from Eudocia, wife of the Byzantine emperor Theodosius II. In response to a vow she visited Jerusalem in A.D. 438. She was received with great ceremony, and she returned to Constantinople with radiant memories and numerous relics. From her generosity came a whole series of new churches, including Saint Sophia of the Praetorium, Saint Peter-of-the-Palace-of-Caiaphas, Saint John the Baptist (this also survives at Saint John of the Hospitalers near the Muristan), and the church at the Pool of Siloam. Eight years later, Eudocia returned to Palestine after being alienated from her emperor husband. She ruled over Palestine in fact for twenty years, until A.D. 460. She restored the walls of Jerusalem that Theodosius II had begun

---

53. Join-Lambert, *Jerusalem,* p. 129.

in A.D. 413. The Golden Gate, the most prominent feature of the eastern wall and the most ornamental gate of the Holy City, has been attributed to Eudocia. In addition she built chapels at the monastery at Saint Euthymius in the Judean Desert, another at Saint Stephen's near Jericho, and a tower at the monastery of Mar Saba. Her major interest was the church north of Jerusalem at the presumed site of Stephen's martyrdom. The modern church on this site is one of the most impressive in Jerusalem. It is now cared for by the Dominicans, whose splendid library in the École Biblique is adjacent to this historic site on the Damascus road.

In the theological struggles of the era, Eudocia sided with the Monophysites—those who insisted that Christ had but one nature but were condemned by the Council of Chalcedon in A.D. 451. The result was a political, religious, and military struggle between the orthodox Christians, who adhered to the Council's decision, and the Monophysites, who did not. Jerusalem was torn by dissension, and many of the Orthodox Christians there were

Interior view of the Church of the agony. The mosaic Gethsemane scene overlooks the altar and the "rock of the agony."

Portion of the Madaba map that shows Jerusalem.

massacred by the Monophysites. Upon the advice of Simon Stylites and the monk Euthymius, Eudocia submitted to the Orthodox patriarch in Jerusalem and was restored to the communion of the Catholic church. Monophysitism, however, spread through Egypt and upper Mesopotamia and became linked with nationalistic rivalries. From that day to the present there has never been a true separation of church and state in the Near East. Consequently, theological dissension and nationalistic rivalries have tended to coincide, with the result that there has been no unified Christian witness in the Near East throughout the centuries. Instead, disgraceful and embittered rivalries prevailed, often leading to conflict.

Greatest of the Byzantine emperors was Justinian (A.D. 527-565). During this time Christianity enjoyed its greatest outward successes. It is believed that underneath the present Aqsa Mosque are the foundations built by Justinian for a great church honoring the Virgin Mary. Also, a church is believed to have been located between the Dormition church and the Tyropoeon Valley; it was built from 531-543 and called Saint Mary the New. The church was dedicated on November 20, 543, when Christian Jerusalem was at the pinnacle of glory. South and east of the

Joppa Gate is the great church that honors Saint James; it also serves as the headquarters of the Armenian church.

At the site of the present Saint Anne Church was the Byzantine Church of the Probaticum (sheep pool), which is now being excavated. Nearby was the Church of Saint Mary, which was believed to be the site of Mary's birth but later became known as Saint Anne's. Below, in the Kidron Valley, was a tomb alleged to be that of Saint James, the second Christian martyr. The famous Madaba mosaic map shows the Jerusalem of this period and in it are listed thirty-five identifiable monuments.[54]

During this period, the few Jews who were in the Holy Land and the Samaritans were mercilessly oppressed by Christians. Theodosius II reduced both Jews and Samaritans to a second-class citizenship and virtually deprived them of all civil rights. The Samaritans revolted several times, but they were finally suppressed in A.D. 556.

Because Justinian's successors could not continue the heavy expenditure on public works, the Byzantine Empire became badly divided and economic resources were strained. During the reign of the emperor Heraclius (A.D. 610-641), the Persians took advantage of this situation to sweep into the Byzantine Empire in 611. By 614 they had conquered Jerusalem after a siege of twenty days. Aided by Samaritans and Jews, the Persians perpetrated a widespread massacre of Christians in Jerusalem. They destroyed all of the beautiful churches except the church in Bethlehem, which was spared only because they saw on the front of the church a mosaic picture of the magi whom they recognized as Persians. Not until 629 was Heraclius able to dispel the Persians and to start rebuilding the country that had been ravaged beyond repair. After repelling the Persians, Heraclius undertook to rebuild portions of Jerusalem, but an even greater catastrophe followed—the Islamic Arab invasion of A.D. 640. Judaism and Christianity have a parent-child relationship, but in the heresy of Islam both faced their most formidable antagonist of the centuries. From A.D. 640 to the present, Jerusalem has been the focal point of the conflict.

---

54. Ibid., p. 140.

One of the source streams of the Jordan River, in upper Galilee.

3

Upper Galilee

Our survey of the land begins in the north and moves south, because the earliest invaders apparently came from the north.[1] Scholars estimate that man appeared in the Jordan Valley a half million years ago. Caves in Galilee and on Mount Carmel revealed skeletons of "early Palestinian man" of Pleolithic time (c. 200,000 B.C.).[2]

It was from the north that Abraham came, the ancestor of Hebrews and Arabs and spiritual father of Christians; "a wandering Aramean was my father" (Deut. 26:5).

OVERVIEW OF GALILEE

Galilee has not received the recognition it deserves in Palestinian geography and history, primarily because Biblical history centers in the south and central regions rather than in the north. Old Testament history touches Galilee only occasionally: the migration of the tribe of Dan; the influence of the Phoenicians on the kingdom of Israel; and the rival sanctuary at Dan, the northern extremity of the portion dominated by Israel. Isaiah refers to Galilee as the place of the Gentiles (Isa. 9:1).

In New Testament times, Nathaniel wondered whether any good could come out of Galilee, out of a town like Nazareth

1. James Parkes, *A History of Palestine from 135 A.D. to Modern Times* (New York: Oxford Press, 1949), p 16. Paleolithic remains were found at the Mughara caves in Mount Carmel and near the Sea of Galilee. See also Emmanuel Anati, "Prehistory of the Holy Land," *A History of the Holy Land,* ed. Michael Avi-Yonah (New York: Macmillan Co., 1968), pp. 10-21.
2. Yohanan Aharoni and Michael Avi-Yonah, *The Macmillan Bible Atlas* (New York: Macmillan Co., 1968), map 17.

(John 1:46). The strict rabbis distrusted the Galileans because they were less strict than the leaders in Jerusalem. Lower Galilee is important for Christians as the scene of the origin of Christianity, and for Jews because rabbinic scholars and pietists (haggadists) brought fame to Galilee during the centuries after the fall of the Jewish state.

From the hills surrounding Nazareth, at an elevation of 1,600 feet above sea level, the viewer can envision the panorama of history. To the north is the fertile oasis around Sepphoris, which during the Roman period was the most important city of the district called Diocaesarea. From these hills by Nazareth, Jesus could see the center of Roman power. Later at Sepphoris on July 4, 1187, the Crusaders rallied for the decisive confrontation with the Saracens.

Safad

To the north and east is "the high rough chain where Safad stands."[3] Safad represents the tenacity and faith of the Jews, who during the Middle Ages and since have made this a religious sanctuary and more recently a summer resort, a mecca for poets and artists. In recent history, a tragic earthquake killed a large number of residents in 1837.[4]

Later, this same city witnessed the victory of the Jewish colonists over their Arab neighbors in the struggle of 1947, resulting in the Israeli victory. Far beyond is the towering height of Mount Hermon, linked in poetic metaphor with Mount Tabor ("Tabor and Hermon joyously praise Thy Name"—Ps. 89:12). To the east on the horizon is the rim of an ancient volcano with two projections on either side called the Horns of Hattin. In 1187, in the decisive battle of the Crusades, the knights in armor—harassed by the Saracen armies under Saladin, seared by the midsummer heat, without water and enveloped by smoke from grass fires—were decimated by the victorious Moslems. The Crusaders fled in all directions or remained to be slain or enslaved. But nearer is Cana, the scene of the first miracle where Jesus "manifested his glory; and his disciples believed in him" (John 2:11). To the southeast is Mount Tabor, where Barak gathered his forces for the confrontation with the Canaanites under Sisera (Judg. 4:12). Apparently a volcanic cone, Mount Tabor is conspicuous from the surrounding fertile plain. The summit is now surmounted by a beautiful chapel,

3. C. R. Conder, *Palestine* (New York: Dodd, Mead & Co., n.d.), p. 92.
4. Edward Robinson, *Biblical Researches in Palestine* (Boston: Crocker and Brewster, 1838), vol. 1, pp. 321-324.

which has become for many weary pilgrims a setting of inspiration and a commemoration of Jesus' transfiguration, since early pilgrims inaccurately identified Mount Tabor as the site of that event in Jesus' ministry. To the south the hill of Moreh comes into view, where Gideon was victorious over the Midianites (Judg. 7), and just beyond is Mount Gilboa, where King Saul met defeat (1 Sam. 31). Between the hill of Moreh and Mount Gilboa and leading to the Jordan is the valley of Jezreel, the corridor through which the Philistines pushed eastward, to occupy the fortress city of Bethshan. At other times Midianites pushed west on raiding parties. Through this valley came Jehu, riding furiously from Rama of Gilead to the village of Jezreel to liquidate the remnants of the dynasty of Ahab (2 Kings 9:17-20).

Directly south of Nazareth across the Esdraelon Plain is Megiddo, which guarded one of the most important highways of the ancient world—the main road between Egypt and Asia. **Megiddo** Fifteen centuries before Christ, Thutmose III, the "Napoleon of

The Horns of Hattin. The peaks of the cliffs (center of photo) comprise the "horns." The Sea of Galilee is in the background.

Structures from the Canaanite period at Megiddo, overlooking the valley of Jezreel.

Egypt," fought here to conquer the gathered kings of Canaan (1468 B.C.), as portrayed in his mighty palace at Karnak. Through this pass came Pharaoh Necho, to be challenged by the young King Josiah at whose death the best hopes of the kingdom of Judah were dashed (2 Kings 23:29-30). Later came the armies of Alexander en route to Egypt. Through this pass marched the Romans, especially during the Jewish revolt when armies led by Vespasian occupied this territory. On this road Napoleon led his army from Egypt to the futile siege of Acre to the northwest. In 1917 came the British forces under Allenby in pursuit of the Ottoman Turks, who were being driven from the Holy Land after four centuries of misrule. After this campaign, Allenby was knighted as "Viscount of Megiddo." In June 6, 1967, columns of Jewish tanks sped toward Jenin from the coastal plain and pursued remnants of the Arab Legion toward the Jordan Valley.

Through Megiddo groups of pilgrims also came throughout the centuries. They traveled from Jaffa to Haifa, or over the hills to Nazareth, and then from Nazareth either east to Tiberias or southeast to Mount Tabor before continuing on to Capernaum. In this fertile plain of Megiddo, which was the scene of some of the world's bloodiest battles but is now the peaceful bread basket of Palestine, it is prophesied that the final conflict in human history between the forces of Theism and those who defy God's rule will take place (Rev. 16:16). Directly to the west is the new port of Haifa and the plain of Acre with its reminder of the departure of the British during the Mandate period and the arrival, clandestinely and otherwise, of Jewish refugees from Europe—an oppressed and long-suffering minority, finding at last a national home.

The Greek poet, Aeschylus, is credited with the statement, "Learning is through suffering." As Arnold Toynbee has noted, Palestine is a spiritual seedbed in which many seeds fell, but only two survived, Judaism and Christianity.[5] Palestine, even more than Asia Minor, is the scene of the perennial struggle between the East and the West, but also between the North and the South. The struggle was between the Nile civilization and the Mesopotamian, with Palestine crushed between these upper and nether millstones, being ruled over first by one master and then another, and only momentarily and precariously enjoying some measure of independence, as in the period of David and Solomon, the period of the Maccabees, and since 1967. Though even now the competitive forces are at work, the land of Israel is being tortured between pressures from the east, from the south, and at a greater distance, from the "super-powers"—Russia and the United States. All converge on Palestine, and the valley of Esdraelon is the focal point of this age-old series of pressures. As Toynbee further points out, the period of intense suffering occurred here following the accession of Tiglath-pileser III in 745 B.C. This "first bout of agony" was between 745 and 522, with the accession of Darius I. The second began in 221 B.C. and was between the Seleucids of Syria and the Ptolemies of Egypt, lasting until the victory of Octavian at Actium in 31 B.C. The third bout of agony was from A.D. 66 to 134, resulting in the elimination of the Jewish state and total control by the Roman invaders. The fourth period of agony was in the seventh century A.D., first with the incursion by the Persians in A.D. 614, and later by the conquest by the Moslems in A.D. 640. The struggle

5. Arnold Toynbee, ed., *The Crucible of Christianity* (London: Thames and Hudson, 1969), p. 11.

between East and West occurred again during the two centuries of the Crusades, with the Crusade challengers bringing in an intrusion of Western culture and ideas only to be engulfed later by the East. The second invasion from the West was by the British and French in World War I, which terminated legally but not actually in 1948. The center of this suffering was Palestine, and the chief sufferers were the Jews compared to the trials of pagans, Christians, and Moslems in that land. Into this maelstrom of strife and triumph, of anguish and hope, came Jesus with His unique message of salvation.

Extent of Galilee

Galilee is bounded on the north by the Lebanons and on the south by the Carmel-Gilboa ranges, on the west by the Mediterranean and on the east by the valley of the Jordan. The name itself means "ring" (Hebrew, "*galil*" means anything that rolls or is round, cf. Esth. 1:6; Song of Sol. 5:14; 1 Kings 6:34). In the Scriptures the term is applied to the area in the north surrounded by Gentiles on three sides, the Phoenicians on the west, the Lebanese directly to the north ("the entrances into Hamath"), and the Syrians, or Arameans, on the east. In Isaiah's time the term applied to the area adjacent to the Sea of Galilee (Isa. 9:1). At the time of the Maccabees it included the plain of Esdraelon (1 Macc. 12:47-49). In New Testament times it extended to the Carmel range. Northern Galilee is, from the standpoint of climate, the most attractive region of the Holy Land. Its elevation means that it is relatively cool in summer; its location plus its elevation means that it receives more than the average rainfall. The soil is deeper than in the hill country of Judea. The hills and the valleys are less precipitous, so that the moisture runs off more slowly. In addition Galilee is the beneficiary of the rainfall on the Lebanons to the north, thus Galilee's copious springs are fed by the mountains to the north. Today from this area, its moisture more than sufficient for itself, an Israel aqueduct conveys surplus water to the parched region near Beer-sheba. The situation is similar to that in North America, where most northern regions have more water than they need, whereas the southwest is semiarid.

UPPER GALILEE

The natural boundary of Palestine is the Litani River as it swings sharply to the west before emptying into the Mediterranean Sea north of Tyre. The canyon of the Litani, however, is so steep that it is not suitable for roadbuilding. Therefore the

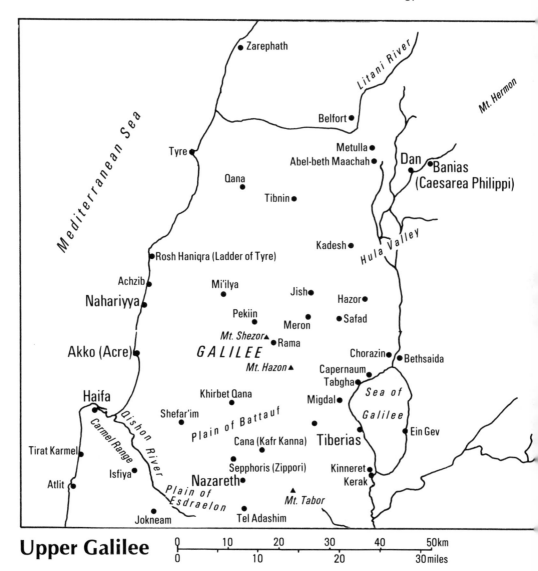

Upper Galilee

highway from Tyre to Damascus lies to the south, passing near Dan and Caesarea Philippi of New Testament times. Three geographical areas are open to Upper Galilee: to the northwest is the seacoast of Phoenicia, now Lebanon; directly north is Coele-Syria, between the Lebanons and the Anti-Lebanons, opening into what the Scriptures speak of as the "entrance into Hamah," and often mentioned as the northern terminus of the land of Israel; to the northwest lies Aram (1 Chron. 2:23) or Syria.

The present boundary, however, is from the white stone promontory on the Mediterranean called the Ladder of Tyre (Rosh Haniqra), which for centuries has been the southern border of Lebanon. From there the border continues east to the heights above the Hula Valley near the ancient mound of Kedesh, then north to the sources of the Jordan River near the present city of Metulla, and southeast to encompass the ancient Tell Kedi, or Qado (Dan), at the base of Mount Hermon, then directly south along the course of the Jordan to the Sea of Galilee. Northern Galilee is separated from southern Galilee by a shallow valley named Biqal Del Keren, leading directly east from Acre to the north shore of the Sea of Galilee.

The northernmost city in Galilee today is Metulla, a modern city founded in 1896. The name in Arabic means "overlooking," since the village views an area extending from Mount Hermon on the east to the Lebanons on the west and into a deep gorge by the name of Iyan. Two miles to the south is Abel-beth-Maachah located on one of the main routes of the ancient world. It guards the road leading in ancient times from Hazor at the northern end of the Hula into the valley of Coele-Syria. It almost is certain that this ancient town witnessed the sad procession of captives led by King Zedekiah and his sons following the fall of Jerusalem en route to meet victorious Nebuchadnezzar at Riblath far up the valley of the Litani. The king saw his sons slain before his own eyes were put out, and he was driven to captivity in Babylon (2 Kings 25:6, 7). Much earlier, Sheba sought refuge here after his revolt against David, while the city was under siege by Joab. Peace was arranged when a "wise woman" agreed to throw the rebel's head over the wall (2 Sam. 20:14-22). This border village was captured by Ben-hadad in response to a request for assistance from Asa, king of Judah (1 Kings 15:20; 2 Chron. 16:4). Later it was captured by Tiglath-pileser III in 734 B.C., and some of its inhabitants were deported to Assyria (2 Kings 15:29).

The topography of northern Galilee is dominated by snow-capped Mount Hermon, standing in majestic isolation at an elevation of 9,232 feet above sea level. When Lieutenant Conder and his survey party camped on Mount Hermon around 1880, they found on the peak a circle of cut stones with ashes, signifying a beacon or perhaps a sacrificial fire. Here also they found a cave hewn in the rock and ground leveled for building, called the Castle of the Youth by the local shepherds. Since 1968, Israeli youth ski down these slopes. From the summit is a breathtaking view. The vast wheat fields of the Hauran stretch out to the southeast. To the south is the deep valley of the Jordan, centering in the oval Sea of Galilee. Damascus presents a conspicuous green oasis adjacent to the trackless desert. The Hauran shows not only the wheat fields among the basalt stones, but also volcanic craters and the ruins of Byzantine villages are visible. To the west the gorge of the Litani River can be seen, surmounted by the imposing Belfort Castle, whereas farther west is the once great city of Tyre. Mount Carmel lies eighty

Mount Hermon

Cedars of Lebanon at the foot of a snow-streaked slope.

Snowcapped Mount Hermon from one of the wheat fields of Syria. The photo was taken in July.

miles to the southwest. "Hermon is the center of every view in northern Palestine."[6] Its snowy dome is visible at times from Jaffa and the valley of Jericho. This mighty mountain was called Shenir by the Amorites, and Sirion by the Sidonians, because of its white crest. From the hot fields south of Damascus an unforgettable view of this mighty mountain is afforded; the snow-filled crevices extend like fingers down the mountain giving visual relief to the harvesters in the basaltic fields of wheat. Almost as impressive, is the view from the Sea of Galilee in midsummer, when the remnants of the winter snow may often be seen. The best view of Hermon is from Birket Ram, at the base of Hermon to the southeast. This pool is perfectly round and may be the cone of a volcano; on the east side lies the modern highway. It was once thought to be the source of the River Jordan (Josephus), but subsequent investigation has not borne this out. This region for centuries has been inhabited by Druzes, an agricultural people who have maintained a sturdy independence from the various conquerors through the centuries.

Springing from the base of mighty Hermon are four perennial streams that unite to form the Jordan. The most famous

6. Conder, *Palestine*, p. 132.

source is from the eastern place called Banias, the Arabic altera-
tion of the Greek name Panias, honoring the sylvan god Pan, the
god of the flocks. An immense spring gushes out of a cave at
the foot of the mountain. The cliff is 100 feet high on the south
side of the western edge of a steep ridge. The roof of the cave
has fallen in, possibly because of an earthquake. Through the
mass of stones the water gushes out in a broad stream. The
clear, clean water pours over the stones at a width of over
fifty feet. Above the debris, in the face of the cliff to the right
side of the cave, are three niches with tablets. The niche nearest the cave is the most perfect and is in the form of an arch
incised into the living rock. It resembles the small apse, or the
mithrab, of a mosque, with a Greek inscription below it. These
niches presumably held statues at one time. Above, on top
of the cliff and to the left of the cave, is the Moslem shrine of
El Khader. There are also some rock-cut tombs and tesselated
pavement with colored marble in that same direction. One of
the most lovely spots in Palestine, this elevation, with its brac-
ing air and the welcome freshwater stream that supports luxurious vegetation, is a tonic for mind and body. The pure water
emerging from the earth is like a gift of God to a thirsty traveler.
It is not surprising that springs of this type were regarded as
favorite abodes of the local deities in pagan times (W. Robert-
son Smith, *The Religion of the Semites*). In Roman times, Herod
Philip honored his emperor by placing on the adjacent hill a
shrine honoring Augustus. To distinguish it from the Casarea
of Herod the Great, it was called Caesarea Philippi. Noteworthy
was his audacity at linking his own name with that of Caesar.
The shrine symbolized the triumph of Rome over Greece.

To this spot came Jesus and His disciples in quest of re-
freshment, rest, and perspective. Here, where the shrine testified to the belief that Caesar is God, Jesus asked His Galilean
disciples to assess His status. Peter's reply, "You are the Christ,
the Son of the living God," perhaps marked the first overt confrontation between Caesar and Christ in a contest that lasted
three centuries. Today, Peter's Lord reigns in millions of lives.
George Adam Smith was at his best in recreating this dramatic
scene.[7]

Now, a modern pavilion graces the site for the convenience

Sources
of the
Jordan

7. George Adam Smith, *The Historical Geography of the Holy Land*, 15th
ed. (New York: A. C. Armstrong and Son, 1909), pp. 476-479.

of tourists who visit the site. Farther on, at the edge of the
ridge, is the village of Banias with its round arches that once
held a Roman aqueduct. The town is surrounded by a wall of
the Crusader period. This is the village that resisted the Moslem
leader Nur Et Din, as portrayed by William of Tyre.[8] Dominating the ridge to the south is the mighty Crusader fortress of
Surbaiya, one of the most imposing structures of its kind that
remain in Palestine. Because of its location on a ridge, it is long
and narrow. At an elevation of 1,570 feet, it overlooks the Wadi
Selukieh. It was built about A.D. 1104 by the Prince of Tiberias.
"The castle has a romantic and beautiful appearance, as it is
not visible until quite close because of a high ground all around."[9]
The rooms and vaults of the structure are still almost perfect.
The stones measure eight to ten feet in length, dressed and
drafted. Round towers protect the walls. It was occupied by the
Hospitalers for twenty years, until A.D. 1164.[10] The entrance is
by a steep and narrow path along the southern side. The eastern
keep, very strongly built, and aided by a rock-cut moat, protected
the rest of the castle. Inside are many large cisterns and the
rooms of the tower are still in perfect condition. This castle,
located one and a fourth miles east of the town, measures 1,450
feet from east to west, and 360 feet from north to south. Robinson termed it "the most extensive and best preserved fortress
in the whole country."[11] Its workmanship compares with the
best of the period. From here, the prospect of the Hula Valley
and the mountains opposite is magnificent. This fortress dominated one of the most strategic sites in the Middle East: the
road between Tyre and Damascus, and also the Damascus-
Acre route via the Jacob Bridge, "the most vital in Northern
Palestine."[12] Robinson, not knowing that it was Crusader in
origin, commented that "the whole fortress made upon us a
deep impression of antiquity and strength, and the immense
amount of labor and expense employed in its construction."

8. William of Tyre, *A History of Deeds Beyond the Sea,* trans. E. A. Babcock and A. C. Krey (New York: Columbia University Press, 1943), vol.
2, pp. 260-263.
9. C. R. Conder and H. H. Kitchener, *The Survey of Western Palestine*
(London: Palestine Exploration Fund, 1883), vol. 1, p. 123.
10. T. E. Lawrence, *Crusader Castles* (London: Cockerel Press, 1936),
p. 44.
11. Robinson, *Biblical Researches,* vol. 1, p. 402.
12. Michael Avi-Yonah, ed., *History of the Holy Land* (New York: Macmillan Co., 1968), p. 236.

A scene near Banias (Old Testament Dan).

The second source of the Jordan is the river Leddan (North Dan), which emerges from the base of a volcanic cone known as Tell Kedi, located four miles west of Banias as stated in the Onomasticon.[13] It is an ancient *tell,* or mound, which is the site of the Old Testament city of Dan (Judg. 18:14), meaning "the judge," with its corresponding Arab equivalent, *kadi.* Prior to the invasion of the tribe of Dan from the Shephelah, as reported in Judges 18:29, the area was known as Laish. The spies from the tribe of Dan, noting that the inhabitants "dwelt in security, after the manner of the Sidonians, quiet and unsuspecting, lacking nothing that is in the earth, and possessing wealth, and how they were far from the Sidonians and had no dealing with any one" (Judg 18:7; cf. Gen. 14:14), urged immediate conquest. The copious stream that takes its name from the village, gushes forth from the base of the tell, creating an area of luxurious vegetation. This delightful spot was also made a shrine by Jeroboam I. His choice of the site was probably

13. Eusebius, *Das Onomastikon der biblischen Ortsnamen,* trans. E. Klostermann (Hildescheim: G. Olms, 1966), p. 122.

partially affected by its pleasant surroundings, linked with an apparently miraculous source of water, together with the fact that it was the outer, or northern, boundary of his realm, which then extended to Bethel on the border of Benjamin (1 Kings 12:29; 2 Kings 10:29). The exposed position of the place, however, invited invasions from the north; thus we read that Ben-hadad attacked the northern cities including "Ijon, Dan, and Abel-beth-Maacah" (1 Kings 15:20; cf. 2 Chron. 16:4; Jer. 4:15; 8:16). The tell today corresponds with the descriptions by early visitors. The area is still surrounded by dense vegetation.

It is significant that both Banias and Dan were religious shrines and that both possess an abundance of water and natural beauty. As W. R. Smith has noted, the ancients believed that nature's beauty spots were favorite abodes of the gods. Even today, villagers in the Lebanese mountains regard with religious veneration the caves out of which emerge life-giving water.

Today, important excavations are being conducted on the site of the ancient tell, sponsored among others by the Albright Institute of Archaeological Research. It also figures in the political turmoil of the area. Archaeologists report working there in 1969 with artillery shells whistling over their heads, as Israeli and Palestinian commandos exchanged fire. Tell Dan is near the border between Lebanon and Israel. This stream, called Ain Leddan, is the shortest and broadest of the four sources of the Jordan.[14] The site was inhabited long before the tribe of Dan settled there, as evidenced by the pottery that abounds at the place. Occupancy, according to this data, was prior to the time of Abraham, reaching as far back as the "Pre-Pottery Neolithic Period, more than seven millennia ago."[15] The Biblical significance of the area was the basis upon which it was decided at the Versailles Conference of 1919 that British Mandatory Palestine should include this ancient site.

Farther west is the third source of the Jordan, called the Nahr Hasbani. This is the longest source of the Jordan and the one most directly in line with it. It is twenty-four miles long, beginning at a spring at the base of Mount Hermon. The watershed between the Jordan Valley and the Mediterranean is just to the west of this stream. West of the watershed is the area

14. Nelson Glueck, *The River Jordan* (New York: McGraw-Hill Book Co., 1968), p. 37.
15. Ibid., p. 37.

drained by the Nahr Litani (Leontes) which empties into the Mediterranean north of Tyre. The two streams flow through parallel valleys southward for five miles before the Litani turns west.

The fourth and westernmost source of the Jordan is called the Nahr Bareighit, meaning the "Flea River." It drains the area from the Biblical city of Ijon (1 Kings 15:20). This stream enters the valley of the Hasbani less than a mile above the place where Hasbani reaches a junction with the Leddan and Banias branches. Thus, the waters of the Jordan Valley owe their common origin to the springs at the base of the Anti-Lebanon range, and Mount Hermon in particular. To the casual observer, the valley of the Jordan and the region between the Lebanon ranges is a continuous depression. Actually, however, the Beqa between the Lebanon ranges divides, as noted previously, west of Mount Hermon, the Litani turning west and the eastern portion draining into the Jordan. This rather complicated source of water has been understood only relatively recently by geographers of the area. Of these, the smaller but by far the most important historically, is the Jordan, which drains not the Beqa Valley but the lower buttresses of Mount Hermon.

BORDER CITIES

The natural boundary of Palestine is the Litani River. The route directly east and west from Dan to Tyre would cut through the country of Lebanon. But for centuries the boundary has been farther south, on a line directly east from the Ladder of Tyre (Rosh Haniqra). As Edward Robinson noted with surprise, this section of northern Galilee was, until recently, almost unknown (*Researches*, vol. 3, 365). Today the region is dotted with agricultural villages. During the period of the Crusades, there were two roads connecting Banias with Tyre; the northern one, a secondary route, was almost a straight line between the two places. The main road led to the south through Tibnin, where a Crusader fortress lies on a hill surrounded by a cultivated plain, described as "an extensive, undulating, cultivated region of great beauty, with the strong castle of Tibnin on an isolated hill in the midst.[16] The village by the same name lies at the base of the castle. Waters from here drain into the Litani River. The fortress of Tibnin, or Toron, was erected in A.D. 1107 by the Lord of Tiberias, as reported by William of Tyre (XI 5).

---

16. Robinson, *Biblical Researches*, vol. 3, p. 376.

A Roman street and arch at Tyre.

A relief from Tyre depicting Hector being dragged behind a chariot and a second chariot bearing gifts for ransom. Priam, king of Troy, begs of Achilles (right) the body of Hector.

The castle was designed, not for protection, but to secure the adjacent countryside as a fief. Saladin captured the fortress shortly after the Battle of Hattin in A.D. 1187. Later, the fortress, then in control of the Saracens, was besieged by another group of Crusaders in 1197. Because of dissension that arose among the Christians, the siege was abandoned although the defenders were twice on the verge of surrender. The castle was dismantled in A.D. 1219 by the Saracens, but apparently it was later reoccupied by Christians, for Sultan Baybars assaulted and occupied the castle in A.D. 1266, after which it passed from history.

Far to the north on the northern banks of the Litani River may be seen the impressive castle of Belfort (Esh-Shukif is its Arabic name). This is one of the greater castles surviving to the present day, but is seldom visited because of its difficult access. It is built on a promontory 1500 feet above the Litani River and can be approached from the south. The castle can be seen for miles, jutting up against the sky, a sight never to be forgotten. What historic scenes occurred within these castle walls: scenes of laborious construction, of ardent prayers, joys, and sorrows, culminating in the noise of battle followed by deathly silence. In 1189, two and one-half years after the Battle of Hattin, Belfort fortress surrendered to Saladin. The Knights Templars acquired the fortress in 1260. It was successively assaulted by Baybars in A.D. 1268. The defenders were enslaved, and the women and children were sent to Tyre.

Castle of Belfort

The once proud city of Tyre, which resisted Nebuchadnezzar for thirteen years and whose fall is so graphically described by Ezekiel (Ezek. 27), is today only a town serving as a modest fishing and trade center of the area. Formerly there was the island fortress and the adjacent mainland city. Since the siege by Alexander the Great, the city has been located on a peninsula formed by the landbridge constructed by Alexander's troops. An extensive series of ruins, now being excavated by French archaeologists, reveals an astonishing extent of Roman and Byzantine remains unknown a decade ago. Today the visitor is amazed to see the hippodrome shaped like an elongated hairpin, which could seat 100,000 spectators. An enormous ceremonial arch dominates the scene. The extensive necropolis features sacrophagi of the Graeco-Roman epoch and a mausoleum with scenes from Homer's *Iliad* (now in the Beirut museum). The Byzantine street is slightly over three feet above the well-paved

Tyre

Roman main street. In the time of the Crusades, the chain of fortresses between Damascus and Tyre included Tibnin (Toron) and Belfort.

In the Hebrew conquest under Joshua, the area embracing the eastern portion of northern Galilee was apportioned to Naphtali. It extended roughly from Mount Tabor in the south to Mount Hermon, Dan, and Ijon in the north. The allotment to Asher lay along the seacoast, from Mount Carmel north to Tyre. Zebulun was between the two toward the south, occupying much of the Esdraelon Valley between Mount Tabor and Mount Carmel and including the present town of Nazareth. The description in Joshua 13 ff. is in terms of the tribal borders and a listing of their cities; presumably the city list was acquired later after the tribal boundaries were originally assigned.[17]

Although assigned to Asher, the Phoenician occupants of Tyre and Sidon were never successfully challenged by the invading Israelites, and the seacoast area has always remained with Phoenicia rather than with Israel. Because of their proximity to the sea, along with the mountain barrier flanking the narrow coastal plain, Tyre and Sidon for years enjoyed the semi-independent status of city-status. Any occupying army from the land had great difficulty in conquering and assimilating them. In contrast, farther south along the coast, in Palestine there are no adequate natural harbors or protective mountain ranges, and the occupying land forces were better able to dominate the seacoast settlements.

Kana

About eight miles southeast of Tyre is Kana (*Qana*) sometimes confused with Cana of Galilee, in an area viewed by Robinson as "an undulating region of cultivated country ... with the large village of Kana on the brow of the valley."[18] Eusebius and Jerome make no distinction between this Kana and the one near Nazareth, describing this as "the Kana adjacent to greater Sidon in the tribe of Asher where our Lord made the water into wine," and the home of Nathaniel (cf. John 21:2).[19] This site was occupied prior to the Israelite conquest and its allotment to the tribe of Asher (Josh. 19:28).

Zarephath

North of Tyre, and along the coast is Zarephath, the city referred to by Jesus as the place where Elijah was sent to be

17. Yohanan Aharoni and Michael Avi-Yonah, *The Macmillan Bible Atlas* (New York: Macmillan Co., 1968), plate 76 (Josh. 19:24-31).
18. Robinson, *Biblical Researches,* vol. 3, p. 384.
19. Eusebius, *Das Onomastikon,* p. 116.

sustained by a widow (Luke 4:25; cf. 1 Kings 17:8-24), thus indicating that God's prophets may find greater receptivity among the non-Israelites. In Elijah's day, the area was under the domain of Sidon. The woman who provided shelter for Elijah was a God-fearing woman, who later came to accept Yahweh as her God. Josephus agrees that the area pertains to Sidon, and Jerome mentions it as having been visited by Paul. It was a small city in the sixth century, and the Crusaders made it a seat of the bishop, under the archbishop of Sidon. William of Tyre also speaks of the place as a bishopric. Crusaders also erected near the port a small chapel where they believed Elijah raised the widow's son from the dead. The chapel later became a mosque. Apparently the ancient city of Zarephath stood near the sea, whereas the modern village of the same name is situated on a nearby hillside; the location probably was changed for greater security. William of Tyre noted that the Crusaders (marching south) left the city of Zarephath on their right near the sea.[20] Today the inconspicuous village of that name is located on the east side of the modern highway between Sidon and Tyre. Local tradition claims that Jesus visited this place, alluding to the statement in Matthew 15:21 that Jesus visited the coasts of Sidon.

Phoenicia was the only nearby country that maintained friendly relationships with Israel (cf. 1 Kings 5). At one time or another, Israel was at war with all the other adjoining countries—Philistia, Syria, Ammon, Moab, Edom, and Egypt. Phoenicia was then as Lebanon is now, a neutral country and an enterprising commercial center with extensive international relations.

Another important site in Biblical history is Kedesh (Naphtali), located on heights overlooking the Hula Valley. When the survey party visited there in 1878, they found impressive **Kedesh** ruins including the main gate of the temple of Baal and the temple of the Sun, which is a Roman construction of the second half of the second century. The doorpost of the Roman temple, still standing, is a monolith fifteen feet in height. There is a road leading to the spring and a rock-cut tomb west of the city. Kedesh is mentioned in the city list of Thutmose III, although there is some question as to which Kedesh is intended.[21]

---

20. William of Tyre, *History of Deeds*, vol. 7, p. 22.
21. Yohanan Aharoni, *The Land of the Bible: A Historical Geography*, trans. A. F. Rainey (London: Burns & Oates, 1967), p. 143.

The village of Banias.

Its modern name is Tel Qedesh. Its king was defeated by Joshua (Josh. 12:22). In the tribal allotments, it was assigned to Naphtali (Josh. 19:32, 37) and designated a city of refuge (Josh. 20:7; 21:32). It was the hometown of Barak (Judg. 4:6). Aharoni notes the absurdity of identifying the place of Barak's birth with Kedesh in upper Galilee, since Kedesh is one of the great Canaanite cities that, according to Joshua 12, fought with the Israelites. Aharoni is among those who identify this Kedesh Naphtali with a larger site from the Israelite period located east of the valley of Jabneel "high on the slopes leading down to the Sea of Galilee, named Khirbet Qedesh."[22] This Kedesh is located between Tiberias and the outlet of the Jordan River at the south end of the Sea of Galilee, approximately a mile from the shore. Actually the narrative does not say the battle occurred at Kedesh Naphtali, but only that Barak was from there, and Deborah joined him there before recruiting the army, which was stationed on Mount Tabor. In Eusebius, it is placed near Banias, twenty miles from Tyre, which agrees with the position of Tel Qedesh. Chelo of A.D. 1334 placed the tombs of

22. Ibid., p. 204.

Barak and Deborah at this site. Josephus, in listing the cities of refuge, notes that Kedesh Naphtali is a place of upper Galilee.[23] The mass of tradition linking Kedesh of Naphtali with its location in upper Galilee rather than near the southwest shore of the Sea of Galilee makes Aharoni's conclusion less than convincing.

One of the most important cities of the Old Testament was Hazor, located at the south edge of the Hula Valley, about six miles west of the Jordan River and nine miles southwest of the former Lake Hula. The site of ancient Hazor ("the head of all those kingdoms"—Josh. 11:10) is one of the largest tells in Palestine and is twice the size of Megiddo. It is a sloping tableland with a flat top overlooking the valley to the east. It was in position to command all of the traffic moving north through the Hula Valley. It was in position also to challenge the traffic moving over the Bridge of the Daughters of Jacob between Damascus and the Mediterranean coast. Near the base of the tell today there is the attractive kibbutz, Ayelet HaShahar, with a small airport nearby. The city is mentioned in the nineteenth century B.C. Egyptian Execration Texts, which list the potential enemies of the Egyptians among the distant provinces. It is also mentioned in the ancient archives of Mari (Tell Hariri) on the middle Euphrates. Some of the letters mention messengers on their way from Mesopotamia to Hazor. Another letter notes the arrival of a caravan from Hazor, accompanied by Babylonian representatives. In the fifteenth century, there are references to Hazor by the Pharaohs of Egypt, including Thutmose III, Amenhotep II, and Seti I, and in some of the El-Amarna letters of the fourteenth century B.C. The letters indicate that the King of Hazor had rebelled against the Pharaoh and had captured several cities under Egyptian rule. Hazor was a Hyksos stronghold during the Middle Bronze period (1750-1550 B.C), "the largest Palestinian city ever built in the Biblical period," and its fall to the Israelites marked the end of the Hyksos empire, at least so far as its dominance of Palestine was concerned.[24]

It is stated that Hazor, a city-state, was the head of all the northern kingdoms defeated by Joshua, who "smote its king with the sword . . . and burned Hazor with fire" (Josh. 11:10, 11). The site later was occupied by Jabin, the king of Canaan, who reigned at Hazor. It was his army, led by Sisera, that was defeated by the forces under Barak and Deborah (Judg. 4, 5).

Hazor

23. Jos. *Antiq.* V. 1. 24.
24. Aharoni, *Land of the Bible,* p. 136.

In the ninth century B.C., Solomon developed Hazor as one of his several chariot cities because of its strategic location, guarding, as it did, the northeastern frontier. The city was conquered by the Assyrian conquerer Tiglath-pilezer III, in 732 B.C. (2 Kings 15:29). This site enters recorded history again in 147 B.C., when Jonathan, leading Jewish forces, fought with Demetrius, the Syrian, in the plain of Hazor (1 Macc. 11:62).

In 1955, Israeli archaeologists, directed by Yigael Yadin, began excavating the site on behalf of the Hebrew University and the government of Israel. Both the artificial mound, or tell, and the rectangular plateau on the north were excavated. The excavation revealed the city to have been founded in the Early Bronze Age (approximately 2500 B.C.). Its period of greatest strength occurred six centuries later, during the Hyksos period, when the area of the rectangular plateau covered 180 acres, making it the largest city in the country. The charred remains of the last Cananite city, destroyed by Joshua in the middle of the thirteenth century (Josh. 11), was "abundantly confirmed" after four seasons of excavation.[25] The archaeologists also discovered later settlements, including the city built by Solomon in the tenth century and the structures erected by Ahab in the ninth. From the standpoint of the history gained from the stratigraphy of the site and from the artifacts recovered, Hazor is one of the most important ancient sites in Palestine.[26] The water tunnel, discovered during the fifth season of excavation (1968), is twice the size of the similar system at Megiddo and is one of Hazor's most spectacular features.[27] The small museum on the site preserves some of the important artifacts uncovered during the several seasons of excavation. Solomon's Gate with its three doors are among the things that a visitor to this site may examine today. Hazor's size, location, and archaeological disclosures confirm the Biblical comment that Hazor "formerly was the head of all those kingdoms" (Josh. 11:10).

Meron

Meron, another town in upper Galilee, is located about six miles west of Hazor and three from Safad. It is situated at an important crossroads southeast of Mount Meron, where the

25. Y. Yadin, "Fourth Season of Excavation at Hazor," *Biblical Archaeologist* 22 (1959): 20.
26. Moshe Pearlman and Yaacov Yannai, *Historical Sites in Israel* (New York: Vanguard Press, 1965), pp. 29-34.
27. Y. Yadin, "Fifth Season of Excavations at Hazor, 1968-1969," *Biblical Archaeologist* 32 (1969): 63-71.

View across a man-made pond in the north end of the Hula Valley.

highway turns west toward the Hula Valley and where a branch road turns north. It is therefore on one of the main roads connecting Acre with the Jordan Valley and Damascus. Meron is among the towns listed by Thutmose III in the fifteenth century and by Ramses II in the thirteenth century. Today it is a small Israeli village. The mountain to the west of the village is the highest summit in Israel, reaching an altitude of 3,962 feet. The village itself was established in 1949. It is important in recent Jewish history as commemorated by a shrine honoring Rabbi Shimon and his son Eliezer. Rabbi Shimon lived in the second century B.C. and was a prime exponent of Talmudic literature. He is the author of " 'The Brightness,' the standard work of the Cabbala."[28] Meron is the scene of an annual pilgrimage sponsored by the Cabbalists to honor Rabbi Shimon.

A second-century synagogue stands nearby with its facade almost intact, consisting of three doors, the two smaller doors flanking the larger central one that is surmounted by a rounded arch. Nearby is the Cave of Hillel, named after the most famous of all the rabbis—the one to whom modern Judaism is chiefly

28. Zev Vilnay, *The New Israel Atlas: Bible to Present Day* (Jerusalem: Israel University Press, 1968), p. 493.

indebted. Local tradition asserts that when the stone falls from the lintel of the synagogue (it now looks as if it would fall at any moment) the Messiah will appear, and a rock situated on the wooded slope above, will be the Messiah's throne. The legend adds that when this occurs, Elijah the prophet will blow his trumpet to herald Israel's deliverance. Nearby, a deep gorge carries water to the Sea of Galilee during the rainy season.

The "waters of Merom" (Josh. 11:5) are difficult to identify.[29] Near the town of Meron is the Wadi Meron, which carries water from the springs under Mount Meron to a place where it joins the Wadi el-Tawahin. As the stream continues southeastward, it is joined by the Wadi Amud. It eventually finds its way to the Sea of Galilee. The perennial springs that feed this stream near the village of Meron are probably the Biblical "waters of Merom." Here Joshua's forces successfully defeated a coalition of Canaanite kings. These kings "came and encamped near one another at the waters of Merom, to fight against Israel. . . . Joshua and all his warriors caught them unawares by the waters of Merom and fell on them. Yahweh delivered them into the power of Israel, who defeated them and pursued them to Sidon the Great . . . until not one was left to escape. Joshua . . . hamstrung their horses and burned their chariots" (Josh. 11:5-9 JB).

The Talmud speaks of Safad as one of a series of hills from which beacons announce the arrival of the New Year. The town gained great prominence during the Middle Ages as a Rabbinic center. Jewish mystics made their headquarters here and it became one of the four holy places of Palestine according to Rabbinic tradition. In the early seventeenth century, Talmudic colleges in this area numbered eighteen. Here was installed the first printing press in Asia. Here, also, the first Hebrew book to be printed in Palestine was published in 1578.[30] During the latter part of the nineteenth century, the population comprised about 3,000 Moslems, 1,500 Jews, and 50 Christians, as reported in the Palestine survey.[31]

Safad

One of the most tragic convulsions of nature, an earthquake, destroyed most of the city in 1837, and nearly 6,000 people were buried under the debris. Not only is Safad on

29. In KJV and RSV it is spelled "Merom"; on modern maps, it is "Meron."
30. Charles F. Pfeiffer and Howard F. Vos, *The Wycliffe Historical Geography of Bible Lands* (Chicago: Moody Press, 1967), p. 132.
31. Conder and Kitchener, *Survey*, vol. 1, p. 206.

a hill, but the city itself is upon an incline on the sides of a mountain dominated on the summit formerly by a Crusader castle and now by a police station. The town itself is on three levels. The Jewish quarter lay immediately below the castle on the summit. The Moslems occupied the south and the eastern portion. When Robinson visited the town in 1838, the Arabs lived in stone houses and the Jews in mud houses on the western slope. In the earthquake of January 1837, more Jews were lost because their houses were poorly constructed. The intensity of the shock was accentuated by the houses higher on the hill falling upon those below. The population before the earthquake was estimated to be 8,000 (nearly 5,000 of those perished in the earthquake), of whom about 1,000 were Moslems.[32] Eighteen months later, during Robinson's visit, they were still digging out of the rubble, but the usual Friday market was well attended by peasants who gathered together from a considerable distance. Today, Safad is a thriving community featuring not only the synagogues and Rabbinic schools but also artists' colonies. It serves as a summer resort, for its height offers a welcome relief from the heat. In the summer of 1958, a group of students sponsored by New York University, failing to find accommodations there during July, were forced to spend a sleepless night in Tiberias, sleepless because of the excessive heat. Safad is the capital of upper Galilee, and its present population is entirely Jewish. It appears to have been founded by the Crusaders who built the castle on this prominent high place. When they were driven out, the Moslems made it their capital. The Jews, especially the Cabbalists, came in the sixteenth century. Here, the chief of the Cabbalists, Rabbi Izhak Luria, died in 1573.[33]

The town was attacked and destroyed by the Druzes in 1833. In 1948, it was inhabited by about 12,000 Arabs and 1,700 Jews. The pious defenders were reinforced when 100 freedom fighters joined them, with the result that the Arab garrison and population fled on May 11, 1948, inspired by a fear that the mammoth mortar used by the Jews was an atom bomb. The war memorial features this primitive mortar, called the Davidka, accompanied by an inscription from Jeremiah 1:18.

A town that is not mentioned in the Scriptures but is fea-

---

32. Robinson, *Biblical Researches,* vol. 1, pp. 320, 322.
33. Vilnay, *New Israel Atlas,* p. 482.

tured in Josephus as the Arabic village of El Jish (Gischala), described by the survey party (1878) as "a well-built village with a modern chapel," with a population consisting of about 600 Christians, and 200 Moslems. On the modern map, it appears as Jish (Gush Halav) and is located northwest of Safad about five miles. This was one of the towns fortified by Josephus and was the hometown of John, a Levite, described by Josephus as "a treacherous person." He was a rival of Josephus, and he attempted to obtain control over Galilee during the revolt of A.D. 66. Josephus reported that he defeated the plans of John to usurp Josephus's authority, but that later John escaped to Jerusalem and was one of the leaders in the factions defending the city in A.D. 70. A secondary road leads from this town in a northwesterly direction to the Lebanese border, and south to the vicinity of Safad.

El Jish

COASTAL CITIES

In contrast to the rolling tableland of Galilee is the area adjacent to the Mediterranean that is largely flat and sandy but highly cultivated with vegetables and citrus crops. This area is bounded on the north by the Ladder of Tyre (Rosh Haniqra), a promontory of white cliffs jutting out toward the sea. These cliffs are visible from Haifa. The area to the north is drained by the Wadi Beset and to the south by the river Keziv, which rises in the mountains of Meron. Halfway between the Ladder of Tyre and Akko is the modern city of Nahariyya, located at the place where the river Gaton enters the sea. This was the region occupied by the tribe of Asher. This stretch of coastland has been intensively cultivated throughout history and even more so now because of the Jewish settlers who migrated there from various parts of Europe. The city of Nahariyya was founded in 1934 by German Jews who were refugees from Nazi Germany. It was the first Jewish settlement in northwestern Galilee. Near the beach are the remains of a Canaanite temple dating back three and one-half millennia. The temple has a holy of holies, a larger holy place, and a narthex. Among the artifacts discovered in the ruins are slender figurines of goddesses, possibly representing Astarte, who is frequently condemned in the Bible. The modern city combines the features of an agricultural colony, which has expanded to become a holiday resort as well. Beautiful beaches lie adjacent to the city. North of the city are the ruins of Achzib, one of the towns of Asher.

Nahariyya

South on the coast is the ancient city of Akko (Acre). It is interesting that this site, rather than Haifa, was the main ancient seaport. Possibly, the smaller ships of antiquity could find a safer harbor here than at Haifa where the Carmel range comes abruptly down to the coast. Today, with the larger modern ships and a modern breakwater, Haifa is more advantageous. The importance of Akko, or Acre, lies not only in its facilities as an ancient seaport, but it is the terminus of a main east-west road separating upper and lower Galilee. This road and valley leads through the pass in the mountains east of Gamal and Gilon to the north end of the Sea of Galilee. Continuing through the broad fertile valley, bounded on the north by Shezor Mountain and on the south by the Kammon and Hazon, the road emerges on the east at the river Hammud, which flows through the plain of Gennesaret and empties into the Sea of Galilee. The road itself does not continue on east, but divides near Qaddarin Mountain, one branch going south, the other north to Safad and Meron.

Akko

Akko was the chief city of the territory of Asher, but during much of its history it has been under the dominion of Phoenicia. In ancient times, the city was located at Tell el-Fukhar. It was not unusual in ancient times for cities to be located at some distance from the sea, probably for protection from pirates. Thus Rome had its seaport at Ostia, Athens had its seaport of Piraeus, and Antioch had its seaport at Salamis. A few, however, such as Byblos, Tyre, and Caesarea, were located on the shore. The shoreland to the north of modern Akko is rocky and extends to the water, but to the south the wide sandy beach extends all the way to Haifa.

During the Middle and Late Bronze ages, Akko was an important Canaanite city-state. It is mentioned in the Egyptian Execration Texts of the nineteenth century B.C. It was conquered by Thutmose III in the fifteenth century B.C., and is the forty-ninth city in his list of conquered cities. Akko has always played an important part in Egypt's control over Palestine. During the El Amarna Age, an Egyptian garrison of 400 men and 30 teams of horses came to strengthen the garrison.[34] During the thirteenth century B.C. Pharaoh Seti I made his first campaign to Canaan. His son and successor, Ramses II, portrayed his conquest of Akko in an Egyptian wall relief. Akko was reported

---

34. *Evangelical Alliance* 85:19-21.

to have been a major town on the coastal route between Tyre and Achshaph in the Egyptian papyrus Anastasi I.

After the conquest by the Israelites, it is noted that "Asher did not drive out the inhabitants of Akko ... but the Asherites dwelt among the Canaanites" (Judg. 1:31, 32). It was not until the reigns of David and Solomon that Akko was incorporated into Israel. But it was returned to Phoenician control by Solomon in his agreement with Hiram, as payment for the timber and craftsmen employed in building Jerusalem (1 Kings 9:12, 13; 2 Chron. 8:1, 2). The city was conquered along with its neighboring cities by Sennacherib, king of Assyria in 701 B.C.[35]

During the Persian period Akko appears to have been independent. Likely it was used as a staging area by Cambyses for his invasion of Egypt.[36] Akko served a similar purpose in 373

---

35. James B. Pritchard, ed., *The Ancient Near East* (Princeton: University Press, 1958), p. 287.
36. Strabo, XVI. 758.

Akko (Acre) across the bay as seen from the south.

B.C. when Pharnabazos, satrap of Cicilia, made a futile attempt to invade Egypt.

After the conquest of Tyre by Alexander the Great, Akko submitted. The name of the city was changed to Ptolemais, when the region came under the dominance of the Ptolemies of Egypt. In 219 B.C. the city came under the influence of the Seleucids, under Antiochus III.[37]

During the Maccabean struggles, Ptolemais resisted the Jews. The city was besieged without success by Alexander Jannaeus, because it was the strongest of the cities of the area. For a short period of time Cleopatra of Egypt acquired Ptolemais.[38] With the arrival of Pompey and his Roman legions, Akko was absorbed into the Roman province of Syria in 65 B.C.[39] In 40 B.C. Ptolemais and Sidon received the Parthian leader Pacorus. About a year later, Herod the Great landed at Ptolemais with authorization from Rome to make de facto his de jure title to the kingdom from his rival Antigonus.[40] Herod welcomed Octavian at Ptolemais in 30 B.C. following the latter's victory over Pompey, and the two rode in a triumphal review of the troops (Jos. Wars I. 20. 3; Antiq. XV, 6, 7). Later, Herod built the gymnasium at Ptolemais although it never became the port of the Herodian kingdom. The emperor Claudius (A.D. 52-74) made Ptolemais a Roman colony and located veterans of his legions there.[41]

During this period the Jews refused to consider Akko a portion of the Holy Land because of the dominance of pagan influences there. However, a small Christian community arose there as evidenced by Paul's visit at Ptolemais with resident Christians in A.D. 57 (Acts 21:7). Ptolemais was the scene of violence during the first Jewish revolt. It was attacked by Jewish rebels; the citizens later retaliated by killing some 2,000 Jews.[42]

It was from Ptolemais that the Romans set out to conquer Palestine and to quell the Jewish revolt in A.D. 66. To Ptolemais came Vespasian, later joined by his son Titus, as together they prepared to conquer Galilee and advance on Jerusalem.[43] A bishop from Ptolemais attended the Council of Nicaea in A.D. 325.

37. Polybius IV. 61.
38. Jos. *Antiq.* XIII. 13. 1.
39. Appian, *Syrian Wars,* 70.
40. Jos. *Wars* I. 11. 1-3; *Antiq.* XIV. 15. 1.
41. Pliny, *Natural History* V. 7.
42. Jos. *Wars* III. 18. 5.
43. Ibid., III. 6. 1, 2.

Local residents ignored the name Ptolemais and its Canaanite name Akko was restored.

Akko entered history again with its capture by the Crusaders in A.D. 1110. Saladin captured it from the Crusaders in 1187, but it was reoccupied by Richard the Lionhearted and given to the knights of Saint John, who renamed it Saint Jean d'Acre. After the fall of Jerusalem, Akko became the capital of the kingdom of Jerusalem. It was the last Crusader fortress to succumb to the Moslems in A.D. 1291. It was rebuilt by Jezzar Pasha ("the Butcher"), who strengthened its fortifications. Napoleon besieged the city without success in 1799, using the adjoining hillock, Tell el-Fukhar, from which to bombard the city. The arrival of the British fleet guaranteed the survival of Akka, or Acre as it came to be called, and the defeat of Napoleon. After a five-month siege, it succumbed to the Egyptian leader Ibrahim Pasha in 1831. During the Mandate period, the British built Haifa as the principal seaport, and Acre has since dwindled in importance.

The visitor today can see the fortified section that was occupied first by the Crusaders and later by the Moslems. He will be impressed by the double walls, the deep moat, the cathedral, and the Jezzar Pasha Mosque. Also interesting are the caravansary and the Oriental *souk* (bazaar). Surrounding the old city are the Jewish residential quarters. Acre is one of the main tourist attractions along the Mediterranean coast because of its place in history and the preservation of much of its medieval character. From its walls is the view of the hills of Nazareth to the east or the broad expanse of the valley of Megiddo to the southeast or the long beaches extending south to the Carmel headland with the bustling city of Haifa nestled at its base. It therefore stands as the most important link between upper and lower Galilee.[44] It has, however, lost its importance as the commercial link between East and West.

Peqiin

Other cities of note in upper Galilee include Peqiin. It is an agricultural village located in the central plateau on a secondary road following the course of the Peqiin Valley. The historic city of Peqiin now includes mostly Druzes with a few Christians and Jews. It is believed that its members are the

---

44. A detailed summary of the history of Akko has been compiled by A. F. Rainey, of the Tel Aviv University, in an unpublished typescript entitled "Historical Geographical Sites" (1969).

The village square of the Druze settlement of Peqiin.

last remnants of the Galilean population of former times. They claim their ancestors were never evicted from the Holy Land. It is a picturesque village, which features a threshing floor, much livestock, the village well, and some two-story houses with grapevines reaching to the second floor roof to form a leafy arbor. The town itself lies in a valley. The ancient synagogue was restored in 1873, as indicated by the Hebrew inscription over the entrance. According to Rabbinic tradition, Rabbi Shimon here compiled the Zohar ("brightness"), a standard book of the Jewish mystics (Cabbalists). Nearby is the new Peqiin, established in 1955 by Jewish immigrants.

Northwest of Peqiin, on the road to Nahariyya, is the Christian village of Mi'ilya, which was built on the ruins of a Crusader fort known as the *Castrum Regis* (Castle of the King), which dates from the twelfth century. Still farther northwest, about five miles distant, is the important castle of Montfort, the castle of the Teutonic knights. This castle was built in A.D. 1226 as an important link in the fortresses guarding Akko, then the capital of the Latin Kingdom. It was a fief in the county

Montfort Castle

of Jocelyn. The fortress dominates the Wadi el-Kurn, which is a deep gorge running through the hills in a straight line to the west. The castle is isolated by the wadi on the north and a smaller valley coming in from the south. It is on a narrow ridge running east and west protected on the landside by a deep ditch, probably the quarry from which the stones for the castle were procured. The stones of the castle are eight or nine feet long and "smoothly dressed." The keep is on the eastern side, and beyond that is a low terrace with a semi-circular end. Farther down the slope is a round tower and another surrounding wall flanked by square towers. This was the outer defense of the castle. Attackers first had to overcome the low wall, then the terrace, then gain access to the second wall, and lastly, "an almost impregnable keep would resist the invader."[45] Close to the river is a large Gothic ruin, with the remains of a bridge and perhaps a mill, as reported by the survey team. The archives of this castle are now in Berlin. In 1271, the castle was captured by the Sultan Baybars who dismantled it and left

45.   Conder and Kitchener, *Survey,* vol. 1, p. 187.

Upper Galilee in the Hula Valley. Swamps that formerly existed here have been drained by the Israelis.

it in its present condition. The site was excavated by the Metropolitan Museum of Art in New York in 1926. Many relics of Crusader armor and other artifacts were recovered. Directly south, ten miles distant, are the ruins of another Crusader castle, Judin, near the modern settlement of Yehi'an. This fortress, with a good view to the Mediterranean, fell to the Moslems in 1291, at the end of the Crusader rule in the Holy Land. These fortresses were designed to protect the coast, with the major forts at Tyre, Tripoli, and Acre. Today, they simply evoke memories of an inglorious past, evocative of misplaced zeal and devotion, in contrast to the peaceful but busy new life evidenced in these congenial rural surroundings.

Arnold Toynbee agrees with Josephus that the Galilean Pharisees tended to be either zealots or backsliders (into paganism).[46] Josephus mentions that the Galileans tended to be rather volatile. It was here that John of Gischala represented the rebel, the fanatic, and the zealot; whereas Josephus, his contemporary, represented the tendency to compromise with the Gentiles. Jesus, who preceded them by two generations, represented a nonmilitant "revolutionary," whose aim was a peaceful revolution against the prevailing traditions and a return to the declarations of the great Hebrew prophets. Upper Galilee probably figured less historically because of its political divisiveness, which in part was caused by the topography—a mountainous terrain, although it was fertile and capable of supporting a more dense population than the hill country of Judea and Samaria. The majority of Galileans today still combine the pietism of the Pharisees and the "worldliness" of men like Josephus. Perhaps this dual tradition in Galilee is why the Israelis effected their most spectacular successes there—in the War of 1948 and in agriculture and in engineering projects such as draining the Hula marshes and building the giant Israel aqueduct to carry water from Galilee to the Negev.

The Galilean Temperament

---

46. Toynbee, *Crucible of Christianity*, p. 34.

Boat on the Sea of Galilee.

4

Lower Galilee and Esdraelon

Lower Galilee is bounded on the north by the broad Hilla-zon Valley extending eastward from Acre to the Sea of Galilee near Capernaum, and on the south by the valley of Jezreel. The Bay of Acre, or the Bay of Haifa, is a broad semicircular sand bar eight miles long and three miles wide. The river Naaman crosses the plain and empties into the sea south of Acre. In earlier years, sandbars kept this river confined, which created marshes to the south and east of Acre. In recent times, the river has been cleared, and the marsh has become a smaller lake, or pond. At the southern extremity of this sandbar, the river Qishon empties into the bay after making a similar cir-cuitous course, again explained by the sandbars which so fre-quently occur along the Mediterranean coast close to the mouths of the streams, creating marshes behind the dunes. The hills of lower Galilee drain into this plain in a series of small wadis including the Hillazon to the north, and the Evlayin. Still farther south is the Wadi Zippori, which drains the plateau north of Nazareth. This is the area of the ancient tribe of Asher, and it also is the region of the twenty cities that Solomon presented to Hiram of Tyre, which cities Hiram contemptuously called "Cabul" (1 Kings 9:13; cf. 2 Chron. 8:2). Their inconspicuous tells indicate civilizations that precede recorded history. The survey party of 1887 discovered what they considered to be a Roman road, extending from Acre southeast toward Bethshan.[1]

1. See also the map of Roman Palestine in Michael Avi-Yonah, *The Holy Land* (Grand Rapids: Baker Book House, 1966), p. 187.

East of the Bay of Acre and eight miles north of Nazareth is the extensive plain of Battauf (Biqat Bet Kerem). The hills north of Nazareth are approximately 1,500 feet in elevation. The plain of Battauf measures nine miles east and west, and spans a mile and one-half in width. The eastern half used to be marshy in the winter time. Tel Kison, located five miles southeast of Acre, is a large, artificial mound surrounded by a plain. Its elevation is about 130 feet above the surrounding plain. It was here that Saladin encamped during the siege of Acre; it formed the campsite of Richard the Lionhearted. It was the scene of a battle between the Crusaders and the Saracens, during which the Crusaders ransacked the camp of Saladin but were so preoccupied with the spoils that they neglected the defense of Acre.

Shefar'am

Shefar'am, located twelve miles east of Haifa, was and still is an important community. The survey party discovered Jewish and Christian tombs here, together with the ruins of a Byzantine church. The tombs were reported to reflect the transition from the earlier *kokim* to the *loculi*.[2] The ruined church seemed contemporaneous with the tombs on the south, which are also Byzantine. One of the seals of the Sanhedrin after A.D. 70 means *Shefar'am*.

Zippori

Zippori (Sepphoris), blessed with copious springs, is an ideal campsite. Located about four miles northwest of Nazareth, it was a very important city during the Roman period. At that time it was the capital of the district and went by the name Diocaesarea, from which comes Seffurieh of the Turkish period, with the modern Jewish spelling Zippori. During the Roman period, it had a synagogue, mausolea, theaters, temples, and an aqueduct.[3] The area governed from here in Roman times included Bet She'arim, Bet Lehem (Bethlehem), Cana, and all of lower Galilee except the Tiberias portion.[4] From the first to the fourth century A.D., it was the largest and most important city in Galilee. Thus Jesus in Nazareth spent His boyhood within walking distance of the Roman administrative center of the province. The term *zippori* means "bird," and the city was said to perch like a bird on a mountain. Later it was the center of Hebrew academies and the seat of Talmudic scholars, including

---

2. *Kokim:* receptacle for the dead arranged in a wall-recess. *Loculi:* trough-like receptacle for the corpse.
3. Jos. *Antiq.* XVIII. 2. 1; *Wars* II. 18. 11.
4. L. Waterman, ed., *Report of University of Michigan Excavations at Sepphoris* (Ann Arbor: University of Michigan Press, 1937).

Tibnin

Kadesh   *Hula Valley*

Rosh Haniqra (Ladder of Tyre)

Achzib   Mi'ilya   Jish   Hazor

Nahariyya   Pekiin   Meron   Safad

Mt. Shezor ▲ Rama

Akko (Acre)   *G A L I L E E*   Chorazin   Bethsaida

Mt. Hazon ▲   Capernaum
Tabgha

Haifa   Khirbet Qana   Migdal   *Sea of
Galilee*

Shefar'im   *Plain of Battauf*

Mediterranean Sea   Tirat Karmel   *Qishon River*   Cana (Kafr Kanna)   Tiberias   Ein Gev

Carmel Range   Isfiya   Sepphoris (Zippori)   Kinneret
Kerak

Atlit   Nazareth

*Plain of
Esdraelon*   ▲
Mt. Tabor

Jo   Jokneam   Tel Adashim

Dor   *Zerka (Crocodile) River*   Afula   Ein Harod   Belvoir

Megiddo   Yizreel   *Jezreel
Valley*

Caesarea   Tanaach   *Gilboa Range* ▲   Bethshan

Pardes Hanna   Jenin

Hadera   Ibleam

Tell Dothan   Salim

Misilya   *Jordan River*

T R A N S J O R D A N

Netanya   *S A M A R I A*   Tirzah

Tulkarm

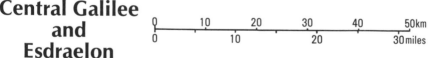

Central Galilee
and
Esdraelon

| 0 | 10 | 20 | 30 | 40 | 50km |
| 0 | | 10 | 20 | | 30 miles |

Rabbi Yehuda Hanassi who is buried in the synagogue at Bet She'arim. Zippori is the reputed home of Anna and Joachim, the parents of Mary, the mother of Jesus. It was visited by Antonius of Piacenza in A.D. 570. The Crusaders built a church here honoring Saint Anne, of which only the apses remain. The castle on the hilltop commands a view to all sides.[5]

The castle measures fifty square feet with walls twelve feet thick; a later addition included an Arabic door. The Crusaders camped here prior to the Battle of Hattin, in July 1187. They came from the south, the north, and the west for this crucial showdown with Saladin and his Saracens. After this decisive battle on July 4, those who were not captured or killed scattered in all directions but mainly retreated to the seacoast. Doubtless, the central location, the ease of access, and the abundance of water accounts for the Romans and later the Crusaders making Zippori their headquarters. Since it could not easily be defended, it remained an administrative center only during relatively peaceful times, such as the period during the first centuries A.D., until the Moslem incursion.

CANA OF GALILEE

Cana of Galilee is an important site to Christian pilgrims. It is mentioned three times in the Fourth Gospel: as the hometown of Nathaniel (John 21:2); as the site of the meeting between Jesus and the nobleman, which resulted in the healing the latter's son (John 4:46-54); and as the place of the wedding feast (John 2:1-11). The location of this Cana is unknown, but four sites lay claim to this distinction. One improbable site is the Qana which was in the vicinity of Sidon (Josh. 19:28), within the tribal territory of Asher. Another improbable site is the ruin known as Kanna, located a short distance west of modern Kafr Kanna (four miles northeast of Nazareth) and linked with the prophet Jonah of Gath-Hepher (2 Kings 14:25). In the nearby Arab village of Mash-had is shown the grave of Jonah, revered by both Jews and Moslems.

In modern times, Cana of Galilee is linked with Kafr Kanna, a Christian village, northeast of Nazareth. Quaresmius, guardian of the Holy Sepulchre from 1627 to 1629, noted a Cana of Galilee north of Nazareth and also a village east of Nazareth named "Sepher Cana." Since then, Kafr Kanna has been on the

---

5. C. R. Conder and H. H. Kitchener, *The Survey of Western Palestine* (London: Palestine Exploration Fund, 1883), vol. 1, p. 335.

Cana (Kafr Kanna) of Galilee is a Christian village located northeast of Nazareth.

regular pilgrim itineraries. The Greek Orthodox built a church there in A.D. 1566. The Greek church has two large ancient stone vats that resemble baptismal fonts. The Franciscans came in A.D. 1620 and purchased a house near the mosque in 1641. The present Franciscan church, with its red dome, was erected in 1879 on the ruins of the mosque, under which was discovered the mosaic floor of a Jewish synagogue dated from A.D. 500.[6]

Near the Franciscan church is a chapel honoring Nathaniel and said to be built on the site of the house of the disciple mentioned three times in John's Gospel and believed to be the Bartholomew of the Synoptic tradition. Notwithstanding the presence of three Christian churches—Latin, Orthodox, and Greek Catholic—and the information given by guides and guidebooks, this village of Kafr Kanna seems not to be the Biblical "Cana of Galilee."

The fourth, and probable, candidate is the ruined site ten

6. Clemens Kopp, *The Holy Places of the Gospels* (New York: Herder & Herder, 1963), p. 146.

miles north of Nazareth called Khirbet Qana. It is known locally as "Kana el-Jilil," the Arabic equivalent of "Cana of Galilee." "Cana," from the Hebrew *kanah* means "reed." The name apparently derived from the reeds in the nearby marshes. This ancient site lies on the northern edge of the long depression known as the plain of Battauf or Biqat Bet Netofa (ancient Asochis). This plain lacks natural drainage and at the end of the rainy season, even as late as April, used to resemble a lake.[7] It was strategically located on the ancient road from Acre (Ptolemais) to Magdala (Tarichaeae) on the Sea of Galilee between Tiberias and Capernaum. It was also near the road leading from Nazareth, north through ancient Sepphoris to Jotapata, two miles north. Josephus lived in a Cana of Galilee, near the "plain of Asochis" (Battauf), which presents strong evidence for the northern site.[8] Early pilgrim itineraries clearly favor the northern site. Theodosius (A.D. 530) reports that, "It is five miles from Diocaesarea to Cana of Galilee. From Diocaesarea to Nazareth is five miles."[9] Antonius of Piacenza (A.D. 570) reports that in traveling from Acre to Diocaesarea (Zippori), "Three miles farther we reached Cana where our Lord was at the wedding; and we reclined on His very couch on which I . . . wrote the names of my parents. There were two waterpots there: . . . and we bathed in the fountain for a blessing. Thence we came to Nazareth."[10] These witnesses both point to the northern site, Khirbet Qana, since it lies on the Acre, Qana, Zippori, Nazareth road. The monk Epiphanius (A.D. 775) noted that the distance from Tiberias to Mount Tabor is a day's journey and it is also a day's journey from Mount Tabor "to the great city of Cana in Galilee, where the wedding took place . . . where the miricle was performed. . . ."[11] This also suggests the northern site since Kafr Kanna actually was less than a day's journey from Mount Tabor. Also, two medieval sources credit Queen Helena with the building of the church at Khirbet Qana. During the Roman period this town was of considerable size. It is understandable, as Dalman noted, that Nathaniel in

7. Gustaf Dalman, *Sacred Sites and Ways: Studies in the Topography of the Gospels.* trans. Paul P. Levertoff (London: Society for Promotion of Christian Knowledge; New York: Macmillan Co., 1935), p. 103.

8. Jos. *Vita* 16. 41.

9. Kopp, *Holy Places,* p. 150.

10. Aubrey Stewart, trans., "Holy Places Visited by Antinius Martyr," *Library of the Palestine Pilgrims' Text Society* (New York: AMS Press, 1971), vol. 2, p. 4.

11. Kopp, *Holy Places,* p. 151.

the then-important city of Khirbet Qana would look past the administrative city of Sepphoris (Diocaesarea) to tiny Nazareth and ask smugly, "Can any good come out of Nazareth?"

The chief arguments against Khirbet Qana, however, are its location in a site without evident water. Also, it was not located on the shortest route from Nazareth to Capernaum. It also is difficult to explain how a site where Helena built a church could have been so easily forgotten by Christian pilgrims from that day to the present. Although the location of Cana cannot be ascertained with certainty, this does not hinder one's appreciation for the fact that near Nazareth, Jesus performed His first miracle "and manifested his glory, and his disciples believed in him" (John 2:12).

NAZARETH

Today, two communities bear the name Nazareth. One is the historic city, inhabited mostly by Christian Arabs; but on the plateau above the old city is the new suburb occupied by Jewish settlers, an area characterized by apartments and newer hotels. Our primary concern, however, is with the historic city.

It was in this town of lower Galilee that Jesus spent most of His life. Luke states that Jesus as a boy of twelve returned to Nazareth with His parents, and He was subject to them (Luke 2:51). His father was a carpenter and Jesus as his eldest son assisted him (Matt. 13:55; Mark 6:3). Today, the inquisitive tourist can visit a "modern" carpenter shop, which has much in common with the shop run by Joseph. In such a shop, a large block of wood served for a workbench, and piled in the corner were several shafts of wood, a few of them straight. In the center the workman fashioned a primitive plow, consisting of a wooden beam to which were joined two shafts to go up on either side of the draft animal. A handle, or tiller, would enable the farmer to guide the plow. A beam projected downward, to which was affixed an iron point. This type of instrument was used for thousands of years in Palestine and is used today by many Arab tillers of the soil. This plow does not have a mold board and therefore does not turn the soil over; it merely stirs it up. Each implement is custom-made, and the reputation of the craftsman depends upon the product of his craft. Rather amazingly, even today in Nazareth a carpenter shop exists very similar to that which must have operated in the first century.

Mary's Well in Nazareth.

The major church in Nazareth is a recent structure, dominated by a large polygonal tower sloping upward to a point. Completed in 1936, it was built on the site of an earlier structure erected in 1730 by Franciscan Fathers. This in turn was built upon the remains of an older Crusader church. This church features a grotto where it is stated that the holy family lived for some thirty years. This could be true, for poor families did live in the numerous caves of Palestine. The cave had the advantage of being "air-conditioned" in summer and winter, and they required a minimum of upkeep. It is somewhat unlikely, however, that a man with a trade like Joseph's would be content to live in a cave on a permanent basis. The tradition is suspect from another standpoint, namely that many Roman Catholic shrines feature grottos almost as a matter of course, perhaps under the assumption that a special sanctity attaches to a subterranean place. The only conclusion is that Joseph and his family might have lived in a cave such as this for a limited period of time.

Adjacent to the grotto, on the floor, is a Greek mosaic inscription that reads, "For Coronus, Dean of Jerusalem." This indicates that the Crusaders built upon the ruins of an ancient Byzantine church. Therefore at least four different structures have been erected on the spot believed to be the place of the communication of the angel Gabriel to a betrothed girl by the name of Mary (Luke 1:26-32). Nearby is the Church of Saint Joseph, claimed to be the site of the carpenter's shop. Between the Church of Joseph and that of Mary is a Franciscan monastery. Not far away is another convent called the Dames of Nazareth. The monastery contains a museum with Crusader remains. Farther up the hill is the Anglican church, and still farther, a small Maronite church. The Franciscans also own a small church adjacent to the Maronite one. This church, erected in 1861, contains a rock called the "Mensa Christi" (table of Christ), which preserves a tradition that Christ dined here after His resurrection. Between these buildings and the water supply of the village (Mary's well), is the Greek Orthodox church, built over the spring that emerges in the public square at "Mary's well." It is called the Church of Saint Gabriel. Before water was piped to the residences, the women of the village gathered here at "Mary's well" for the family supply of water and carried it home in four-gallon jars balanced on their heads. In this part of the world, especially among Moslems, it is a woman's chore to provide the family with fuel and water. The Moslem community is served by a mosque near the village market. Like most Arab villages, Nazareth has its *souk*, where a buyer can purchase such items as ropes or tin vessels fabricated by hand. In another section, a wide variety of freshly grown, colorful vegetables is sold from stalls lining the street. Most of the narrow cobblestone streets leading up the hillside have in their centers (rather than in gutters at either side) a storm sewer to carry off the winter rainfall.

Other churches, of lesser importance, are located in Nazareth. Toward the southern edge of the town is the Convent of Saint Clair. At the south edge of Nazareth is the Convent of Mary's Fear ("Notre Dame de l'Effroi"), which belongs to the Franciscan fathers and preserves a tradition that Mary stood here in fright as she saw her son led by the crowd to the brow of the hill to be cast down headlong. This prominence, known as the "Precipice of the Lord's Leap" is a conspicuous feature of the terrain south of the city.

Fruit stands along a Nazareth street. Note the drain gutter in the center of the street.

On a mountain overlooking Nazareth from the north is a basilica commemorating Jesus' youth. It is owned by the monks of the Salesian Order. It reminds one of the New Testament statement concerning Jesus' physical, mental, social, and spiritual growth (Luke 2:52). Today, Nazareth has the largest community of Arabs in Israel (30,000). Its growing suburbs contain, in addition, nearly 12,000 Jews.

Recent archaeological excavations by Franciscans near the Church of Annunciation have brought to light the foundation of an ancient village and the walls and floors of Byzantine and medieval churches. Here were found some additional "Nazareth Capitals" believed to be the work of French artists. These elongated faces are assumed to represent the prophets of Israel. Some of the capitals are in the Palestine Archaeological Museum in East Jerusalem. A torso has also been discovered here recently, perhaps depicting the angel Gabriel.[12]

---

12. Moshe Pearlman and Yaacov Yannai, *Historical Sites in Israel* (New York: Vanguard Press, 1964), p. 74.

It takes little imagination to envision Jesus growing up in the stimulating environment of Nazareth. From the hills surrounding this village He could look to the south and see caravans headed toward Acre or Ptolemais. An hour's walk to the northwest could take Him to Diocaesarea (Sepphoris), the Roman administrative center of the whole province. It would be obvious to Jesus that "those who are supposed to rule over the Gentiles lord it over them" (Mark 10:42). As He watched dignitaries with their retinue come and go He would note the contrast between the "faith of the fathers" and the pomp and circumstance that the Gentiles considered to be important. The contrast between master and servant prompted His conviction that "he that would be greatest of all shall be servant of all" (Mark 10:44). He undoubtedly shared in the aversion of the pious toward their fellow countrymen and villagers who eagerly curried the favor of the Gentile "establishment." Jesus saw the difference between an attitude of servility that was willing to sacrifice principle for convenience and the attitude of genuine service that was inspired by love for God and man.

In the immediate environs of Nazareth, Jesus also could appreciate the "lilies of the field" and note the grass that appears suddenly in the spring but soon after withers under the blazing May sun.

He observed women of the village, perhaps His own mother, grinding the meal in the cool of the morning with a circular stone about fifteen inches in diameter, probably made out of nearby basalt rocks. Later He would use this familiar chore in a parable: "One shall be taken, and the other left" (Matt. 24:41). Jesus probably knew some neighbor boys who furnished the precedent for His parable of the prodigal son. There were those who left the village to spend their lives in careless living in Tiberias, Ptolemais, or Diocaesarea, responding to the passion of the flesh. From the brow of the hill He could see to the south more caravans traversing the broad valley below Him, perhaps pilgrims returning from Jerusalem. Jesus was a member of these pilgrimage parties more than once during His growing years.

Nazareth then was a conservative Jewish community, but not isolated. It was surrounded by a world filled with constant tension between the East and West—between the true God and pagan idols, between the flesh and the spirit, between the old and the new. One world was represented by the Hebrew prophets and the other world, by the Greco-Roman environs. The tension that had broken out, more than a century before Jesus' time, in the Maccabean struggle would emerge again three decades after Jesus' death, in the first Jewish revolt of A.D. 66. These political tensions doubtless occupied the thoughts of Jesus as He grew into manhood. Today, Nazareth, as much as any community in the area, attempts to mediate between Jew, Christian, and Moslem. Previous efforts to entice the Arabs of Nazareth to militant action against Jewish authorities have proved ineffective. The Arabs of Nazareth today demonstrate the possibility of diverse groups working together effectively to rebuild the Holy Land.

THE SEA OF GALILEE AND ITS CITIES

Deep in a bowl, with an open end to the north and south, lies the lowest freshwater lake in the world, nearly 700 feet below the level of the Mediterranean. It is to many the most beautiful spot in the Holy Land, whether it is viewed from the Horns of Hattin, or from the heights near Safad, or from the slopes of Mount Hermon, or from the Golan Heights to the east. This usually placid body of water, thirteen miles long and eight miles wide, presents an unforgettable sight. Its shape is like a heart and its place in the country is not unlike that of a heart in the body. Here, more than at any other locality on the globe, is the scene of the origin of Christianity. Indeed Jerusalem was the place of Christianity's confrontation and challenge to the world and Antioch was the springboard of its Gentile mission, but the Sea of Galilee is the place of its origin and its formative period. Capernaum, on the north shore, was the center of Jesus' public ministry. From here He recruited the apostles, who would continue the movement after His departure to become the authentic definers of His message and mission. On these shores sturdy laborers and businessmen "rose up without a word" to follow Jesus and, through the discipline of obedience and suffering, became His martyrs (witnesses).

The northernmost city bordering the lake was Chorazin, whose lack of response to Jesus' ministry called down His malediction. It has been identified with Khirbet Korazim, less than three miles north of Tell Hum, the probable site of Capernaum. Jesus linked it with Bethsaida and Capernaum in His condemnation (Matt. 11:21; Luke 10:13). At the time of Eusebius (c. A.D. 340) it was uninhabited. Today it is only a field of ruins. Excavations

Chorazin

Synagogue ruins at the site of Chorazin.

in the area were conducted in May and June of 1962, forty years after an earlier excavation. The town was considerable in size, comprising about fifteen acres on the hilltop and on the southwestern slopes. The houses were of basalt; some walls are still about ten feet high. There was a synagogue on the hilltop in the center of the town. Jesus probably preached in this one or in an earlier one on the same site. Three building phases were identified by the excavators, one in the second to fourth centuries A.D., another in the Byzantine period, and the last in the thirteenth to the fifteenth centuries A.D.[13]

Bethsaida was the hometown of Peter and Andrew (John 1:44; 12:21). Peter's house was close to the synagogue in Capernaum (Mark 1:29). A question persists as to whether there were two Bethsaidas or one. In favor of two is the fact that one is called "Bethsaida in Galilee" (John 12:21), which implies another Bethsaida elsewhere. It is generally agreed that there was a

Bethsaida

13. Z. Yeivin, "Chorazin," *Israel Exploration Journal,* 1962, pp. 152-153.

Bethsaida near the northeast shore of the Sea of Galilee just east of the Jordan River, the Roman town of Bethsaida Julius. It is about a mile from the Sea of Galilee (Tiberias), situated 100 feet in elevation above the lake. It was located in Gaulanitis and was enlarged to be the capital by Philip Tetrarch, who named it Julius after Julia, daughter of the emperor Augustus. This Roman city stood on the ruins of the ancient village of Bethsaida at Khirbet el Araje (Zizyphus tree).[14] In support of this identification, the Gospel accounts, Matthew 14:13 and Mark 6:31, 32, indicate that Jesus withdrew with His disciples to "a lonely place." Luke agrees by stating that they "withdrew apart to a city called Bethsaida" where they could be by themselves (Luke 9:10). John indicates that it was on "the other side of the Sea of Galilee" (John 6:1), and some distance from Capernaum (John 6:16; John 6:24). In the light of Mark 6:32 and 8:19, this would be the location of the first miracle of the feeding of the multitude. The preponderance of evidence makes it clear that at least the major miracle of the loaves occurred east and south of Bethsaida Julius, on the northeast shore of the lake, where there is a grassy location much smaller in extent than the plain of Gennesaret, yet large enough to accommodate a multitude.[15] The second miracle of the loaves appears to have been in the Decapolis, near the eastern shore of the lake, opposite from Magdala (cf. Dalmanutha, Mark 8:10).[16]

Capernaum

All four Gospels indicate that Capernaum was the center of Jesus' public ministry. It was His home away from home. It was here at Peter's house that He healed the disciple's mother-in-law, and here, also, on several occasions He preached and healed the sick in the synagogue. Nevertheless Capernaum is one of the cities condemned by Jesus for its lack of receptivity of His gospel. In any case, it is the most important single site in this area from the standpoint of Christian history.

14. Eugene Hoade, *Guide to the Holy Land,* 4th ed. rev. (Jerusalem: Franciscan Press, 1962), p. 697.
15. Kopp, *Holy Places,* pp. 180-186; Jos. *Antiq.* XVIII. 2. 28; G. A. Turner, *The Gospel According to John* (Grand Rapids: Eerdmans Publishing Co., 1964) pp. 153, 154; Emil G. Kraeling, ed., *Rand McNally Historical Atlas of the Holy Land* (Chicago: Rand McNally & Co., 1959), pp. 386, 387.
16. Several ancient manuscripts have *Mageda,* others *Melegada,* and still others *Magdala.* See Kurt Aland, *Synopsis Quattor Evangeliorum,* 3d ed. (Stuttgart: 1965), p. 223.

There are two rival claims for this site. One is Tell Minyah and the other is Tell Hum. When Edward Robinson visited the area in 1838, he carefully and critically surveyed the site at Tell Hum, which consists of, then and now, basalt ruins lying some two miles west of the Jordan River and on the northwest shore of the lake. Robinson, not at all adverse to disputing church ecclesiastical tradition, was not surprised that this tradition identified the site as Capernaum. He describes the area as about a half a mile in length and a quarter mile from the shore and consisting of foundations, falling walls, and other buildings of unhewn stones. Nearby were "ruins of an edifice, which, for expense of labor and ornament, surpasses anything we have yet seen in Palestine."[17] He concluded that the impressive ruins must have been the church or heathen temple, but he concludes: "the confusion is too great and hopeless, to admit of any certainty." Because literary sources (Josephus especially) linked

17. Edward Robinson, *Biblical Researches in Palestine and in the Adjacent Regions* (Boston: Crocker and Brewster, 1838), vol. 2, p. 407.

The site of Capernaum, on the northwest shore of the Sea of Galilee.

Synagogue ruins at the site of Capernaum. This building dates from the second century A.D. but was probably built on the same site as the synagogue of Jesus' day.

A Roman inscription on one of the columns of the Capernaum synagogue.

A millstone on its base, in Capernaum.

Capernaum with the plain of Gennesaret, Robinson was sure that these ruins were not those of Capernaum.

In the spring of 1864, the area was visited by H. B. Tristram. After the examination of various sites, he concluded that Tell Hum was not the site of Capernaum, basing his conclusion chiefly on the literary source of the New Testament and of Josephus. Nor did he accept Khan Minyah as the probable site. Instead, at "the round fountain of Ain Mudawarah, we find a spot of perfect harmony with the accounts of the evangelists and of Josephus, and in fact the only possible locality which harmonize all the accounts."[18] He believed that this site agrees with Josephus's description of a place which abounds in water and with fish like those of the Nile. Colonel Wilson agreed that the site of Capernaum was the Bay of Et Tabighaa because of the great spring that corresponds with the description of Josephus as the fountain of Capernaum.

With this, William Thomson agrees. Thomson was a missionary for forty-five years in Syria and Palestine and a careful observer of historical sites. He agreed with Wilson saying, "there can be no reasonable doubt that Ain et Tabighaa is the fountain which Josephus calls Capharnaum and probably the fish—coracinus—mentioned by him are still found there."[19]

At Tell Hum, however, Thomson found a mass of shapeless ruins, very extensive—the most impressive found anywhere on the lake shore. He found that the limestone for the synagogue was cut from the mountains to the northwest and that it was the same date as synagogues at Kedesh, Berim, and Meron. Despite the testimony of Josephus, Thomson concluded that Tell Hum is the authentic Capernaum, partly because of the impressive ruins and also because of its proximity to Chorazin.[20]

Robinson believed that Khan Minyah, lying at the northern edge of the plain of Gennesaret, was the site of Capernaum. The khan was in ruins during the nineteenth century, but was obviously a large and well-built structure like other important ones along the Damascus road. Robinson noted that the testimony of Quaresimius clearly identified Capernaum with the khan called by the Arabs "Minyah." By the process of elimination, Robinson

18. H. B. Tristram, *The Land of Israel: A Journal of Travels in Palestine* (London: Society for Promoting Christian Knowledge, 1865), p. 442.
19. William M. Thomson, *The Land and the Book* (Hartford, Conn.: S. S. Scranton Co., 1908), vol. 2, p. 416.
20. Ibid., pp. 421-423.

agreed with this identification in spite of the fact that most maps of ancient and medieval times show Tell Hum off the main road to Damascus in the Roman period. It was a custom station and the seat of a small Roman garrison. It was also the center of small commercial routes.[21] It was east of the main highway in 1878, 1924, and 1967. That it had customs and police indicates its proximity to the border between Galilee and Gaulanitus.[22]

In literal fulfillment of Jesus' prophecy, the sites of Bethsaida, Chorazin, and Capernaum were deserted. The sites were unknown at the time of Eusebius (265-340). The moral degeneracy of the inhabitants a hundred years after Jesus' ministry is testified to in the Rabbinic writings, which state that "the people of Kefar Nahum were sinners."[23] We learn that a Christian church was begun in the vicinity in A.D. 352 by Joseph, Count of Tiberias.[24] Its early name seems to have been Kefar Techumin, meaning boundary or Sabbath limit.

Colonel Wilson, in 1866, explored the ruins and described them as those of a synagogue. The Franciscans were able to purchase the site in 1894. The ruins were explored by Professors Kohl and Watzinger in 1905. The Franciscans continued excavation, and in 1922 they published a preliminary report. The synagogue faced south toward Jerusalem and included an upper gallery to the north, called the matronaeum, where the women could worship. East of the synagogue was an enormous hall with eight doors, probably a school adjacent to the synagogue. Partial reconstruction of the building was made by Franciscan Gaudence Orfali in 1926.[25]

The large eastern hall is of basalt as is the retaining wall north of the synagogue. The synagogue is made of limestone with elaborately carved capitals and friezes of Biblical motifs. Wilson noted that north of the ruin are "two remarkable tombs, one with limestone blocks below ground level, the other a rectangular building above ground. The synagogue measured nearly fifty-seven by seventy-five feet.[26] Wilson found here a remarkable stone block engraved with a pot of manna and with the words, "I am the bread of life, your fathers ate manna here

---

21. Hoade, *Guide to the Holy Land*, p. 704.
22. Conder and Kitchener, *Survey,* vol. 1, p. 416.
23. Midrash Koheleth, 14. 2; 109. 4.
24. Hoade, *Guide to the Holy Land*, p. 712.
25. Ibid., p. 714.
26. Conder and Kitchener, *Survey,* vol. 1, p. 416.

A bas-relief of the Ark of the Covenant, sculptured in rock at the synagogue in Capernaum.

and are dead."[27] Its importance is evidenced by the fact that it was the residence of a centurion with at least a hundred-man garrison (Matt. 8:5; Luke 7:2). Herod Antipas would naturally keep the big garrison near the frontier.

In recent decades archaeology and medieval tradition tend to establish Tell Hum as the site of Capernaum. This is seen in the coins found by the Franciscans at the site and by the witness of medieval pilgrims. It seems clear that the ruins of the existing building are those of the second or third century A.D., when the Jews flourished under the Antonines and when other important Galilean synagogues were built. Benjamin of Tudela (A.D. 1160) found that Capharnaum is the same as Kaphar Nachum. Later witnesses change it to the similar name of Tanchun.[28] From Tanchun, the Arabs modified it to the present Telhum, or Tell Hum. South of the synagogue, recent excavations have revealed the mosaic floor, apparently of the Byzantine period and perhaps linked with the house of Peter. To the east

27. Ibid.
28. See footnote cited in Kopp, *Holy Places,* p. 178.

is a small Greek Orthodox church decorated with cupolas. A parklike area to the west now contains basalt stones including flour mills and olive presses. A pier projects out into the sea from which boats regularly ply from Tiberias and which in former times was frequented by fishermen. It is a delightful place to meditate and to re-create mentally the stirring events of New Testament history.

Jesus found His reception at Nazareth not encouraging to say the least (Luke 4:28-29). After His rejection at His hometown, He moved to Capernaum, which Matthew saw as a fulfillment of the prophecy of Isaiah (Matt. 4:14-15). Jesus began His ministry at the synagogue, probably in the building that antedates the existing ruin. His teaching created a profound impression. Even more impressive was His casting out of an unclean spirit, and the later healing of the man with a crippled hand. It was here that He healed the centurion's servant and raised a dead girl to new life (Mark 5:41). It was here that Peter's mother-in-law was cured and many others thereafter (Mark 1:21-31; Matt. 8:14-16). At this place He called Matthew from the customs house to discipleship (Mark 2:13-15). Later, at the synagogue He explained to His disciples and others that unless they ate His flesh and drank His blood they had no life in themselves. After this "hard saying" many forsook Him (John 6:1-66).

Southwest of Capernaum, along the shore, are a cluster of sites of importance in Christian tradition. About a mile and a half from Capernaum is Tabgha, from the Greek term *eptapagon*, meaning "seven springs." Here is the Church of the Multi-

Tabgha   plication of the Loaves, believed by many to be the site of at least one of the miracles of the loaves and fishes. The area is located at the northern end of the plain of Gennesaret under the Mount of Beatitudes, traditional site of the Sermon on the Mount. The Christian pilgrim, Egeria (A.D. 390-395), found near Capernaum at the place called "seven springs," that which coincides with recent discoveries made by Drs. Mader and Schneider in 1932. They discovered a basilica with three naves resting upon a foundation of an older church, probably the one visited by Egeria. Beneath the altar, they found the stone which was pointed out as being the place where the Lord placed the bread. There is a splendid mosaic exposed to view today, probably of the Byzantine period, representing a basket of loaves and fish. It is one of the finest mosaics in the land, comparable to that of Khirbet el Mafjir near Jericho. It includes pictures of various plants and birds. There is, for example, a heron and a dove on a lotus flower, a goose with an oleander bush, ducks on a lotus flower, and a bird attacking a snake.[29]

Next to this church is a church over a rock by the seashore commemorating Jesus' interview with Peter (John 21:15, 16). This tradition states that here Jesus prepared fish for the disciples' breakfast and challenged Peter to prove that he loved and was loyal to Jesus. This church was erected by Franciscans in 1943 upon ancient ruins. It is called Saint Peter's Church or the Chapel of the Primacy or the Mensa Christi ("Table of Christ"). Across the road from this church is a grotto, which Franciscans excavated in 1933. They discovered a little chapel with Byzantine mosaics, probably the place mentioned by Egeria as the place where Christ pronounced the Beatitudes.

Where was the Sermon on the Mount delivered? Matthew locates it on a mount, but Luke, on a plain. Both are reflected in Christian tradition. The most specific witness is that of Aetheria (A.D. 385). While at the Church of the Muliplication of Loaves, she reported that "in the direction of the mountain nearby is the hill which the Redeemer ascended and where he uttered the Beatitudes." She mentions both a mountain and a nearer hill (*specula*). In 1935, B. Bagatti excavated a little church, with a single aisle, fifty-four yards northeast of the Church of the Loaves. It included a natural cave some thirteen feet in length. This chapel was built perhaps toward the end of the fourth century.[30] Medieval tradition preserves the witness of Aetheria, stating that two miles from Capernaum is the place where Jesus preached to the crowds, and that one mile from this place is where He fed the 5,000.[31] This location coincides with a site on a mountain range about a mile from the lake, locally called "the Blessed Trees." Until recently there were three trees on this height. The local inhabitants believed these trees to have been blessed, and stone fragments found here include the word in Greek for blessed (Matt. 5:4; Toblar: quoted by Kopp, p. 209). The top of this hill affords a panoramic view of the lake and the plain of Gennesaret. Directly above this hill is the beautiful Hospice

Sermon on the Mount

---

29. Zev Vilnay, *The New Irsael Atlas: Bible to Present Day* (Jerusalem: Israel University Press, 1968), pp. 450-453; Pearlman and Yannai, *Historical Sites*, p. 58.
30. See footnote cited in Kopp, *Holy Places*, p. 208.
31. Ibid.

of the Beatitudes owned by an Italian missionary society (Associazione Nazionale per soccorrere i Missionari Italiani).[32] Included in the decor of this small chapel are symbols of the seven virtues: charity, justice, providence, faith, hope, fortitude, and temperance (cf. Gal. 5:22), reminiscent of the Sermon on the Mount.

Another possible site of the Sermon on the Mount is the Horns of Hattin, a mountain height near Tiberias. The site overlooking Gennesaret, however, seems the more probable one; it is nearer Capernaum and more accessible by a multitude. It also has the support of ecclesiastical tradition, especially the link with the "Trees of Blessings."

---

32.   Hoade, *Guide to the Holy Land,* p. 699.

The plain of Tabgha, at the north end of the Sea of Galilee, is the traditional site where Jesus fed the five thousand.

As the main highway ascends the mountain of upper Galilee, the slight mound to the right between the road and the sea is perhaps the ancient city of Kinneret (Arabic *Ureine*). This city belonged to the ancient tribe of Naphtali. Here were found Stone-Age implements and a fragment of an Egyptian stele erected by Thutmose III, on which is his claim that he repelled the Mitanni.

Kinneret and its vicinity

A short way farther along the shore of the lake are the remains of Khirbet Minyah. It lies at the northern edge of the plain of Gennesaret. Robinson found that it coincided both with the Gospel description and with Josephus that Capernaum was related to Gennesaret. The most specific witness is that of Quaresmius, who stated that Capernaum was at a place with a *khan* called Minyah.[33]

The survey party of 1878 found only "slight mounds of ruins, a few walls about 200 yards square." It is accepted as Capernaum by Robinson, McGregor, and Conder, whereas Guerin thought it to be Bethsaida. The Conder and Kitchener survey party also is inclined to identify Minyah with Capernaum. In addition to Quaresmius, Isaac Cheio (A.D. 1334) mentions a town occupied by the Minai and containing the tomb of the Rabbi Nahum mentioned in the Jerusalem Talmud.[34]

Some authorities have labeled the site as the second Bethsaida of Galilee. It was first proposed by Reland and later supported by Dr. Thomson and Colonel Wilson. The *khan* itself is almost square, measuring about sixty-one by sixty-nine yards. The main entrance is on the east, and on the southern wall is the prayer niche (mihrab). The structure dates from the seventh century and is one of the most ancient prayer places in the land.[35]

Nearby this ruin is the Kinneret pumping station, a major engineering project of the state of Israel. Water is pumped from the lake into a reservoir north of Nazareth; from there it travels in a concrete aqueduct, about nine feet in diameter, to a major installation on the Yarqon River near the site of Antipatris. From there it flows into the area of Beer-sheba and the Negev to the south. By this engineering project desert areas to the south are made to blossom "like the crocus . . . abundantly" (Isa. 35: 1-2).

A village of considerable significance historically is known

33. Robinson, *Biblical Researches,* vol. 3, p. 288.
34. Conder and Kitchener, *Survey,* vol. 1, p. 369.
35. Vilnay, *New Israel Atlas,* p. 448.

variously as El Majdel, or Migdal, or Magdala. It is believed
to be the home of Mary Magdalene. The survey party found
it only a mud and stone village consisting of eighty Moslems.
The site lies at the southeast corner of the plain of Gennesaret
and opposite the Wadi el-Haman, which comes down the gorge
north of Hattin. This could be the same place that Mark called
Dalmanutha (Matt. 15:30; Mark 8:10).[36]

Magdala

In the fall of the year this site presents a green, smooth
mound covered with grass. It is two and three-quarter miles north
of Tiberias. The Talmud speaks of Magdala in seven places
that links it with the modern site. The name itself means "tower,"
and therefore it is not an unusual term. Josephus mentions the
town under the Aramaic term *taricheae* ("fish tower"). The
influence of the Greeks is reflected in this type of name. It possessed a hypodrome, and thus the predominant influence must
have been non-Jewish (Jos., *Wars.* II. 21, 3). It was apparently
the most important town on the lake before the building of
the town of Tiberias. Josephus cited its population as 40,000.[37]
Several Christian pilgrims mention the town with its Biblical
name, such as Theodosius (530), Willibald (724-26), and Epiphanius (750-800). By the seventeenth century, however, Quaresmius (1616-26) could find only some ruins on the site.[38]

In Rabbinic tradition, the town was important but wicked.
The Gospels do not report that Jesus was ever at this place. Because of its location near the junction of two roads, it had been
the most important city on the lake. About a mile from the shore
is a modern Jewish village, which began in 1910, to which the
name Migdal is attached. Arab farmers who once lived in the
area have vanished. That there are not more remains honoring
Mary Magdalene in this place is probably explained by the
fact that medieval tradition erroneously linked her with Mary
of Bethany. An evidence of this error is the Russian church
honoring the Magdalene on the Mount of Olives. The medieval
pilgrims were shown places honoring this Mary in the vicinity
of Bethany and in Jerusalem. There seems to have been a church
honoring Mary Magdalene in Jerusalem as early as the ninth
century. A later church honoring Mary, which was near Herod's
Gate, disappeared in 1892.[39]

---

36. Robinson, *Biblical Researches,* vol. 3, p. 278.
37. Jos. *Wars* II. 21. 4.
38. Kopp, *Holy Places,* p. 194.
39. Ibid., pp. 196, 197.

Mary Magdalene has gripped the imagination of Christians from the earliest times to the present. The second century Gnostic gospel of Thomas mentions her as Jesus' sweetheart, in that Jesus stood foremost in her affections. This may have been occasioned by the fact that the sinner who wiped Jesus' feet, as reported in Luke 7, is a woman who loved Jesus much because much had been forgiven her, and in John 11 Jesus is said to have loved Mary and Martha and Lazarus. Even more eloquent is the figure of Mary Magdalene, reported in John 20, as lingering at the sepulchre in tears after the others had departed. Her devotion was rewarded as she was the first to see the resurrected Christ (John 20:16).

Today no community near or on the Sea of Galilee carries either a Jewish or Christian name. The only name preserved is that of the Roman emperor, Tiberius. It is now a tourist center of growing importance. It is said to have occupied the site of **Tiberias** Rakkath, an ancient town of Naphtali. According to Rabbinic tradition, Tiberias was built on the ruins of Rakkath and over an ancient cemetery. It was constructed in A.D. 26, and thus was a very new city in the time of Jesus. Herod had difficulty attracting inhabitants to it. Jews avoided it because it had violated an ancient cemetery. Its location proved to be wise, however, because it was adjacent to the south end of the Sea of Galilee near roadways and was convenient to the ascent into the hills of lower Galilee. It was also near hot springs. Cities built by and for the Romans were always located near a copious supply of water. These baths at that time were famous throughout the Roman world.[40] The evidence of Josephus places the date of its founding in A.D. 26, but evidence from coins places it as early as A.D. 20.[41] Since Herod could not persuade the "best people" to inhabit his new city, he welcomed the less desirable elements. It was an extensive city; the wall measured three miles in length.[42]

The Fourth Gospel is the only one that mentions Tiberias. It is stated there that hosts from Tiberias came across the lake to the scene of the feeding to talk with Jesus (John 6:23). George

---

40. Pliny, *Natural History* 5. 15.
41. George Adam Smith, *The Historical Geography of the Holy Land,* 15th ed. (New York: A. C. Armstrong & Son, 1909), p. 448; Vilnay, *New Israel Atlas,* p. 436.
42. Schumacher, *Palestine Exploration Fund, Quarterly Statement* (1887); 85 ff.

Adam Smith and some other travelers have found the area "repellent" and noted that, in Smith's words, "Schürer is here quite incorrect" in praising the city. During the summer months the heat is excessive. Aside from that, as one stands overlooking the city of Tiberias, he is inspired by the panorama before him. And the very conditions that make it unpleasant in the summer, make it pleasant at other seasons of the year. Today, in an air-conditioned hotel, a visit to Tiberias is likely to be very pleasant. The water of the lake in midsummer is approximately eighty degrees.

Today's tourists find the place not at all unpleasant, as witnessed by the many new hotels that are appearing on the northern and western edges of the city. Herod Antipas built his fortress and palace on the heights above the city. The ruin today carries the name, "Palace of the King's Daughter" *(Kasr Bint el-Melek)*. The fortress remained until medieval times, and Saladin, after conquering the city itself, found the subjugation of the fortress a much more formidable problem.

Fishing is still done at night and drying nets are commonly seen in the area. Boats catering to tourists ply regularly between Tiberias and the site of Capernaum, and between Tiberias and the new Jewish community of Ein Gev, directly across the lake. From the hill west of the city one can see the western shore of the lake stretching on toward Capernaum in the distance, the scene of many of Jesus' words and deeds. He can see across the lake to the Golan Heights, from which for twenty years Syrian soldiers gazed from their bunkers upon Jewish farmers and fishermen below them.

Farther south toward the east, one can see the corner of three nations: the Syrians, north of the Yarmuk River which empties into the Jordan below the lake; the Hashemite kingdom of the Jordan, to the south of the Yarmuk and east of the Jordan River; and Israel on the west. Near the Yarmuk is the site of one of the decisive battles of the world, a conflict in which Arabs, inspired by Islamic faith and a new-found nationalism, defeated the Christian forces under Heraclius in A.D. 639. One can also see the place where Saladin marshaled the united forces of Arabs of Egypt and Syria prior to the decisive Battle of Hattin, which marked the end of Crusader dominance in the country. In 1918, British forces under Allenby drove the retreating Turks in the direction of Damascus. In 1948 and again in

Structure from Roman times on the western shore of Galilee. The square section was a flour mill, which was powered by the water entering it by the aqueduct.

One of the hot springs at Tiberias.

1967, Jewish forces compelled the Arabs to retreat in the direction of Damascus. Farther south is the northern end of the Beisan Valley, dotted like a patchwork quilt with fish hatcheries. Below, on the shore of the lake and to the right, is the little mound of Khirbet Kerak (Tel Bet Yerah) famous for its Kerak pottery, whereas to the north near the Wadi Amud is the gorge where the Galilean skull was discovered in 1925, believed to be that of a human being from 100,000 B.C. It is now in the Palestine Archaeological Museum. From this ancient man to today's tourists on the top story of a "skyscraper" hotel, the scene is a panorama of human existence that has few parallels on the globe. The population of Tiberias today is approximately 24,000.[43]

Gradually Jews settled here and Tiberias eventually became one of the four most sacred cities of the Jews, containing some thirteen synagogues. They were drawn here probably by the hot springs where today the tombs of Maimonides, R. Yohanan, R. Eliezer, and R. Akiba may be seen. Most important of these is the tomb of Maimonides. This medieval philosopher spent most of his years in Egypt and he died in 1204. Akiba was martyred by the Romans about A.D. 150. The tomb of R. Meir is regarded as one of the holiest of Israel's sanctuaries. His tomb is located south of Tiberias near the hot springs. Nearby are many other tombs of famous rabbis and other holy men. The memory of Saint Peter is preserved in a Franciscan monastery on the shore of the lake.

Here in this Jewish community, the Mishna was completed about A.D. 200, and A.D. 400 saw the completion of the Palestinian Talmud. Here, also, vowels were added to the Hebrew Bible making it the Masoretic text. The Jews preferred the name Tabur for this city, meaning "navel," for after the destruction of Jerusalem in A.D. 70 it became the center of world rabbinism. During the days of the Ottoman Empire the city of Tiberias was the administrative capital, replacing Sepphoris of the earlier period. The black basaltic walls of the Turkish city are still a reminder of their long residency here. Even more impressive than the present activity around the Sea of Galilee are the cities mentioned in ancient records but which no longer can be identified. In addition to Bethsaida and Gennesaret there was Gergesa.

---

43. Misha Louvish, ed., *Facts About Israel, 1970* (Jerusalem: Keter Books, 1970), p. 53.

At Ein Gev, on the east side of the Sea of Galilee, fish just caught are freed from the nets and put in containers for processing.

Across the lake, above the modern settlement of Ein Gev, are the ruins of a fortress dating from the Roman period known as Hippos, with its alternate term Susita. During the Roman period, the chief activity was fishing and its related industries. Today, due in part to Rabbinic links with Tiberias but even more to links with Christianity, the chief industry of Ein Gev is tourism. In 1968, the number of tourists arriving in Israel amounted to 432,272, the majority of whom included this area in their itinerary. Wadi Fik, near Ein Gev, where "a spur runs out to the shore," would have been the likely spot for the swine to have rushed into the lake (cf. Matt. 8:31-34).[44]

Ein Gev

In the area of the Sea of Galilee the chief appeal is to the countryside rather than to the cities, whether in Tiberias or elsewhere. The Gospels present Jesus as working mostly in the open countryside so that one gets closest to Christian traditions not in buildings or in city streets but in the out-of-doors. It was in the out-of-doors that Jesus preached His most important sermons and taught His most important lessons rather than making formal pronouncements from inside the synagogues. Most of

44. Conder and Kitchener, *Survey,* vol. 1, p. 13.

the miracles of healing were performed outside. The man with the withered hand was in the synagogue, but this is an exception. Most of Jesus' ministry was that of an itinerant rather than that of a settled lecturer or pastor. Most of the episodes remembered and reported by His followers occurred in informal situations, often in transit. In this Jesus was much in the tradition of the patriarchs, who were wanderers and nomads, and Jesus was not ashamed to say, "... the birds of the air have nests; but the Son of man has nowhere to lay his head" (Luke 9:58).

Qedesh

South of Tiberias and near the shore of the lake is Khirbet Qedesh, believed by Aharoni to be the Kedesh of Naphtali. He finds that this "fits the Kedesh Naphtali of Barak in every respect."[45] The remains of this mound do indeed date back to the age of the judges.

Kerak

The important site of Khirbet Kerak, far down on the southwest shore of the lake, is mentioned in the Talmud as Beth-Jarah (House of the Moon), but in the Hellenistic period it was known as Philoteria. Excavators have disclosed strata going down to the Chalcolithic remains. It is the source of the now famous Kerak Ware, a distinctive type of red and black burnished pottery. It seems to have been an important place in the Canaanite period, and from the Roman period there are remains of baths and a theater. Visible also are remnants of a synagogue from the fourth century and of a church of the Byzantine period. Excavator Pesach Bar-Adou also discovered a city wall twenty-five feet wide built in the Early Bronze Age (c. 2700 B.C.), contemporary with the Egyptian pyramids.[46]

ESDRAELON

Bethshan

The ancient Canaanite city of Bethshan is familiar to Bible readers as the place where the bodies of Saul and his sons were hung after the Philistine victory on nearby Mount Gilboa. The importance of this fortress lay in its command of the Jezreel Valley, which leads from the plain of the Jordan to the plain of Megiddo (Esdraelon). It is one of the more conspicuous tells in the Holy Land, dominating the entire valley and sloping at nearly a forty-five-degree angle, with a flat top.

Bethshan (Bet She'an) lies between the river Jalud to the

45. Yohanan Aharoni, *The Land of the Bible: A Historical Geography,* trans. A. F. Rainey (London: Burns & Oates, 1967), p. 204.
46. Pearlman and Yannai, *Historical Sites,* p. 66.

north, which rises from Ein Jalud near Yizreel (ancient Jezreel), and a broader ravine to the south. Just south of the mound is the modern village of the same name. Because of its strategic location, dominating not only the valley of Jezreel but the Jordan Valley as well, Bethshan controlled major traffic arteries. It is 320 feet below sea level and the rich soil to the east has made it largely sought as a place of residence. The name apparently honors the god Shan, though it has been interpreted as "House of Rest." Between 1921 and 1933, the site was excavated by the University of Pennsylvania. Archaeologists have identified eighteen strata, the lowest going back to the Chalcolithic Age. Above it was the Early Bronze Age through the sixteenth level. The Middle Bronze, represented in stratum ten, has not yet been published. The best known period is the Late Bronze (levels nine, eight, seven) which coincide with the Egyptian occupation. Thutmose III mentions Bethshan as one of his conquered cities. Egyptian scarabs were found in levels nine and seven. The stele of Seti I (1303 B.C.) was found in stratum nine. It abounds in Egyptian artifacts. At this time it apparently was the main Egyptian base in the area, held with a strong garrison. The invading Israelites did not conquer it, nor were they in conflict with it. This is consistent with the report that "the people of Scythopolis had always treated the Jews well" (2 Macc. 12:30). Gradually Egyptian influence waned and Philistine influence increased so that by the end of Saul's reign, the latter were in complete possession. As in the manner practiced in the battles described in Homer's *Iliad*, the heads of the fallen leaders, Saul and his sons, were carried by the Philistines to their gods in the pentapolis whereas the victims' bodies were hung on the city wall of Bethshan to be rescued by citizens of Jabesh-Gilead, grateful for Saul's earlier intervention in their behalf (1 Sam. 11:1-14; 31:1-13).[47] The Philistines, descendants of these "Sea Peoples," were acting consistently with the traditions of their contemporaries as described by Homer. Later, Solomon placed a garrison here (1 Kings 4:12). The Israelite level has been identified with strata five and four.

During the Persian period the city seems to have been relatively unimportant. During the Hellenistic period the Greek name Scythopolis was given to this city (Judith 3:10; 2 Macc. 12:29). The first to mention the city as Scythopolis was Polybius

---

47. Aharoni, *Land of the Bible*, p. 36; cf., Homer, *Iliad*, Bk. 23.

The mound of Bethshan with an excavation of Roman ruins in the foreground.

(V. 70) in connection with the conquest of Palestine in 218 B.C. by Antiochus III of Syria.[48] The origin of this name is obscure. Scholars now are skeptical of the claims by Eusebius and Syncellus that link it with the Scythian invasion of 624 B.C. (Herodotus I, 103-105; IV, 1). Against this view, it has been noted that Scythians did not found cities and their invasion of Palestine lasted only a short time. Avi-Yonah suggests that it was perhaps named by Scythian units of the Ptolemaic armies who settled there,[49] perhaps in the autumn of 254 B.C. It was the only city of the Decapolis located west of the Jordan. It was ignored by Tiglath-pileser III and was not included in the first deportation of exiles (2 Kings 15:29; 1 Chron. 5:26). During the Maccabean struggle its residents tried to remain neutral (1 Macc. 12:40, 41). Gradually Jews settled here and became numerous by the time of the first revolt.[50]

The Talmud indicates that both Jews and non-Jews had shops in the town, though the Gentiles apparently predominated since the Sabbath was not strictly enforced. By the third cen-

---

48. Michael Avi-Yonah, "Scythopolis," *Israel Exploration Journal* 12 (1962): 123.
49. Ibid., p. 127.
50. Jos. *Wars* II. 466-476.

tury of our era, Armenian Christians were resident here.[51] During the Roman period, it was the capital of Palestina Secunda, the province that included Esdraelon, Galilee, and northern Trans-Jordan.[52]

During the Byzantine Age, represented by stratum two, the city was the seat of a bishopric. Its several churches included a round one similar to the original plan of the Church of the Holy Sepulchre. North of the tell a sixth-century monastery with excellent mosaic floors was excavated. With the Arab conquest, the former name, Bet She'an, came back into use. The town was destroyed by the Crusaders and never prospered thereafter. Outside the town, the Mosque of the Forty Warriors has the date 1403 as the time of its completion. Most impressive today is the well-preserved amphitheater containing not only a vomatorium, but places where bronze pipes were placed for sounding tubes.[53]

51. Avi-Yonah, "Scythopolis," p. 133.
52. Aharoni, *Land of the Bible,* p. 37.
53. Conder and Kitchener, *Survey,* vol. 2, p. 102.

The mound of Bethshan from an old photo that shows the strategic position of the site above the surrounding valley.

Bethshan, or Scythopolis, was not the only fortress bordering the upper Jordan Valley. Approximately eight miles north of Bethshan on the eastern edge of the plateau overlooking the Jordan Valley and the Tavor Gorge on the north is the Crusader fortress of Belvoir. It is well named, for this fortress commands a view of a vast area of the upper Jordan Valley—from the Sea of Galilee to nearly twenty miles south; Bethshan itself, however, is hidden from view. To the east one can see the Yarmuk Valley, with Syrian territory to the north and the state of Jordan to the south and east. This fortress was built in the twelfth century by the Frankish knights. It was successful in holding out against the Saracens for months after other fortresses had succumbed. After the decisive Battle of Hattin, Acre fell on July 9, 1187, but Belvoir did not fall until January 1189. It was an isolated fortress, however, and it had little control over its immediate environs. The Egyptians, Canaanites, and Philistines had fortified Bethshan because of its strategic location; the Crusaders preferred Belvoir because of the view and defensibility. But its remoteness rendered its strength irrelevant.[54]

Few sites in Palestine besides Bethshan, by virtue of physical prominence, strategic location, and historical importance, conjure up such an awesome sequence of events and peoples— Thutmose III, Seti I, Saul, Judas Maccabeus, Pompey, Vespasian, Byzantines, Saladin, Turks, British, Arab Palestinians, Israelis, and archaeologists.

From Bethshan, the Midianites of old, later the Arabs, and then the Palestinian commandoes of recent years infiltrated up the valley of Jezreel between Gilboa and Mount Issachar, along the path of the river Harod toward Jezreel (Arabic Zerin; Hebrew Yizreel). To the south of this valley a copious spring emerges from the foot of Mount Gilboa called Ein Harod. It is mentioned as the site of Gideon's camp (Judg. 7:1, "all the people who were with him rose early and encamped beside the spring of Harod; and the camp of Midian was north of them, by the hill of Moreh, in the valley"). It is here that Gideon's army was drastically reduced to 300 men prior to their victory over the Midianites, who were encamped to the north and west. Today, it is a pleasant, grassy campsite that surrounds a clear circular pool from which water gushes to irrigate the surrounding villages. The site now includes a modern youth hostel and park.

Ein Harod

54. Smith, *Historical Geography,* pp. 358-360.

It is slightly below sea level at this point. The survey party of 1878 witnessed a raid of Bedouins upon the farmers of the area, but the farmers drove back the marauders by shouts and the discharge of firearms, reminiscent of the forays of the more formidable Midianites in the days of Gideon. Almost nightly episodes of armed conflict in the Bethshan area were reported during the summers of 1968 and 1969. This quiet spot witnessed the ravages of war in Bible times not only during the time of Gideon but by the assault of the Philistines on the defending Israelites on Mount Gilboa to the south. Here the battle swirled; then the victorious Philistines stripped the slain. They carried the body of Israel's king down the valley to Bethshan, but his head they triumphantly took with them down the shallow valley of Jenin to their Philistine coastal cities.

Two miles farther up the valley of Jezreel is the site of ancient Jezreel. Here Jezebel secured the death of Naboth, but later met her own death at the hands of a vengeful Jehu (2 Kings 9:30-37). It was through this valley that Jehu made his **Jezreel** charge with the intent of destroying the remnants of the family of Ahab. Jezreel (Yizreel), less than one mile west of the sea-level gradient, marks the point of distinction between the Jezreel Valley leading to the southeast, and the central valley, sometimes called the valley of Megiddo or Esdraelon, leading to Haifa Bay at 164 feet above sea level. The watershed between the Jordan and the plain of Acre is farther west, near Afula. Whereas the river Harod drains the eastern valley (valley of Jezreel), the Qishon drains the valley of Esdraelon, with branches mainly originating between Jezreel and Jenin but with a northern branch originating west of Tabor.

This central valley is triangular in shape; its base, some twenty miles in length, extends from Tel Yokneam along the base of Mount Carmel southeast to Jenin. From Jenin it is a distance of fifteen miles north to a point beyond Tel Adashin south of Nazareth and west of Mount Tabor. It is then fifteen miles to the place of origin at Jokneam. The valley floor is 330 feet above sea level near Jenin, but it drops to 80 feet at Jokneam and Tel Qashish where the Qishon enters the plain of Acre. The rich alluvial soil of this sheltered area is the most fertile section of Palestine, richly deserving the tribute paid by Hosea that the rich harvest was emblematic of divine blessing (Hos. 2:21-23). Military strategists have said that whoever controls

Esdraelon controls Palestine. Bible history confirms this. Indeed, it is predicted that the climactic battle in human history will occur here (Ezek. 38; 39; Rev. 20).

This was the scene, in Bible times, of the decisive battles of Barak against the Canaanites, Gideon against the Midianites, Josiah against Pharaoh Necho (2 Kings 23:29, 30), along with the confrontation with Holofernes (Judith 12) and the Persians (1 Macc. 9:4). In more recent times, the Turks were pursued by Allenby in World War I and the Israeli tanks drove back the Arab Legion (June 6, 7, 1967) through Jenin to the Jordan River. As one views the peaceful agricultural villages today shimmering under the bright sun, it is difficult to envision the stormy scenes and the blood-soaked fields of this historic battle area.

In the middle of the base of this triangle is its most strategic area historically—Megiddo. For years its site was unknown. **Megiddo**   Conder thought it was to be sought south of Bethshan, and George Adams Smith located it at Lejjun, the Roman camp east of this site. Excavations by the University of Chicago established it at Tell el Mutasallin. It was here that the well-docu-

A storage pit uncovered at the site of Megiddo. Two circular stairways lead into the pit.

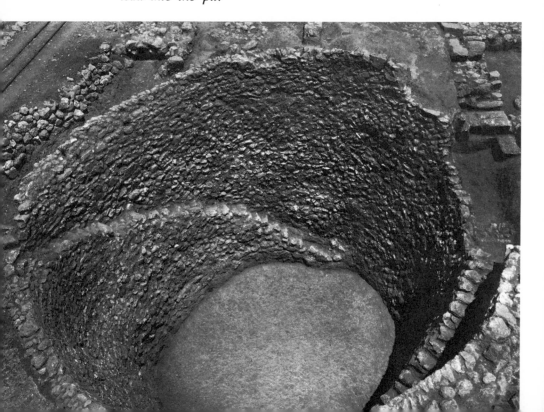

mented battle between Thutmose III and the Canaanite kings occurred.

Megiddo was one of the four Canaanite fortresses not subdued by the Israeli incursion (Judg. 1:27). These four fortresses dominated the passes through the Carmel range separating the plain of Sharon from the plain of Esdraelon. From northwest to southeast they are Jokneam, Megiddo, Tanaach, and Ibleam (Jenin). Of these four, Megiddo is the central and most important, because it commands both the most direct route between the plain of Sharon and Jezreel, but also the main road between the Jordan Valley and the plain of Acre. Prior to the twentieth century, this area was almost impassable. Pilgrims going from Jerusalem to Nazareth as late as the nineteenth century often found it more convenient to go by way of Jerusalem to Joppa (by ship) to Haifa to Nazareth than to go directly overland from Jerusalem to Nazareth, a distance of seventy-five miles. The survey party in the 1880s found it covered with dust so deep that it was difficult even for horses to traverse it. At other times of the year it was an area of swampy marsh. The exception to this was a basaltic causeway that led from Megiddo northeast past the hill Moreh and Mount Tabor and permitted virtually an all-weather route.[55]

Yokneam dominates Wadi Yokneam, Megiddo dominates the valley of Iron Wadi, Tanaach controls Wadi Zavaon (Wadi Abdullah), and Ibleam oversees the shallow valley of Dothan (Wadi Abu Nar).[56]

Jenin (En-gannim) is believed to be the place where Jesus healed ten lepers, one of whom was the Samaritan who returned to give thanks (Luke 17:11-18). The tradition could be true since the town is on the border between Galilee and Samaria, a border marked in general by the Carmel and Gilboa ranges. The name means "guarded spring." It was partly in the tribe of Issachar (Josh. 19:21; 21:29). Josephus mentioned it as Ginea located between Samaria and Galilee. Here the Samaritans killed a large number of Galileans who were passing through Samaria on their way to Jerusalem.[57] In recent times this village, along with Nablus and Hebron, was deeply resented by the Zionists and appreciated pan-Arab nationalism. In the summer of

Jenin

---

55. Denis Baly, *The Geography of the Bible* (New York: Harper & Row, Publishers, 1957), p. 152.
56. Ibid.
57. Jos. *Antiq.* XX. 6. 1.

1968, one Arab merchant in Jenin refused to stock soft drinks made in Israel though his competitor across the street was less scrupulous and hence attracted more customers among tourists.

Less than seven miles northwest of Ibleam and Jenin is the site of ancient Tanaach, only five miles southeast of Megiddo. Previously it was assumed that Tanaach and Megiddo could not flourish simultaneously since the two were so close together.[58] Thus Tanaach had to compete, it was believed, with nearby Megiddo and with the easier pass near Dothan. Recent archaeological excavations, however, indicate that both Tanaach and Megiddo prospered and suffered reverses simultaneously. Both sites were prosperous during the Bronze Age, and both suffered destruction after about 1125 B.C.[59] The close proximity of the sites are not surprising when compared to a similar situation that existed around the shore of Galilee, where villages very close together prospered and suffered simultaneously. Beginnings of occupancy at Tanaach apparently coincided with Et Tel (Ai) near Deir Dibwan, roughly contemporary with the great Pyramid Age of Egypt. These Early Bronze Age fortifications circled a city fourteen acres in extent as compared with contemporary Megiddo of thirteen acres.[60] "Its first substantial occupation involved a major planning and construction project."[61] In this respect, it was similar to the Early Bronze city of Et Tel (Ai), a contemporary site of twenty-seven acres near Bethel. Both indicate an operation far exceeding the resources of the local community, but reflecting a very broad-based and simultaneous building program that could only have been achieved by a major power. Egyptian influence is indicated at Et Tel in construction found there that was practiced only by the Egyptians at that time. This would coincide with the Old Kingdom period of Egypt, a time of Egypt's greatest international influence. Egyptian influence then extended as far north as Byblos (on the Phoenician coast). The next two centuries were the period of Tanaach's greatest glory, and pottery remains link it with the Early Bronze city-state system, its ceramics resembling those of Khirbet Kerak. It prospered again in the Hyksos period as

The label "Tanaach" appears in the left margin.

58. William F. Albright, *The Archaeology of Palestine* (London, 1960), p. 117; Baly, *Geography of the Bible,* p. 153.
59. Paul W. Lapp, "Tanaach by the Waters of Megiddo," *The Biblical Archaeologist,* February 1967, p. 9.
60. G. W. Van Beek, "Megiddo," *Interpreter's Dictionary of the Bible* (Nashville: Abingdon Press, 1962), p. 336.
61. Lapp, "Tanaach," p. 7.

the strong fortifications and beautiful artifacts attest. During the twelfth century there occurred a violent destruction followed by a century in which no occupation is noted. It is suggested that this is contemporary with the victory celebrated in the Song of Deborah (Judg. 5).[62]

During the Iron Age, Megiddo seems to have been an administrative center whereas Tanaach was an agricultural town. A strong fortress was constructed on the acropolis at Tanaach by the Abbasids, which may well have been used later by the Crusaders. Thereafter, the site was abandoned. The modern village by the same name on the eastward side of the tell numbers some two hundred inhabitants. Tanaach is mentioned seven times in the Scriptures. Joshua defeated its king (Josh. 12:21), it was allotted to the tribe of Manasseh (Judg. 1:29), the famous battle between Barak and Sisera occurred at "Tanaach by the waters of Megiddo" (Judg. 5:19). The town itself, however, remained undefeated by Joshua (Judg. 1:27). It was a Levitical town (Josh. 17:11; 1 Chron. 7:29), and was included in one of Solomon's administrative districts (1 Kings 4:12).

Five miles farther along the road to Haifa is Tel Megiddo, south of the highway and west of the road from Sharon to Galilee, guarding the Valley of Iron. "A more strategic site than Megiddo is difficult to find."[63] It is twenty miles from Haifa, eleven from Jenin, and one mile from the site of the Roman camp Lejjun. From its summit, the hills of Nazareth are visible to the north. Northeast is the profile of Mount Tabor, whereas nearer, although a little farther to the east, is the volcanic cone of Mount Moreh. Immediately below and five miles distant to the northeast is the modern city of Afula, the present commercial and communication center of the entire area. From here the main highway between Egypt and Asia lies from the plain of Sharon through the Iron Pass across Esdraelon toward Damascus. Thus Megiddo was in a position to challenge passage between the Fertile Crescent and Egypt and the passage between Phoenicia and the central Jordan Valley. Thus Megiddo was a main communication center in the Near East. This was largely true because of the basaltic causeway across the plain in the direction of Mount Tabor; otherwise the plain of Dothan at Jenin might have been used more widely, as it is used today. The

Tel Megiddo

---

62. Ibid., p. 8.
63. Van Beek, "Megiddo," p. 336.

route by Jenin, however, was much less direct than that by Megiddo, as a topographical map indicates. The Megiddo route was more susceptible to ambush, as the advisors of Thutmose III pointed out, but it was more direct and saved considerable time. It also had the advantage of lying nearer to the Akko Plain and the Phoenician coast. Carmel projects out too close to the sea to permit the passage of armies along the coast. Also, the rivers and marshes along the bay at Acre made passage more difficult during many seasons of the year.

Excavations at this important tell were initiated by Shumacher in 1903-1905. This was continued by the University of Chicago in several seasons between 1925 and 1939. In 1960, Israeli archaeologist Yigael Yadin conducted some soundings to clarify the stratigraphy of Megiddo because he had noted that identical gates at Gezer, Hazor, and Megiddo were adjacent to casemate walls in Gezer and Hazor, but at Megiddo the gate was joined to a wall with insets and offsets. He found it strange that a wall contemporary with Hazor and Gezer would be different in a city midway between them. Several seasons of excavation were undertaken, but were interrupted by excavations at Masada and in the Bar Kochba caves. They excavated again in the summer of 1966 and 1967. The detailed report has not yet been published, but a preliminary report states Yadin's conclusions that the inset-outset wall was built over an earlier casemate wall. He concludes that the city that Solomon built at Megiddo (1 Kings 9:15) was a royal city and not merely a chariot city with horse stables as previously supposed. It contained "many splendid public buildings."[64]

Above a four-chambered Middle Bronze Age gate on the north edge, Solomon built a six-chambered gate with a casemate wall. It appears that the access to the water was planned at a later date than previously supposed. In other words, it was an Israelite construction rather than Canaanite. The Biblical data plus the pottery and such archaeological evidence as the style of stone dressing and building plans indicate that the city Solomon built was "a metropolis with stately buildings of official and ceremonial character . . . surrounded by a casemate wall with a gigantic gate of six chambers and two towers" with "a secret passage (the gallery) leading to the water spring."[65]

64. Y. Yadin, "Megiddo of the Kings of Israel," *The Biblical Archaeologist,* September 1970, p. 84.
65. Ibid., p. 95.

A restoration of Megiddo from the time of Solomon.

Five miles farther toward Haifa is another, smaller tell, set at an angle in the highway between the main road to Haifa and the side road leading to Jokneam. It is Tell Keimun, identified with Jokneam (Josh. 19:11). From the Mount Carmel range, above at the place of Elijah's sacrifice, the round tell is conspicuous. It can be scaled only with extreme difficulty because of the thirty-eight-degree slope to the sides. The onomasticon of Eusebius calls it Cimona. The survey party of 1878 found on its summit foundations of an Arabic fortress. It has never been excavated, and is now covered with dense growth of weeds, making it almost impenetrable. A few ruins scattered on top include a giant millstone. A survey party of the American Schools of Oriental Research, at this site 1969, found on it sherds going back to the Middle Bronze and Iron ages. It is a relatively small tell, but it invites excavation.[66]

Jokneam

---

66. Carl Grasser, Jr., unpublished "Newsletter" of the American Schools of Oriental Research (July 1970).

Towering over this site on the west is the frowning precipice of the highest portion of the Carmel range. It is the traditional place of fire, commemorating the scene of the confrontation between Elijah and Yahweh and the prophets of Baal, witnessed by King Ahab and Israelite leaders during the ninth
century B.C. (1 Kings 18). This marked the highlight of the
confrontation between the religion of the patriarchs and of Moses
and that of the Phoenician deities imported by Jezebel, wife
of King Ahab. A monastery is on the site, which includes a
statue of Elijah. From this height is a sweeping view of the
plain of Esdraelon, one of the most impressive views in the
whole area. Below can be seen the small conical tell of Jokneam,
and stretching to the southeast, the spine of the Carmel range
culminates in the plain of Dothan, or Jenin, on the horizon.
To the south and east are the roads leading from the plain of
Sharon through the passes in the Carmel range. To the northwest is the headland of Mount Carmel as it juts into the
Mediterranean and overlooks the modern city of Haifa.[67] This
site commemorates one of the most dramatic events in Old
Testament history, and this incident, more than any other one
factor, gave Elijah the large place he fills in both the Old and
New Testaments.

Mount
Carmel

Mount Carmel is presented in the Old Testament as one
of the beauty spots of Palestine. It is often linked with Hermon,
as when the psalmist says "Carmel and Hermon rejoice in Thy
name." From the Carmel headland at Haifa southeasterly toward
the plain of Dothan, Carmel is an outcropping of limestone
stretching about eleven miles at an average elevation of about
1,500 feet. The name *Carmel* in Hebrew means "vineyard" and
suggests the horticulture of an earlier time. In addition to separating the plain of Esdraelon from the plain of Sharon, it formed
the boundary of four tribes: Asher to the north; Zebulon to the
northeast; Issachar to the east; and Manasseh to the south. In
olden times, it afforded a sanctuary from the marshes on either
side, and in modern times it provides a welcome relief from
summer heat. At its northern base, the Qishon River drains the
Esdraelon into Haifa Bay. The distance from the traditional
place of Elijah's sacrifice to the winter capital at Jezreel is
approximately eighteen miles—a long way to run, even for one

67. The elevation at the place of sacrifice (Muhrakah) is 1,697 feet; halfway between Muhrakah and Isfia the height is 1,818 feet.

of Elijah's constitution. But the Scripture states that "he ran before Ahab's chariot until he came to Jezreel."

It was while Elisha was residing on Mount Carmel that the Shunamite came in haste to seek the prophet's help because her son was suddenly stricken. The woman refused to leave until Elisha himself promised to accompany her back to Shunem (located at the base of Mount Moreh), where the child was restored to life (2 Kings 4:30). Mount Carmel had a sanctity from times immemorial as evidenced by the fact that Elijah "rebuilt the altar of the Lord that was broken down." Pagans also saw something holy in this mountain. These included the philosopher Pythagorus and the Roman general Vaspasian; Roman historians Suetonius and Tacitus report that the mountain was believed to be divine.[68] During the Byzantine period many monks went to the mountain to pray and meditate.

One of the Crusader knights, Bethold of Limogenes, founded the Carmelite Order. Soon the Carmelite Order spread all over Europe. The convent of the order now stands on the western tip of Carmel, overlooking Haifa and its harbor. At the foot of the mountain below is "Elijah's cave," together with a smaller grotto with the Arabic name El Khader, for "Saint George." The spot is sacred to Christians, Moslems, and Jews alike, who believe that it was here that Elijah found refuge from Ahab. The monastery over the site, the headquarters of the Carmelite Order, was destroyed with the fall of Acre in 1291. The Carmelites erected a new monastery in 1767, which was used as a hostel by the soldiers of Bonaparte after the siege of Acre. After the French departed, the monks and soldiers were massacred and the convent burned.[69]

The main village on the summit of Carmel is Isfiya, a Druze village, built on the site of the ancient Jewish village of the same name. Here are remains of a Byzantine synagogue of the fifth or sixth century with beautiful mosaic floors. The Druzes are the heretical sect of the Moslem faith who do not follow the Koran nor have any outward religious ceremonies or chapels. Their origin dates from the "mad" Caliph Hakim of Egypt (died A.D. 1021). They did not join with the Arabs in their struggle against the Zionists in 1948 or since, and they are considered loyal citizens of the state of Israel. Another Druze village nearby

---

68. Hoade, *Guide to the Holy Land,* p. 640.
69. Ibid., p. 641.

is Daliya. Today 34,000 Druze live in Israel, scattered in seventeen mountain villages. The details of their religion are secret even from most of its adherents.[70] Younger members of the Druze agricultural villages are becoming restive, both with respect to family traditions and their status in Israel.

Haifa

Until recent times, Haifa was an inconsequential village at the northern foot of the Carmel headland, not far from the mouth of the Qishon River. Today, Haifa is the third largest city in Israel, with a population over 212,200.[71]

Until recently, guidebooks listed Haifa as the second most populous city, but this rating has given away to Jerusalem, which

70. Y. Friedler, "Revolt of the Druze," *Jerusalem Post,* 30 March 1971, p. 9.
71. Louvish, *Facts About Israel,* 1970, p. 53.

The city of Haifa and the bay as viewed from Mount Carmel.

now numbers more than 275,000 including East Jerusalem. Until
the twentieth century the main seaports were Joppa and Acre.
The Turks, however, gave some promise to Haifa by making it
the terminus of the Haifa-Damascus railroad. The British took
up where the Turks had left off by expanding and modernizing
the port and building an oil refinery there. Until the end of the
Mandate (1948), it was the terminus of the oil pipeline from the
Persian Gulf. With the advent of Jewish immigration, the size
of the city greatly increased. The saying among contemporary
Israelis was, "Jerusalem is a city of the past, Tel Aviv the city
of the present, and Haifa the city of the future." It is the center
of Israel's heavy industry, including such industrial activities
as the Nesher cement factory. The oil refinery continues to function. In addition, it has car-assembly plants, foundries, and glass
and textile plants. Jews who formerly lived in Holland now pursue their trade of cutting diamonds in Haifa, making it the
home of Israel's diamond-cutting industry. Haifa replaces Acre
as the main seaport on the coast and the chief means of access by sea to the inland portions of the Jezreel Valley and
Galilee. A perplexing question is: why throughout history until
modern times was Acre rather than Haifa the major port?
Haifa has the natural advantages of the headland—the altitude of the adjacent mountain and a natural beauty that Acre
does not share. It also has the advantage of access to the Sharon
Plain to the south as well as the plain of Acre to the north,
advantages which Acre does not possess. The question remains
unanswered. Air travel has reduced Haifa's importance, as has
the loss of the Arabian pipeline. Haifa's future may be more
tied in with industry and tourism than as a transportation center.

Ruins of the Herodian-built harbor at Caesarea.

5

The Maritime Plain — North

The plain of Sharon, extending from the Carmel range on the north to the Yarqon River on the south and between the Mediterranean Sea and the hill country of Samaria, is one of the beauty spots of Palestine. The "Rose of Sharon" designates the bridegroom in the Song of Solomon (Song of Sol. 2:1), and in modern Christian hymnody the figure is applied to the Messiah—"He is the rose of Sharon, the bright and morning star." It is mentioned three times in the prophecy of Isaiah. It is linked with other beauty spots such as Lebanon, Carmel, and Bashan as beautiful areas that were to experience devastation (Isa. 33:9). Again it is linked with the beauty of Lebanon and Carmel in Isaiah 35:2: "The glory of Lebanon shall be given to it, the majesty of Carmel and Sharon." It is also promised to be "a pasture for flocks ... a place for herds to lie down" in a description of future blessings upon the land (Isa. 65:10). Toward the end of the nineteenth century, Sharon impressed one writer on horseback as having "a quiet, but rich beauty. If the contours are gentle, the colors are strong and varied.... Over corn and moorland a million flowers are scattered—poppies, pimpernels, anemones, the convolvulus, and the mallow, the narcissus, and the blue iris ... with the twittering of small birds. ..."[1] Today, by contrast, it is one of the most densely populated portions of the Holy Land and the center of Israel's citrus industry.

Plain of Sharon

1. George Adam Smith, *The Historical Geography of the Holy Land*, 15th ed., (New York: A. C. Armstrong and Son, 1909), p. 149.

Sharon marks the northern half of the Maritime Plain, which extends from the Brook of Egypt to the foot of Mount Carmel, the lower half being Philistia. Historically the northern half was divided into two divisions—the plain of Sharon designated the plain south of the Crocodile River, and the plain north of the same river was called the plain of Dor. The total length for the plain of Sharon today, from the mouth of the Yarqon to the Carmel headlands, is about fifty-five miles. The "coasts of Dor," from the Crocodile River (Zerka) to Mount Carmel, was approximately twenty miles, whereas the Biblical plain of Sharon, from the Crocodile River to the Yarqon, was approximately thirty-five miles. This was the territory allotted to Manasseh. The shoreline is rather extensive as compared with that given to Ephraim, but this is explained by the fact that in ancient times this area was largely marsh and therefore remained relatively useless until modern times. The plain of Sharon today is triangular in shape, narrow at the north and widening southward, with an average width of about ten miles.

A prominent feature of the plain of Sharon is the outcropping of Mousterian red sand forming an "island" extending twenty miles north and south at an elevation of approximately 180 feet, bounded on the south by the Yarqon and on the north by the Iskanderuna River (Nahar Alexander). This red sand makes possible the citrus crops which are so characteristic of modern Israel and which produce some of the finest fruits to be found anywhere on the globe.

Rainfall from the hill country to the east drains to the sea through the plain of Sharon by five perennial streams. To the modern geographer, the problem is complicated by the frequent changes of the names of these streams. The changes often reflected the political changes by each successive occupying nation, who sought to erase the memory of its predecessor by "improving" the nomenclature of its natural features. On the south is the Yarqon, which unites four wadis. Twenty-five miles north is the Iskanderuna River (Nahar Alexander). Some five miles north of this is the Mifjar (Nahar Hadera), and another five miles up the coast is the Crocodile River (Nahar Tanninim). Still farther north is the Wadi Me'arot. The coastline is one of the most regular shorelines in the world. It is characterized by a narrow strip along the border of the sea, backed by a line of sand dunes comprising sand carried by sea currents from the Nile River,

Palestinian coastline along the Mediterranean.

washed ashore, and blown inland to form dunes. These dunes
in old times prevented most of the streams from draining directly
into the sea; marshes were formed instead. This coastline was
always difficult to traverse because of the sand and the numerous
small streams to cross. The Yarqon, for example, presented a
formidable obstacle to the advance of Allenby's troops in the
fall of 1917.[2] To avoid this stream, the *Via Maris* detours inland
at this point.

THE COASTS OF DOR

As one looks at the map today or travels through the area,
the likely conclusion is that this entire area is one geographical
and political unit. Historically, however, the area designated as
the "coasts of Dor" often formed a province by itself and was
more often than not connected to Phoenicia rather than to Palestine. This situation was caused by the extensive marshes that
in ancient times effectively blocked travel between the north and

2. E. H. H. Allenby, *The Advance of the Egyptian Expeditionary Force,
July, 1917, October, 1918* (London: His Majesty's Stationery Office, 1917),
pp. 15 ff.

the south. Even during the dry season, these soggy areas remained so wet and treacherous that travel was hazardous. All-weather roads in this area were unknown until the coming of the Romans, who built bridges across the small streams. The bridges and roads, however, disappeared during the Middle Ages and, under the Ottomans, the situation reverted to primitive conditions until the arrival of the Zionists and the British.[3]

The link between the plain of Dor and Phoenicia is reflected in the statement that "... in Asher, Manasseh had ... the inhabitants of Dor and its villages..." (Josh. 17:11) implying that Dor originally was allotted to the tribe of Asher to the north, but that Manasseh actually had inhabited its villages. In New Testament times, this area was linked with the northern district of Ptolemais (Acre) and remained outside the territory of the Herods.[4]

3. Denis Baly, *The Geography of the Bible* (New York: Harper & Bros., 1957), p. 134.
4. Ibid., p. 131.

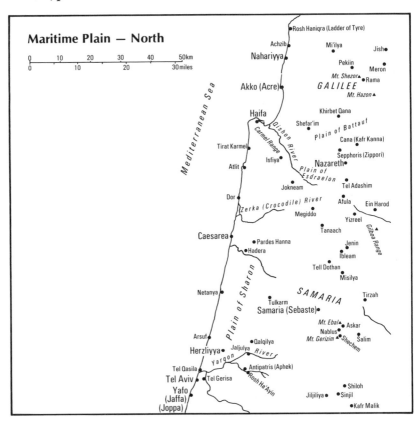

Dor was a prominent port city during the Bronze Age when trade along the coast was abundant and Phoenicia's power was extensive. Phoenicia's influence waned after the arrival of the sea peoples farther to the south (Philistia). The Israelites did not gain control over the area until the time of Solomon. After the Assyrian conquest in 722 B.C., it remained a province of Dor, extending from Carmel to Joppa, an arrangement that continued until the period of the Seleucids. After Herod built his new harbor in Caesarea, Dor never regained its importance. Dor was linked to the plain of Esdraelon primarily by the Wadi Keimun (Jokneam). Otherwise it remained relatively isolated, on the landward side by the Carmel range to the north and east and by the marshes to the south.

Dor, the chief city of this plain in ancient times, was visited by Wen Amon, a representative of the Pharaoh, about 1000 B.C. Later the king of Dor was among the thirty-one kings conquered **Dor** by Joshua (Josh. 12:23). It was one of the twelve administrative districts organized under Solomon (1 Kings 4:11). It was besieged by the Seleucid leaders in 217 B.C. and again in 139 B.C. (1 Macc. 15:13, 14). It was occupied by the Maccabean leader Alexander Jannaeus and liberated by Pompey in 65 B.C. It became an episcopal city in the Byzantine period, although the onomasticon says that the site of Dor was deserted. The ruins, as seen by the surveyors in 1876, included a strong tower built by the Crusaders, with a deep moat separating the tower from the town. The tower itself was then about forty feet in height, measuring twenty by forty feet with a circular staircase; Byzantine ruins were in evidence. It is still nearly one hundred feet above the sea.[5]

North in the cliff are rock-cut tombs, believed to be Jewish. A few remains of a small harbor are still in evidence. The visitor to the area today will encounter the new village of Dor "settled mostly by newcomers from Greece" near the kibbutz Nahsholim ("breakers").[6] A sandy beach invites swimmers. Hopefully, archaeologists will investigate this site before it vanishes completely.

The other important site is the Crusader castle of Atlit a few miles to the north. This was called the Castle of the Pil-   **Atlit**

5. Carl Grasser, Jr., unpublished newsletter of the American Schools of Oriental Research, July 1970.
6. Zev Vilnay, *The New Israel Atlas: Bible to Present Day* (Jerusalem: Israel University Press, 1968), p. 335.

Remains of the Crusader castle at Athlit, south of Haifa.

grims. The Crusader remains are still impressive, especially the high wall of the citadel, which the visitor approaches as he nears the beach. The Castle of the Pilgrims was built by the Templars in A.D. 1218 near a small port called Detroit.[7] From the southeast, one looks across the curving beach that constitutes the harbor. Across the former moat separating the peninsula from the mainland, the remains of the church on the southwest corner of the ruins is the most conspicuous feature. The high eastern wall extended 800 yards on the east with three gates. The southern wall was 300 yards in length. Beyond the outer wall is a ditch cutting across the promontory and the main wall is beyond the ditch to the west. The main wall, which is still standing, extends 200 yards north and south. The wall extends to a height of 80 feet at the northern tower, and the wall is 16 feet wide. The entire area inside the outer wall is about fifty acres. The church, nearly destroyed, once had three apses facing the west. Much of it was destroyed in the earthquake of 1837. A year

7. C. R. Conder and H. H. Kitchener, *The Survey of Western Palestine* (London: Palestine Exploration Fund, 1883), vol. 1, p. 123.

later, Ibrahim Pasha removed much of the stone to build Acre. There are a series of vaults, impressive for their size and construction. The largest one runs along the east side beneath the two great towers and measures more than 270 feet in length. The vault on the south is 240 feet long and 35 feet wide. This large, strong castle was the last to be abandoned by the Crusaders, in 1291, when it was dismantled. Many of the building stones are now not only in Acre, but also in Jaffa and Beirut. After being dismantled by the Moslems in 1291, wrecked by an earthquake in 1837, its building stones carried away in 1838, and worn through the passage of time, these ruins can still be assessed as "perhaps the finest Crusading remains in Palestine."[8]

Excavations were conducted on the site in 1930 by the Antiquities Department. Among the important finds were some sculptured heads—perhaps those representing Jesus and Mary— and some Crusader coats of arms. Today, a salt plant operates less than two miles to the south; the salt is collected in evaporating pools. From Atlit (the ancient site and modern village) a secondary road leads northeast into the Carmel range past Beth-horon to the summit, where the road branches to the right to Isfiya and to the left toward Haifa. Both the railroad and the modern highway, however, continue north along the coast. On the right, the Carmel caves are visible in the Wadi Mugharet where, among other remains, a skeleton was found believed to be that of a man who lived 40,000 years ago. Here also lived the Natufians, cave dwellers who began to cultivate grain about 8,000 years ago. Higher up on the Carmel range is the modern town of Daliyat el Karmil, five miles south of Isfiya.

The coastal plain narrows at the north to a point, where Mount Carmel meets the seashore. The modern village of Tirat Karmel lies between the railroad and the highway, between mountain and beach. Before reaching Haifa by this shore road, the tell on the southwest shore is that of ancient Shiqmona. Founded by the Greeks, it was once the twin city of Haifa. Its name is taken from the sycamore trees that once grew in the area. Excavations here revealed a beautiful mosaic of birds standing beneath a shrub; the mosaic now is in the museum at Haifa.

In summary, it may be concluded that the "coasts of Dor," or "Dor and its cities," have not played any strategic role in Palestine since the departure of the Crusaders. Little in the fore-

8. Ibid., p. 299.

seeable future envisions this area doing more than its present role of providing agricultural products, seaside resorts, and a communication corridor between north and south, east and west. Its most flourishing modern settlement, at the southern border, is Zikhron Ya'aqov and its twin city, Binyamina (both near the site of Caesarea). Named after Baron Rothschild, Binyamina is a "prosperous settlement," near which are the remains of an ancient Roman theater from the second century.[9]

Nearby, on a plateau, is the Rothschild tomb. This great benefactor of Zionism is honored here amid the several nearby villages that resulted from his philanthropy. The largest of these communities, Zikhron-Ya'aqov, is one of the first Jewish establishments sponsored by Rothschild, in 1882. It is called Jacob's Memorial, thus honoring his father. The highway to the northeast reaches the Esdraelon Valley via Tell Yoqneam, the northernmost of the four passes through the Carmel range.

THE PLAIN OF SHARON

Three miles south of the Crocodile River (Zerqa) are the important ruins of Caesarea, the city built by Herod the Great on the site of Strato's Tower. Strato's Tower was established by the Phoenicians in the third century B.C. and was incorporated into the Hasmonean Kingdom by Alexander Jannaeus.[10] Herod determined to make this the chief seaport on the coast, and he succeeded. The project is fully described by Josephus.[11]

Caesarea

In recent years the ruins have been excavated by Israeli archaeologists, and the port itself was surveyed by a team of marine archaeologists from Princeton University. Christians remember that the gospel first came to Gentiles when Peter visited the house of Cornelius. From here, Paul, after being detained two years in prison, set out for Rome to present his case at "Caesar's judgment seat." At this time, Caesarea was the administrative capital of Judea and Samaria.

Caesarea was one of Herod's major building projects, comparable in scope to his works in Jerusalem and in Samaria. Primarily a port city, its harbor was as large as the Athenian harbor at Piraeus. Herod spared no effort or expense on the project, and it took twelve years to complete it. The harbor was artificial,

9. Vilnay, *New Israel Atlas,* p. 332.
10. Moshe Pearlman and Yaacov Yannai, *Historical Sites in Israel* (New York: Vanguard Press, 1965), p. 132.
11. Jos. *Antiq.* XV. 9. 6; *Wars* I, 23.

and it included a sea mole, or barrier, fifty feet in length, eighteen feet in width, and nine feet in depth, built in water thirty fathoms deep. In the form of a semi-circle opening to the sea, a tower dominated each end of the semi-circle, between which the ships had to pass. Before Herod's project, ships had to unload their cargo anchored at some distance from the shore, just as ships had to do in recent times until the modern port at Haifa was constructed. Some of the stones Herod used in the Caesarea harbor construction were said to be fifty feet in length. One of the towers at the entrance was called Drusus, thus honoring Caesar's son-in-law. Dominating even these towers was a temple, visible at a great distance, with two statues—both honoring Rome, one specifically honoring Caesar. Provision for sanitation utilized the sea; its tides flushed the city, keeping it clean.[12]

Here Pontius Pilate received a delegation of Jews from Jerusalem, who implored him to remove the pagan effigies from Jerusalem. Later, the massacre of Jews in this city touched off the great revolt of A.D. 66. By the end of the first century, this

12. Jos. *Antiq.* XV, 9.6.

A replica of the theatre inscription that bears the name of Pontius Pilate. The original, found at Caesarea, was taken to Jerusalem for protective reasons.

The Roman theatre at Caesarea.

city had enough Christians to be the seat of an archbishop. Eusebius served here as archbishop from A.D. 313 to 337.[13]

The city was captured by the Moslems in the year 638 and remained in Moslem hands until taken over by the Crusaders under Baldwin I in A.D. 1102. Saladin retook it from the Crusaders in 1187, but the Crusaders recaptured it in 1191. Saint Louis rebuilt the citadel and walls, but it was again captured by Baybars in 1265; the latter dismantled it. The chief periods of Caesarea's history were the Phoenician, the Maccabean, the Roman, the Byzantine, the Moslem, and the period of the Crusades.

Existing ruins are chiefly those of the Romans and of the Crusaders. The walls of Herod were in the form of a half-circle 1,600 yards in extent from north to south and 900 yards east to west. An impressive aqueduct parallel to the seashore brought water from the north, a conduit which is still well preserved. At the southern edge near the sea is the theater, excavated and

13. C. W. Wolf, "Eusebius of Caesarea and the Onomasticon," *Biblical Archaeologist* (September 1964): 69.

in part reconstructed, which presently serves as the scene of contemporary theatricals. Within the Roman town was the hippodrome, or race course, 1,056 feet in length, 264 feet wide, which accommodated about twenty thousand spectators. The hippodrome featured in the center three conical blocks of highly polished granite, which were designed to shine like mirrors for the purpose of exciting the horses. The blocks bore the name *taraxippos* (horse frighteners).[14] On a nearby mound, excavations led by Professor Michael Avi-Yonah in 1956 uncovered synagogues of the fourth to seventh centuries A.D. Later the fourth-century synagogue site yielded a hoard of several thousand bronze coins, the largest of which was struck in A.D. 351 and honored Gallus Caesar.[15]

Nearby are the ruins of a Byzantine home and some remains from the Phoenician structures of Strato's Tower. The harbor itself was explored in 1960, aided by a special vessel contributed by Edwin Link. Excavations in the theater near the seashore at

14. Vilnay, *New Israel Atlas*, p. 328.
15. Pearlman and Yannai, *Historical Sites,* p. 142.

the southern edge of the enclosure were undertaken by the Italians under the direction of Professor A. Frova. The Hebrew University pursued excavations north of the harbor in 1956 and again in 1962. Excavations are continuing, and the entire area is of increasing interest to scholars and tourists.

The contributions of the Crusaders was the fortress, approximately one-tenth the area of the Roman Caesarea; the walls of the fortress measured 60 yards long and 250 yards wide east and west, and comprised some 30 acres.[16]

Excavations along the east wall reveal a moat about 38 feet in width, and the main gate consists of Gothic vaults. The remains of the cathedral are located near the south gate and another church is found at the north end of the harbor. The southern gate is well preserved with an entrance 8 feet wide. The castle, built on the southern leg of the harbor, measures 142 feet in length and 59 feet in width. It is fairly well preserved and extends to a height of 70 feet above sea level.[17]

As was characteristic of the Crusader work, the walls of the fortress featured granite columns laid horizontally through the walls, designed to prevent sappers from undermining the wall from without. The ruins of this important city have provided building materials within the last 200 years for Acre, Jaffa, and even distant Venice.[18]

Discovered recently is a stone bearing the name of Pontius Pilate, a striking supplement to the description of this Roman governor by Josephus and the New Testament. Among the most impressive ruins recovered are two statues inside the ancient Roman walls. They are of gigantic size. A third-century figure is in white marble. The other statue is of reddish porphyry, perhaps a representation of the emperor Hadrian.[19]

Caesarea is now an expanse of sand and stone, visited by tourists, a few archaeologists, and occasionally some dramatists making use of the ancient theater. The ruins are reminders of man's ineffectual attempts to achieve his own personal immortality.

Why did Herod choose Strato's Tower as the site for his major seaport? Why not either ancient Jaffa or Akko? Herod

16. Conder and Kitchener, *Survey*, vol. 2 ,p. 23.
17. Ibid., p. 25.
18. Pearlman and Yannai, *Historical Sites*, p. 142.
19. Michael Avi-Yonah, "The Caesarea Porphyry Statue," *Israel Exploration Journal* 20: 203-208.

A vaulted street of Crusader construction at Caesarea.

The Roman aqueduct at Caesarea that supplied water to the city.

chose it either because of its better strategic position or because he wanted to provide a scope for his engineering and political ambitions. If the latter, then it is easy to understand that neither before nor since has Caesarea figured significantly in the history of the area. After the Roman period Jaffa and Akko resumed their former supremacy, but today it is Jaffa and Haifa especially that carry this role.

When the Romans under Vespasian sought to quell the first Jewish revolt, they began at Acre (Akko) rather than at Caesarea, the Roman administrative center. This was done, probably, to protect their flank while they moved on Jerusalem rather than to risk being caught between Jewish forces on both sides had they made a direct attack by way of Caesarea. Obviously, Caesarea provided the easiest access to the interior. It lay on the coastal road. It had easy access to the plain of Esdraelon, either by way of Megiddo or Dothan. It was the terminus of the main road to Jerusalem by way of Antipatris. Even though the revolt started in Caesarea, in A.D. 66, the Romans launched their attack in Galilee from Acre, and the Galilean city of Jotapata was the first key battle in the campaign. Caesarea did not figure prominently in the second Jewish revolt (A.D. 132), except that it was to Caesarea that the Romans retreated after the Jews' initial successes in the Jerusalem area. Instead, Roman armies gathered from the south, the east, and the north to converge on Judea, since upper Galilee was not involved in this revolt.

East of the site of Caesarea, across the sand dunes, is the modern settlement of Pardes Hanna, astride the main road to Haifa. This settlement of approximately 30,000 people is at the fork of the road, one branch goes north to Haifa, and the other travels northwest by way of the Iron Road and the Megiddo Pass to Afula in the Esdraelon Valley.

Just north of Caesarea is the place where the ancient *Via Maris* (The Way of the Sea) left the coastal area to go inland over the Carmel range. The pass through the Carmel range, known as the Iron Road, was guarded at the upper end by Megiddo and at the lower end by Tel Esur. It was one of the most important highways in the world, joining as it did Africa and Asia. The route of countless caravans through the centuries, it also witnessed the passage of great armies. Over this route Thutmose III invaded Palestine in 1468 B.C., inflicting severe defeat on Canaanite kings near Megiddo, as reported on the walls of the palace at Karnak in upper Egypt. Centuries later, Assyrian armies under Sennacherib used this route to attack the coastal cities, as did also the Chaldean armies of Nebuchadnezzar in his thrust into Egypt. Alexander the Great came this way for the same intent. Cambyses, the Persian, conquered Egypt by this same route. Napoleon passed through in 1799 from Egypt, penetrating to the Esdraelon for the siege of Acre. Allenby used this route to pursue the Turks in December 1917. The *Via Maris* was far enough from the sea to avoid the sand, the rivers, and the marshes, and on the right it avoided the hills and mountains of the central highlands. As George Adam Smith observed, the plain of Sharon is noted historically for its convenience of passage from Africa to Asia.

A few miles farther south is the settlement of Hadera, with a population numbering about 30,000. This town was founded in 1890 after the draining of the marshes in the area was begun, **Hadera** a task that was completed only in 1945. Hadera is surrounded by eucalyptus groves, citrus orchards, and farther to the east, irrigated grain fields. The Hadera River to the north was named "Dead River" by the Crusaders because its outlet to the sea was at that time stopped by sand dunes. This area is one of the most thickly settled in Palestine, largely due to the success of Jewish immigrants in reclaiming marsh and sand lands. Several miles south is the Alexander River, so named for the Maccabean ruler Alexander Jannaeus.

In this section the maritime plain is crowded with small settlements, and approximately twelve miles separates the sea and the Samaritan hills at Tulkarm. At the railroad junction, trains from Tel Aviv meet with those coming from Jerusalem before proceeding on to Haifa. Five miles south of the Alexander River is the coastal city of Netanya, now numbering about **Netanya** 21,000. Established in 1928, it honors the memory of Nathan Strauss, an American philanthropist. Although starting as a citrus-growing center, Netanya has grown to be the "capital" of the Sharon. In addition to important industries, it is an attractive resort center with beautiful parks, an open-air theater, and a beach which attracts throngs of people during the summer.

From Netanya there is a good road east leading to the Arab city of Tulkarm, and continuing on to Nablus (Shechem). This area used to be called the valley of Hefer, and was mentioned in the list of districts organized by Solomon (1 Kings 4:10). The area was characterized by sand dunes and swamps until 1929 when the land was purchased with the help of Canadian Jews and reclaimed. Among the numerous agricultural villages of the area is Herev Laet, inhabited by war veterans, the name meaning "swords and plowshares" (Isa. 2:4).

Ten miles farther south on the coast is the site of an ancient town known by various names including Rishpon, Apollonia, and Arsuf, the Arabic name changed by the Crusaders **Arsuf** into Arsur. In 1874, little of its former importance was in evidence. Dusty mounds covered the foundations of the ancient structure.[20] The existing remains are mostly of the Crusader town. The total area is some twenty-two acres (660 by 1,452 feet). The town is isolated by a ditch averaging 40 feet in width. Its irregular shape is approximately twice as long as it is wide. A drawbridge led across the ditch on the east side. A spring was available on the southwest corner and there were numerous cisterns. The fortress itself was in the northwest corner, entered by another drawbridge over a small moat. The castle faced the harbor, which was created by two piers protected by an outer breakwater. This harbor measured 100 yards north and south, and 40 yards in width. The entrance to the harbor between the jetty on the south and the reef of rocks is only thirty feet. It is located twenty-two miles south of Caesarea.

The city is linked with both ancient history and mythology. C. Clermont-Ganneau did research that led him to the conclusion that the ancient name of the city was Reshef, the name of a god of the ancient Phoenicians and also of a modern suburb of Herzliyya. The word means "flame." Excavations at Atlit discovered the god Reshef, which held in one hand what appears to be a plate, and the right hand held a sword. Reshef, according to this theory, corresponds to Perseus of the fable linking him with Andromeda. It also corresponds to the Egyptian god Horus. The combat of Horus is similar to that between Perseus and Andromeda and also between Saint George and the dragon. The god Reshef is equivalent to the Greek god Apollo. The name Apollonia may have been conferred on the city when Seleucus Antipater controlled the area from Damascus. Josephus states that the area formerly belonged to Phoenicia. After the site had remained in ruins for many years, the Romans

---

20. Conder and Kitchener, *Survey,* vol. 2, p. 137.

rebuilt it in 57 B.C. It was besieged in vain by Crusaders Raymond of Toulouse and Godfrey of Bouillon. It was captured, however, by Baldwin I, and it was here that Richard Coeur de Lion defeated Saladin in 1191. It was completely restored by Louis IX in 1251, but was destroyed by Baybars in 1265 and never rebuilt.

This site, together with Lydda, leaves the widespread interest in Saint George to merit some explanation. He was reverenced not only by Christians but also by Mohammedans under the name El Khader. This transfer of the battle of Horus to Perseus and Andromeda, and then to Saint George and the dragon, focuses attention on a soldier who served as a military tribune under the emperor Diocletian.[21] This soldier was martyred in A.D. 103 either near Lydda or in Nicomedia. Thanks to Richard Coeur de Lion and to Edward III, Saint George became the patron saint of England. Perseus slew the mythical dragon either here or in Joppa, thus rescuing the virgin. It is not unusual for Christian heroes to inherit the fame of pagans, since the gods of one religion are easily transferred to become the gods of another. In any case, Saint George is honored not only here and at Lydda, but throughout the Middle East, especially along the Mediterranean coast from Phoenicia southward. In Moslem legends, the story is linked with Jesus' battle with the anti-Christ.[22]

Arsuf is on the northern edge of Herzliyya, a city of 36,000 inhabitants. Herzliyya was named in honor of the founder of Zionism, Theodor Herzl. It was established in 1924. Now a prosperous suburb of Tel Aviv, it features luxury hotels along the beach. Formerly it was the center of the citrus and banana plantations and a predominantly rural village until World War II. Its prosperity today chiefly lies in its proximity to Tel Aviv, whose inhabitants find in Herzilyya a delightful weekend resort or residential suburb.

Herzliyya

From Herzliyya east to the border of the west bank of the Jordan at Qalqilya is only ten miles, the narrowest portion of the state of Israel. Qalqilya is an Arab village of about five thousand, taking its name from Gilgal. From here, in June 1967, the guns of the Arab legion shelled suburbs of Tel Aviv. They were soon silenced by the Israeli army, and the village of Qalqilya was almost completely destroyed. It has since been rebuilt. This sali-

---

21. Smith, *Historical Geography*, p. 162.
22. C. Clermont-Ganneau, "Horus et Saint George," *Revue Archeologique* (1877).

ent for twenty years had presented Israel with its most serious danger as it threatened population centers in and north of Tel Aviv. Less than two miles south is another village with a similar name, Jaljulya (Gilgal).

Rosh Ha'Ayin

Three miles south of Jaljulya is Rosh Ha'Ayin, near the site of ancient Antipatris, which is adjacent to Tel Aphek, an important Old Testament site on the *Via Maris* where the Philistine armies assembled before the battle of Ebenezer (1 Sam. 4:1) and again before the battle of Mount Gilboa (1 Sam 29:1). It has always been one of the most copious springs of Palestine, and it feeds into the Yarqon River. Presently, it is the site of a major pumping station in the Israel aqueduct that brings water from Galilee to the Negev. Large walls of a square khan, or caravansery, are built over foundations from the Roman period. The Crusaders had a structure near here to guard the springs, called "Le Toron aux Fontaines Sourdes" (Tower of the Southern Springs). Josephus states that during the period of Seleucid dominance, Alexander Jannaeus dug a deep ditch from "Chabarzabi [Antipatris] to the Sea of Joppa."[23]

Josephus further recounts that after Herod had instituted a vast celebration at Sebaste in the twenty-eighth year of his reign, he "erected another city in the plain called Capharsaba, where he chose out a fit place, both for plenty of water and goodness of soil . . . where a river encompassed the city itself, and a grove of the best trees for magnitude was round about it: this he named Antipatris, from his father Antipater."[24]

Antipatris

The only mention of Antipatris in the Bible is with reference to the night journey of Paul from Jerusalem to Caesarea. In Jerusalem he had been rescued from a mob that threatened his life, and he was taken under the protection of the tribune. The episode provides an excellent example of the determination of the Roman administration to protect the civil rights of Roman citizens. Paul was committed to the barracks for his own protection after it was learned that a plot to kill him was under way. When the tribune learned of the danger to Paul, he acted decisively. In the dead of night, to elude the forty who vowed to assassinate Paul, the tribune alerted two hundred foot soldiers, two hundred spearmen, and seventy horsemen. With this guard, Paul was escorted out of the city in the early evening.

23. Jos. *Antiq.* XIII. 15. 1.
24. Ibid., XVI. 5. 2; *Wars* I. 21. 9.

Before morning, they had reached Antipatris, about half the distance to Caesarea, their destination. From here, the foot soldiers returned to Jerusalem, whereas the cavalry escorted Paul to Caesarea the following day (Acts 23:6-32).

Farther down the Yarqon, on its north bank near the main coastal highway, is one of the more important archaeological sites, Tel Qasila, excavated under the direction of Professor Mazar. Some of the antiquities are housed in a small adjacent museum. The first settlement of the site was by the "Sea Peoples," invaders from the Greek Islands who arrived about the twelfth century B.C. Artifacts indicate commercial relations with Phoenicia. This settlement was destroyed in the tenth century, and an Israelite city was built on its ruins. It was destroyed again by Tiglath-pilezer III in 732 B.C. It has been suggested that this was the port city through which building materials from Phoenicia reached Jerusalem (2 Chron. 11:16; Ezra 3:7). The site also presents evidence of Hellenistic, Roman, and Byzantine occupancy, up until the Mameluke period through the fifteenth century A.D.[25]

Tel Qasila

Also near Yarqon, in the northeast section of Tel Aviv, is the site of Tel Gerisa. Professor E. L. Sukenik began excavating here in 1927. He found evidences of occupancy from the Hyksos period in the eighteenth century B.C. Napoleon used this site as a campsite, and it consequently has been named Napoleon's Hill. Thus the banks of the Yarqon, the major river of the south of the Litani, has been inhabited for at least four millennia, but never more densely than now.

Tel Gerisa

---

25. Pearlman and Yannai, *Historical Sites,* pp. 148, 149.

Captive Philistines are portrayed at Medinet Habu, Egypt. An interesting feature is their feathered helmets.

6

The Maritime Plain — South

The southern half of the maritime plain can be defined as extending from the south bank of the Yarqon River through Tel Aviv and other cities along the coast to the brook Besor, five miles southwest of Gaza. The southern boundary of Palestine coincides with the southern boundary of Judah, which was designated as extending from the southern edge of the Dead Sea to the "Ascent of Akrabbim," which ascends from the Arabah to the Negev Plateau, past the springs at Kadesh Barnea and terminates along the Brook of Egypt approximately fifty miles southwest of Gaza (Josh. 15:2-4). Thus the southern boundary of Judah was a loop far to the south of Beer-sheba and included the wilderness of Zin, passing through Kadesh Barnea (Meribah) and Azmon.[1] The plain of Philistia, however, extended from the coast south of Joppa to the brook Bezor, far to the north of the line assigned originally to Judah.[2]

The distance from Beer-sheba to the coast near Gaza is about 30 miles. The altitude of Beer-sheba, however, is nearly 1,500 feet. The entire distance from the Mediterranean coast from Khan Yunis, south of Gaza, to Mount Carmel is about 115 miles. Although the maritime plain is less than a mile in width at its northern tip, it widens markedly from Tel Aviv south; the entire plain, shaped like a curved sword, increases gradu-

1. H. G. May, ed., *The Oxford Bible Atlas* (Cambridge: At the University Press, 1962), p. 58.
2. Yohanan Aharoni and Michael Avi-Yonah, *The Macmillan Bible Atlas* (New York: Macmillan Co., 1968), plate 107.

ally in width until it reaches the Negev at Gaza. Part of this can be explained by geological factors. There is an outcropping of Cenomanian limestone that serves as a demarcation line between the plain and the mountains. This outcropping appears near Aijalon at the 1000-foot level, whereas west of Hebron, it is 1,600 feet about sea level. East of this line, the elevation rises rapidly, but to the west it drops gradually toward the sea. Between the two is a narrow line of Senonian chalk, extending from the valley of Aijalon approximately to the Gaza-Beer-sheba road. The maritime plain here consists of Pleistocene alluvium, whereas the lowlands, or Shephelah, just west of this area contains Eocene limestone, extending from the area west of Ramla to Beer-sheba and beyond. Of the two areas, the plain and the Shephelah, the plain is the more important historically; the Shephelah was often a border zone between the country of the Philistines and the hill country of Judea. Today, the Shephelah is primarily devoted to raising grain and fruit; the plain along the coast is devoted more to commerce and is more thickly settled, now as in ancient times.

JAFFA AND ENVIRONS

This is one of the better known places of the Holy Land. It has been continuously occupied since prehistoric times. Historic Jaffa stands on a promontory jutting into the sea and forming a shallow harbor, similar to that of Haifa but on a much smaller scale. Toward the end of the nineteenth century, its population numbered only about 8,000 persons, mostly Moslems with a Christian minority of Greek and Roman Christians. It is the ancient port of Jerusalem, thirty-five miles inland. It has never been an adequate port, with vessels having to unload at some distance from the shore and the cargo conveyed by tender to the dock. This was true of both freight and passengers, as many pilgrim itineraries dramatically witness. Its chief claim to fame is as a trading center, although the adjacent area is fertile, both for fruit and flowers as well as garden produce. As at Haifa, here also a German colony pioneered the modern settlement in this area. Today there are some restaurants overlooking the bay, a large Latin church and hospice, a Greek monastery, and an excellent archaeological museum high on the hill. A good view is obtained across the shallow bay north in the direction of Herzilyya. The broad beach is thronged with weekend bathers in the summer months.

The harbor of Jaffa, looking northeast.

Here, by special revelation, the gospel was first presented to the non-Jewish world. While residing with a Jewish tanner by the name of Simon, the apostle Peter was on the roof of the house overlooking the bay. Before his noonday lunch, while engaged in prayer, Peter saw the vision that led to his journey to Caesarea and the bringing of the gospel to Cornelius and his household, an event reported three times in the New Testament. Interestingly, this Simon was a tanner by trade, and when one reads the itinerary of Benjamin of Tudela, he will be impressed by the many times Benjamin refers to Jews he met who were tanners by trade. It seems likely that the processing of leather was a specialty among the Jews living in Palestine during the Middle Ages. It was in Jaffa also that Peter, summoned from Lydda, saw the corpse of Dorcas return to life, one of the few recorded incidents of the restoration of life in answer to prayer and faith. It is not surprising, therefore, that in Jaffa, "many believed in the Lord" (Acts 9:42). It was from Jaffa, also, that the less dedicated but almost equally effective minister of the Lord, Jonah, set sail rather than proceeding to Nineveh.

The largest all-Jewish community in the world is claimed for Tel Aviv, with a population of nearly 400,000. In 1909, Jews residing in Jaffa purchased an area of sand dunes east of the city. They gave it the name Tel Aviv ("Hill of Spring," cf. Ezek. 3:15), the name taken from the title of a book by Theodor Herzl. During World War I the Turkish general ordered all the residents to disperse, but at the conclusion of the war they returned, later joined by thousands of new immigrants from Europe. In 1921, the suburb was separated from Jaffa and became an independent municipality. Today the two cities are again merged. Some Samaritans from Nablus, visiting their relatives in 1947, were caught in the war that followed the termination of the British mandate. Thus there is a small Samaritan community here also. Only remnants of the Arab community are found in Jaffa, for many Arabs had left during the same conflict. The British general of World War I is remembered in Allenby Road. Other streets commemorate Jewish heroes, including Herzl, Montefiore, and Rothschild. Also, Balfour is remembered. In Tel Aviv modern Israel proclaimed itself an independent nation on May 4, 1948. Because the United Nations passed a resolution in 1947 that Jerusalem should become an international city, all embassies are located at Tel Aviv rather than at Jerusalem, which is the *de-facto* but not the *de-jure* capital of Israel, although legations are commonly stationed in Jerusalem as well. Tel Aviv depended upon Jaffa for its harbor until an Arab boycott in 1936, which resulted in the supplemental harbor for Tel Aviv alone. Jaffa no longer serves as a harbor; sea trade is carried out at Haifa and the new harbor at Ashdod. But Tel Aviv maintains its cultural and economic superiority, assisted by the airport at nearby Lydda (Lod).

At few places on the globe is the past and present more dramatically set in juxtaposition. Tel Aviv is one of the newest important cities in the world and Jaffa is one of the oldest. As if almost by accident, they are now united. On the high ground above the harbor near the museum, Professor Kaplan, in 1955-61, found remains going back to the eighteenth century B.C. Included in the finds was a Hyksos citadel, the walls twenty feet thick. The city gate was inscribed with the name of Ramses II, which would date this particular artifact before 1234 B.C.

This would place it near the time of the Exodus. The French archaeologist, C. Clermont-Ganneau, in 1871, found tombstones near the Russian church inscribed in Hebrew, Aramaic, and Greek, going back to the first centuries of our era.[3]

Down a slope, but overlooking the harbor, is the Franciscan monastery of Saint Peter, built in the nineteenth century on the ruins of a thirteenth-century Crusader fortress. Adjacent to the monastery, at the end of a winding alley, is a mosque built in 1730. It is on the presumed site of the house of Simon the Tanner, and like Simon's house it overlooks the sea. The tomb of Tabitha (the Dorcas for whom Peter prayed) is said to be a cave in the courtyard of the Russian monastery, on the site of a much more ancient Jewish cemetery. A short way down the hill is the village square with a quaint Turkish clock on a column in the center of the square.

A few miles east of Jaffa is the site of the Crusader battle (1192) of Bombrac; the name is given to a Crusaders fortress nearby. To the south of this is another Crusader fortress, called the Castle of the Plains, at the ancient site of Yazur, four miles east of Jaffa. The Crusaders had three fortresses guarding the approaches to Jaffa, a fortified city. The southernmost castle was Casal Maen-Beit Dagan.[4] Two miles south of this is Beth Dagon (House of Dagon), an ancient city honoring the god of the Philistines. The name is preserved in a modern settlement of that same name at the site.

The most important city south and east of Tel Aviv is the ancient city of Lod, which is on the ancient road to Jerusalem. Today, the railroad forks here, one branch going to Haifa, the other to Tel Aviv. This city, more than 2,000 years old, was built by one of the descendants of Benjamin (1 Chron. 8:12). Later it became known as Lydda and was the place where the sick man Aeneas was cured in response to the faith of the apostle Peter (Acts 9:32). During the first Jewish revolt, A.D. 66-70, it was demolished by the Romans en route to Jerusalem. Later it flourished as the Jewish seat of learning, its fame enhanced by the residence of the famous Rabbi Akiba, co-sponsor of the second Jewish revolt (A.D. 132-134). When the Roman emperor,

Lod

---

3. Moshe Pearlman and Yaacov Yannai, *Historical Sites in Israel* (New York: Vanguard Press, 1965), p. 154.
4. See map, "Palestine of the Crusaders," in F. J. Salmon, *Survey of Palestine* (Jaffa: 1937).

Septimius Severus, visited the country in A.D. 200, the name of the city was changed to Diospolis (City of God).

The most prominent church here, however, honors not Peter but rather, Saint George. This church is pictured in the Madaba mosaic map in which the city is called by three names, including Lydea. As noted earlier, George was a Christian soldier who rebelled against the anti-Christian edicts of the Emperor Diocletian and was martyred in A.D. 303. The Christian community buried him in his native city and for a while the city itself bore his name (Georgeosopolis). The legend of Perseus slaying the dragon at Andromeda and rescuing the virgin from danger was transferred to Saint George and was carried by Richard Coeur de Lion to England. A twelfth-century Crusader church was erected on the ruins of an older Byzantine church, and in 1870, the church was restored to its present condition. Therefore it is not surprising that the English cathedral in east Jerusalem carries the name of Saint George. The legend of the hero attacking the monster of evil is very common and prevalent. Even in India, an annual festival popular in many parts of that country represents Dirga, the goddess of light, slaying the demon of darkness.

Ramla The only city built by the conquering Moslems in Palestine from the seventh century to the present was Ramla. They destroyed Lod and built Ramla in its stead four miles to the southwest. The town was founded in A.D. 716 by the son of Abdel el Malik, the Omayyad caliph who built the Dome of the Rock Mosque in Jerusalem. As the name indicates, it was built not upon the ruins of a previous city but on the sand. Even more than Lod, Ramla was in a position to command the main trade routes—the north-south route from Egypt to Syria and the east-west route from Jaffa to Jerusalem. It is not clear whether the foundation of Ramla was necessitated by the prior destruction of Lod, or whether Lod was destroyed to make room for Ramla. Today they are virtually twin cities. The international airport, however, is located nearer to Lod than to Ramla. The most conspicuous feature of the city is the "white tower of Ramla," built by Arabs in the fifteenth century A.D. It is also known as the "Tower of the Forty Martyrs," probably built by the sultan Baybars after he had taken Ramla from the Crusaders in A.D. 1268. A view from the top of the tower is impressive. From it is visible not only the coastal cities but also the valley of Aijalon where Joshua defeated the Canaanites while the sun stood still. From the top of this tower, Napoleon watched his troops successfully assault Jaffa in 1799. East of this tower is the "great mosque," which originally was one of the best preserved Crusader buildings in the country. "It is an expression of the power, ingenuity and grace of Crusader architecture."[5]

On the west is the Franciscan monastery and hospice, where pilgrims could tarry while awaiting permission to proceed to Jerusalem. During the four centuries of Ottoman rule, such permission was frequently delayed. North of the monastery is a cistern, perhaps Moslem in construction, where medieval pilgrims refreshed themselves, calling it the "Pool of Saint Helena" in honor of the mother of Constantine. Water was apparently a problem as the vast reservoirs of the area testify. Also in Ramla is the hospice of Saint Nicodemus, honoring the one who shared with Joseph the responsibility for Jesus' burial. According to one tradition, Ramla was the home of Joseph of Arimathea.

But today there is little to remind one of Bible times or

5. Pearlman and Yannai, *Historical Sites*, p. 159.

The town of Ramla, near Tel Aviv. The Tower of the Forty Martyrs is visible on the extreme left.

even of the Medieval period. This area, lying in the hinterland of Tel Aviv-Joppa, is the scene of farming and commercial activity. The international airport nearby is busy. Auto routes converge upon it from all directions, and some wend their way through congested city streets to reach it. Where once Israel and the Philistines were in confrontation, and where armies from Egypt and Asia crossed and recrossed, traffic today on land and in the air competes for space and time. Where medieval pilgrims spent their night in fitful sleep after arriving in this land, modern pilgrims are more likely to be efficiently whisked away to Jerusalem, Tel Aviv, Haifa, or Ashqelon instead. Yet in spite of the modern hustle, much of the Biblical aura persists.

PHILISTIA

The
Philistines

Few problems in Palestinian geography and history present more complexities than the story of the Philistines. They left no written language, and there are only a few references to them in other than Biblical sources. Their arrival to the southern coast of Palestine appears to be linked with the sudden collapse of civilizations in Greece and Asia Minor, including the Mycenaens in Crete. The earliest reference to them is from Egypt, where they are called the "Sea-peoples." Their unsuccessful attempt to invade Egypt is graphically portrayed in the wall of the temple of Ramses III (ca. 1175-1144 B.C.) at Medinet Habu near the Valley of the Kings in upper Egypt.[6]

Apparently, after their attempted landing near the mouths of the Nile was repelled by the Egyptians, they moved up along the coast and settled from Gaza northward. That they did not attempt to land first on the Palestinian coast is explicable by the fact that there is no natural harbor in that area, so they chose the Nile delta. There is also evidence that the termination of the Hittite Empire and the fall of Ugarit coincides with this invasion of the "Sea-peoples," approximately 1230 B.C.[7]

According to the Biblical evidence, the Philistines came from Crete, which finds added significance as coming after the collapse of the Minoan and Mycenaean civilization in that large island. In the words of Amos, "Did I not bring up Israel from the land of Egypt, and the Philistines from Caphtor, and the Syrians from Kir?[8] Thus the Pentateuch, an eighth-century proph-

---

6. George Ernest Wright, *Biblical Archaeology* 29 (1966): 70.
7. Ibid., p. 73.
8. Amos 9:7; cf. Jer. 47:4, "For the Lord is destroying the Philistines, the

et, and a sixth-century prophet harmoniously agree that the Philistines, inhabitants of the coast near Gaza, originated in Caphtor, the Biblical name for Crete. The name itself appears first in the Egyptian form, then in the Assyrian sources, and later, transliterated, into Hebrew. Since there was no comparable Semitic etymology, the name is probably of Indo-European origin.[9]

In the Old Testament, the Philistines are often referred to as "the uncircumcised," thus distinguishing them from Semitic peoples, though there is some evidence that they originally were Semites who migrated west and then returned. In so doing, they may have given up the practice of circumcision. The name of these obscure people, who comprise a minor episode in history, who left no literature, and who erected few buildings, has been given to the entire land of Palestine, whereas the Israelites, who figure so importantly in the history of this land, are not so honored.

During the tenth century, however, the very existence of Israel was threatened by Philistine expansion—during the time between the fall of Saul and the rise of David, the Philistines extended themselves to the west edge of Jerusalem, only to be repulsed eventually by David (2 Sam. 5:17-25). After this, the Philistines never became a major threat either to the united monarchy of Israel or to the later kingdom of Judah.

An attempt to answer the strange anomaly of the changing fortunes of the Philistines has been undertaken by George Adam Smith, who suggests two reasons: first, the Philistines were vulnerable—located as they were on the road between Africa and Asia, they were constantly subject to opposing forces. This restricted their ascendancy to only short periods of time. The second reason is the unusual stability of Israel—influenced as she was by her prophets who gave their fellow tribesmen a reason to exist. This stability enabled Israel to survive whereas the Philistines, without this undergirding, were assimilated by their stronger neighbors.[10]

The gods worshiped by the Philistines were Dagon, the fish god (1 Sam. 5:15), and Baal-zebub, the god of Ekron (2 Kings

remnant of the coastland of Caphtor." Cf. Deut. 2:23, "As for Avvim, who lived in villages as far as Gaza, the Caphtorim, who came from Caphtor, destroyed them and settled in their stead."
9. J. C. Greenfield, "Philistines," *Interpreters Dictionary of the Bible* (Nashville: Abingdon Press, 1962), vol. 2, p. 791.
10. George Adam Smith, *The Historical Geography of the Holy Land,* 15th ed. (New York: A. C. Armstrong and Son, 1909), pp. 476-479.

Herzliyya
Yarqon River
Tel Qasila
Antipatris (Aphek)
Tel Aviv
Tel Gerisa
Rosh Ha'Ayin
Yafo
(Jaffa)
(Joppa)
Shiloh
Jiljiliya
Sinjil
Lod (Lydda)
Jifna
Bethel
Ramla
Upper Beth-horon
Ramallah
Tel Gezer
Beth-horon
Ram
Mukhmas
Imwas
Qubeiba
Jaba
Ashdod
Latrun
Nabi Samwil
Anata
Tel Miqne (Ekron)
Kiriath-jearim
Abu Ghosh
Jerusalem
Tel Zafit (Gath)
JUDEA
Ein Karem
Eizariya
Tel Bornat (Libnah)
Beth-shemesh
Matta
Betar
Shephelah
Tel Zakariyeh (Azekah)
Bethlehem
Mar Saba
Ashkelon
Artas
Herodium
Tel Erani
Adullam
Tekoa
Qiryat Gat
Bet Guvrin
Bet Zur
Ein el-Arrub
Tel Mareshah
Halhul
Tel Lachish
Hebron
Gaza
Tel Zif
Maon
Tel Sera
Lahav
Samu
Philistia

Maritime Plain
— South
and the
Shephelah

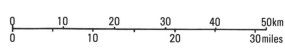

0   10   20   30   40   50km
0   10   20   30 miles

1:2-6). Philistia remained stubbornly polytheistic and pagan. The Syrian goddess of fertility, Atargatic (Babylonian Ishtar and Phoenician Astarte), was worshiped in the form of a mermaid at a great shrine in Ashkelon under the name Derceto. Images of this goddess were also found in Nabatean shrines to the south and east.[11] Not until the fourth century of the Christian era was paganism finally dominated by Christianity. Before this, not even did the zeal of Alexander Jannaeus succeed in converting Philistia to monotheism during the Maccabean ascendancy.

The arrival of the Israelites and of the Philistines to this area occurred at approximately the same time, as witnessed chiefly by archaeological evidence of the Canaanite population at this period, both in Philistia and in the Judean cities. The Philistines came from the west and the Israelites came from the east and south—one from the sea, the other from the desert. The Philistines, however, had a monopoly on iron from the very beginning of the Iron Age, approximately 1200 B.C. Until the time of David, the Philistines were militarily superior to the Israelites. Also, the Israelites were economically dependent on their Philistine neighbors: "There was no smith . . . throughout all Israel . . . but everyone of the Israelites went down to the Philistines to sharpen" his tools (1 Sam. 13:19, 20).

During the period of their greatest strength, the Philistines not only occupied the coasts from Gaza to Dor, but they sent three prongs eastward up into the valleys to the edge of the Jordan. The southernmost thrust, although temporary, reached west Jerusalem through the valley of Rephaim, where they were defeated by David in two separate battles (2 Sam. 5:17-25). Another thrust brought the Philistines through the valley of Aijalon to the vicinity of Geba and Michmash (1 Sam. 13). On still another campaign they reached as far east and north as Shiloh, using Aphek as the source of their attack (1 Sam. 4:1-11). Excavations indicate that Gezer, in a position to control the valley of Aijalon, came under Philistine control in the twelfth century B.C.[12] Archaeological as well as Biblical evidence indicates Philistine presence in Bethshan in the twelfth century. Archaeological evidence reveals also that they were in the Jordan Valley as far south as Tell Deir Alla. Thus they had the Israelites almost surrounded at the time of Saul's death or shortly there-

---

11. Theodor F. Meysels, *Israel in Your Pocket* (Tel Aviv: Ben-Dor Israel Publishing Co., 1956), vol. 3, p. 27.
12. Wright, *Archaeology,* p. 77.

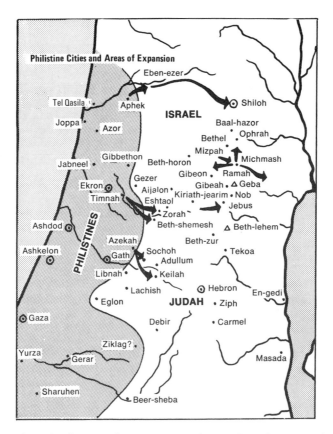

Philistine Cities and Areas of Expansion

after.[13] The rapid expansion of Israel under David and Solomon, however, effectively and finally reversed this trend, and the Philistines were confined to their coastal strongpoints.

Philistia suffered a far more serious threat from Assyria, beginning with the expeditions of Tiglath-pileser and lasting until the decline of Assyrian power, about 630 B.C.[14] The conquest of Philistia followed the Assyrian dominance over Phoenicia, which occurred in approximately 734 B.C. This coincided roughly with the period of Philistine resurgence following the defeat of Judah at the hands of Israel (the northern kingdom) and Damascus (2 Chron. 28:5-15; Isa. 7:1-3, cf. 2 Chron. 28:18). Soon after this, Tiglath-pileser captured Gaza and extended Assyrian dominance as far south as the Brook of Egypt, near modern Tell El-Arish, where he set up his stele to mark the boundary between his empire and that of Egypt.[15] Tiglath-pileser and his successors next turned their attention to Syria

13. Ibid.
14. H. Tadmor, "Philistia under Assyrian Rule," *Biblical Archaeologist* 9 (1966): 86 ff.
15. Ibid., p. 88.

and the northern kingdom of Israel, as readers of the Bible know, with Damascus succumbing in 732 and Samaria in 722. The siege of Ekron, and also the siege of Gibbethon by Sargon II, is portrayed in bas-relief at Khorsebad.[16] No doubt encouraged by Egypt, and perhaps also by Hezekiah, the city of Ashdod revolted in 712 B.C. The story is told in Assyrian records and also in the Bible where it is stated that the Assyrian "commander in chief . . . came to Ashdod and fought against it and took it" (Isa. 20:1). The same campaign apparently resulted in the fall of Azekah (Tell Zakariyeh). The battle for Ekron (Tel Miqne occurred during Sennacherib's campaign in 701.[17] The campaign apparently conquered El-ekeh (Tel Esh-Shelaf) also. Sennacherib's son Esarhaddon adopted a more aggressive policy, and Philistia was thoroughly subjugated during that monarch's campaign against Egypt. The sudden fall of Assyria afforded little relief to Philistia or Judah, for the armies of Nebuchadnezzar soon conquered both. The last mention of Philistine kings appears in a list of high court officials at Nebuchadnezzar's palace.[18]

The First Book of Samuel frequently mentions the five lords of the Philistines. These were the local kings, or tyrants, of the Philistines' five main cities—Ashdod, Ashkelon, Gaza, Ekron, and Gath. The first three were coastal cities, the latter two were inland. The three coastal cities were by far the most important. The two inland cities, the locations of which are still uncertain, were on the border with Israel and often changed hands.

There are several sites that bear the name *Ashdod*. The name itself is seen in the Assyrian term *As-du-du-*, whereas in the Babylonian cuneiform of Ugarit, it appears as *As-da-di*. The Hebrew term is derived from an older Canaanite term, *Attadu*. The Hebrew name *Ashdod* means "stronghold" or "fortress" and is perhaps related to the old Akkadian root meaning "to measure."[19] The southernmost Ashdod is Ashdod by the Sea (Ashdod Yam). The port of Ashdod was Tel Mor, located on the south bank of the Lachish River. In addition, there is a nearby Arabic village of Ishdud, now in ruins. Still another is the modern settlement that takes the name Ashdod. The new town was established in 1957 on desert sands near the shore. Several industries,

---

16. See note cited by Tadmor, ibid., pp. 90-93.

17. J. Navey, *Israel Exploration Journal* 7 (1958): 87-100.

18. Tadmor, "Philistia," p. 102.

19. F. M. Cross, Jr. and D. N. Freedman, "The Name of Ashdod," *Bulletin of the American Schools of Oriental Research* 175 (October 1964): 48.

including the Leyland Bus factory, have recently grown up around the site. The tell, or ancient city, is three miles south of the mouth of the Lachish River on the *Via Maris*. As one of the larger tells in Palestine, it is currently being excavated by the Israel Department of Antiquities, the Carnegie Museum, and Pittsburgh Theological Seminary. Initial results have just recently been reported in detail.[20]

At the northern extremity of the mound, evidences of Early Bronze Age occupancy were discovered. Above these were evidences of the Middle Bronze Age stratum. At various times in the city's history there were three ports that served it. One was Tel Mor (also Minat Isdud) and the previously mentioned Ashdod-Yam (also Neby Unis, to honor the prophet Jonah). The modern city encompasses three of these ancient sites, and

20. M. Dothan and D. N. Freedman, *Ashdod I: The First Season of Excavations, 1962* (Jerusalem: Antiqot, 1967), pp. 1-171.

The modern harbor and breakwater at Ashdod.

it is planned to become the largest seaport in Israel. Ashdod began as an important commercial and military center at the earliest phase of the Late Bronze Age, although there were evidences of much earlier settlements at the site.[21] The influence of Egyptian Middle Kingdom period of the eighteenth dynasty is in evidence. It was then that the Hyksos were expelled and Egypt was able to regain possession of Palestine. Ashdod served Egypt both as a military fortress and a commercial center. At this time Ashdod, Akko, and Ugarit had mutual commercial relationships.

The Late Bronze Age city "came to a violent end about the middle of the thirteenth century B.C., as indicated by a layer of ash three feet thick."[22] This date would coincide in time with the invasion of the Israelites under the leadership of Joshua.

Philistine occupancy was in evidence a century later. Excavators found a structure from this period consisting of a brick wall about four feet thick. One portion of the excavation revealed a large number of religious objects reflecting "ritual practices connected with the fertility cult, which must have been very popular."[23] The upper strata gave evidence of violent destruction, possibly by Uzziah (2 Chron. 26:6) or more likely by Sargon II of Assyria, who conquered Ashdod in 712 B.C. (Isa. 20:1). Fragments of a stele disclosed by the excavators include the commemoration of the victories of Sargon, "thus offering direct confirmation and vivid illustration of the Biblical and Assyrian accounts."[24]

With the coming of the Greeks, the name of the city was changed to Azotus. The town is mentioned in Jewish literature of the Maccabean period as well as in the writings of Josephus. The Maccabean general Jonathan destroyed the temple of Dagon, the deity with which Samson was linked much earlier. Coins of Alexander Jannaeus were found at the site. Nehemiah was scornful of the strange dialect of those who came from Ashdod (Neh. 13:23, 24). This city was among the first to hear the gospel of Christ. After Philip had baptized the pilgrim from Ethiopia, he went to "Azotus, and passing on he preached the gospel to all the towns till he came to Caesarea" (Acts 8:40). Ashdod became the seat of a bishop during the Byzantine period.

---

21. D. N. Freedman, "The Second Season at Ancient Ashdod," *Biblical Archaeologist* 26 (1963): 135.
22. Ibid., p. 136.
23. Ibid., p. 137.
24. Ibid., p. 138.

Today, Ashdod is planned to fill the role that it had in ancient times, when it was a major trading center on the *Via Maris* between north and south and also between east and west, linking the caravan trade of the Negev with the European lands to the west. Today it is a commercial link between the Red Sea by way of Eilat and the Mediterranean coast.

Ashdod had incurred the curse of Israel's prophets, "I will cut off the inhabitants from Ashdod . . . and the remnant of the Philistines shall perish" (Amos 1:8). In the Arab-Jewish conflict in 1948, the Egyptian army penetrated as far as Ashdod before being thrown back by the Israeli defenders, reminiscent of a statement in Isaiah: "In that day the Egyptians will be like women and tremble with fear before the hand which the Lord of hosts shakes over them. And the land of Judah will become a terror to the Egyptians" (Isa. 19:16-17).

The second major city of the Philistines lay approximately halfway between Ashdod and Gaza. It is located on one of the few cliffs that rise along the shore. It has a narrow beach for swimming but no adequate harbor.

The name Ashkelon is probably derived from the root of the word "shekel," a reflection of the city's involvement in commercial transactions. The name is also linked with "onions," one of its main exports, and from which comes the English term "scullion." At least four sites bear the name Ashkelon. There was an Ashkelon by the sea in old times, and an Ashkelon inland during the Middle Ages. In recent times, a small Arab town bore that name, but now a rebuilt ultra-modern city lies between the medieval site and the sea. In ancient times, the Wadi Ibrahim reached the sea and provided a small sheltered harbor at its mouth. Ashkelon was the only city of the Philistines that had its own harbor nearby. It appears to have been a cultural and religious center of ancient Philistia. It is one of the oldest cities on the earth, as witnessed by more than one ancient writer. It was primarily a trading center rather than a military strongpoint. Numerous wells made it an oasis and a very attractive spot. The town is first mentioned in the "Meriut Ostraca" of the twelfth Egyptian dynasty.[25]

In Tel Ashqelon, there are six levels of early settlement: Canaanite, Philistine, Graeco-Roman, Byzantine, Moslem, and Crusader. The fertility of the adjacent environs made the Ash-

---

25. Meysels, *Israel*, p. 25.

Ancient relics, from different eras, found in the region of Ashkelon are restored and preserved at the Ashkelon Antiquities Park.

At the Ashkelon Antiquities Park, the center relief in this section shows Nike, the goddes of victory, standing on the world which is supported by the shoulders of Atlas.

kelon of old and the Ashkelon of today a center of vintage and fruit. Established at the end of the third millennium B.C., it was one of the Canaanite cities mentioned in the nineteenth-century Execration Texts, when Egypt was at the height of its power, and later in the Amarna Letters.[26]

Ashkelon was dominated by the Hyksos during the eighteenth century. They fortified the city with a bank of beaten earth, consistent with their practice at other sites. They were expelled, however, by the Egyptians, and the country again came under Egyptian sovereignty. Revolts occurred nonetheless, and the palace of Ramses II, about 1280 B.C., shows Egyptian troops subjugating the rebellious people of Ashkelon. Later, the Egyptian pharaoh Merneptah, about the year 1225, made this important notation in a stele, the earliest reference to Israel in

26. Edward E. Hindson, *The Philistines and the Old Testament* (Grand Rapids: Baker Book House, 1961), p. 48.

contemporary records: "Carried off is Ashkelon; seized upon is Gezer . . . Israel is laid waste, his seed is not."[27]

In 701 B.C., Sennacherib deported the rebellious king of Ashkelon, and the city remained under Assyrian suzerainty. The city later was conquered by the Babylonians and its king deported along with the Judean king Jehoiakim. During the Persian period, Ashkelon reappeared as the southernmost town of Phoenicia under the leadership of Tyre. During the time of Greek dominance, Ashkelon was under the influence of Ptolemaic Egypt. This came to an end, however, with the Seleucids from Antioch acquiring Ashkelon in 200 B.C. The city was granted political independence by the Romans in 104 B.C. It then became an autonomous Greek city. During this time Ashkelon sought to maintain an independent status amid the swirling tides of political and military change. As a trade center, her prosperity continued, and she enjoyed semi-independent status. Her beauty and culture were often praised. Ashkelon was an important trade center until World War I. On the Madaba mosaic map (sixth

27. James B. Pritchard, ed., *The Ancient Near East* (Princeton, N.J.: Princeton University Press, 1958), p. 231.

A closeup of another relief at Ashkelon.

century A.D.), Ashkelon territory extended to Ashdod in the
north, and to Bet Guvrin in the east. For several centuries thereafter it was more important than Gaza. Abdul el Malik, builder
of the Dome in the Rock in Jerusalem adorned Ashkelon with
a magnificent mosque in A.D. 685.[28] After the Crusades, however,
Gaza was the main market of the area until 1914.[29]

Excavations indicate the total destruction of the Canaanite
city on which the Philistines built their own new city and new
civilization. The arrival of the Israelites coincided with this
date. The Bible records Samson's involvement in the struggle between the Philistines and the Israelites. At Samson's wedding feast, after his riddle was discovered, "he went down to
Ashkelon and killed thirty men of the town, and took their
spoil . . ." (Judg. 14:19). Several generations later, when Saul and
Jonathan were slain by the Philistines during the battle of Gilboa, David lamented, "Publish it not in the streets of Ashkelon; lest the daughters of the Philistines rejoice, lest the daughters of the uncircumcised exult" (2 Sam. 1:20). In the middle
of the eighth century B.C., Ashkelon received this prophetic
warning, " 'I will cut off . . . him that holds the scepter from
Ashkelon . . . and the remnant of the Philistines shall perish,'
says the Lord God" (Amos 1:8). The triumph of the Israelites
over the Philistines is announced in the sixth century by Zephaniah, "The seacoast shall become the possession of the remnant
of the house of Judah . . . in the houses of Ashkelon shall they
lie down at evening . . ." (Zeph. 2:7). Today, a street in Ashkelon bears the name Zephaniah Boulevard. There is none named
after Amos!

During the Maccabean period, Ashdod seems to have been
more prominent than Ashkelon, but Herod the Great adorned
the city of Ashkelon by building waterworks, baths, and "large
and beautiful piazzas and cloisters," as stated by Josephus. Ashkelon became a strong Christian center and continued so even
after the Moslem conquest.

During the Middle Ages, its importance continued, and
the Egyptians controlled it for much of this period. The Crusaders, in one of their most difficult tasks, finally brought this
city under their control by the efforts of Baldwin III in A.D. 1153.
When Benjamin of Tudela visited the city in 1171, he found
it to be "a very large and handsome city; merchants from all parts

28. Meysels, *Israel*, pp. 29-31.
29. Ibid., p. 30.

resort to it, on account of its convenient situation on the confines of Egypt."[30]

Benjamin, however, distinguished this city from old Ashkelon, which lay in ruin "four parasangs" distant. Ashkelon was the scene of several subsequent battles between the Saracens and the Crusaders until it was destroyed by Sultan Baybars in A.D. 1270. The city lay in ruins until it was rebuilt by the Israelis after the establishment of their state in 1948. The strategic importance, however, was recognized by Ibraim Pasha, who built a fort on the site.

The fabled treasures of buried Ashkelon have long intrigued treasure hunters and archaeologists. Lady Stanhope sought in vain for treasure here in the nineteenth century. The first scientific excavations were initiated by Garstang and Adams in 1920-1922. In Biblical times Ashkelon was a center of hostility to Israel and in Christian times it was one of the last cities to renounce paganism. In the words of Jeremiah: "The Lord has given it a charge. Against Ashkelon and against the seashore he has appointed it" (Jer. 47:7). The principal deity of Ashkelon was the fish goddess (mermaid) Derceto, and fish dedicated in her honor were kept in a special pool.[31]

On the east edge of the old city, protruding above the sand dunes, is a high wall of the Crusader period. In the relatively small portion excavated, in an area looking like a sunken garden, are the remains of the building of Herod the Great. Once his courtyard, the area includes many of the columns belonging to that structure. Among the sculptured figures uncovered is the winged goddess of victory, standing on the globe of the world, which rests on the shoulders of Atlas. Another goddess, Isis, holds a child named Harpocrates.[32] Recently uncovered are ancient baths illustrating the ducts that conveyed heat to the water from the furnace where the heat originated.

A mile north of the Herodian ruins is a painted tomb similar to the one in Bet Guvrin. It is a pagan inscription with two naked nymphs sitting beside a brook in which are some fish. In one corner, an ox drinks from the water; on the other side, a crane is looking for fish. The background is filled with ducks,

---

30. Benjamin of Tudela, "Travels . . . ," *Early Travels in Palestine,* ed. Thomas Wright (New York: KTAV Publishing House, 1968), p. 88.
31. Zev Vilnay, *The New Israel Atlas: Bible to Present Day* (Jerusalem: Israel University Press, 1968), p. 225.
32. Pearlman and Yannai, *Historical Sites,* p. 171.

reeds, fruit, flowers, and leaves. On the ceiling are further decorations which include the representation of Demeter, the goddess of cereals.

The modern city caters to tourists and features an attractive park, a beach area, and a shopping center. Ashkelon has been made into one of the most attractive areas in Israel. It includes one of the favorite campsites in the land. The population is approximately 40,000. The future of Ashkelon looks bright, especially as a cultural and tourist center, although Ashdod to the north will become a major seaport and Beer-sheba on the southeast continues to be the gateway to the Negev.

As Beer-sheba is the gateway to the Negev, so Gaza is the portal to Egypt. During much of its long history, Gaza has been a border city—sometimes under the dominance of Egypt, at other times under control of the inhabitants of Palestine. The strategic importance of Gaza is readily apparent to the traveler or to the map reader. Historically, the traveler from Egypt found Gaza to be the first oasis of importance after crossing the stretch of sand from the Suez, whereas the traveler to Egypt here prepared for his desert journey into Egypt. The fertility of the soil in the area has been an asset through the centuries, and Gaza has been a terminal for commercial traffic from Arabia to the east. It was recognized as the southern extremity of the land of Canaan (Gen. 10:19) and the northern limit of Sinai (Josh. 10:41; Judg. 6:4). Ancient Gaza (Tell el-Ajuul) was located on a low hill about two hundred feet above the surrounding plain, separated two and a half miles from the sea by sand dunes. Tell el-Ajuul is six miles south of modern Gaza. It was excavated in 1930-1934 by Flinders Petrie. The site flourished during the Middle Bronze Age. When Edward Robinson visited the city in May of 1834, he found on the southern half of the tell a village of mud huts constructed of unburnt bricks made with straw. It then had extensive suburbs to the east and north. A few remnants of the ancient gates of the city were in evidence at that time; one gate on the southeast was pointed out as the gate whose doors and bars were carried off by Samson. Toward the east is a line of hills, the highest of which was called Samson's mount; the claim was made that this was the hill toward Hebron, where, according to the Bible (Judg. 16:3), Samson carried the gates of the city.[33] Robinson

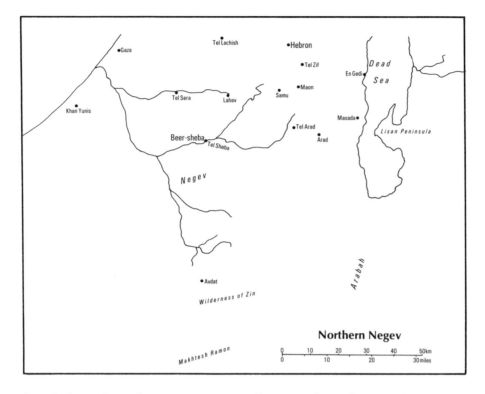

found the soil in the region very productive, abounding in olive orchards and watered by the many wells in the area. Today, irrigated gardens extend to a considerable distance south and west of Gaza, as far as Khan Yunis in the Sinai. Robinson noted "The fertile soil produces in abundance grains and fruits of every kind and of the finest quality." Cotton and soap products were also commodities of Gaza. The city of Gaza has a population of 120,000, and by adding the inhabitants of the Gaza Strip the number totals nearly 360,000. In the Gaza Strip, however, 175,000 people are in refugee camps.[34]

Gaza first appears in historical records in connection with the march of Thutmose III on his first campaign to western Asia. It appears to have served as a staging area for the invasion of Palestine.[35] The text of Thutmose III implies that Gaza was

33. Edward Robinson, *Biblical Researches in Palestine* (Boston: Crocker and Brewster, 1838), vol. 3, p. 39.
34. Misha Louvish, ed., *Facts about Israel, 1970* (Jerusalem: Keter Books, 1970), pp. 52, 53: "The population of Gaza has usually been rated as much too low, as that of Jerusalem has been overestimated."
35. James B. Pritchard, ed., *Ancient Near-Eastern Texts Related to the Old Testament* (Princeton: Princeton University Press, 1953), p. 235.

the southern limit of the area in revolt, which extended from there north to the area of the Euphrates. Gaza apparently performed a similar function as the base of operations for Pharaoh Amenhotep II, as witnessed by the cuneiform letters of Tanaach (Nos. 5 and 6).[36] According to the Bible, the original inhabitants of this area were the Avvim, who were later subjugated by the invading Caphtorim, or Philistines, from Crete (Deut. 2:23).

Under Joshua, this area was assigned to Judah in the division of the lands, but it was not actually conquered until some time later (cf. Josh. 13:2, 3; Judg. 1:18; 3:3). The city figures largely in the narratives concerning Samson. After Samson had patronized a prostitute at Gaza, his enemies planned to apprehend him at daylight. But Samson arose at midnight and carried the doors of the city gate to the hilltop toward Hebron, (Judg. 16:1-3). Later, at Gaza, Samson was blinded by his enemies and set to grinding grain (Judg. 16:21). In Gaza, at the great temple of Dagon, Samson perished in one last effort that killed three thousand of his tormentors (Judg. 16:24-30). Gaza was the southern boundary of Solomon's kingdom (1 Kings 4:24). In the eighth century, Gaza was condemned by Amos for its slave trade with the Edomites (Amos 1:6, 7). This is consistent with Gaza's historic role as a trading center between the East and the West, between the desert and the coast.

Egypt's authority was challenged in the eighth century by the Assyrian conqueror Tiglath-pileser III, who established his authority there in 734 B.C.[37]

Sargon II reestablished Assyrian dominance in Gaza in 720 B.C., as a result of a battle at Raphia twenty miles south of Gaza, slightly west of the modern city of Khan Yunis. Gaza apparently did not join in the rebellion sponsored by Hezekiah (2 Kings 18:7, 8). As a result, the area was conquered by Hezekiah but recaptured later by Sennacherib, who rewarded Gaza by making it the headquarters of that district. Gaza was later attacked and conquered by Pharaoh Necho, as implied in Jeremiah 47:1-7 ("Gaza a shorn bear"). Gaza, on the borderland, therefore suffered capture alternately by the rival empires of the Nile and the Euphrates. Although the prophets typically were scornful of Egypt's ability to be an effective ally of Judah,

---

36. Yohanan Aharoni, *The Land of the Bible: A Historical Geography,* trans. A. F. Rainey (London: Burns & Oates, 1967), p. 143.
37. Pritchard, *Ancient Near-Eastern Texts,* pp. 282-284.

Jeremiah nonetheless described Egypt as used by the Lord to punish the Philistine cities. The prophet Jeremiah gave no reason for this judgment, as did Amos.

Herodotus (fl. 430 B.C.) was impressed by the size and importance of Gaza, and indicated that it was under the control of the king of Arabia.[38]

Thus during the period of Persian ascendency, Gaza was placed under a third power, Arabia, for commercial as well as political purposes. Under Persian patronage, Gaza became a major seaport on the coast rivaling the Phoenician cities to the north. Gaza resisted Alexander's advance for two months during a bitter siege after which the male population was slaughtered and the women and children sold into slavery. In the centuries that followed, Gaza changed hands frequently—under the dominion variously of the Ptolemies, of the Seleucids, and of the Maccabeans (Josh. *Antiq.* XIII. 13. 2, 3; *Wars* I. 4. 2).

That Gaza was referred to as "desert" (Acts 8:26) leads to the supposition that the new Gaza was a coastal port, whereas the old Gaza, two and one-half miles distant, was on the alternate "desert road" to distinguish it from the "coastal" path. During the third century of our era, old Gaza remained pagan whereas new Gaza on the coast was Christian.[39]

Later, Gaza was the seat of the bishopric, and the city was reunited until conquered by the Moslems in A.D. 634. During the Crusader centuries, it was the southernmost of the fortified cities along the coast, and had the name Gadres and was included in the county of Schelor. Gaza's checkered history as a border city is evidenced also by the defeat of the Mamelukes by the Turks in the sixteenth century, which opened Egypt to the Ottomans. It was conquered by Napoleon in 1799. In World War I, it was the scene of three important battles. During the first two, in March and April of 1917, British forces were unsuccessful. Only after General Allenby had broken through the Turkish lines near Beer-sheba was Gaza evacuated by the retreating Turks. This victory opened the way of the British armies to take Jerusalem and, later, Damascus.[40]

Today Gaza's inhabitants are restive. Many men of the refu-

---

38. Herodotus, *History* III. 91.
39. Sozomenus, *History Ecclesiastical* V. 3.
40. E. H. H. Allenby, *The Advance of the Egyptian Expeditionary Force, July, 1917-October, 1918* (London: His Majesty's Stationery Office, 1917), p. 6.

Ruins at the site of Tel Gath.

gee camps are at work on highway building and other construction projects in Israel. Others make products marketed
throughout Israel, in "west bank" Jordan, and in Trans-Jordan.
Some residents of the Gaza Strip are being relocated near Khan
Yunis. If this trend continues, the Gaza Strip will be incorporated into the state of Israel and the refugee situation solved
through rehabilitation. Current tensions within the Strip are
less the result of hostilities of Arabs against the Jews than of
threats from Arabs to other Arabs who accept employment by
Israelis.

Of the locations of the coastal cities of the Philistines, there
has been little uncertainty as to identification. This is not true,
however, of the two inland cities, Ekron and Gath. Of these,
Gath is the most frustrating and elusive. Several ancient sites

have been nominated by different scholars as the true Philistine Gath. The name itself means "winepress." It is not an unusual name, for there are several Gaths; but only one is linked with the Philistines. Logically, the two inland cities of the Philistines would be near the border between the plain and the hill country. Since Ekron is farther north, the location of Gath would be sought at a strategic place to the south. The phrase, "from Ekron to Gath" seems to imply a considerable distance between the two towns (1 Sam. 7:14). On the basis of this text, of the topography, and the strategy that such topography would indicate, W. F. Albright, a half-century ago, identified Gath with Tel Erani. This site is in a position to dominate the valley that leads past Maresha and up through the hills to Hebron.[41]

In consequence of this early idenification, Israeli maps, on which Arabic names were changed to older Hebrew names, name this site Tel Gat. Nearby, there grew up the new Israeli city taking the name Qiryat Gat, a community now numbering about 17,000. An Israeli archaeological expedition excavated at this site in 1956-58, but failed to locate any Philistine artifacts. They learned that it was an Early Bronze Age city.[42] In this case, a topographical probability is ruled out by archaeological investigation. Since a back-up strongpoint for Ashkelon and Gaza argue for a southern site, Gath was sought twelve miles south, at Tel Nagila, which is at an elevation of 686 feet. Archaeologists Ruth Amiran and R. A. Mitchell excavated here in the early 1960s and found the site to date mainly from the eighteenth to sixteenth centuries B.C., with only small amounts of material to be dated later, hence the improbability of Philistine occupancy."[43]

Kassis, however, argues that Philistine artifacts were not indispensable in identification of Gath; that although Gath was under Philistine control, it was not necessarily inhabited by Philistines as such. The king of Gath was Achish, whose status, some argue, was higher than that of the five "lords" (Seranim) of the Philistines because he was "king." He may have been,

41. William F. Albright, *Annual of the American Schools of Oriental Research* 2, 3 (1923): 7-12.
42. C. S. Yeivin, "First Preliminary Report on the Excavations at Tel Gat, 1956, 1958," *Israel Exploration Journal* 9 (1961): 191.
43. S. Bulöw and F. A. Mitchell, *Israel Exploration Journal* 9 (1951): 101-110; R. Amiran and A. Eitan, "Yediot," *Bulletin of the Israel Exploration Society* 28 (1964): 193-203.

however, their inferior, since his name was Canaanite in origin and not Philistine.[44]

Acting upon this hunch, G. Ernest Wright suggests still another identification for Gath. Wright suggests that there are at least two Gaths in Philistia; therefore the one to which the Philistines fled after their defeat in the Elah Valley (1 Sam. 17:52) was probably the northern Gath-Gittiam.[45] The other Gath he finds southeast of Gaza on the Wadi Shariah (Nahar Gerar) called Tell esh-Shariah. On the modern Israeli map it is labeled Tel Sera, between Beer-sheba and Gaza. Wright finds that this is in "precisely the right area."[46]

Founded in the Late Bronze Age, Tel Sera falls in the period of 1500-1200 B.C. It lies on the border between the Negev and the hills of Judea, thus conforming to the requirements of the story of David's relationship with Achish. It is the only feature of military significance for the southeasterly defense of Gaza. It would be appropriate as a defense of the Israelites against the Philistines, the other fortresses being Tel el-Hesi (Eglon) and Tell Zafit (Libnah). To the objection that this site contained no Philistine artifacts, Wright reports seeing several in the nearby museum. One objection to this hypothesis is that it is based upon the assumption that there are two distinct Gaths belonging to the Philistines. More seriously, it places the last-named site too far south to be linked with Ekron, according to the Biblical account of the conflict between Philistia and Judah (1 Sam. 5:6—6:16; 17:52). Furthermore, it is difficult to explain how David could deceive Achish about his raids if they both were in the south (1 Sam. 27:5-12). On the other hand, how could Achish give David Ziklag if it were not near his "royal city" of Gath (1 Sam. 27:5, 6)? Aharoni is among those who conclude that Tell Sera is Ziklag rather than Gath, and that Gath is in the north.[47]

Another candidate for the site of Gath is in the north, the large and impressive Tel Zafit, located on the Wadi Elah approximately midway between Tel Erani and Tell Miqne and about twenty miles east of both Ashkelon and Ashdod. Among the first to make this identification was J. L. Porter in 1857.

44. H. E. Kassis, "Gath and the Structure of the 'Philistine' Society," *Journal of Biblical Literature* 84 (September 1965): 261.
45. George Ernest Wright, "Fresh Evidence for the Philistine Story," *Biblical Archaeologist* 29 (1966): 80.
46. Ibid., p. 82.
47. Aharoni, *Land of the Bible,* pp. 376, 385.

This view was supported by C. R. Conder of the British Survey. This was, of course, too early to make a judgment on the basis of archaeological evidence. Among the features urged to favor this site are Scripture passages that support a site in northern Palestine. Also, impressive topographical advantages are possessed by this site, such as the domination of the valley leading into the Judean hills south of Jerusalem. It is the most prominent site in the northeast edge of the Philistine Plain. The view today is as described by Conder's survey party, "the site is naturally of great strength. Precipitous white cliffs, 100 feet high, exist on the north and west, and a low narrow neck of land on the south joins the Tell to a range of low hills. . . ."[48]

In 1874 the highest part of the tell (the northwest corner) was occupied by a village of mud houses. Today the site is overgrown with weeds, and no dwelling exists on or near the site. Only secondary roads lead to the area. In the time of the Crusades, there was a fortress here named *Blanche Garde,* built by King Fulke in A.D. 1144. It was described as having four towers of equal height.[49] It was dismantled by Saladin in A.D. 1191. The foundations of a castle would indicate a building about fifty yards square, on the northeast portion of the tell, above the white cliffs.

The following specific considerations have led some to make this identification. The Gath of Joshua 11:22 was described in the onomasticon "near in the fifth milestone from Eleutheropolis (Bet Guvrin), as one passes along from Eleutheropolis towards Diospolis (Lydda)."[50] Josephus defines the limit of the tribe of Dan as having "all Jamnia and Gath, from Ekron to that mountain where the tribe of Judah begins."[51]

This would place Gath in the north. In short, the terrain, the size and importance of the tell, and its alleged harmony with accounts by Josephus and the Scriptures led Conder to support Porter's identification. The objection to this is its proximity to a site widely agreed to be that of Ekron, only five miles to the

---

48. C. R. Conder and H. H. Kitchener, *The Survey of Western Palestine* (London: Palestine Exploration Fund, 1883), vol. 2, p. 440.
49. William of Tyre, *A History of Deeds Beyond the Sea,* trans. E. A. Babcock and A. C. Krey, Jr. (New York: Columbia University Press, 1943), vol. 15, p. 25.
50. Eusebius, *Das Onomastikon . . . ,* trans. E. Klostermann; translated into English by A. F. Rainey, *Christian News from Israel* 27 (September 1966): 31.
51. Jos. *Antiq.* V. 1. 22.

north, namely Tell Miqne. This objection was sustained, among others, by G. Ernest Wright after he visited the site in 1965. In his judgment, it would seem foolish to have a defensive fortification so far north and so near Ekron.[52]

A. F. Rainey argues with considerable cogency against this objection stating that proximity to Tell Miqne is not a decisive argument against identifying Gath with Tel Zafit. Rainey maintains that Tell Miqne was settled after the selection of Tel Zafit because of its water supply.

Considerable Biblical evidence seems to favor this identification. When the Philistines captured the Ark, it was taken first to Ashdod, then to Gath, and then to Ekron, and thence returned to Israel by the Sorek Valley (1 Sam. 5:6-10; 6:9-12). The flight of Philistines after David's defeat of Goliath can be cited in support of this identification. The Philistines were camped near Tel Azekah in the valley of Elah, which leads east in the direction of Bethlehem. After Goliath's death, the Philistines fled west down the valley of Elah "as far as the approaches of Gath at the gates of Ekron." This is strong evidence for the proximity of Gath and Ekron. Also in favor of a northerly location is the report that Uzziah fought the Philistines, demolishing the walls of Gath, Jabneh, and Ashdod (2 Chron. 26:6). Another argument is that since Ziklag was in the south, Gath must be located in the north. Otherwise it would have been easy for Achish to check up on David's activities near Ziklag. The same evidence, however, has been used to argue for the southern location of both Gath and Ziklag, since David asked to live in "one of the country towns" rather than "in the royal city" (1 Sam. 27:5-7). Ziklag was apparently one of the villages belonging to and not far from Gath.

The problem is complicated by the fact that Biblical Libnah ("white") also has been located at Tel Zafit (Arabic for "bright"). The Crusaders named it "Blanche-garde" or "Alba Speaila." This site alone has the white cliffs that could account for the Hebrew, Arabic, French, and Latin names all meaning "white." The objection to this identification is that it places Libnah farther to the north than other villages of its province (Josh. 15:42) and requires a boundary line through the middle of the valley of Elah. The favored alternate site for Libnah, therefore, is Tel Bornat, (Burna) farther south.

---

52. Wright, "Philistine Story," p. 19.

On balance therefore Gath can be tentatively located at the impressive site of Tel Zafit, which lies fairly close to Ashqelon. Hence David's warning "tell it not in Gath, publish it not in . . . Ashkelon" (2 Sam. 1:20).

The fifth member of the Philistine pentopolis was Ekron. The name apparently means "deep rooted" (cf. Zeph. 2:4). It was not acquired by the Israelites on their initial invasion (Josh. 13:3), but later the Biblical record states, "Judah took . . . Ekron with its territory" (Judg. 1:18). The territory of Ekron was initially assigned to the tribe of Dan (Josh. 19:43) and was later absorbed by Judah (Josh. 15:45, 46).

Ekron, therefore, a border city, was the scene of repeated conflicts between the Israelites in the Shephelah and the Philistines in the plain. The captured Ark, after being taken from Ebenezer to Ashod to Gaza, then to Ekron, was returned to Israel at Beth-shemesh (1 Sam. 6:2-12). When the Philistines retreated after the defeat of their hero Goliath, they retreated through the valley of Elah toward Gath and Ekron (1 Sam. 17:52). The deity of Ekron was Baal-zebub (2 Kings 1:2-16).

The city was included in the denunciation of the Philistines by Amos (Amos 1:8). Ekron enters Biblical history again during the time of Hezekiah, when several Palestine states were rebelling against the Assyrians. The king of Ekron, whose name was Padi, refused to join in this rebellion and was taken captive by Hezekiah to Jerusalem. When the Assyrians under Sennacherib came in 701 B.C. to punish the rebellious territories, the city of Ekron was captured, and its leading citizens impaled on stakes around the city. Hezekiah was forced to give up Padi, who was reinstated by Sennacherib (2 Kings 18:14).[53]

The surrender of Padi is mentioned in Sennacherib's *Annals* ("Taylor Prism" III. 8-10): "The officials, the patricians and the (common) people of Ekron—who had thrown Padi, their king, into fetters (because he was) loyal to (his) solemn oath (sworn) by the god Ashur and had handed him over to Hezekiah, the Jew" who "held him in prison, unlawfully, as if he (Padi) be an enemy . . ." "I made Padi, their king, come from Jerusalem and set him as their lord upon the throne."[54]

Ekron's conquest by Babylon was predicted during the reign of King Josiah (Zeph. 2:4). After the Exile the city was warned

---

53. Ralph W. Rogers, *History of Babylonia and Assyria* (New York, 1900), vol. 2, p. 200.
54. Pritchard, *The Ancient Near East,* p. 200.

of further suffering (Zech. 9:5, 7). In the Maccabean period Jonathan acquired the city (c. 151 B.C.).[55]

Ekron was identified by Robinson and others with Aqir on the basis of similarity of name, and is so indicated on many of the older maps. Archaeological evidence, however, fails to support this hypothesis. Recently, excavations plus literary evidence favor the site known as Tel Muqanna (Arabic), or Miqne (Hebrew). This site is south of the Wadi Timnah in the valley of Sorek. A survey by Naveh in 1957 discovered Philistine ware and evidence that the Philistines had built this city on the site of an abandoned Early Bronze village.[56] There is an ample water supply here that probably attracted the Philistines. Archaeological data is reinforced by literary evidence. This evidence, as summarized by A. F. Rainey, includes the boundary

55. 1 Macc. 10:89; Jos. Antiq. XIII. 4. 4.
56. J. Naveh, "Khirbet al-Muqanna—Ekron," *Israel Exploration Journal* (1958): 87-100, 165-170.

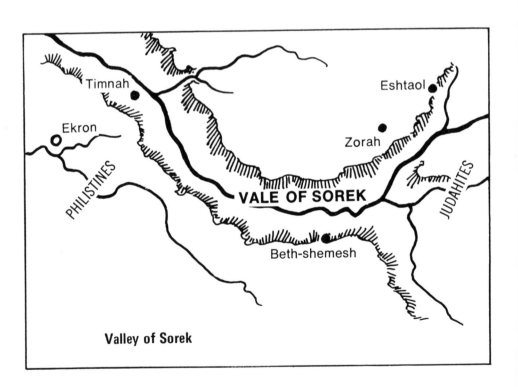

Valley of Sorek

The site of ancient Beth-shemesh.

description of Judah as following a line from Beth-shemesh to Timnah and to "the shoulder . . . north of Ekron" (Josh. 15:10-15).[57] This agrees with topography of the site.

Furthermore, the flight of the Philistines after their defeat by David is said to favor this site: it is nearer than Aqir and only five miles from Tel Zafit (Gath). "The wounded Philistines fell on the way from Shaaraim as far as Gath and Ekron" (1 Sam 17:52).

Finally, Beth-shemesh lies farther up this same valley (Sorek). If Ekron was at Tel Miqne it would be natural for the Ark to proceed up this valley from Ekron to Beth-shemesh. When they saw it arrive at the border, the five Philistine "lords" returned to Ekron (1 Sam. 6:1-16).

The episode of the Ark occurred in the Sorek Valley, which leads past Beth-shemesh toward Jerusalem. The contest between David and Goliath occurred south of this in the valley of Elah, which leads toward Bethlehem. Ekron (Tel Miqne) lay between these valleys and was easily accessible from each. Located on the boundary between the hill country and the lowlands it knew continued tension and exchanged hands many times dur-

57. Eusebius, *Das Onomastikon. . . .*, translated into English by A. F. Rainey, *Christian News from Israel,* 27 (1966) : 26.

ing the centuries. It enjoyed peace and prosperity during the early Christian centuries at least, until the Moslem invasion in the seventh century.

The identification of these inland Philistine cities and their neighbors in the nearby Shephelah presents a nearly insoluble problem for geographers, archaeologists, and historians. As other tells are excavated, perhaps more light will come.

It is important to locate Gath and Ekron near to each other and to Ashdod, to agree with the requirements of the narratives of the Ark and of Goliath (1 Sam. 5:6–6:16; 17:52). A location of Gath at Gath-Gattaim is too far north to meet this requirement. A Gath located at Tell esh-Shariah or nearby would be too far south for the Philistines to seek refuge after Goliath's defeat. Therefore Tel Zafit, in the same valley as the scene of battle and on the way to Ashdod, the shortest and easiest place of refuge, has a strong claim to being Gath. Tel Zafit, with Libnah, requires a provincial boundary in the valley of Elah.[58] The alternative is to place Libnah at Tel Bornat, a more southern site on the Wadi Zeita.

Opposed to this is the likelihood of the white cliffs of Tel Zafit to be Libnah (Hebrew for white) and also that Libnah was Jerusalem's defense in 701 B.C. (2 Kings 19:8), whereas in 587 B.C. both the Lachish letters and Jeremiah 34:7 designate Azekah (Tel Zakariyeh)—both on Wadi Elah—as Jerusalem's defense, Libnah having fallen.[59] No one theory fits all the facts, and the problems remain unsolved pending further evidence.

THE SHEPHELAH

The Shephelah is the name given to the area in Palestine lying between Philistia (the plain) and the Judean hills. The name Shephelah means "lowland," and the term occurs twenty times in the Scriptures. The distinction between the lowlands and the plain is clear in 2 Chronicles 26:10 and 28:18. King Uzziah "built towers in the wilderness . . . for he had large herds, both in the Shephelah and in the plain . . . vinedressers in the hills and in the fertile lands, for he loved the soil" (2 Chron. 26:10). With the exception of Joshua 11:2, 16, it applies to the piedmont area between the plain of Philistia and the hill country of Judea. Today, in addition to vineyards, it produces an

58. R. W. Corney, "Libneh," *Interpreter's Dictoinary of the Bible* (Nashville: Abingdon Press, 1962), vol. 2. p. 123.
59. Wright, "Philistine Story," p. 80.

A typical watchtower in the Shephelah.

The valley of Aijalon.

abundance of small grain, and other crops. In Biblical times it was famous for its forests, so much so that the phrase "as plentiful as the sycamore of the Shephelah" became proverbial (1 Kings 10:27; 1 Chron. 27:28; 2 Chron. 1:15; 9:27). Today it is dotted with agricultural communes, and the frequency of ancient ruins testifies to the relatively dense population in its ancient history as well. During the Byzantine period Christian churches were built there in abundance.

Geologically, the Shephelah consists of Eocene limestone lying between Cenonian chalk and the harder limestone of the hill country, whereas to the west is the soft loess soil of the plain. It is similar to part of eastern North America, where the states of North and South Carolina are in three clearly defined zones—the mountains, the piedmont, and the coast. The "moat," or narrow valley, of Cenonian chalk may be seen from Aijalon, northwest of Jerusalem, to Debir (Beit Mersim).[60]

The Shephelah is wedge shaped, narrow at the north and wider at the south. The hills of the Shephelah are separated from the high ridges to the east by a "moat," or shallow valley, through which runs the modern highway from Latrun via Beth-shemesh, Tel Azekah, and Bet Guvrin, to Lahav.

It is bisected by five rather prominent streams. From the north is the valley of Aijalon, leading from Beth-horon to Gezer. This is a historic warpath, where Joshua defeated the Canaanites by commanding the sun to stand still (Josh. 10:10-15) and where the Israelites defeated the Philistines after Jonathan's brilliant strategem (1 Sam. 14:31). It is where Judas Maccabeus defeated the Syrians (1 Macc. 3:13-24). Through this valley likewise the Crusaders came to gain access to the hill country, and to launch their attack on Jerusalem from the northwest. In 1917, the British under Allenby came through this valley to force the Turks to withdraw from Jerusalem. In 1948, the Arab Legion pushed down this valley to cut off the corridor from Tel Aviv to Jerusalem at Latrun. Because Latrun is a western projection of the hill country, it is able to command the approach to Jerusalem either through the valley of Aijalon on the north or the Wadi (Sorek) to the south. The modern highways reflect this topographical phenomenon. Today a monastery stands at Latrun, but the nearby village of Imwas (Emmaus?) was

Valley of Aijalon

---

60. Denis Baly, *The Geography of the Bible* (New York: Harper & Bros., 1957), p. 144; Smith, *Historical Geography,* pp. 206, 207.

destroyed by the victorious Israelites in 1967, when they reversed the tide of war by thronging up the valley of Aijalon to approach Jerusalem, then Ramallah, and on toward the Jordan Valley.

In ancient times Gezer dominated this corridor. Gezer (Tel Gezer) lies about five miles west of Latrun and in ancient times was a frontier town in every sense of the word, as the boundary stone discovered by C. Clermont-Ganneau in 1874 attests. Situated on the northeast corner of the Philistine territory, it was in a position to command both the important north-south road and the east-west road into the hills. Thutmose III recorded his capture of Gezer, and Egyptian scarabs at the site verify this identification. Three of the Tell el-Amarna letters include a reference to Gezer. In the Merneptah stele (ca. 1230 B.C.) it is reported that "Canaan is despoiled, Ashkelon is taken, Gezer is seized . . . Israel is laid waste, his seed is not. . . ." The city was captured by Shishak of Egypt, as reported in the temple at Karnak (cf. 1 Kings 14:25; 2 Chron. 12:2). Gezer was conquered by the Israelites under Joshua (Josh. 10:33; 12:2). It was later designated as a Levitical city (Josh. 21:21) though Canaanites continued to inhabit it (Josh. 16:10; Judg. 1:29). David chased the Philistines down the valley of Aijalon, the same valley through which King Saul had pursued them, from Geba to Gezer (2 Sam. 5:25; 1 Chron. 14:16). The city was presented to Solomon by the king of Egypt as a dowry for one of Solomon's wives (1 Kings 9:16). In the second century B.C., it played a strategic role in the struggle between the Jews and the Syrians (1 Macc. 14:34; 9:52; 13:33-38). It remained under Jewish control until Roman times, after which it was a "ghost town" for two millennia.

It has meanwhile made a major contribution to the modern science of archaeology. It was excavated by R. A. S. Macalister (1902-1905). Of the many important finds there is the so-called Gezer calendar, inscribed in ancient Hebrew characters on soft limestone, which includes a list of the agricultural seasons, including the olive, grain, flax, barley, and vineyard harvests. Since olives are harvested in the fall, it appears that this Canaanite calendar had its new year beginning in the fall. In recent years, excavations of Gezer have continued under the leadership of Hebrew Union College in Jerusalem, a ten-year project. Beginning in 1964, a long trench to date the stratification of the mound was begun. During the fourth season (1968), bedrock was reached in all areas. Fourteen strata were identified to a total depth of nearly thirty feet. The earliest town, consisting of a campsite and fire pit, was of the Chalcolithic period. One of the more important results was the clarification of a gate of the Solomonic period, contemporary with that of Hazor and Megiddo. Archaeologists since Macalister have been intrigued with the so-called high place, which features ten large stela, dating back to the late Middle Bronze Age. The scanty evidence available suggests that the high place was abandoned during the Solomonic period, when the Israelites displaced the Canaanites.[61]

Wadi Sorek   The second important valley leading from the hill country of Judea to the Philistine Plain is the Wadi Sorek. The exploits of Samson took place here, and it is through this valley that the modern railway reaches Jerusalem. Wadi Sorek has three main branches extending to the Judean hills. The northernmost prong,

61. W. G. Dever, *Archeological Newsletter of Hebrew Union College* (Jerusalem, January 1969).

The valley of Sorek, west of Jerusalem.

named Kesalon, has its source at Kiriath-jearim, the site of modern Abu Ghosh, where the Ark came to rest after it had been returned from the Philistine city of Ekron. The Ark lodged here for twenty years before it was taken to Jerusalem by David (1 Sam. 7:2; 2 Sam. 6:2; 1 Chron. 13:6; Ps. 132:6). The confrontation between the king of Israel and the king of Judah occurred farther down the valley at Beth-shemesh (2 Kings 14:11). The second arm of the Wadi Sorek goes from Beth-shemesh up the winding valley called Refaim on the modern maps. Through this winding valley, with walls crowding in on either side, the railroad, built by the British, reaches Jerusalem 2,000 feet above the Philistine Plain. Over the same route presumably the Israelite king Joash reached Jerusalem. Apparently, it was his pursuit of the Philistines to the borders of Judah that led Amaziah to challenge his presence there, to his own humiliation and undoing (2 Chron. 25:17-24). The southernmost prong of the Sorek Valley extends southeast from Beth-shemesh into the Judean foothills toward the village of Matta.

The third valley, farther south, is the valley of Elah, where David encountered Goliath. Guarding this valley is Tel Zafit (Gath) and Tel Azekah, one of the last fortresses of Judah to fall to the Babylonians (Jer. 34:7). Here in this wide valley between the Philistines encamped on hill Azekah to the west and the Israelites on the hill opposite, occurred one of the most dramatic confrontations in Old Testament history—the contest between the Philistine giant and the inexperienced youth from Bethlehem (1 Sam. 17). This dramatized the larger contest between Israel and Philistia and between Dagon and Yahweh. The valley has several prongs, one of which extends almost to Bethlehem. It would be natural for David, coming from Bethlehem, to reach his brothers through the eastern end of this valley.

Valley of Elah

The southern branch of this valley goes to Adullam (Gen. 38:1), which was assigned to the territory of Judah (Josh. 15:35). Adullam was fortified by Rehoboam (2 Chron. 11:7). Desolation to Adullam was prophesied by Micah (Mic. 1:15), but the town was inhabited by Jews after the exile (Neh. 11:30). If the identification of Tel Zafit with Libnah (whiteness) is correct, then it was here that Joshua was victorious (10:29-31), and it was here where Sennacherib was fighting while simultaneously attempting to subdue Jerusalem (2 Kings 19:8). Adullam was a constant point of struggle between the Israelites and

A Roman milestone near the valley of Elah.

the Philistines, being held by Israel under her stronger kings and lost during the reign of the weaker ones, including Joram (2 Kings 8:22; 2 Chron. 21:10).[62]

The fourth valley of the Shephelah approaches the outskirts of Hebron, and is called the Wadi Guvrin, taking its modern name from Bet Guvrin, a very important crossroads town on the boundary between the low country and the maritime plain. Bet Guvrin is a relatively young city, dating from the Roman period when Emperor Septimus Severus decided that there should be a control point at this road junction instead of at the neighboring tells of Lachish and Maresha. The Romans called the new city Eleutheropolis ("Free City"), and it flourished until its destruction by the Moslems in A.D. 796. Built over the older site of Baitogabra ("House of Giants"), it flourished as a trading post between the desert and the coast. Impressive remains of churches dating to the Byzantine period

---

62. Baly, *Geography,* p. 146.

are still visible. Under the Moslems, Bet Guvrin acquired the name Beit Jibrin, Arabic for "house of Gabriel."[63]

Christianity won its most important triumphs in this area during the early centuries. Bet Guvrin apparently was the center of Christianity in the Shephelah as reported in the histories of Eusebius, Socrates, Sozomen, and also in the letters of Jerome and in his work *Life of Hilarion*. Here, many early converts were influenced by the Christians both from Egypt and from the north. From this area came some of the first Christian martyrs, among them, Zebina of Bet Guvrin.[64]

In the area were many natural caves as well as many artificial caves made in the soft chalk. These extensive caverns contain many evidences of Christian habitation. The extensive underground labyrinth may have been occupied either by the ancient Horites (cave dwellers), as implied by Jerome, or by the Idumeans, who were expert in cave structure (cf. Petra).[65]

After centuries of neglect, the Crusaders built a strong wall and a fortress on this site. Later the structures were largely destroyed by Saladin, but even today the ruins, located near the highway, are most impressive. A short distance to the south is the impressive Tel Maresha, which was a chief city of the Shephelah (Josh. 15:44). Earlier it had been the fortress guarding the highway. It is located three miles northeast of Lachish and one mile southeast of Bet Guvrin and was identified by archaeological excavations in the last decade of the nineteenth century by archaeologists Frederick Bliss and R. A. S. Macalister.

It also was one of the sites fortified by Rehoboam. "He rebuilt Bethlehem, Etam, Tekoa ... Gath, Maresha, Ziph. ... He fortified them strongly and put commanders in them with stores of food, oil and wine. In each of these towns were shields and spears, he made them very strong to keep Judah and Benjamin under control" (2 Chron. 11:8-12 JB). A major crisis arose when Zerah the Ethiopian with a vast army "of a million men and three hundred chariots" confronted King Asa at Maresha. After prayer, Asa's forces chased the enemy as far south as Gerar (2 Chron. 14:9-15).

---

63. Meysels, *Israel*, pp. 16, 17.
64. Eusebius, *Ecclesiastical History* IX.
65. For excellent descriptions of the caves and nearby structures, see George Olaf Matson, *The Palestine Guide*, 5th ed. (Jerusalem: Joshua Simon, 1946), pp. 282-286; Smith, *Historical Geography*, p. 242; Meysels, *Israel*, pp. 16-21; Robinson, *Researches*, vol. 2, pp. 22-29.

The mound is very conspicuous and its profile is quite regular. Among the interesting features near this site are two burial caves with paintings and inscriptions, one of which conveys in Greek the message of a maiden to her lover: "I lie with another, though loving thee dearly."[66]

For awhile Maresha was the capital of the Idumeans, who were later dislodged by the armies of the Maccabees. Rebuilt by the Romans, it was destroyed by the Parthians and then rebuilt by the Crusaders. Their church was called the Church of Saint Anna, hence the Arabic appellation—Tell Sandahannah.[67] About a mile and a half north of Bet Guvrin is Micah's hometown, Moreshet–Gath (Tel Judeidah, or Goded). Nearby are the remains of a church honoring the prophet.

LACHISH

A few miles farther to the southwest is the important tell of Lachish, the area which drains past Tel Erani (Qiryat Gat) northeasterly through the Nahar Lachish to Ashdod. This city

66. Matson, *Palestine Guide*, p. 244.
67. Pearlman and Yannai, *Historical Sites*, p. 174.

This Assyrian bas relief shows Sennacherib seated on his throne at the scene of the siege of Lachish.

Two closeups of the bas relief of Sennacherib. The top photo shows the city of Lachish (the oval pattern is the city wall) and the bottom photo portrays one of Sennacherib's soldiers beheading a captive.

figured prominently in Israel's conquest of the Shephelah (Josh. 10:31, 32). Lachish is prominent, not only in Biblical history, but in the military history of Assyria. Its siege and conquest was one of Sennacherib's proudest achievements in his western campaign of 701 B.C. (Isa. 36:2; 37:8). The stone walls of his palace at Nineveh were adorned with elaborate bas-reliefs of the assault on Lachish, pictures which provide one of the most informative portrayals of siege warfare of the seventh century B.C.[68] In one of the scenes showing the conquest of Lachish is this inscription: "Sennacherib, king of the world, king of Assyria, sat upon a throne and passed in review the booty taken from Lachish" (*Ancient Near-Eastern Texts*, J. Pritchard, p. 201; cf. 2 Kings

68. Pritchard, *Ancient Near-Eastern Texts*, plates 101, 102.

18:14; 19:8). The famous Lachish letters were found in 1935; thirty-eight were discovered just inside the gate in what was probably the guard room. They are written in Hebrew and are contemporary with the latter years of the kingdom period. Most important is the fourth letter, which ends with a statement: "We are watching for the signals of Lachish, according to all the indications which my lord hath given, for we cannot see Azekah" (which was twelve miles north).[69] This letter has a remarkable similarity to the statement in connection with Jeremiah's message to King Zedekiah: "While the army of the king of Babylon was attacking Jerusalem and the towns of Judah which still held out, namely Lachish and Azekah, these being the only towns of Judah that still held out, since they were fortified" (Jer. 34:7 JB). Soon after this, these three cities also succumbed to the king of Babylon.

Today the Shephelah presents a striking contrast between the turbulent past and the peaceful present. Amid the numerous hilltop ruins, which witnessed one ruthless destruction after another, Israeli farmers now harvest winter wheat with modern combines. The sycamore trees that filled the lands in Biblical times are now replaced by numerous fruit orchards. Water is more widely available because of the modern water conduit that extends from upper Galilee to the Negev. The numerous fortified city-states that once dominated the hilltops are replaced by energetic agricultural communes occupied by resourceful kibbutzniks. The numerous tells challenge archaeologists to probe more deeply into the secrets they enclose. Uncertainty, however, still lingers as to the exact location of important towns such as Libnah, Ekron, Gath, and Eglon. One constant factor through the centuries is that this area remains a frontier; it is always coveted and hence is subject to sudden changes. Until recently, as in times past, the occupants of the Shephelah were unable to dislodge the inhabitants of the hill country to the east. This pattern was changed in June 1967, with the Israeli conquest of the "hill country," but it was an exception to the rule.

---

69. Ibid., p. 213.

7

Joseph's Allotment

This area, so important in Biblical and subsequent history, extends from the maritime plain to the Jordan Valley and from the Carmel-Gilboa mountain ranges to a line approximately ten miles north of Jerusalem extending from Jericho to Bethel to the Beth-horon descent to the maritime plain (Josh. 17:12-13). This southern boundary, separating the territory of Ephraim and Benjamin, fluctuated, especially during the reigns of Baasha and Asa (2 Chron. 13:19; 16:1-6). The geography of Samaria coincides roughly to the allotment of Ephraim and Manasseh (Josh. 16:1-10; 17:7-12). There is some topographical justification for the division between Ephraim and Benjamin. From the west is the valley of Aijalon leading up past Beth-horon toward Bethel, and from Bethel eastward the Wadi Makkuk leads to Jericho and the Jordan River. The forces under Joshua marched through the Wadi Makkuk from Jericho to Ai and Bethel (Josh. 7:2-5).[1]

THE HILL COUNTRY OF MANASSEH

In this extensive "hill country of Samaria" occurred many of the most important events in Old Testament history. The religious and political center of this area through the centuries was located in or near Shechem—the site of Abraham's first campsite on the promised land (Gen. 12:6), the scene of the renewal of the covenant after Joshua's conquest of the country (Josh. 8:35; 24:1, 2), and the area of the northern kingdom's

---

1. Denis Baly, *The Geography of the Bible* (New York: Harper & Bros., 1957), pp. 171, 172.

political center until it fell to the Babylonians. Even after the captivity, Mount Gerizim remained the chief rival to Jerusalem as a religious shrine. Here Jesus conversed with the woman of Samaria, and here, the gospel was first received by those other than Jews, thanks to the labors of Philip (John 4:4-42; Acts 8:4-24).

From the north, entrance to this country is gained by crossing the plain of Dothan, which begins at modern Jenin near the ancient fortress of Ibleam. It is a broad and fertile valley, lying between Gilboa on the east and Carmel on the west. The Dothan Valley extends in a southwesterly direction emerging at the western edge of the maritime plain at ancient Aphek, the place from which the Philistines twice attacked the armies of Israel, and the sixty-sixth town in the list of Thutmose III. Aphek is located north of Tulkarm, near modern Tel Gat in the Hadera Valley.[2]

The modern road probably follows the ancient route, trailing through what is now called the Hadera Valley, which extends as far as the ancient site of Dothan. This was the route that Thutmose III was advised by his officers to take during his campaign against the Canaanites in 1468 b.c.[3] It is the southernmost of the three possible routes across the Carmel range. This route begins at the Gath located in Sharon (its alternate name is Jatt), which is also identified as Gath-Padella; the route enters the Jezreel Valley near Jenin.[4]

Tell Dothan Tell Dothan is located at the northeastern head of this broad valley. It is a large tell, situated a half mile east of the modern north-south highway. It is famous as the scene of the sale of Joseph by his brethren (Gen. 37:14-17) and is the traditional scene of Judith's triumph over Holofernes and his armies (Judith 3:9; 4:6; 7:3). Its location is about twelve miles north of Samaria (Sebaste).[5]

This impressive mound was excavated by Joseph Free, formerly of Wheaton College, who spent several seasons (1953-

---

2. F. M. Abel, *Geographie de le Palestine* (Paris: Gabalda, 1933-1938), vol. 2, p. 246.
3. James B. Pritchard, ed., *Ancient Near-Eastern Texts Related to the Old Testament* (Princeton: University Press, 1953), p. 176; Yohanan Aharoni and Michael Avi-Yonah, *The Macmillan Bible Atlas* (New York: Macmillan Co., 1968), p. 32.
4. Yohanan Aharoni and Michael Avi-Yonah, *The Macmillan Bible Atlas* (New York: Macmillan Co., 1968), pp. 38, 40.
5. Abel, *Geographie,* vol. 2, p. 308.

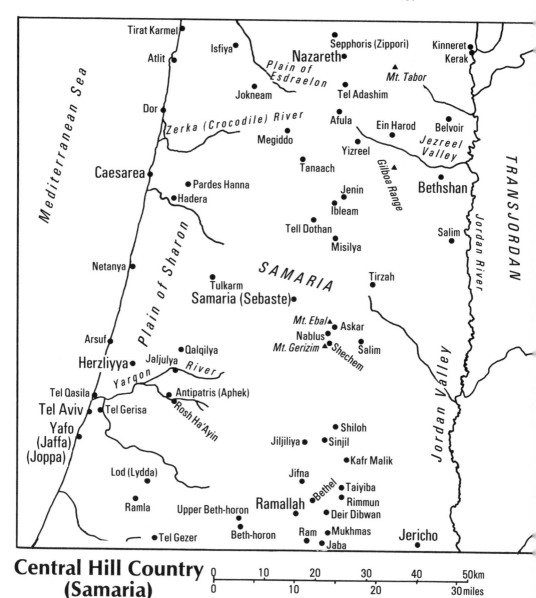

Central Hill Country (Samaria)

1964) at the site. The top covers ten acres, and it stands 175 feet above the plain. In the fifth season, a massive Early Bronze Age city wall, thirteen feet thick, was uncovered.[6]

During the same season, the lines of several of the walls were exposed and a water course was discovered. Examination of stratigraphy indicated a settlement extending from the Early Bronze (3000-2000 B.C.) to the Iron Age. There was abundant evidence of a Middle Bronze city in the time of Joseph and an Iron Age city in Elijah's day. The end probably came shortly before the fall of Samaria, about 722 B.C. The 1964 expedition at the same site resulted in the excavation of a cave-tomb in which were found more than three thousand artifacts. It is said to be one of the richest tomb discoveries to be found anywhere in Palestine.

The prophet Elisha was living in Dothan when the king of Aram, or Syria, learned that Elisha was warning the king of Samaria about the movements of enemy troops. Upon learning this, the king of Syria sent an army of horsemen, who surrounded the city. As a result of the prophet's prayer, however, the army was stricken with blindness and the city was spared. Elisha then led the army to Samaria, probably over the route

---

6. J. P. Free, "The Fifth Season at Dothan," *Bulletin of the American Schools for Oriental Research* (1958): 11 ff.

Excavations in progress at Tell Dothan.

that the modern road now follows. In Samaria the invaders were treated to oriental hospitality and sent back to Damascus (2 Kings 6:8-23). This indicates that the normal road of approach from Damascus to Samaria was through the low pass at Jenin, Ibleam, and Dothan. Not long after this, residents in and near Dothan saw the funeral train of the Judean king Ahaziah, whom Jehu had slain, traveling along this road from Megiddo to Jerusalem (2 Kings 9:27-29). Later they saw Jehu driving furiously along this route, from Jezreel to Samaria, intent upon exterminating the remnants of the household of Ahaz (2 Kings 9:27, 28; 10:1-28). Throughout history, peasants and villagers, intent on wresting a living out of the soil and from their flocks, regarded political realignments and the passing of armies with relative indifference.

Today a small Arab village is lodged on the southern slope of Tell Dothan, and to its large and generous well, not far distant, flocks still come for water. From the top of the tell, broad fields stretch as far as eye can see southwest toward the Mediterranean coast. Here archaeologists uncovered an ancient *tabun,* or "dutch oven," used by the ancients for baking bread. Today, in many Arab villages, the same type of oven is used both in private homes and public bakeries. This Arab bread, round and flat in shape, is very tasty. Hosea had watched the local baker and sadly characterized his countrymen as "a cake not turned" (Hos. 7:8). Thus from Bible times until today, village life continues with a minimum of change in the mode of life. The exception to this is the flight eastward of Arab refugees in the wars of 1948 and 1967, and their replacement in many instances by Israeli immigrants, recalling the mass deportations by the Assyrians (2 Kings 17).

The tribe of Manasseh occupied more territory than any other tribe. Their allotment from Gilboa and Carmel to the plain of Sharon to the Jordan Valley and to the wide area in Gilead east of the Jordan, fulfilled the ancient prophecy that "Joseph is a fruitful creeper near the spring, whose tendrils climb over the wall" (Gen. 49:22 J.B.). The average attitude of this territory west of the Jordan is considerably lower than the hill country of Ephraim to the south. It has been described as a broad saucer rimmed with hills with some mountain peaks in the center.[7]

Manasseh's Territory

7. Baly, *Geography,* p. 178.

The soil of the central area from Nablus northward is predominantly from Eocene–Oligocene rock and tends to be less
fertile than land lying to the north or south or west. Access to
this area is also much easier than is true of the hill country
of Ephraim or the hill country of Judea. Furthermore, the
territory assigned to Manasseh includes major trade routes,
especially through the Sharon and Dothan plains, also from
the west coast through Tulkarm and Nablus to the Jordan
Valley. Because of this, Manasseh, though much larger in extent,
was less influential in Biblical history than was Ephraim. This
recalls the episode recorded in connection with Jacob blessing
his grandsons: although Manasseh was the older, Jacob crossed
his hands, placing his right hand on the head of Ephraim, thus
predicting the younger brother's dominance (Gen. 48:13-22).
Judah and Ephraim, more mountainous and hence more isolated,
were less exposed to foreign influences than were the other tribes.
Unlike areas to the north and south, the territory of Manasseh
had few natural fortresses or strongpoints. The approach from
the north via Dothan was guarded by Jezreel whereas to the
south lay Jenin and the nearby Bronze Age fortress of Ibleam.
These, however, were frontier posts but hardly fortresses. Bethulia is mentioned in the book of Judith as a fortified city
which defied Holofernes, but its location cannot be identified
with any assurance except that it lay near Dothan. Among places
suggested are Misilya (by Conder) and Sanur. It is generally
assumed to be southeast of Dothan.[8] By others it conjecturally
is placed north of Dothan in the foothills of the Carmel range.

The Crusaders placed one fortress (Beleism, or Khirbet
Belame) near Jenin to guard the road. They also had a small
fortress at Tanaach and another near the present site of Afula.
These three were in a position to dominate the highway. On
the east the Crusaders built a fortress (Burjel Malih) over
the Jordan Valley, but it was isolated and strategically had
little practical strength.[9] Another fortress was built near Aphek
where the plain of Dothan joins the plain of Sharon. The Crusaders apparently had a fortified castle south of Jenin named
Bethulia and a little south another fortified castle called "Tower,"
which was visible from Nazareth.[10]

8. Aharoni and Avi-Yonah, *The Macmillan Bible Atlas*, fig. 211.
9. See map, "Palestine of the Crusades," in F. J. Salmon, *Survey of Palestine* (Jaffa: 1937).
10. Ibid.

Many of these were fortified castles designed for control of the surrounding hinterland by the nobleman, as in medieval Europe, rather than for the strategic defense of the wider area. During the Mandate period, one of several "Taggert forts" was located south of Dothan in a position to control highways going north and south and the one going to the Sharon Plain.

Today in much of this area there are small Arab villages of stone houses located normally on the hilltops whereas the broad and shallow valleys are under cultivation. Though the soil is not rich, it lends itself readily to the growing of small grain fields while the hills support pasturage for herds and flocks.

Many of the place-names mentioned in the Fourth Gospel are difficult to locate and identify, none more so than Aenon and Salim where John is said to have baptized because of "much water" (John 3:23). The hypotheses are many. One theory locates them east of Nablus at *Beit Ainum* ("House of Springs"), north of *Beni Salim*.[11] Another suggestion is a Wadi Farah, ten miles northeast of Jerusalem,[12] which became since the Mandate period one source of Jerusalem's water. Tell El Farah (ancient Tirzah) with its copious spring (Ein Farah) has supporters also.

Aenon and Salim

Some favor the Salim located about four miles east of Nablus. Supporters of this site point to a village called Ainun, seven miles north of Salim, as supporting evidence.[13]

A discriminating traveler in 1879 made a strong case for this site. Professor J. W. Garvey's party located the village of Salim three miles northeast of Shechem (Balata), through which the road led eastward to Aenon, which was located, in Conder's words, "four miles north of the stream."

This Wadi Farah rises at Ein Farah (Tirzah) and is joined by the Wadi Bedan as it descends to the Jordan Valley. This picturesque valley was once lined with oleanders and numerous water mills, but now the stream is flanked with small, well-irrigated gardens. As J. W. McGarvey noted: about four miles below the junction of the two streams, the valley broadens into

11. Mader, *Altchristliche Basiliken,* pp. 38-47, cited in Clemens Kopp, *The Holy Places of the Gospels* (New York: Herder and Herder, 1963), p. 136.
12. J. T. Barclay, *The City of the Great King* (Philadelphia, 1858), p. 559.
13. See E. Robinson, *Neuere biblische Forschungen* (Berlin, 1857), p. 438; C. R. Conder, *Tent-work in Palestine* (New York: Appleton, 1878), p. 50; W. F. Albright in *Harvard Theological Review* (1924): 194.

an area a mile wide and two in length. He concludes, "No prettier mountain valley is seen in Palestine and none more suitable for John's purpose."[14]

This setting, plus the fact that nowhere else are the name Salim and Aenon applied to nearby villages, support Conder's conclusion that "the two names, the fine water supply, the proximity of the desert, and the open character of the ground" are a combination found only in Wadi Farah.[15]

However, this Aenon has no water; it is not next to Salim, and it lacks a tradition.

The site that seems to best fit all available evidence is near the springs located seven and a half miles south of Bethshan. Eusebius and Jerome designate Aenon as "near Salim, where John baptized ... eight miles south of Scythopolis, near Salim and the Jordan."[16] This is supported by the Madaba map which shows an "Aenon near to Salim" near a Jordan ferry south of Scythopolis, with the pool of water designated probably with a cluster of cubes.[17] Furthermore, the area south of Bethshan is indicated by Cyrillus, *Life of Saint Sabas*, as dedicated to John the Baptist.[18]

This reflects a tradition that is consistent with early pilgrim itineraries, including Aetheria (A.D. 385) and other witnesses. Aetheria reported visiting a village called Sedima (Salim) near Bethshan, with a large pool in "a garden of John the Baptist." These evidences are convincingly set forth by Kopp.[19] Today there is no village at the site, but there are numerous fountains. Here in the vicinity of the Decapolis city of Scythopolis, John would have been relatively safe from Herod Antipas, whose domain was limited to Galilee and Perea.

No town of much consequence is to be found between Jenin on the north and Nablus on the south and Tulkarm to the west. There is easy access to the Jordan Valley from Ein

14. J. W. McGarvey, *Lands of the Bible* (Nashville: Gospel Advocate Co., 1957), p. 92.
15. C. R. Conder, *Tent-work in Palestine* (New York: Appleton, 1878), p. 92; McGarvey, *Lands of the Bible,* p. 294.
16. Eusebius, *Das Onomastikon der biblischen Ortsnamen,* trans. E. Klostermann (Hilescheim: G. Olms, 1966), p. 40.
17. Michael Avi-Yonah, *The Madeba Mosaic Map* (Jerusalem: Israel Exploration Society, 1954), pp. 35 ff.
18. Schwartz, ed., "Kyrillos von Skythopolis," *Texte u. Unters* (Leipzig, 1939), p. 163, as cited in Avi-Yonah, *Madaba Mosaic Map,* p. 36.
19. Clemens Kopp, *The Holy Places of the Gospels* (New York: Herder and Herder, 1963), pp. 130-137.

Farah, site of ancient Tirzah; but strangely enough no significant fortress seems to have guarded this important route. Tirzah itself, although serving for a time as the capital of the northern kingdom, was soon abandoned in favor of Samaria. Tirzah has an ample spring and is potentially, as no doubt it once was (cf. Song of Sol. 6:4), a place of great beauty. The modern road that follows the Wadi Farah to the Jordan and the site of ancient Adam is a delightful way to enter the valley of the Jordan. Extensive use is made of the water for irrigating vegetable gardens along the banks. The eastern edge of this valley was guarded by the fortress of Herod the Great, which he named Alexandrium. It is on a high conical hill, which, after a strenuous climb, presents an inspiring view to the north, east, and south. Farther east across the Jordan is the strong Saracenic fortress of Ajlun. Thus the Wadi Farah has a strong fortress at its lower eastern end, but apparently none at its upper end except Tirzah. Jeroboam moved his capital from Shechem to Tirzah. There his son Abijah died as the prophet Ahijah had warned (1 Kings 14:17). Nadab reigned for two years (1 Kings 15:25). Baasha reigned from here for twenty-four years (1 Kings 15:33) while continuously fighting with Asa of Judah. Elah reigned in Tirzah only two years. He was murdered by Zimri, who later burned himself in the royal palace (1 Kings 16:18). The next king, Omri, after living here six years, moved the capital to Samaria—a place more central, of easier access, and facing west as well as east (1 Kings 16:23, 24). Recently Tirzah has been partially excavated by a team of French archaeologists led by the late Pere de Vaux of the École Biblique in Jerusalem.[20] It was occupied from about 3500 B.C. to the beginning of the sixth century B.C.

A few miles south is the site that has the soundest claim to be the worship center of the Holy Land. It is Shechem, now identified with Tell Balata, a small mound nestled between Mount Ebal and Mount Gerizim at the point where they almost touch. Its chief interest to readers of the New Testament is its proximity to Jacob's well and the scene of Jesus' conversation with the woman of Samaria. Modern Askar, lying a half mile to the north at the foot of the Ebal mountain, is widely acknowledged as the site of ancient Sychar. To the west, the narrow valley extends beyond Nablus, passing the hill of ancient Sa-

Tirzah

Shechem

20. R. de Vaux and A. M. Steve, in *Revue Biblique* 62 (1955): 587-589.

From inside the fortification walls of ancient Shechem, remains of
the East Gate indicate that rebuilding from time to time eventually
raised the passageway within the gate to a level five steps above the
inner street. Walls of large bricks interlaced with wooden beams once
stood on the stone foundations visible here.

Nestled behind lines of Shechem's Middle Bronze Age fortifications
lie the largest extant temple-ruins in Palestine, very likely "The House
of Baal-berith" mentioned in Judges 9:4, 46. The structure probably
was begun about 1650 B.C. during the Hyksos expansion of the city.

maria (Sebaste), three miles farther, continuing from there to Tulkarm and the Mediterranean coast.

To the north, east, and south of Shechem stretches a broad fertile plain (Mikhmetat), beyond which to the east are low hills. As one considers the terrain he senses at once the strategic importance of ancient Shechem. It stands guard over one of the two most important east-west passages from the Jordan to the coast. As Bethshan guards the north–east approach to Samaria, so Shechem guards its south–east border.

The name Shechem means "shoulder." When Abraham came from Ur of the Chaldees, Shechem was the first place he stopped; there he built an altar (Gen. 12:6, 7). When Jacob returned from his twenty-year sojourn in Haran he purchased land at this place from the sons of Hamor (Gen. 33:18-20). It was here that the rape of Dinah occurred (Gen. 34). Joseph came here in quest of his brothers, whom he later found in Dothan (Gen. 37:12-14). Joseph is said to be buried at Shechem (Josh. 24:32). It was here that Joshua made his farewell speech, urging his countrymen to keep inviolate their covenant with Yahweh (Josh. 24). Here, the Israelites, in compliance with the instructions given in Deuteronomy 26 and 27, gathered to reaffirm the covenant under the leadership of Joshua (Josh. 8:30-35). Many scholars regard this incident at Shechem as the inauguration of the Hebrew twelve-tribe "amphictyony."[21]

Very instructive is the attempt of Abimelech to make himself king of Shechem and its environs (Judg. 9). Here Rehoboam was crowned and here he established his capital (1 Kings 12).

Archaeologists have been busy at Tell Balata at intervals beginning in 1903. The work was continued in the early 1930s by Sellin. In 1956, a series of expeditions was begun under the direction of a G. Ernest Wright (the Drew-McCormick Expedition), which continued through 1968. City gates going back to the Middle Bronze Age (c. 1650 B.C.) were exposed. The city was apparently occupied during the Hyksos period (c. 1750-1550 B.C.). An impressive temple area was uncovered which the excavators surmised might date from the time of Abimelech. Evidence from the coins indicate that the city continued its existence until its destruction by John Hyrcanus in 107 B.C., twenty years after he had destroyed the Samaritan temple.

21. Martin Noth, *The History of Israel,* 2nd ed. (New York: Harper and Row, 1958), p. 93.

The occupation of the mount thereafter apparently ceased. There is no record of the conquest of Shechem by the Israelites, which is one of the major remaining mysteries of Old Testament history. How could Joshua and the Israelites renew the covenant here if the area were dominated by hostile Canaanites? One theory is that Shechem had already been occupied by Israelites or kinfolk who welcomed Joshua.[22]

In short, the city seems to have been dated from the Amorite period (1900 B.C.) about the time of Abraham's visit and near the time when the city was mentioned in Egyptian texts. Excavations, which continued into 1970, include the exciting disclosures linked to Hadrianic temples on a spur of Mount Gerizim (Tell er-Ras) overlooking Shechem.[23]

A chief interest in this area centers upon the nearby well of Jacob, where Jesus conversed with the woman from the village of Sychar.[24] Travelers until recent times described the well as reached through an opening in a pavement over which was a broken vault. The well was often described as about seventy-five feet deep and containing only mud. When the Latins tried to purchase the property the Greek Orthodox began the rebuilding of the present walls, a structure which still lacks a roof. The first church was built toward the end of the fourth century; the present structure on the Crusader foundations was built in 1903-1914.[25] Currently, the well is about six feet in diameter and is about a hundred feet in depth. It contains clear, potable water, to be reached by pail and windlass, by which the thirsty traveler still finds the water that relieves thirst only temporarily (cf. John 4:13). This woman, as re-

22. George E. Wright and Floyd V. Filson, eds., *The Westminster Historical Atlas to the Bible* (Philadelphia: Westminster Press, 1945), p. 39; G. E. Mendenhall, "Hebrew Conquest of Palestine," *Biblical Archaeologist* 25 (September 1962): 84.

23. G. E. Wright, "Shechem (Tell Balata)," *The Biblical World,* edited by Charles F. Pfeiffer (Grand Rapids: Baker Book House, 1966), pp. 518-522; L. E. Toombs and G. E. Wright, "The Fourth Campaign at Balata (Shechem)," *Bulletin of the American Schools of Oriental Research* (February 1963):1-60; "Balata: 1969," unpublished newsletter of the American Schools of Oriental Research, January 1969, July 1970.

24. For an effective defense of the identity of modern Askar (one mile north) with the Johannine Sychar and of the latter's trustworthiness see George Adam Smith, *The Historical Geography of the Holy Land,* 15th ed. (New York: A. C. Armstrong and Son, 1909), pp. 367-375.

25. Kopp, *Holy Places,* p. 166.

Jacobs' Well (center) and the surrounding Samaritan countryside from the slopes of Mount Gerizim.

ported, knew Biblical history. Few sites in the Holy Land have a better claim to authenticity and antiquity.[26]

Wells and rivers do not migrate for the convenience of pilgrims! Jacob purchased a campsite here (Gen. 33:19) and gave it to Joseph (Gen. 48:22). Nearby was laid to rest the mummy of Joseph (Josh. 24:32; cf. Gen. 50:25) forty years after it left Egypt. The name "shoulder" seems to have been alluded to in Genesis 48:22. When one considers the centrality of this site since the Late Bronze Age and its prominence in Old Testament history, one can understand better the centuries of bitter rivalry with the much less venerable site of Jerusalem. It helps explain the tenacity of the Samaritan tradition and the bitterness that followed the massacre of the inhabitants by John Hyrcanus (and later by Pontius Pilate) and the desire of the unnamed woman for a reassessment of the rival claims. We may be thankful that she raised the issue, for as a result the world received one of the most important statements ever made concerning the nature of true worship (John 4:21-24). Today the spot is quiet and unspoiled.

Mount Ebal, rising abruptly to the northwest is higher (3,044 feet) than its sister opposite, Mount Gerizim (2,890 feet).

---

26. Ibid., pp. 155-166.

Mount Ebal

From its summit a vast area unfolds in all directions before the viewer, but the most impressive sight is to the southeast overlooking the fertile plain of Shechem below. To the north the ground falls gently. Small grain is grown amid the rocks on the treeless summit. Below is the midportion of the modern city of Nablus, which has a population of 45,000. Its name comes from Neapolis, the "new city" west of Shechem (Balata), founded in A.D. 72 by the veterans of the armies of Vespasian and Titus. It is the birthplace of Justin Martyr the second-century apologist. Of special interest is the Crusader Church. The "Great Mosque" (*Jamia el Kebir*), largest of the eight mosques in the city, lies on the eastern side and features a Gothic-like portal similar to the entrance to the Church of the Holy Sepulchre at Jerusalem. The Crusaders built upon the

Mount Gerizim.

ruins of the great Byzantine basilica a structure that the Moslems converted into the present mosque.[27]

The Jenin-Tulkarm-Nablus triangle was the theater of Arab intrigue during the British Mandate.[28] Nablus's reputation for turbulence has been witnessed by many travelers. British tanks were seen here in December 1955. Israelis occupied the city in June 1967. Restiveness against the governments of Jordan and of Israel has not been unusual during recent decades. The inhabitants were "in constant revolt against the Ottoman authorities," and in 1918 they resisted two French calvary units.[29]

27. C. R. Conder and H. H. Kitchener, *The Survey of Western Palestine* (London: Palestine Exploration Fund, 1883), vol. 2, p. 208.
28. James Parkes, *A History of Palestine* (New York: Oxford University Press), p. 324.
29. Eugene Hoade, *Guide to the Holy Land,* 4th ed. (Jerusalem: Franciscan Press, 1962), p. 528.

In the fall of 1967 the public school teachers staged an ineffective boycott. The city today, however, presents the appearance of industry (soap and fruit juice) and tranquillity, except for the large barracks, built during the Mandate period, which now house captured Palestinian guerrillas.

From the high western portion of Mount Ebal, an excellent view encompasses Safad, Mount Hermon, Jaffa, Ramla, and Caesarea. To the east the broad valley spreads eastward to the Jordan, north toward Tirzah, and southeast toward Jerusalem. Between Ebal and Gerizim, as on a picture postcard, lie Jacob's well, Balata, and Nablus. It was here that the Israelites heard the curses and blessing of Deuteronomy 27, 28, pronounced antiphonally at one of the earliest recorded instances of public education (Josh. 8:30-35).

The other unique feature in Nablus is the Samaritan synagogue with its scroll of the Samaritan Pentateuch and the small community of Samaritans, now numbering fewer than 200. The scroll itself, enclosed in an elaborately embossed silver cylinder, is not, as alleged, "the oldest book in the world," but dates from about A.D. 900. They still observe the Passover by the slaughter of a lamb on the southeast portion of Mount Gerizim's summit near the wely (sheik's tomb). Nearby are remains of what they claim is their temple, which was destroyed during the Maccabean regime. They also show "twelve stones" said to have been carried from the Jordan by priests of Joshua's day.

Mount Gerizim At the present time the top of Mount Gerizim is mostly barren except for myriads of stones. In addition to the Samaritan place of sacrifice on the southeast portion, there is a locality called Luz on the western side, giving rise to the tradition that Biblical Bethel was located on Mount Gerizim rather than at Beitin on the border with Benjamin.

Near the center of the mount are the foundations of an octagonal church, a structure not unlike the Dome of the Rock in Jerusalem. The inner octagon consisted of pillars, the middle octagon furnished the main support of the roof, the outer octagonal wall enclosed an apse at one end, the narthex at the opposite end, and six chambers opening out of the center. The church is said to have been erected in A.D. 474 by the Emperor Zeno in honor of the Virgin Mary.[30] Later it was con-

---

30. Conder and Kitchener, *Survey,* vol. 2, p. 189.

verted into a mosque. It was once surrounded by a fortress, honoring Sheik Ghanim, a friend of Saladin.

On the northern spur of Mount Gerizim, overlooking Shechem and separated from the summit by a moat or ditch, is the site of the temple built by Hadrian about A.D. 130 and dedicated to Zeus Hypaistos. The 1968 expedition exposed the enormous platform on which the temple was erected, also six large vaulted cisterns on the north, and several of the 1,500 steps by which the temple was reached from the valley below, according to Epiphanius (A.D. 315-403).[31] Over a hundred coins found in the cisterns indicated occupancy during the period of Constantine (A.D. 307-337). Traces of the Samaritan temple were also identified on Tell er-Ras conforming to the description by Josephus of the temple authorized by Alexander the Great and destroyed by John Hyrcanus.[32]

Here Abimelech and his supporters in Shechem were cursed by the sole survivor of Gideon's household, Jotham, from the summit of Gerizim (Judg. 9:7-15). Below, in the valley, is the base of the ancient sanctuary (Baal-berith) where Baal was worshiped and where Abimelech burned the defenders before his own death at Thebez (modern Tubas) in fulfillment of Jotham's prophecy (Judg. 9:22-41).[33] Here the Israelites renewed the covenant and chose Yahweh as their only God (Josh. 8:30-35; Judg. 24:1-28) in the natural amphitheater below.

Thus from "the Canaanites" to Abraham's altar (Gen. 12:7), to Jacob's purchase (Gen. 33:18-20), to Joshua's two visits, to the half-Canaanite Abimelech, to the armies of Sargon II and the Exile, to the erection of the Samaritan temple and its destruction soon after, to Pilate's massacre of the Samaritans, to the Roman war veterans, to the shrine of Hadrian, to the arrival of the Moslems, to the constructions of the Crusaders on Byzantine remains, to the present political tensions, Mount Gerizim has been a microcosm of Middle East history. Small wonder that it is called "the navel" of the land (Judg. 9:37); it is central in many ways and it rivals Jerusalem in this respect.

---

31. Robert J. Bull, unpublished newsletter of the American Schools of Oriental Research, January 1969, pp. 5-8.

32. Jos. *Antiq.* XI. 11. 6; XIII. 10. 2.

33. Abimelech, son of Gideon and his Canaanite concubine from Shechem, ruled for three years over both Canaanites and Israelites. This illustrates the earlier amicable relations between Israelites and Cananites at Shechem and helps explain Joshua's presence here under peaceful conditions (Josh. 24). See also the note in *The Jerusalem Bible* at the place cited.

The village well in Sebaste, on the hill of Samaria, the site of the capital of the northern kingdom of Israel.

Hill of Samaria

Three miles west of Nablus is the famous hill that chiefly owes its importance to Omri and to Herod the Great. It is a rounded hill about fifty acres in extent on the summit. With the exception of the east it is surrounded by hills on all sides, like a rounded cone in a huge saucer. It has no natural defenses like Jerusalem or Tyre, but its location, elevation, and distance from the surrounding hills, when joined with defensive walls, made it almost impregnable. Thus it was able to sustain itself even against the Assyrians for three years (until its fall in 722 B.C.). It is a relatively young city but a very influential one. When purchased from Shemer by King Omri it was, as now, farmland (1 Kings 16:24). It served as the capital of the northern kingdom from 882 to 722 B.C.[34]

During this time Amos and Hosea warned constantly and emphatically of the consequences of apostasy. Omri's son, Ahab, married a Phoenician princess named Jezebel. Here in Samaria, Ahab and Jezebel supported a vast company of priests and

34. Wright and Filson, eds., *Westminster Historical Atlas*, p. 15.

prophets of Baal and built for them a temple (1 Kings 16:31; 2 Kings 10:18-27).

After the Exile, the Samaritans opposed the erection of the temple in Jerusalem, as attested by the books of Ezra and Nehemiah. Their city was destroyed by Alexander the Great in 331 and again by John Hyrcanus in 108 B.C. It was rebuilt by the Roman general Pompey in 63 B.C. In 27 B.C. the city was given to Herod the Great by Emperor Augustus. In gratitude Herod rebuilt it on a magnificent scale, including a forum, public basilica, columned streets north and south of the city, and a temple on the summit honoring Augustus.[35] The site still bears the name Herod gave it—Sebaste, the Greek equivalent of Augustus. Thus at either end of the valley between Ebal and Gerizim are cities named by or in honor of Romans: Nablus and Sebaste.

Archaeological excavation began here in 1908-1910 under Lyon; Reisner of Harvard continued it in the early 1930s. Seven levels of Israelite occupancy were identified.[36] Numerous incised ivory decorative pieces were found, apparently designed as furniture overlays, probably accounting for the reference to the "ivory house" (1 Kings 22:39; Amos 3:15), a symbol of the selfish luxury which Amos denounced: "Woe to those . . . who feel secure on the mountain of Samaria . . . who lie upon beds of ivory, and stretch themselves upon their couches . . . they drink wine in bowls and anoint themselves with the finest oils, but are not grieved over the ruin of Joseph" (Amos 6:1-6). From the summit, the columns with which Herod lined his streets are still visible below on the north and the south of the hill. Excavations reveal the impressive city gate on the west, probably where the lepers made their desperate foray which resulted in a breaking of the siege (2 Kings 7:1-20). On the north are the strong rounded towers of the Hellenistic period and also a recently excavated theater.

Here the preaching of Philip resulted in the first "breakthrough" of the gospel outside of Judaism and here the phenomena of Pentecost repeated itself, calling for official investigation by Peter and John and earning the admiration of Simon the magician (Acts 8). Here, where established Baal worship was finally terminated by Jehu, occurred the establishment of

35. Jos. *Antiq.* XV. 8. 5.
36. Pfeiffer, *Biblical World*, p. 494.

the first Christian community of non-Jews! Although the city was burned in A.D. 66, was restored by Septimus Severus in A.D. 196, and possessed a bishopric in the fourth century, it lost influence in favor of Nablus. The Crusaders built a cathedral in Sebaste in 1187, the ruins of which now serve as a mosque. Some impressive Roman tombs can also be seen nearby. The local traditions that Salome danced for Herod Antipas here and that John the Baptist was beheaded here appears to be without foundation in view of Josephus's statement that these events occurred east of the Dead Sea at Machaereus.[37]

Tulkarm

From Nablus the highway extends in the four directions of the compass; west to Tulkarm and the coast, east to the Jordan, north to Jenin via Tubas, and south to Jerusalem. Tulkarm, on the west edge of the "mountains of Samaria," numbers 15,000 inhabitants and has two agricultural colleges, one for Arabs and the other for Jews. Formerly a border town, it now serves as a transportation center between Natanya and Nablus.[38]

Qalqilya

Qalqilya, on the west border south of Tulkarm, recalls the site of one of the Gilgals. This town, on the border between Israel and Jordan's "West Bank," was severely damaged during the 1967 War. It lay only ten miles from the coast and hence at Israel's narrowest and most vulnerable "waist."

The boundary between the portion allotted to Manasseh and that of Ephraim may be fixed at Jasif (Josh. 17:8), modern Yasuf, and Tappuah (Josh. 16:8), or modern Tell Sheich Abu Zarad.[39] Manasseh's domain was far more extensive than that of Ephraim, for the latter's portion did not extend to the Jordan and had far less shoreline on the west. Manasseh's territory was bounded on the south by the brook Kansah and the Yarqon, as previously noted. The boundary is very irregular in that Manasseh had a large share of the low country both east and west whereas Ephraim had more of the hill country. In spite of this, Ephraim had the greater influence in Biblical history, greater because it was more isolated and hence less open to amalgamation with foreign influences.

THE HILL COUNTRY OF EPHRAIM

The hill country of Ephraim, lying between Benjamin and

37. Jos. *Antiq.* XVIII. 5. 2.
38. Hoade, *Holy Land,* p. 530.
39. Aharoni and Avi-Yonah, *Macmillan Bible Atlas,* p. 236; Hoade, *Holy Land,* p. 517.

Manasseh and between the Jordan Valley and maritime plain, has higher elevation than either of its neighbors, Baal Hazor being 3,334 feet above the Mediterranean. The soil is based upon a "dome" of hard Cenomanian limestone, extending north-east into Gilead.[40] From this comes the rich red *terra rossa*, in which olive trees and vineyards thrive. When a large lime-stone boulder of this area is broken, the interior is reddish in color; after further disintegration reddish soil results.

Of the northern tribes, Ephraim was the most influential. This is seen particularly in the eighth century, when Hosea usually referred to the northern kingdom simply as Ephraim. Why this dominance? The Ephraimites, in several instances, were not presented in a particularly favorable light. They are pictured as proud, sensitive, volatile, and peevish on at least two occasions. When Gideon was pursuing the Midianites, the men of Ephraim were incensed because their aid was not enlisted, but they later were soothed by Gideon's flattery (Judg. 8:1-3). When they later demanded of Jephthah why he had not sought their help against the Ammonites, he answered with civility, but after their continued hostility, Jephthah attacked them at the fords of the Jordan and had those Ephraimites slain whose pro-nunciation (Shibboleth) disclosed their identity (Judg. 12:1-6). Hosea criticized them for their vacillation and treachery against the Lord—"Ephraim is a cake not turned . . . they are like a treach-erous bow," was his despairing lament (Hos. 7:8, 16).

The instances reported in which Ephraimites were con-tentious and divisive may have a bearing on the fact that the division of the united kingdom, including the formation of the northern kingdom, came about under the influence of Jeroboam, who was an Ephraimite (1 Kings 11:26-40). The most beautiful part of central Palestine is the hill country of Ephraim. Even today, its rich soil and the fact that it receives more rainfall than portions either north or south make it ideal for the culti-vation of the grape and the olive. This, together with the scenic beauty, could easily have given the Ephraimites their feeling of superiority over their neighbors, an attitude which their isolation fostered.

Their territory, although less extensive than that of either Manasseh or Judah, was nevertheless more productive. The lime-stone soil *(terra rossa)* in the "mountains of Ephraim" was richer

---

40. Baly, *Geography,* p. 175.

than the more chalky soil to the north and it had more rainfall than the "hill country of Judea." Although more exposed to foreigners than Judah, it was less vulnerable than its neighbor to the north. Its proximity to Jerusalem helped to make it more influential than the tribes to the north. This was reinforced by the former religious sanctuary at Shiloh and the one at the border village of Bethel established by Jeroboam (1 Kings 12:26-32).

The chief cities of this area in Old Testament times included Aphek, Ebenezer, Lod, Tappuah, Shiloh, Ophrah, Bethel, Beth-horon, and Joppa. Strangely enough for a tribe of this importance, they had no major border fortress or commercial center. With the exception of Joppa, none of its cities played a major role as in the development of the land. The important religious centers were Shiloh and Bethel, but their importance was due to religious factors rather than any strategic location. Although their territory was much greater than that of Benjamin, it was far less than that of Manasseh. Also, Ephraim had no access to the Jordan River and possessed only a small portion of the Mediterranean coast, even though that coast did include Jaffa and its environs. Gezer was a border town between Dan and Ephraim, the only town not conquered by the Ephraimites. Being more isolated than most of the other tribes no doubt contributed to the Ephraimites' spirit of independence. The influence it wielded, however, was far out of proportion to its size.

Two main highways ran through their territory. One route, later called the *Via Maris*, extended along the coastal plain, and the other route was a trunk road on the mountain spine that linked its major cities. The Ephraimites, therefore, could retire to their mountains, as Judas Maccabeus later did, or they could intervene in the affairs of their neighbors at will. On the western border, where the Shephelah meets the plain, is the site of ancient Aphek. It was here that the Philistines captured the Ark of the Covenant from the Israelites (1 Sam. 4). Herod the Great rebuilt the city about 25 B.C., naming it Antipatris after his father Antipater. The apostle Paul stopped here on his way from Jerusalem to Caesarea under armed guards (Acts 23:31). Its copious springs (Ras el-Ein) are a major source of water for Jerusalem. This site was excavated in 1946 by the Palestine Department of Antiquities. It lies on a branch of the Yarqon River and is today an important pumping station for

Aphek (Antipatris)

the Israeli aqueduct. Located about halfway between Jerusalem and Caesarea, it formed a major rest stop during the Roman period. During the Crusader period, it served as "Le Toron aux Fontaines Sourdes," the ruins of which the visitor sees today. The site nearby was involved in a major phase of Allenby's push against the Turks in the autumn of 1917. Josephus knew that this Aphek was near Antipatris.[41]

Aphek was important as a border fortress. The name Aphek means "fortress." Its strategic importance is exemplified by the ease with which the Philistines, having won a victory here, were able to penetrate as far east as Shiloh, to destroy this religious center (1 Sam 4:2; cf. Jer. 7:12). Later, after victory over the Philistines, the name of Ebenezer was given to this site located "between Mizpah and Jeshanah" (1 Sam. 7:12).

The city of Lod, south of Antipatris, was another important bordertown between the maritime plain and the Shephelah. It is noted, that by the times of Joshua it was a "walled city according to the Talmudic tradition."[42] Built by an offspring of Benjamin (1 Chron. 8:12), it was known in later centuries as Lydda, scene of the healing of the sick man, Aeneas, through the prayers of the apostle Peter (Acts 9:32). Nearby is Modin, where the Maccabean Revolt had its origin, in 168 B.C. Lod was destroyed by the Babylonians in the sixth century, but some of its inhabitants returned with the Restoration (Ezra 2:33; Neh. 7:37). It suffered destruction again at the hands of the Romans during the first Jewish Revolt, in A.D. 66. After the visit of Septimus Severus, about A.D. 200, the city was given special privileges and renamed Diospolis. In 351, Byzantine armies put down a series of Jewish outbreaks, including one at the Rabbinic school at Lod. Today's Greek Orthodox church stands on the ruins of a twelfth-century Christian church erected by the Crusaders on the ruins of a sixth-century Byzantine church. The present structure is a restoration of the Crusader church, completed in 1870, in honor of Saint George, the patron saint of England and a hero honored along the Mediterranean coast. According to legend, he was born here, served as a soldier in the Roman army where he became converted, and was martyred at the beginning of the fourth century because of his faith. In popular romance, he is equated with the dragon-slayer

Lod

---

41. Jos. *Wars* II. 19. 1.
42. Moshe Pearlman and Yaacov Yannai, *Historical Sites in Israel* (New York: Vanguard Press, 1965), p. 160.

of Greek legend and is pictured as a medieval knight slaying the dragon and rescuing the princess. In European churches and museums this "event" frequently is portrayed.

In the hill country, about ten miles down the main road south of Shechem through the broad valley of Mikhmetat is Ain Berkit (Anuat Borkos), the border between Samaria and Judea of New Testament times. West of the highway lies the Arabic village Sawiya, on the edge of the high ridge (elevation 2,320 feet) overlooking the fertile plain through which the highway runs. Three miles farther south and west is the village of Lubban, the ancient Lebonah (Judg. 21:19), one of the five villages which, according to the Talmud, supplied wine for temple services. The highway skirts Mount Rahwat (2,296 feet) on the east, crosses the plain and climbs by hairpin curves onto the plateau of Mount Batin, in recent years the border between "Samaria" and "Judea."[43]

On the central mountain ridge, on both sides of the main highway, are numerous villages including some that are important in Biblical history and the Crusader period. One of these hilltop villages is Jiljiliya, one of the numerous Gilgals of Palestine. It is identified with Galgala of 2 Kings 2:1 and 4:38, where the prophet Elisha multiplied the barley bread. East on the same road is Sinjil, taking its name from Raymond Saint Gilles, count of Toulouse. It is the highest village in this area (2,274 feet) and it affords a good view of Mount Hermon. Crusader buildings here include a tower and a church.

Shiloh

To the east is Shiloh. The only remains are a series of ancient tombs in the rock, like cisterns, a jumble of stones, and the roofless walls of a restored Byzantine church. This was the site of the Hebrew tribal assembly and cult center (amphictyony), which fell to the Philistines during Samuel's youth (1 Sam. 4).[44] The Philisines probably destroyed both the city and shrine before returning to Ashdod with the Ark. Shiloh thus became a symbol of divine judgment against a backsliding Israel (Jer. 7:12). Israel's defeat at Ebenezer (1 Sam. 4:2) opened the way for defeat at Shiloh (Selun). Noth locates Ebenezer and Aphek at El Mejdel, but it is probably at Rosh Ha'Ayin, as on modern Israeli maps, since the Wadi Deir Ballut (Nahar Shillo) runs directly east to Selun (Shiloh)

43. Hoade, *Holy Land*, p. 516.
44. Noth, *History of Israel*, p. 95.

whereas El Mejdel is on the watercourse far to the north, which leads to Dothan rather than to Shiloh.

Farther south on the main highway is the picturesque "Valley of the Robbers" winding along the bottom of the Wadi Haramiyeh with tree-covered hillsides pressing in on either side. It is named "Robber's Valley" because it proved a profitable place for highway brigands, who could swoop down on the travelers from the shelter of the surrounding hills. It was like the "Jericho road" in this respect. Baldwin's Tower lies east of the road, a Crusader's fort named to commemorate the Crusader chieftain. West of the highway is 'Ein Sinya (ancient Jeshanah—2 Chron. 13:19). Some, including W. F. Albright, consider this to be the Ephraim of Saint John's Gospel. It was destroyed in World War I. Farther south and west of the highway is Jifna, the Gophna of Josephus, an important city of the Roman period. It was the leading city of one of ten toparchies into which the Romans divided Judea. Here may be found remains of a Byzantine church on the south, and another on the north, now replaced by a Roman Catholic church.

Other villages cling to the hillsides, but one that should not be ignored lies on another road to the east: Taiyiba, believed by most scholars to be identified with Ophrah of Joshua 18:23 and 1 Samuel 13:17. It is usually identified with Ephron of 2 Chronicles 13:19 and as an important political center during the Maccabean period, when it was called Aphairema (1 Macc. 11:34). The latter term is cognate with Ephraim, a city "near the wilderness" to which Jesus retired, as reported in John 11:54. It is now a Christian community with several ancient structures, including the remains of a Crusader tower owned by Boniface of Mont Ferrat in 1185. A youth of the village told us that Jesus had visited his city. Saint George is honored in a Crusader church on the eastern hill built on the ruins of a Byzantine church of the sixth century, the apse of which still remains. The Arabic name is El Khader, an Arabic term meaning "evergreen," and is applied to Saint George and the prophet Elijah. It is one of the highest cities in central Palestine, and the view to the south is most impressive. The Jordan on the east and Jerusalem on the south are easily discernible. North of this village is Baal Hazor, the highest point between Galilee and Sinai, with an elevation of 3,334 feet. It was here, "near Ephraim," that Absalom had much land and flocks (2 Sam. 13:23). The fact that it is a high place and bears the name Baal implies that it was once a pagan shrine. Later investigators have confirmed the persistence of the Baal cult on this great high place. To the northwest is Kafr Malik, slightly off the main road. East and below this village is Ain Samieh, which some identify as the Johannine Ephraim. At this latter place, there are many ancient structures, including caves in the side of the cliff near the wadi. As a result of recent excavations, a series of Middle Bronze shaft tombs were cleared. About forty inches in diameter, these tombs are vertical, extending down as far as thirty feet.

An ancient Roman road once led from Taiyiba to the Jericho Plain, and it still is followed in some sections by the modern road. The road winds down precipitous terrain into the awe-inspiring valley of the Jordan, a descent of more than 3,000 feet in a few miles, one of the most picturesque roads in Palestine.

Bethel

The most important city in this area is Bethel. It is east of the main highway and on a side road linking Ramallah with Taiyiba. In Bible times it was a major religious center, the original name being Luz, scene of Abraham's campsite (Gen. 12) and later of Jacob's first night away from home (Gen. 28). According to this Biblical source, the name was changed from Luz to Bethel as a result of Jacob's awareness that "this is the house of God, the gate of heaven." An ancient Byzantine church, now converted into a mosque, is on the south side of the road and commemorates Jacob's dream. The modern village, which bears the name Beitin, lies to the north in a shallow valley. To the east on a hill, the remains of the Crusader fortress (Burj Beitin), a small square structure, are now about fifteen feet in height. A small tell can be seen northwest of the village and still farther are the remains of monasteries (Deir esh She-bab) which commemorate Elisha's cursing of the children who taunted him and who were later attacked by bears (2 Kings 2:23-25). There are some small caves nearby. A Byzantine baptismal font is among the remains of a Christian community.

Archaeological excavations north of Beitin (Bethel) were conducted in 1927 and 1934 by W. F. Albright and continued on the east side in 1950 by Kelso and Gogner. They uncovered a Byzantine pavement and remains dating back to the Persian period. Kelso's excavations in 1954-1960 indicate that the city

Calf images from Egypt. Calf-worship in ancient Israel probably was borrowed from the Egyptians.

dates back to the Midde Bronze Age, with an Israelite settlement on the hill to the south. The Byzantine city street ran north and south through the present village. Middle Bronze sherds would date it at the time of Abraham. Today the rather small village has little to remind the visitor of its ancient prestige and importance.[45] Here was the shrine housing the calves worshiped by the Israelites and served by priests subservient to Jeroboam (1 Kings 12:26-33).

Later when King Jeroboam presumed to burn incense at Bethel, he was rebuked by an unnamed prophet (1 Kings 12:33–13:2). The prediction was that Josiah of Judah would

45. Contemporary Beitin has been studied definitively by A. Lutfiyya, cf. Abdullah Lutfiyya, *Baytin, A Jordanian Village* (London: Mouton and Co., 1966).

Clay female figurines, from Palestine, that date from the Middle and Late Iron Age. Such figurines were widely used at such worship centers as Bethel.

sacrifice the bones of the priest on this altar. When the king rebuked him, his arm was paralyzed. An old prophet who lived in Bethel learned of the episode and pursued after the anonymous prophet urging him to return and dine at his house. Later, after dining the prophet was slain by a lion as he returned to Judah (1 Kings 13). In the sixth century, during Josiah's reforms, this king, after removing bones from the nearby tombs, burned them upon the altar, thus defiling it in fulfillment of the earlier Scripture (2 Kings 23:15-19). The event is evidence of the extent of Josiah's reforms and of the control by Judah over territory once claimed by the northern kingdom.

The "hill country of Ephraim" even today remains fertile, attractive, and relatively prosperous, with numerous villages of stone houses usually located on the sides of hilltops. The hillsides are mostly covered with vineyards or olive orchards, and in the narrow valley floors small grain is grown.

Ephraim's coastal city, Joppa, seaport of Jerusalem, was a walled town during the time of Thutmose III (1490-1435 B.C.). According to a legend, the Egyptian general, Thoth, while besieging the city, placed two hundred of his soldiers in baskets or sacks. He pretended to surrender to the men of Joppa, saying that these baskets, or sacks, were filled with presents for the city. After the city gates were opened the soldiers leaped out of the sacks, and the Egyptians took the city, reminiscent of the deception that allegedly led to the fall of Troy.[46]

Joppa

Originally assigned to Dan (Josh. 19:46), Joppa was incorporated in the territory of Ephraim when the tribe of Dan migrated to the north. It was here that Solomon received his timbers for the temple, and from here Jonah tried to sail for Tarshish. Here Peter received the vision, which led to the conversion of Cornelius. Later the city was destroyed by the Romans and fought over during the Crusades. Today, the ancient city is linked with modern Tel Aviv. The archaeological museum on the hill overlooking the harbor is an important depository of remains of nearby Tell Qasila, recently excavated by the Israelis. Until recent days, Joppa remained the place where pilgrims traveling to Jerusalem first set foot on the Holy Land. For much of the time, the city was controlled by the governor of Gaza, who often extorted huge sums from Christian pilgrims on one pretense or another. On several occasions they were prevented from landing until the captain of the galley paid a huge sum to the governor. For example, Canon Pietro Casola, who made the pilgrimage in 1494, reports that the governor of Gaza displayed ten prisoners—Christians who had become shipwrecked and had sought refuge. He threatened to skin them alive unless he received a thousand duggats ransom. He finally agreed to accept 250 instead, which was all that the pilgrims could collect, and the refugees (hostages) were freed.[47]

---

46. Pfeiffer, *Biblical World*, p. 332.
47. Pietro Casola, *Pilgrimage to Jerusalem, 1494*, trans. M. N. Newett, (Manchester: University Press, 1907), p. 225.

Excavation at the Old Testament site of Jericho and the traditional "Mount of Temptation" in the background.

8

Benjamin

From the standpoint of Old Testament history the small territory assigned the tribe of Benjamin is one of the most important areas of the Holy Land. This region was the center of Samuel's long ministry. King Saul here established the first capital of the emerging nation. The area remained prominent during the kingdom period because frequently it was the scene of border clashes between Judah (the southern kingdom) and Israel (the northern kingdom).

The northern border of Benjamin extended westward from the Jordan to Bethel, and then southwest to lower Beth-horon. The western border traced southward between the hill country and the Shephelah to Kiriath-jearim, and the southern border went eastward to the valley of Hinnon, on the south edge of Jebus (Jerusalem), past En-rogel (Job's well), in the lower Kidron Valley, and continued east to the Dead Sea at the delta of the Jordan (Josh. 18:11-20). It therefore encompassed, but did not include, the Jebusite city, which remained independent until conquered by David. The Jordan River formed the eastern border. The eastern portion, from the Jordan to the hills was and still is desolate—a "wilderness"—and sparsely inhabited (the oasis of Jericho was the exception, then as now). The most important cities of Benjamin, including Bethel, Gibeah, Ramah, and Nob, lay on the main north-south road, which still skirts the eastern edge of the "hill country." West of this line lies the undulating tableland extending to the edge of the Shephelah at

Qubeiba and Beth-horon. Excluding Jericho, the inhabited portion of Benjamin is only ten miles square. The most prominent feature of the topography is Nabi Samwil which, at an elevation of 2,942 feet, provides the most extensive panorama in central Palestine.

Approaches from both east and west nearly meet at the center of this territory. From the west is the Wadi Beit Hanina, reaching eastward nearly to the watershed and leading in from the east is the Wadi es Somar and the Wadi Saleim from the Jordan Valley. This made Benjamin vulnerable to invasion from both west (via Latrun and Imwas) and east (via Jericho). This was demonstrated in recent times by British forces in 1917 and again in 1967 by Israeli forces. Allenby, however, encountered stubborn resistance by the Turks near Beit Iksa. Most invaders preferred the northern approach by the Beth-horons.[1] It is interesting to note that during the Maccabean struggle, Syrian armies attempting to subjugate Jerusalem attacked first by the northern route at the Beth-horons and later by the southern approach from Imwas, or Emmaus (1 Macc. 3:21; 2 Macc. 8:23).

Most invaders, however, came from the north. A most impressive sight seen either from the east edge of Mount Scopus looking northward or from the village of Rimmun looking southward, is the string of villages that were terrorized by the approach of Sennacherib in 701 B.C. as anticipated by Isaiah:

> "He advances from the district of Rimmun, he reaches Aiath, he passes through Migron, he leaves his baggage train at Michmash. They file through the defile, they bivouac at Geba. Ramah quakes, Gibeah of Saul takes flight. Bathgallim, cry aloud! Laishah, hear her! Anathoth, answer her! Madmenah is running away, the inhabitants are fleeing. This very day he will halt at Nob. He will shake his fist against the mount of the daughter of Zion" (Isaiah 10:28-32 J.B.).

At certain places, notably at Bethel, the ancient road lay somewhat east of the main highway today. The traveler, however, can take virtually the same course as Isaiah's description of the Assyrian invasion. Beginning his journey at Taiyiba (Ophrah), he can see from its elevation of nearly 3,290 feet most

---

1. E. H. H. Allenby, *The Advance of the Egyptian Expeditionary Force, July, 1917 to October, 1918* (London: His Majesty's Stationery Office, 1919), pp. 15 ff.

of these agricultural villages as they extend south through the
slight haze as far as "French Hill" and the Mount of Olives
northeast of Jerusalem. Rimmun, just below and south of the
viewer, is believed to be the "Rock Rimmun" where six hundred
Benjamites found refuge for four months (Judg. 20:47). From
Rimmun the road leads down, crossing the Wadi Asas, a branch
of the Wadi Makkuk, east of Ai (Et Tel) near Hayan, or
Aiath, at the edge of Deir Dibwan. Traces of an old road
can be discerned leading through grainfields to Tell Miriam
and to nearby Michmash (Mukhmas); from there across the
upper part of the Wadi Suweinit to Jaba (Geba) on its south
bank. From Jaba the road swings slightly west to the east edge
of Rama (Ramah) and to Tell el Ful (Gibeah of Saul) now
crowned with the abandoned shell of a new structure, which
was begun for King Hussein.

From this hilltop (2,758 feet) another vast panorama is
visible in every direction. It commands a view of the Jordan
Valley to the east, and of the broad valley of Beit Hanina lead-

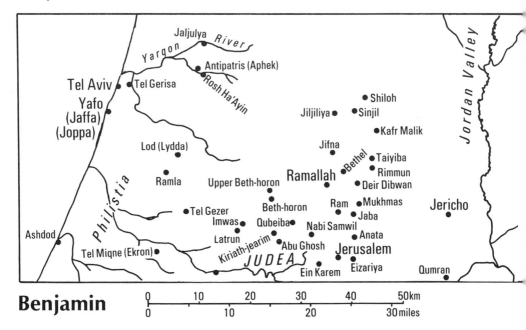

Benjamin

Gibeah of Saul (Tel el Ful), at the site of King Saul's fortress palace.

ing westward and revealing the villages of Gibeon (El Jib), Beit Iksa, Nabi Samwil, Jerusalem, and Qubeiba. Directly north is the three-crowned "French Hill" on the northeast edge of Jerusalem where high-rise apartments may now be seen. A panorama of history lies within this perspective. Immediately below are visible the foundations of King Saul's palace, or fortress, one of the earliest of Iron Age structures built by the Israelites, which was disclosed by a team of archaeologists (W. F. Albright, *et al*) in the 1920s. This rather inauspicious site, now called "hill of beans" (Tell el Ful) by the Arabs, was host to the beginnings of the tribal confederacy under Saul Ben Kish. From here this courageous leader rallied support for besieged Jabesh Gilead (1 Sam. 12:1-11). From here also at a later time the same now-distraught leader gave orders to kill all the priests of nearby Nob (now Shufat) merely because of fancied assistance to his rival David (1 Sam. 22:6-19). King Hussein's projected palace stands as it did on June 5, 1967, when the Six Day War erupted. Three millennia of turbulent history

separates this contemporary structure and the Iron Age foundations below as they do the first and last king of the land. A
short distance to the southeast is Anata (the ancient Anathoth
of Jeremiah), formerly a hometown of priests sent there by
Solomon on a "perpetual vacation"; so decreed because Abiathar
had sponsored the claim of Adonijah to be king (1 Kings 2:26,
27).

Faintly discernible beyond the main highway and parallel
to it is a fork in an ancient road or path. It is the remains of
the Roman road, one fork bearing northwest through Beth-horon
to Antipatris and Caesarea, the right fork leading to Samaria
and Damascas. Saint Paul had traveled this road at least twice,
first to Damascus and later, under armed guard, to Caesarea—
first as the hunter, last as the hunted; first as the reactionary
opposing the new, last as the innovator who had "turned the
world upside down" (Acts 9:2; 23:23-35).

From Nabi Samwil with its minaret now thrusting toward
the sky, the Christian knights wept for joy when they first be-
held the Holy City in July 7, 1099, after a campaign of three   **Nabi Samwil**
years (they had left Europe in the spring of 1096); henceforth
they called this the *Mons Gaudii*—"Hill of Joy." They could
not have seen much of the Old City itself, which lies in a valley,
but the Mount of Olives is clearly visible from Nabi Samwil.
The Arabic name derives from the belief that Samuel was buried
here. This was based upon a Christian tradition that goes
back at least to the fifth century when a church was built above
the grotto believed to be Samuel's tomb.[2] A new church was
built there upon authorization of Baldwin II (1118-1131) and
given the name Saint Samuel of Montjoy. In the eighteenth century, Moslems converted it into a mosque.

The site honors the man who made the transition from
theocracy to monarchy and who himself represents the last of
the judges and the first of the prophets. It serves as a reminder
of Samuel's insight that "to obey is better than sacrifice, and
to hearken than the fat of rams" (1 Sam. 15:22), a transition
from a religion of ritual to one of faith and ethics.

Was this the site of Mizpah of Benjamin, as believed by
Edward Robinson, G. A. Smith, and W. F. Albright, or is Mizpah
to be sought at Tell en Nasbeh as excavations by W. F. Bade

---

2. Eugene Hoade, *Guide to the Holy Land,* 4th ed. (Jerusalem: Franciscan
Press, 1962), p. 554.

would seem to indicate? Very plausible is Hoade's suggestion that this is the "Mountain of the Lord" where seven of Saul's sons were executed to expiate the blood-guiltiness incurred by Saul when he sought to exterminate the Gibeonites, thus violating the covenant made by Joshua (Josh. 9:15; 2 Sam. 21:1-14).[3]

The fact that it is the highest mountain within a radius of twenty miles could account for the shrine there from the days of David and for later attracting the church to honor Samuel at this place. The Bible, however, places Samuel's burial place at Ramah (1 Sam. 25:1; 28:3).

Jerusalem from Nabi Samwil

The view from the minaret atop Nabi Samwil is among the most impressive in Palestine. To the east lie the "mountains of Moab," rising like a blue wall forty-five air miles distant and six hundred feet higher in elevation. Amman, the capital of Jordan and site of Uriah's "murder" (2 Sam. 12:9), is directly east. Conspicuous on the right is Tell el Ful (Gibeah of Saul), surmounted by its "new palace" (the recent Jordanian structure). Here stood the tamarisk, on the "high place," under which King Saul consulted with his staff as to the steps to be taken to eliminate his rival, the youthful David (1 Sam. 22:6). To the south and slightly east is the profile of Mount Scopus–Mount of Olives–east of Jerusalem, with the two spires–Victoria Tower and the Russian Tower–probing the skyline. On the Mount of Olives Jesus was last seen before His ascension (Luke 24:50). The British war cemetery and the newly renovated Hebrew University campus are also on Mount Scopus. The cemetery is a reminder of the stirring wars of these environs.

Panorama from Nabi Samwil

Jerusalem is now rapidly spreading northward and the suburbs are now clearly visible. Nearer is the Arab village of Beit Hanina, in the valley of that name, located on the main highway. The unchecked erosion during the four centuries of

---

3. The Hebrew in 2 Sam. 21:6 says, "at Gibeah of Saul, the chosen of the Lord," but the Hebrew in 2 Sam 21:9 and the Greek in 2 Sam 21:6 state, "mountain of the Lord." This seems more likely. Furthermore, Gibeah was much farther from Gibeon. The NEB renders it, "hurl them down to their death before the Lord" at 2 Sam. 21:6, 9, but there seems to be no textual or topographical justification for this rendering; neither hill has a precipice which would make this form of execution feasible. The "great high place" near Gibeon, where Solomon offered sacrifice (1 Kings 3:4; cf., 1 Chron. 16:39; 21:29; 2 Chron. 1:3, 13), is probably to be found here; if so, it would be *near* Gibeon rather than *in* Gibeon.

View of Mount Scopus from inside Jerusalem.

Ottoman rule is obvious in the exposed ridges of limestone looking like a series of ribs or terraces.

Directly south over the western suburbs of Jerusalem, the
top of ancient Herodium is visible on the horizon, a reminder
of the prominent role played by the Herods in New Testament
and Palestinian history; in the foreground is the village of Beit
Iksa. This presents a beautiful panorama in early spring, when
below are the rich brown parcels of ground, from which spring
wheat is emerging, bounded by innumerable stone walls. The
rounded slopes are terraced both by native ribs of rock and also
by field-stone walls. Paved roads and occasional tracks wind over
and around the hills. In every direction, stone villages perch
atop hills or cling to the sloping sides. The limestone soil is rich
for small grain, olives, and grapes but for little else. In the
same scene in summer, villages, fields, and roads blend together
in grayish brown softened by the slight haze under the cloudless skies of the six rainless months, from May until November.
Turning to the southwest, the viewer from the minaret can dis-

cern the Arab village Beit Surik, comprising small stone houses and its own slender minaret. In the same direction but invisible beyond the horizon lies Kiriath-jearim (Abu Ghosh) from whence David brought the Ark to Jerusalem (1 Sam. 7:1; 2 Sam. 6:2). Directly west, beyond the villages of Beit Biddu and Qubeiba (Emmaus?), the terrain drops gradually to the coastal plain south of Jaffa, and the Mediterranean is visible through the haze. To the northwest lies nearby Beit Ijza in a shallow valley, whereas over the horizon is upper and lower Beth-horon, so prominent in Biblical and Maccabean history. Nearby and directly north, is Gibeon (El Jib), and at a distance is Ramallah with its television towers. Gibeon was the chief city of the Hivites in Joshua's times, an enclave among the Canaanites who made a separate "deal" with Joshua on the basis of false pretenses (Josh. 9:3-18). Its residents escaped death at the hands of the Israelites but became their servants. Here was located the "great high place," where Solomon received a vision from Yahweh and chose wisdom over the less worthy objectives that kings usually prefer (1 Kings 3:4-15).

To the northeast lies Beit Nabala, the Qalandia Airport, and

The pool at Gibeon and the stairway leading into it.

Samuel's ancient village of Ramah (Ram). Taiyiba (Ephraim) is far beyond, backed up by Baal Hazor some 500 feet higher than where the viewer stands.

To the west, long before the Crusaders, Joshua's troops, assisted by a hailstorm and the "long day," chased the five Amorite kings down the valley of Aijalon to Makkedah and their doom (Josh. 10). Up the same valley came the Philistines to battle with the armies of Saul and Jonathan (1 Sam. 14:31). Also in this valley, Judas outflanked and outfought the vastly superior Syrian forces near Emmaus (1 Macc. 4:1-25) in a manner similar to that of Joshua.

Directly south were once amassed the forces of Assyrians, then Babylonians, then the Romans, and, still later, the Crusaders to confront Jerusalem. Allenby's forces toiled up the slopes from the west in late 1917, and the Turks withdrew after four centuries of misrule. Finally, on June 6, 1967, Israeli tanks emerged on the Beit Hanina Valley below, forcing the defending Arab Legion to return eastward to the Jordan.

Such are some highlights of events that swirled around this watchtower at Nabi Samwil, events not only reported in Scripture but recorded in every history book on the Near East. The Biblical account of the vast armies of Sennacherib at the height of Assyrian dominance who were "smitten like frost at the glance of the Lord" (Lord Byron, "Destruction of Sennacherib"), led to the mistaken conviction that Jerusalem was forever inviolate (cf. Jer. 7:1-10). As a noted geographer has stated, the territory of Benjamin for the ten miles north of Jerusalem became the site of more fortresses, sieges, forays, battles, and massacres, than perhaps any other part of the country.[4] If this is so, it is because nearly all successful invaders have approached Jerusalem from the north—either from the Jordan through Ai and Bethel, or from the coast through Beth-horon, or through Samaria.

For the reader of the New Testament, the eastern portion of Benjamin is especially important because of its relation to the ministries of John and Jesus. It was where John baptized multitudes, where Jesus fasted and prayed, where Herod the Great spent his last days, and where Jesus healed the blind Bartimaeus and dined with Zacchaeus, "a chief tax collector."

But it also is important for Old Testament readers. The

4. George Adam Smith, *The Historical Geography of the Holy Land*, 15th ed. (New York: A. C. Armstrong and Son, 1909), p. 289.

crossing of the Jordan under Joshua's leadership probably occurred east of Jericho. The implication is that it occurred opposite Jericho and south of Adam (Josh. 3:16). The stoppage
of the water occurred at Adam, about twelve miles north of
Jericho. From there to the Dead Sea the waters stopped running and piled up north of Adam as far as Zarethan (Tell es-
Saidiyeh), twelve miles still farther north. Earthquakes occur
in this locality and have been known to dam up the Jordan
River causing the water to pile up above the dam and leave
the channel below it dry. Such an event is reported to have
occurred in A.D. 1267, when landslides in this area dammed
the river for several hours.[5]

Gilgal, where the Israelites set up their base camp after
crossing the Jordan, has never been identified with any certainty. A low tell east of Jericho was excavated but without
decisive results.[6] Pilgrims of the twelfth century were shown a
place: "three miles from Jericho, two from the Jordan, is Beth-
aglah ... the place of turning" ... the aforesaid Galgala, where
Joshua for a second time circumcised the people and kept the
Passover.[7]

Jericho itself is the most famous city in the ancient territory
of Benjamin. It is now believed to be the world's oldest con-
Jericho   tinuously inhabited city. Excavations by Kathleen M. Kenyon
have revealed a settlement of a pre-pottery people going back
ten millennia, to 8000 B.C.[8] Although cultivators of food grain
lived in caves of Mount Carmel, Jericho is the earliest known
city, the earliest residences belonging to the Mesolithic Age.
Visitors today can view the most ancient tower known to man,
but may not now, as was formerly done, climb its inner stairway.
This circular tower dates from Neolithic times (ca. 7000-5000
B.C.). Jericho, like Damascus, owes its longevity to the fact that
it is an oasis, the place where a perennial and copious stream
reaches the plain of the Jordan.

There are now three "Jerichos." The Old Testament site

---

5. Nelson Glueck, *The River Jordan* (McGraw-Hill Book Co., 1968),
p. 118.
6. J. L. Kelso, however, reported finding remains of five Byzantine churches
at this site, which lends probability to the identification, *Biblical Archaeologist* 121 (February 1951): 6-8.
7. *Anonymous Pilgrims* (London: Palestine Pilgrims' Text Society, 1894),
vol. 6, p. 47.
8. Kathleen M. Kenyon, *Archaeology in the Holy Land* (New York:
Praeger Publishers, 1960), pp. 42 ff.

A remaining section of a Roman aqueduct along the road leading to Jericho.

The New Testament section of Jericho as seen from the old Roman road.

Air view showing the mound of Jericho in the foreground and a section of the present city, the Dead Sea, and the mountains of Moab in the background.

is at Tell el Sultan, near Elisha's Fountain which issues from its base. It is strange that the succession of cities that constitute the tell were not located near rather than on the source of the spring. Perhaps the proximity was necessitated by the desire to deny enemies the use of the water, hence the ancient walls enclosed it. The Jericho of the New Testament is located a mile south, at the Wadi el Qilt. Here Herod the Great built his winter palace complete with a brick-lined swimming pool, the honeycomb pattern of bricks reflecting the influence of Rome on its architect. On either side of the wadi he built two fortresses, of which now only a few vestiges remain. The third Jericho is the modern one, located between the Old Testament and New Testament sites. Its present inhabitants number about 6,800. Jericho seldom has been held in very high esteem in spite of the fact that it is often a paradise compared with its environs. In 1893, one pilgrim found Jericho "the most loathsome place in the world," where sleep was impossible because of white ants.[9] It is virtually defenseless and through-

9. Matilda Serao, *In the Country of Jesus,* trans. Richard Davey (London: Thomas Nelson and Sons, n.d.), p. 139.

out history it was vulnerable to invasion. Jericho has always been a commercial and travel center with little political influence. In summer it is too hot; in winter it is sometimes wet but always warm. Jericho can claim a certain distinction by the fact that, at 820 feet below sea level, it is the lowest city on the globe.

A palace exceeding in splendor that of Herod the Great was built about two miles north of Jericho at Khirbet el Mafjir. It was built by Omayyad Caliph Hisham (A.D. 724-743) as his winter palace. It included a vast mosaic floor and gorgeous heated baths. Many of its artifacts are now in the Palestine Museum in east Jerusalem.

Jericho has known better days. Famed as the "City of Palm Trees" in the Old Testament (Deut. 34:3) because of its semitropical climate, it later embraced Christianity and by A.D. 325 it was the seat of a bishopric. Luxuriant gardens then as now were nourished by water from Elisha's Fountain and from Ain Duk to the north. The Crusaders restored it and established sugar refineries there. Subsequent invasions have reduced its

One of the mud-brick houses at Jericho. The thatch roof is highly typical of the valley structures of ancient Palestine.

influence. Since 1948, large refugee camps have been established
north and south of the town, thus taking advantage of its mild
climate. Prior to World War I, pilgrims by the thousands would
come from Jerusalem to be immersed in the Jordan and would
often spend the night in Jericho and its environs. Daily bus
services now connect the city with Taiyiba, Ramallah, and
Jerusalem.

As one moves south along this great trunk road in the
highlands, a track leads east from modern Beit Hanina toward
Hizma, the ancient Biblical Azmaveth (Neh. 7:28), a village
founded by the descendants of Saul (1 Chron. 8:36). This
village, which has many grottos and cisterns, is near a strange
megalithic monument called the Tombs of the Israelites. This
strange structure is in an open field. These enormous stone
structures are five in number, the smallest of which measures
98 feet, 6 inches long and 16 inches wide, and the largest of
which is 176 feet long and 14 feet, 7 inches wide. One of
them is 22 feet in width. Their height varies from 3 to 6 feet.
The stones are undressed and piled rudely in courses. The
walls are 5 or 6 feet thick. Some of the chambers have roofs
consisting of stone slabs 7 feet in length. The largest structure
has a square hole in its eastern side that leads to a small square
room. They stretch end to end in a northeast–southwest direction. Local inhabitants call them the Tombs of the Children
of Israel, or the Tombs of the Amalekites.[10] In size and rough
construction, though not in shape, they resemble the Dolmans
of East Jordan. They may be characterized as prehistoric com-
munal tombs, as their local names attest. One of the names
supports the theory that they were built by Amalekites prior
to the arrival of the Israelites.

Ramah

To the right of the main north-south highway, on a side
road leading northwest toward Jaba (Geba) and Mukhmas
(Michmash), is Ram, site of ancient Ramah ("High Place"),
a Levitical city of Benjamin (Josh. 18:25) and the hometown
of Samuel. It lies on the summit of a low rounded hill, which
is rather isolated and prominent. West of the village is a small
Christian basilica, now a tomb of the Moslem sheikh. It is
Ramah of Benjamin (Josh. 18:25), mentioned by Jerome in his
commentary on Hosea as being near Geba, seven Roman miles

---

10. Edward Robinson, *Biblical Researches in Palestine* (Boston: Crocker
and Brewster, 1868), vol. 1, p. 287.

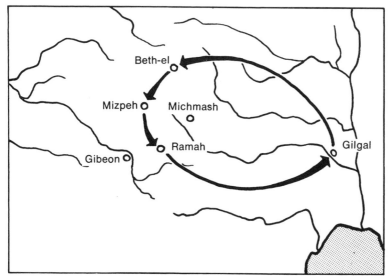

Samuel's Circuit

from Jerusalem (actually six English miles). Formerly it was a fief of the Church of the Holy Sepulchre[11]

This was one of the main places that Samuel visited as a circuit judge ("and he went on a circuit year by year to Bethel, Gilgal, and Mizpah; and he judged Israel in all these places. Then he would come back to Ramah, for his home was there, and there he also administered justice to Israel. And he built there an altar to the Lord"—1 Sam 7:16, 17). Since Ramah was near the border between Benjamin and Ephraim, Baasha, king of Israel, strengthened these fortifications against Asa, Judah's king. When Baasha withdrew to meet a threat from the north, Asa occupied Ramah and dismantled the fortifications (1 Kings 15:17). In the sixth century, after the fall of Jerusalem, Jeremiah was released there by his captors (Jer. 40:1). After the Exile, it was resettled by Benjamites (Ezra 2:26; Neh. 11:33).

East of Ramah is Geba (Jaba), a small Arab farming village with a clear view to the east, north, and south. It was a Le-

11. C. R. Conder and H. H. Kitchener, *The Survey of Western Palestine* (London: Palestine Exploration Fund, 1883), vol. 1, p. 13.

vitical town (Josh. 12:17). To the northwest over the Wadi Suweinit (Arabic *accacia?*) lies Mukhmas, the Michmash of the Bible. South of Michmash, the Wadi deepens into a gorge with two rock buttresses facing each other, the northern called *Bosseh*, and the southern, *Seneh*. It was here that Jonathan with his armor bearer won a great victory over the Philistines camped at Michmash. This led to a rapid retreat of the Philistine garrison later pursued "from Michmash to Aijalon" by Saul's troops rushing northwest from Gibeah (1 Sam. 14:31). Geba was on the route of the Syrian invaders, as reported in Isaiah 10:27-32, although the main road now leads through to the twin cities of Bira and Ramallah. Bira is east of the highway and is the traditional site where Mary and Joseph made their first stop after leaving Jerusalem and the child Jesus behind (Luke 2:44). This seems probable because it is a convenient rest stop, since a large spring, dating from Roman days, is here.

Ramallah, an educational and commercial center, is now the largest village between Nablus and Jerusalem. It is a Christian village—largely Protestant because of the Quaker school located here. Ramallah is situated on a high ridge at a good elevation

The gorge between Michmash and Geba.

An ancient olive press near Deir Dibwan.

providing for cool weather in summer and therefore has been a summer resort. It is a possible site for Ramathaim-zophim, birthplace of Samuel (1 Sam. 1:1). Located here is a Latin convent, a Quaker school, and a Greek church. Its population today is listed as 25,000. From here water is piped to Beitin and to Deir Dibwan to the northeast.

Deir Dibwan is an unusual Arab village, both in its prosperity and its familiarity with western ways. Although Christians formerly lived there, its population now is entirely Moslem. It has a school, a mosque, and a gristmill. The village consists of two main sections, the lower village of older, more simple homes, and the upper village on the north, including modern, more costly homes. The latter is said to have been built by money sent from the New World—the United States and South America —by Arabs who migrated there and sent their money back home. Recently, Deir Dibwan has become the base for archaeological expeditions at the monastery at El Kedria in the valley to the northeast, and also the nearby Et Tel, the Biblical Ai (excavations at the tell were also conducted in the 1930s). Excavation at this imposing site, which earlier had been dismissed by Robinson as containing no antiquities of note, was by John Garstang in 1928. The conclusion then was that the city

had fallen to Joshua in the fifteenth or sixteenth century B.C.
In the mid-1930s, the Rothschild excavation was conducted
under the direction of Mme. Marquet-Krause. They explored
the acropolis and identified part of the southern wall and no-
ticed that it was an early Bronze Age site of great strength
and size. This was destroyed in about 2200 B.C., but Iron Age
ruins point to a later, brief occupation on the acropolis. Excavation was continued by Joseph A. Callaway of Southern Baptist
Seminary in 1964-1966, 1968 and 1969. The citadel, featuring
Egyptian influence, was further excavated, and search was made
for the Iron Age remains on the eastern summit. In the summer
of 1968, excavations on the eastern edge, supervised by G. H.
Livingston, revealed a massive Early Bronze wall twenty feet
in height, consisting of three parallel walls totalling about forty
feet in width. A small "postern" gate was discovered at the southeast corner built nearly five millennia before, adjacent to a vast
cistern paved with limestone slabs.

Emmaus

The site of Emmaus is not clearly established. Four possible
sites have been proposed: (1) at Colonia, (2) at Abu Ghosh
(both on the Jerusalem-Joppa Road), (3) at Imwas, and (4) at
Qubeiba. Emmaus is mentioned in Luke 24:13 as the place of
Jesus' appearance to two disciples on Easter Sunday, and also
in Josephus, *Wars* (VII, 6, 6) as the place where Titus's veterans
were settled. It is stated in Luke and Josephus to be sixty stadia,
about seven miles from Jerusalem. In the onomasticon, Emmaus
is identified with Nicopolis, or Imwas.[12] It has been suggested
that "Emmaus" comes originally from the Hebrew form "hammath," meaning "a thermal spring," or "warm bath."[13] Josephus
links "a warm bath" with Emmaus. It is known that the modern
Imwas was noted for its healing spring in the early Christian
centuries.

Nicopolis, or Imwas, is known from ancient times as Emmaus, where Judas Maccabeus in 165 B.C. defeated the armies
of Nicanor and Gorgias (1 Macc. 3:40; 4:3). The city was fortified in 160 B.C. by Bacchides (1 Macc. 9:50), but it was destroyed in 4 B.C. by Varus in revenge for an attack on a Roman
military convoy. A Roman legion located here in A.D. 67. In A.D.
70 Titus gave it the title of Nicopolis ("victorious city") in
memory of his conquest of Jerusalem. A Byzantine church was

---

12. Eusebius, *Das Onomastikon . . .*, trans. E. Klostermann (Hildesheim:
G. Olms, 1966), p. 91.
13. Jos. *Wars* IV. 1. 3; *Antiq.* XVIII. 2. 3.

erected here and later a Crusader church was built over it. The ruins are still in evidence. The church was excavated in 1880 and again by Dominican Fathers in 1924 and 1925. Vincent and Abel, in 1932, believed it was the Emmaus of the Gospel.[14]

Edward Robinson concluded that Emmaus is Nicopolis, or Imwas, sustaining it on the argument that the entire ancient church until the Middle Ages accepted this as the site. The reading of sixty stadia in Luke's Gospel and in Josephus, he concluded, is a mistake. He pointed out that there are some manuscripts that read 160 stadia rather than the 60 that is found

14. H. Vincent and F. M. Abel, *Emmaus, sa basilique et son historie* (Paris, 1932), cited in Clement Kopp, *The Holy Places of the Gospel* (New York: Herder and Herder, 1963), p. 398.

An old olive tree in the garden at Qubeiba, the traditional site of Emmaus since the sixteenth century.

in most manuscripts. He further indicated that if the ancient manuscripts had 60 stadia, the early church would not have fixed it as far away from Jerusalem as Nicopolis. As to the argument of the great distance, Robinson states that this distance could have been traversed in five hours, that the two disciples could have left Jerusalem in the early afternoon to arrive at Nicopolis about 5:00 P.M. and return to Jerusalem by 11:00 P.M., a roundtrip of about forty miles. Kopp agrees that "a robust Arab nowadays can easily" do this.[15]

Captain Conder of the survey party, however, accepts Qubeiba as the Emmaus of Luke on the assumption that merely the prominence of Emmaus Nicopolis "caused it immediately to be assumed, in the fourth century, as identical with the New Testament site."[16] In addition to the best earliest manuscripts reading "sixty" is the fact that the walk from Jerusalem to Emmaus Nicopolis and back would require at least sixteen hours, "far more than an ordinary day's journey to the Palestinian accustomed to walking."

The survey party of 1876 found at Qubeiba "a village of moderate size, standing on a flat ridge with a few olives [trees] to the west. It commands a fine view to the north over the low hills. To the west is a monastery of Latin monks, established in 1862. In the grounds are remains of a Crusading Church. This place has been the traditional site of the Emmaus of the New Testament from the sixteenth century."[17]

Later, a German hospice was built at this lovely site, and today there is a park where gazelles graze. The survey party concluded that of the various alternatives, the most probable site is Qubeiba, chiefly because its proximity to the main road, its attractive countryside, its name, and its distance from Jerusalem make this "identification ... evidently the most satisfactory yet proposed" (p. 40). Today, the small Moslem village is the site of a German hospice, a Franciscan compound, and also "the first Ave for the German sisters."[18]

The name El Qubeiba means "little dome" and is recorded in Arab documents of the twelfth century. It perhaps received its name from the dome of the Crusader structure. Because of

---

15. Clemens Kopp, *The Holy Places of the Gospel* (New York: Herder and Herder, 1963), p. 399.
16. Conder and Kitchener, *Survey,* vol. 1, p. 38.
17. Ibid., p. 17.
18. Hoade, *Guide to the Holy Land,* p. 544.

the distance to traditional Emmaus, the Crusaders selected a site nearer Jerusalem. Since the arrival of the Franciscans in A.D. 1335, it has been a place of pilgrimage. Excavations in 1940-1944 by Italian Franciscans determined the origin of the nearby village. They found that the Crusader structures rested on Byzantine habitations on ground inhabited from the third to the sixth centuries. Excavators concluded that this village arose in the Hellenistic period and was inhabited in Roman and Byzantine times.[19] The beautiful church, built in 1901, stands 260 feet above sea level and affords a splendid view that encompasses Jaffa to Mount Carmel. Above the door is a picture representing the Gospel scene. The structure is designed to preserve the ancient remains. The stained glass windows and the painting above the door are reminiscent of the supper described by Luke's Gospel. East of the Franciscan's property is a dispensary of the German sisters. The ancient Roman road between these buildings was the shortest from the city to the plain, but was not the most widely used. There is also a German hospice underneath the pines, admirably suited as a guest house.

The small tribe of Benjamin, therefore, despite its having been in Old Testament times nearly exterminated in civil war, played a major role in Biblical and subsequent history, a role which belies its present peaceful agrarian pursuits. So important did little Benjamin become that whereas Saul of Gibeah felt his tribal connection to be a handicap (1 Sam. 9:21), Saul of Tarsus considered it an asset (Phil. 3:5).

---

19. Ibid., p. 548.

The convent building southwest of the Church of the Nativity in Bethlehem.

9

Judea

Of all of the twelve tribes Judah was the most influential. Its leader and head was both earthy and noble. His patronizing of a harlot in Adullam, and his irresponsibility to his daughter-in-law, Tamar, speaks strongly against him (Gen. 38). On the positive side, Judah, the fourth son of Leah and Jacob, first revealed his leadership qualities at Dothan, where he objected to the murder of Joseph (Gen. 37). Later he volunteered to go surety for his younger brother Benjamin prior to their second trip to Egypt (Gen. 43:8-10). Confronted later by Joseph, Judah rose to the occasion and spoke one of the noblest pleas in Scripture or in any other literature. Judah interceded with Joseph in behalf of Benjamin and their father, offering to himself serve as a slave in lieu of his younger brother Benjamin (Gen. 44:18-34). This plea marks the climax of the exciting story of Joseph and his brothers. In Jacob's farewell blessing, Judah and Joseph received the most encouraging prophecies in spite of the fact that Reuben was the firstborn. Judah is presented as the recipient of his brothers' praise; he is compared to a lion and is assured that "the sceptre shall not depart from Judah . . . until he comes . . . to whom shall be the obedience of the peoples" (Gen. 49:10), a veiled reference to the dynasty of David and a prediction of the Messiah.

The borders assigned to Judah were extensive. The southern boundary stretched from the south end of the Dead Sea,

Boundaries of the Tribe

247

west to Kadesh Barnea, and to the Mediterranean at the mouth
of the "Wadi of Egypt," near modern El Arish. The east border
was the west shore of the Dead Sea. The north boundary extended west from the mouth of the Jordan at the Dead Sea,
along the southern border of Benjamin, past Kiriath-jearim and
continuing west to the Mediterranean. The Mediterranean comprised its western border (Josh. 15:1-63). This vast area included the hill country of Judea north of Beer-sheba and Arad,
the wilderness of the northern portion of the Negev, Judea west
of the Dead Sea, and all of the maritime plain south of the
plain of Sharon, including Philistia. The territory actually possessed by Judah however was considerably smaller, leaving much
of the southern area to the Edomites and the western area to
the Philistines. The territory allotted to the tribe of Simeon
was gradually absorbed by Judah, whereas Dan migrated from
its allotment on the west to the extreme north, in the vicinity
of Dan (Judg. 18:1-30). It seemed to be a case of the survival
of the fittest rather than the imposition of the fixed boundaries
guaranteed by a central authority. The most important area in
Judah from the standpoint of Biblical history lay between Hebron and Jerusalem, a twenty-five mile stretch running north
and south along the mountain spine.

THE WILDERNESS OF JUDEA

The northeast corner of Judah's territory comprises the extensive plain of chalky marl, which is like powder when dry
but like grease when wet. This wilderness extends south of the
modern road between Jerusalem and Amman, and spreads between the Dead Sea and the central highlands on the west.
Here, many believe, lay the valley of Achor, where Achan was
exposed and executed (Josh. 7). On the heights to the west overlooking this area, Herod the Great built the fortress Hyrcanus.
Later this was occupied by Byzantine monks, and today is only
a ruin (Khirbet el Mird). This area leaped into worldwide fame
during the past two decades as a result of the discovery of the
Dead Sea Scrolls in the numerous caves in the cliffs near the
shore of the Dead Sea. To the south is the oasis of Ein Fashkah,
a beauty spot consisting of a circular pool of clear fresh water
thirty feet in diameter surrounded by tall grasses.

A mile to the northwest of this oasis lies a narrow plateau
of white marl, on which now stands exposed the Essene sanc-
Qumran   tuary of Qumran, excavated by Jerusalem archaeologists from

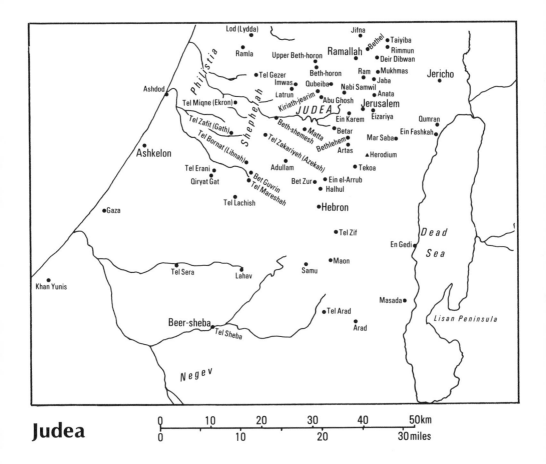

Judea

Map scale: 0 10 20 30 40 50km / 0 10 20 30 miles

1951 onward.[1] This excavation reveals a community dating back to the Iron Age, believed to be ancient Ir ham-Melah (Town of Salt), which was abandoned about the time of the Babylonian invasion.[2] The Essenes, a Jewish group of disciplined ascetics who had "dropped out" of the existing evil world to lead a holy life, settled here in the second century B.C. It was apparently destroyed by an earthquake, which, according to Josephus, occurred in 31 B.C. A crack in the stairs leading down under one of the larger cisterns seems to correspond with this evidence. Approximately thirty years later, it seems to have been reoccupied until the arrival of Vespasian's troops during the first Jewish revolt in A.D. 68. The excavations were carried out with great care by the École Biblique and the Jordanian Department of Antiquities. Visitors today can readily note the

1. Kurt Schubert, *The Dead Sea Community: Its Origin and Teachings,* trans. J. W. Doberstein (London: Adam & Charles Black, 1959), pp. 21-27.
2. Robert Boulanger, *Hatchette World Guides: The Middle East,* trans. J. S. Hardman (Paris: Hatchette, 1966), p. 576.

Archaeologists and students from the Hebrew University searching for remains of the past in the Judean wilderness.

tower on the north edge of the community, the aqueduct that
once brought water from the hills, the numerous cisterns that
conserved it, the remains of the bakery, the potter's kiln, the
dining hall, the town wall leading south, and the remains of
the thousand graves discovered on the hillside.[3]

Across a deep ravine, burrowed in a projection of the plateau into the adjacent wadi, one discerns the artificial cave,
known as Cave No. 4, where hundreds of thousands of tiny
fragments of priceless parchments were discovered. The original cave (No. 1) lies about a mile north. First discovered by
a Bedouin shepherd in 1947, this cave contained the seven best-
preserved of the scrolls, which are now located at the Scroll of
the Book in the Israeli Museum in Jerusalem. The scrolls were
first studied scientifically in the Rockefeller Museum of Jerusalem. The process still continues. Scholars had long since despaired
of finding material of this kind in Palestine, which, in contrast
to the climate of Egypt, makes preservation of such documents
very difficult. But the arid condition by the Dead Sea and the
care taken for their preservation has preserved, for scholars,
scrolls exceeding the age of the then-known Old Testament manuscripts by a thousand years. Scrolls produced by this Essene community include every book of the Bible except Esther. These
scrolls were apparently hidden before Vespasian's armies appeared in A.D. 70.

The area south of this, between the shores of the Dead Sea
and the cliffs to the west is one of the most desolate places on
the face of the globe. Even Bedouins and their flocks avoid it
because of its arid condition and rugged terrain. Israeli engineers have now completed a highway through this area, linking
the Qumran oasis with the oasis at En Gedi where David once
sought refuge from Saul.[4] Tourists can now be driven from
upper Galilee to Masada and back to Jerusalem in one day.

The late Bishop James A. Pike died in this desolate country
east of Bethlehem while attempting to gather information for
his book on the life of Christ. To the south, the caverns on the
Wadi Murabbaat between En Gedi and Masada yielded scrolls
and other artifacts of Jewish rebels of the second great revolt,
known as the Bar Kochba Revolt of A.D. 132-134. The writings

3. Frank Moore Cross, Jr., *The Ancient Library of Qumran and Modern
Biblical Studies* (Garden City, N.Y.: Doubleday and Co., 1958), pp. 37-39.
4. R. Vickers, "Israelis Push Tourism," *Wall Street Journal,* 27 April 1971.

and remnants of clothing fill important gaps in our understanding of the era.[5]

Still farther south is the site of Masada, a towering flat-topped and isolated mountain frowning over the southern end of the Dead Sea, across from the Lisan Peninsula. Here, Herod the Great found refuge from the Parthian invasion, and it was here that he provided for his own last defense. The strongest and best preserved of the Herodian fortresses is to be found here. The visitor today finds important places easily identified and is provided with a brochure describing in some detail what is to be seen. It is a vast outdoor museum of the final resistance movement of the First Revolt A.D. 66-73. From the top, the Roman walls below, surrounding the mountain, can easily be discerned, especially the camp of its leader Silva, under whose guidance a vast white ramp was built against the mountain which permitted the attackers to overcome a stubborn defense. Here 967 Jewish defenders chose to commit mass suicide rather than to face death at the hand of the besieging Romans. The site was skillfully excavated by archaeologist Yadin and his helpers. His published reports together with the site itself provide one of the most vivid descriptions of the siege.[6]

Masada testifies to the vigor and foresight as well as the ingenuity of Herod the Great in utilizing this natural rock for defense. It attests also the determination and resourcefulness of Roman armies. By far its most eloquent evidence concerns the resistance movement. Masada was perhaps the best fortified bastion of the ancient world, and it presented Rome with its most difficult wartime assignment.

Tourists today marvel at Herod's engineers in their construction of the three-story sumptuous palace on the extreme northeast corner of the cliff and of the provisions that enabled the garrison to withstand siege nearly four years.[7] In contrast to modern warfare, defense in the first century was relatively easy and attack relatively difficult.

South of the Lisan Peninsula the waters of the Dead Sea are very shallow. It is believed that this was once dry land and that the cities of Sodom and Gomorrah lay in the vicinity now

Masada

---

5. Moshe Pearlman and Yaacov Yannai, *Historical Sites in Israel* (New York: Vanguard Press, 1965), pp. 181-194.
6. Ibid., pp. 181-194.
7. Yigael Yadin, *Masada, Herod's Fortress and the Zealots' Last Stand*, trans. Moshe Pearlman (New York: Random House, 1966).

Air view of Masada rock, showing several of the excavated areas.

Cliffs along the western shore of the Dead Sea, looking north from the ascent to Masada rock by aerial car.

Dead Sea

covered by the saline water. The sea itself is "dead" in many aspects. The Hebrews called it the "Salt Sea"; Greeks, the "Asphalt Sea"; Latins, the "Dead Sea"; and Arabs, the "Sea of Lot." Its length is forty-seven miles and its average width, ten. The surface lies 1,286 feet below the level of the Mediterranean, whereas the bottom at its deepest point lies 2,601 feet below the Mediterranean surface. Evaporation under cloudless skies is so extensive that it balances the water constantly brought in by the Jordan, the Arnon, and other streams. The water is six times more salty than that of the ocean. Fish that are carried down by a floodtide into the sea soon die, becoming encrusted with salt. At the southern end, at the settlement of Sedom, one plant extracts potash and another magnesium from the waters. The road now continues south along the Arabah to the Gulf of Aqaba and the "twin" cities—Al Aqaba on the Jordan side and Eilat on the Israeli side of the frontier, which lies at the bottom of the Ghor. It is about 120 miles from the Dead Sea to Aqaba. The highest elevation in the valley of the Arabah

The Dead Sea, from the north shore.

The Judean wilderness as seen from the Jericho road halfway between Jerusalem and Jericho.

is 250 feet. Here in the "Valley of Salt" David's army defeated the Edomites in a great slaughter (2 Sam. 8:13).

From the north end of the Dead Sea across the northern boundary of Judea, the Jericho road ascends. There were actually three such roads—one built by the Romans and used at the time of Christ, one built during the British Mandate (1918-1948), and the modern road built in the early 1960s. It is fifteen miles to Jerusalem and the ascent is one of approximately 3,800 feet. Until the advent of the automobile and modern highways, travelers would often stop at the halfway point between Jerusalem and Jericho. At present, there are beside the old road, the ruins of a caravansary, or khan, where beasts and their riders could find accommodation. It is wild and rugged terrain. Anyone can sense the appropriateness of the locale for the parable of the Good Samaritan and his "neighbor" who "fell among thieves" (Luke 10). During the Ottoman period, pilgrims or merchants taking this road bought protection of the local Bedouin sheik or paid for an armed guard to accompany them.[8] During the

The
Jericho
Road

8. Pietro Casola, *Pilgrimage to Jerusalem, 1494,* trans. M. N. Newett (Manchester: University Press, 1907), pp. 260 ff.

Mar Saba, the Greek Orthodox monastery from the Byzantine period, which is situated along the Kidron canyon in the Judean wilderness.

Panorama of the Judean wilderness.

political riots of 1955, pilgrims moving from Amman to Jerusalem avoided the agitated rioters on the main road near Jericho by ascending to Jerusalem on the old Roman road, thus eluding harassment. The Greek and Russian Orthodox churches sponsored pilgrimages from Jerusalem to the Jordan for baptism at the traditional site of Saint John's ministry during the Feast of the Epiphany. Moslem leaders sought to offset this enthusiasm for Christian pilgrimages by establishing, off the Jericho road, a sanctuary entitled the Tomb of Moses, known locally as Nabi Musa (the prophet Moses). This is the grazing ground of the Taamireh Bedouins, discoverers of the Dead Sea Scrolls and subsequently the most successful finders of scrolls. A difficult trail leads south from here toward a famous Christian site known as Mar Saba. This Greek Orthodox monastery is perched on the west edge of the canyon of the Kidron which is known locally as the "Valley of Fire." John of Damascus, author of a well-beloved hymn, lies buried here. The founder of this and similar monasteries was Saint Saba, who inspired thousands by his example. During the centuries, the monastery has been attacked repeatedly and is now surrounded by protective walls. The travelers can expect to find here a cordial welcome and a place for quiet reflection. During the Byzantine period, the surrounding area was occupied by some 5,000 monks seeking a life of holiness in the desert of Judea.

Many readers of the Bible, impressed by the frequent references to the "wilderness of Judea," are surprised to find this area anything but a forest. The "wilderness" refers not to trees, but to its desolation and the absence of civilization. It is actually far less habitable than the Negev, the area lying to the south. In this virtually rainless wilderness of Judea, flora and fauna are nearly absent, and the landscape is not unlike that of the "Badlands" in the Dakotas. It has never supported a thriving population as has the Negev at certain times. The "wilderness of Judea" was a place of refuge. Both David and Herod found protection here. The Maccabeans retreated to this region awhile. The Bar Kochba rebels found refuge here, and the Jewish Essenes and later the Christian monks sought recluse here from an encroaching "evil world." The area lends authenticity to the psalmist's declaration that Yahweh could provide the protection that the sun would not smite him by day (Ps. 121:6). Isaiah spoke longingly of the "shade of a great rock in a weary land"

Wilderness of Judea

(Isa. 32:2). Just a short visit to this area leaves an indelible impression on the visitor, contributing a startling new significance to Biblical references regarding the "wilderness of Judea."

THE HILL COUNTRY OF JUDEA

A traveler ascending the Judean escarpment en route to Jerusalem passes the sea level mark about halfway up the hill. The grade itself is about twelve miles in length. After passing the traditional Inn of the Good Samaritan, the halfway point between Jericho and Jerusalem, he comes to a small spring, called the Apostles' Fountain, where the Jordanian government recently began a small tree nursery. The sight of Jerusalem's environs from this vantage point is impressive; the Mount of Olives dominates the horizon with two towers—the tower of Augusta Victoria and the Russian tower to the south. To the right lies the Arab village of Isawiya and farther to the north is Jeremiah's hometown, Anata (Anathoth). The modern highway makes a wide loop to the southeast through more tolerable terrain than the old road, but still visible on the old road are remnants of the trenches made during World War II by the British to stop anticipated German tanks (later, the one who planned the tank traps defected to the Germans). Also visible is part of the ancient aqueduct, which dates back to the Roman period. South of the Jericho road is the Arab village of Abu Dis, and farther ahead, the road bends around to the base of Mount Olivet at the Arab village of Eizariya, the Arabic version of "Lazarus." It is Lazarus who lends his name to this village referred to in the New Testament as Bethany, the home of Mary, Martha, and Lazarus, a suburb two miles east of Jerusalem, lying on the southeast slope of Mount of Olives. Lazarus's so-called tomb is reached by a modern entrance down some thirty steps to a vacant cubicle hewn out of a rock. The older entrance has long since been closed up. Over the site of the ancient church the beautiful new Chapel of the Resurrection has been erected. It consists of four arms of equal length with scenes on the four walls recalling Jesus' ministry in Bethany, especially His interview with Martha and Mary. Somewhat nearer Jerusalem is the church at Bethphage, marking the traditional spot where Jesus mounted a donkey for the ride to Jerusalem for His triumphal entry. The Mount of Olives is dominated by the Russian bell tower with its bells and platform 214 steps above the level of the ground. Here the White Sisters of the Russian convent lead

The Chapel of the Resurrection in Bethany; its walls include scenes recalling Jesus' ministry to Mary, Martha, and Lazarus.

their quiet life and attend the Russian Chapel of the Ascension. The domed ceiling of this structure features Jesus' ascension into the clouds watched by His wondering disciples, one of the most impressive chapel interiors in the whole area. The bells were "dragged" up to Jerusalem from Joppa. Moslems opposed the use of bells.

The view from this tower is superb. To the north is the Augusta Victoria Hospital beyond which lies a grove of pine trees, and beyond that, the east campus of the Hebrew University, now being rebuilt. To the east lies the whole expanse of the Jordan Valley and the wilderness of Judea, whereas to the south, rolling hills lead the eye to Tekoa, Herodium, and Bethlehem to the southwest. To the west, Jerusalem spreads out like an open book before the viewer. Beyond the Kidron Valley below, the old walled city blends imperceptibly with the extensive "new city" beyond. When Jesus surveyed the scene and reflected on Jerusalem's role in Biblical history, He was moved to compassion and wept over the wayward city—"because you did not know the time of your visitation" (Luke 19:44). That this Russian tower is nearer than the Latin chapel to the site of the Ascension is borne out by Luke's account which says that, "He led them out as far as Bethany" before His ascension (Luke 24:50).

Mount of Olives

Few places in the Holy Land are more thickly beset with churches than the Mount of Olives. More than twenty-five churches, chapels, and convents, past and present, can be identified. A short distance below and to the southwest lies the large and impressive Carmelite convent and the Church of the *Pater Noster*. The opening words of the Lord's Prayer in Latin give the name to this edifice. On the walls of the cloister, the Lord's Prayer is reproduced in nearly fifty languages on beautifully colored tiles. The most revered spot here is the shallow cave where some believe Jesus taught His disciples to pray in response to their request (Luke 11:1 ff.). In recent years, the new Intercontinental Hotel, built to resemble a caravansary with its seven arches, views the Kidron Valley and the former "City

The Church of All Nations and other religious structures on the slopes of the Mount of Olives.

of David" now south of the walls. The new road to this hotel leads through an ancient Jewish cemetery, below which is the extensive tomb known as the Tomb of the Judges. A Benedictine convent lies slightly to the west.

The most frequently visited place on the mountain is the site of the Latin Chapel of the Ascension, now converted into a mosque. Its central feature is the circular enclosure containing the rock from which Jesus is said to have ascended. Here was one of the four churches built by Helena, the mother of Constantine, as reported by Eusebius. The site thus marks one of the first imperial churches of the Christian era. From the roof of the mosque visitors get an impressive view of the Kidron Valley and old Jerusalem. The east wall of the old city presents an especially impressive sight. The limestone used for the wall, probably taken from "Solomon's quarries" underneath the north edge of the city, has now turned to a golden brown, and therefore is less dazzling than when described by Josephus or by the psalmist; but the wall is still very impressive.

The Dome of the Rock as seen from inside the Dominus Flevit Chapel on the Mount of Olives.

Not far to the east is the site of another medieval church on the ruins of which, in recent times, has risen the reconstructed chapel known as *Dominus Flevit* ("The Lord wept"); its onion-shaped dome testifies to its Russian Orthodox architecture. The temple area is beautifully framed by the west window of this chapel. Below, amid olive trees, is a portion of the Garden of Gethsemane.

Below this is the Latin Garden of Gethsemane, featuring eight gnarled olive trees, very ancient and said to date from the first century. Adjoining it, built over the remains of an older building, is the relatively modern Church of All Nations. The facade, facing the Kidron, is of mosaics featuring Gethsemane, and inside, surrounded by wrought iron resembling thorns, is the bare rock where Jesus is said to have sweat great drops of blood while His disciples slept. The garden is a beauty spot, tended by Franciscans who are designated by the Pope as the official custodians of the Holy Land. Although this spot is beautiful and well attended, the Russian Gethsemane, higher on the hill, is probably more like the olive orchard Jesus knew. Across the road and toward the bottom of the Kidron Valley is a low structure that honors the Virgin Mary; tradition claims it to be the place where she was laid to rest before her ascension into heaven. This was the crypt of a church demolished by Saladin in A.D. 1187 along with the adjacent Benedictine abbey founded by Godfrey of Bouillon. Before the Crusades, this upper church was octagonal in form, similar to the one on Mount Gerizim, and dates back to about A.D. 455. East of this ancient church lies the Greek Garden of the Agony. So the "garden of Gethsemane" is presented in three versions—the Russian, the Latin, and the Greek. The exact place, however, where Jesus prayed is unknown. The Mount of Olives and Mount Scopus to the north are actually part of the same ridge with merely a slight depression separating the two summits. This slight depression is linked by some with the prophecy in Zechariah, that when the Messiah returns the Mount of Olives shall be cleft in two (Zech. 14:4-5). A severe earthquake rent Olivet in 1927. On the crest of Olivet is a large Greek Orthodox monastery called *Viri Galilee* ("men of Galilee"), an allusion to Acts 1:11 when the angel said, "Men of Galilee, why do you stand looking into heaven?" Between this monastery and the Russian Chapel of the Ascension is a large modern hospital. For two decades members of the Arab Legion kept watch here during the period of armistice from 1948 to 1967. It is a reminder of the condition Jesus recognized when He indicated that Jerusalem was a city of peace and yet was famous for its wars. The city has experienced war some forty-eight different times during its turbulent history.[9] Prayers for the peace of Jerusalem, such as requested by the psalmist (Ps. 122:6), have often gone unanswered. Yet this venerable living museum remains the symbol of peace and hope.

Job's well (En-rogel) is listed as one of the original boundaries of the tribal allotment (Josh. 15:7). It lies at the confluence of the Brook Kidron and the Hinnom Valley. It is also called the Dragon's Fountain, and it was here that Adonijah rallied his friends in support of his claim to be David's successor as king, only to be thwarted by the quick action of Nathan, Bathsheba, and Solomon (1 Kings 1:9). On the south bank of the Hinnom Valley are ancient sepulchres, under the jurisdiction of the Greek Orthodox church, which are linked with Acaldema, the Field of Blood, or Potter's Field. Jesus' corpse would have been

Hinnom Valley

---

9. George Adam Smith, *Jerusalem ... to A.D. 70* (New York: A. C. Armstrong and Son, 1908), vol. 2, p. 580.

abandoned here had it not been for the courageous intervention of Nicodemus and Joseph. On the summit to the southwest of the old city is the compound built as the Government House for the British Commissioner during the Mandate, which has since 1948 served as the headquarters of the United Nations Truce Commission. It is near the traditional site where Judas bargained to betray Jesus, and therefore has been called by church tradition the "Hill of Evil Counsel." In recent years, complaints were brought here to the United Nations Truce Commission by both Arabs and Jews with the result that both sides agreed that it was still a "hill of evil counsel" since neither agreed with the Commission's decisions. It is now an international enclave surrounded by Israel. About noon on June 5, 1967, elements of the Jordanian army took possession of the area, only to be rebuked by the United Nations in session in New York. Later they were driven out by the Israeli counterattack. To the west is the vicinity of Ramat Rahel, an Iron Age fortress honoring Rachel, Jacob's favorite wife. Jewish archaeologists have recently uncovered important structures illustrating life at this Jerusalem suburb during the Old Testament Kingdom period. Below this vantage point to the northwest is the valley of Rephaim. This was the scene of a Philistine attack when King David came to power by occupying Jerusalem. David's forces successfully routed the invaders by following the Lord's instructions to hold off their attack on the Philistines from ambush until they heard a sound of marching in the balsam trees. The valley of Sorek reaches Jerusalem at this point and through this valley British engineers built the railroad that linked Jerusalem with the maritime plain. Today travelers can ride through an impressive canyon to Tel Aviv and to Haifa. At one time pilgrims would arrive in Jerusalem from Cairo or Joppa by this means. In December of 1917, the Turkish mayor of Jerusalem borrowed a white bedsheet from the American colony and went forth to reach the vanguard of the British army while the Turkish garrison was rapidly retreating in the opposite direction. The dramatic event marked the end of four centuries of Ottoman rule.

On the west bank of the Hinnom Valley lies the Monastery of the Cross, a medieval structure that prizes as a relic a portion of the tree from which the "true cross" is alleged to have been taken. An anonymous pilgrim of the eleventh century was shown an altar which stood where the stump of the tree is said to have been.[10] Ever-growing west Jerusalem spreads over the hills and valleys of this area.

To the west of Jerusalem, on the traditional border of Judah, lies Kiriath-jearim where the Ark came to rest and where the Crusaders built a church with walls as thick as a fortress. High **Kiriath-** on the hill looking over this medieval church is an example **jearim** of misguided veneration for the Virgin Mary. On the roof of the church is a picture of the Ark, of the time of Samuel, and astride it is a statue of Mary. The modern name for the town is Abu Ghosh (Father of Ghosh). The name is that of an Arab robber-chieftain who in the early nineteenth century controlled this territory and exacted tolls from pilgrims ascending to Jerusalem. His clan was tolerated by the Turks but broken by Ibrahim Pasha of Egypt.[11] From this place, where the Ark rested for so long, it is a short distance to Bet-Shemesh (Beth-shemesh) on the border with ancient Philistia. From here, the distance to the Dead Sea is eighteen miles and to the Mediterranean Sea about twenty miles.

Just southwest of Jerusalem is Ein Karem, the traditional birthplace of John the Baptist. Viewed from the highway that leads from Jerusalem to the coast, the village lies in a deep, picturesque valley between the viewer and Nabi Samwil, which **Ein Karem** dominates the horizon to the northeast. The name, "Fountain of the Vineyard," is appropriate to describe this village. The population numbers about 2,000. The valley is linked with the Wadi Beit Hanina, north of Jerusalem, and a branch of the Sorek Valley, west of Jerusalem. Ein Karem appears to be linked with the Jearim of Joshua 15:60 (LXX) and perhaps is the Beth-haccherem of Jeremiah 6:1. Since the fourth century, it has been regarded as the home of Zechariah, Elizabeth, and John. The Virgin Mary came here after the annunciation to greet Elizabeth, who was then six months pregnant (Luke 1:46-55). Here may be found the monastery of Saint John, which houses the Franciscans and also encloses the Church of John the Baptist. Adjoining is the Chapel of Elizabeth. The first fifth-century church was destroyed during the Samaritan revolt. At the bottom of the hill is the fountain called Spring of Our Lady Mary (Ain Citti Miryam). Farther west on the hillside is the

---

10. *Anonymous Pilgrim No. 2* (London: Palestine Pilgrims' Text Society, 1894), vol. 6, p. 11.
11. William M. Thomson, *The Land and the Book* (Hartford, Conn.: S. S. Scranton, Co., 1908), p. 61.

Church of the Visitation. Excavations reveal Byzantine remains followed by Frankish buildings. Nearby is the Russian Church of Saint John with a bell tower. West of Ein Karem is a region designated the "Desert of Saint John," where the Franciscans erected a chapel commemorating Elizabeth's retirement and probable death. Thus there are at least five religious structures linking this area with John the Baptist. Ten sites have been proposed as the place of John's birth. Theodosius (530) is one of the earliest writers to have designated Ein Karem, and by the end of Crusader rule the tradition was well established.[12] There is nothing to suggest that the "Desert of Saint John" is the "wilderness" (*arabah*) referred to by Luke as the area where John spent his youth. It is more likely that this would be found in the vicinity of Qumran near the Dead Sea.

This is the main historic road from Jerusalem to Jaffa. Over this route, or one near it, presumably came the material for building the temple and palaces of Jerusalem. In Solomon's day, material that had been rafted down from Lebanon was labori-

---

12. Clemens Kopp, *The Holy Places of the Gospels* (New York: Herder and Herder), pp. 88-96.

The town of Ein Karem, the traditional birthplace of John the Baptist, just southwest of Jerusalem.

ously transported overland. This is the road over which Russian women pilgrims struggled up the hills bringing the great bells that now hang in the Russian tower on the Mount of Olives. Pilgrims of many centuries, after landing at Jaffa, made their way toward Jerusalem by mule, horse, donkey, or on foot. Today, paralleling this road on the north, a modern four-lane highway links the coastal area with the Holy City, this new road having been constructed after 1968. Traces of the old Roman road are in evidence from the vicinity of Ein Karem ascending the last hill before Jerusalem. Paralleling this, and to the south, is the so-called Burma Road built by the Israelis as a by-pass to reach besieged Jerusalem in 1948 while the Arab Legion commanded the regular road from the fortress at Latrun. In the struggles of 1947 and 1948, Israeli forces were unable to dislodge the Arab legion from the heights of Latrun from which they commanded two major highways leading to the hill country—the southern branch leading to Jerusalem, the northern branch leading past Imwas to Beth-horon. Latrun was repeatedly one of the major military command posts in Palestine. This prominence jutting from the Judean headlands into the coastal area forms a conspicuous point of strategic importance. To the west of Latrun lies ancient Gezer, a Canaanite city never conquered by the invading Israelites under Joshua. For centuries it was under the control of Egypt, as recent archaeological excavations indicate.

Traveling south on the modern highway running along the Shephelah between the hill country and the lowlands one comes to Bet-Shemesh (Beth-shemesh) on the ancient border of Judah. Philistine country lay to the west, the Judean hill country to the east. Bet-Shemesh ("House of the Sun") is now a tell of modest size, encrusted by ruins that are partially excavated. Eusebius described it as being ten miles north of Eleutheropolis (Beit Jibrin). It was identified by Edward Robinson as the mound west of the village of Ain Shems, which lies in the valley of Sorek. The site was excavated by the Palestine Exploration Fund under the direction of D. Mackenzie in 1911 and 1912. Between 1928 and 1933, Haverford College conducted five seasons of excavation. The city flourished especially during the Late Bronze Age (stratum four), but it enters Biblical history during the Iron Age of Israel's early period, revealed in stratum three where an excellent collection of Philistine ware was un-

Beth-shemesh

covered. Apparently it was occupied by the Israelites but still under the "political and economic domination of the Philistines." The city ceased to have significance after its destruction by the Babylonians in the sixth century.[13]

Beth-shemesh is the village to which the oxen carting the sacred Ark returned from Ekron (1 Sam. 6:9-19). It was obviously a border village at that time and continued as such for some years thereafter (2 Chron. 28:18). The confrontation between Amaziah the king of Judah and Jehoash the king of Israel, who "looked one another in the face" at Beth-shemesh, also indicates that it was on the border between Judah and Israel. A glance at a modern map indicates that Beth-shemesh was a strategically located site lying at the crossroads—the road to Jerusalem through the valley of Sorek and also the north-south highway between the Shephelah and the hill country.

Azekah

Farther south, about six miles, is Tel Azekah, scene of the conflict between David and Goliath. Azekah lies adjacent to the valley of Elah, which leads toward Bethlehem. In this dramatic event the Philistines camped between Socoh and Azekah on the west side of the valley, and the Israelites camped on the east side at Kefar Zekharya (1 Sam. 17:1-3). The Elah Valley between is a shallow vale extending in a southeasterly direction. Through the valley runs a small brook presumably where David and the Philistine met and where David selected extra stones for his arsenal. David could have reached the site from his home in Bethlehem in a half-day's downhill journey. The victorious Israelites, following David's victory, pursued the Philistines westward down the valley to Gath (Tel Zafit) and to Ekron (Tel Miqne). For centuries this was disputed territory between the Philistines and the men of Judah. The Philistines at one time penetrated as far as the suburbs of Jerusalem, only to be driven back by David.

Other border villages include Adullam, to the south and east of Azekah, and Kielah, the city that betrayed David's whereabouts to his enemy Saul (1 Sam. 23:11-13). The presumed cave of Adullam is east of Bethlehem, but the city of Adullam is to the southwest. These border villages existed in constant uncertainty between the political fortunes of the powers to the west and to the east, between the hill country and the maritime plain.

---

13. George Ernest Wright, "Beth-Shemesh," *The Biblical World,* ed. C. F. Pfeiffer (Baker Book House, 1966), pp. 145-149.

This usually led to a policy of expediency in which they would ally themselves with the dominant power without any firm political alliance of their own, other than that of self-preservation. This helps explain the betrayal of Samson and later the betrayal of David to his enemies (Judg. 15:11; 1 Sam. 23:12).

Later, when the kingdom of Judah was even smaller, Betar (Battir), a strongpoint ten miles southwest of Jerusalem, became a border fortress between Judah and Edom (later, Idumea). During the Bar Kochba Revolt A.D. 132-135, the rebels had to abandon Jerusalem during the third year of the revolt. Driven from Jerusalem and menaced on all sides, the defenders gathered in Betar. The fortress, situated on a hill, overlooked a deep canyon and was protected by a ditch on the south. It was a strong site except for the lack of water. The Romans surrounded the defenders and starved them into submission in the summer of A.D. 135, killing the defenders including the leader, Bar Kochba. The road from the ruins of the fortress (Betar) leads east from the railroad that goes through Wadi Sorek and leads toward Bethlehem.

Betar

To the east lie two important cities from the Biblical standpoint, namely Bethlehem and Tekoa. Just northeast of Bethlehem is the village of Beit Jala. This suburb of Bethlehem which numbers 2,000 inhabitants, is situated on a hill higher than Bethlehem, affording a view of the vast area to the east, north, and south. Jerusalem is clearly visible on the north horizon, but between Jerusalem and the viewer lies Ramat Rahel. Nearer, on the recently reopened direct route from Jerusalem to Bethlehem, is the monastery of Mar Elias, a Byzantine sanctuary rebuilt in A.D. 1160. According to a tradition, Elijah was given nourishment by the angel at this spot before continuing his route to Sinai (this actually occurred farther south—"into the wilderness"—1 Kings 19:4-8). Opposite is a stone seat honoring the artist Holman Hunt, who painted "The Scape Goat" here. Just north of Bethlehem is Rachel's tomb (Gen. 35:19-20; 1 Sam. 10:2). The present building has two sections—a Moslem sanctuary erected by Sultan Murad I (1623-1640) and an addition by the Jewish philanthropist, Montefiore, in 1847.[14]

To the east lies Bethlehem and beyond that Herodium, Tekoa, and the wilderness of Judea with its numerous caves,

---

14. Rappoport Angelos, *History of Palestine* (New York: E. P. Dutton and Co., 1931), p. 316.

Terraced slopes below Beit Sahur, a suburb of Bethlehem. The Herodium is visible on the horizon.

many of which formerly housed numerous Anchorites or hermits. The city of Beit Jala is supposed by some to be the Old Testament city of Giloh, the birthplace of Ahithophel (Josh. 15:51; 1 Sam. 10:2; 2 Sam. 15:12). It is believed that many of its 3,000 inhabitants are descendants of the Crusaders. Its elevation makes it a favorite summer resort for residents of Jerusalem.

Bethlehem

One of the most important attractions in the whole area is Bethlehem; its claim to wide recognition is its intimate association with Biblical history throughout both the Old and New Testaments. It is linked not only with Rachel's burial, but with Naomi, Ruth, Boaz, and their child Obed. It is the "city of David," and shepherds to the east can still be seen tending flocks in much the same manner in which David did when Samuel came to the home of Jesse in quest of the future king (1 Sam. 16:1-13). The city is hailed by Micah as the birthplace of Israel's redeemer (Mic. 5:1). It is Bethlehem's link with David's greater Son, however, that gives the city its chief claim to fame today. The same fields where the shepherds first heard

the "good news" lie east of the city, on the plains extending eastward toward the Dead Sea.

Bethlehem's population numbered 32,000 in 1967.[15] Most of the Bethlehem residents are Christian Arabs. Their main industry is catering to tourists. Since 1967, Bethlehem has been seeking to be included in the municipality of Jerusalem to enjoy some of its economic benefits, but the Israeli authorities have not yet done so. For the Christian, Bethlehem is one of the most holy places in Palestine. This was recognized first by Helena, mother of Constantine, who built one of the four first Christian churches of the Constantine era here on the presumed site of the nativity. The present structure on this site was built by Justinian, who intended it as one of the best examples of churches in his extensive empire. His builders did well. This is the only church in Palestine that was not destroyed by the Persians in 614. They spared the struc-

15. Misha Louvish, ed., *Facts About Israel, 1970* (Jerusalem: Keter Books, 1970), p. 53.

ture because they saw on the walls pictures of three wise men, who they recognized as Persians. The exterior now resembles a grim fortress. The interior, by contrast, reveals a beautiful basilica of the Byzantine period, one of the best of its kind in the world. The steps on either side of the altar lead to the cave below, where the birth-site of Jesus is identified by a fourteen-point silver star. The adjoining chapels commemorate the slaughter of the innocents and the longtime residence there of Jerome, the leading church scholar (fl. A.D. 400) of the ancient church.

East of the city are the traditional shepherd's fields; one field has structures built by the Byzantines, another field is owned by the Anglican Church, and still another features a cave owned by other Protestants. Extending over these plains are occasional small stone houses now owned by the Taamireh tribe of Bedouins, who have become relatively affluent and sedentary after their success in finding and selling Dead Sea Scrolls. Another suburb of Bethlehem is Beit Sahur a community of about 3,000

A street scene at Manger Square in Bethlehem.

The prominent hill southeast of Bethlehem known as Herodium, where Herod built one of his fortresses.

people. The name means "village of shepherds." The village itself, which has a history dating back to the Bronze Age, includes a Latin church, a girls' school, a Greek church, a small seminary, an Orthodox church, and a Lutheran school. Eusebius mentioned a nearby "Tower of the Flocks" (Tower Ader), but this, along with many other religious structures, is in ruins.

Four miles southeast of Bethlehem is a conspicuous hill known by several names—including Frank Mountain, *Jebel Foureidis* (Hill of Paradise), and Herodium. This is the site where Herod the Great won a victory over Antigonus in 42 B.C. To commemorate this, Herod built a fortress on the summit, called Herodium, and at the base of the hill he established a town called Herodia. Herod died in Jericho, but he was buried in this mountain fifteen days later. Excavation of his fortress began in 1962. The burial place of Herod, who played such a major role in the history of the Near East, is visited primarily by archaeologists, whereas the birthplace of the infant he sought to destroy is visited by millions. It is a vivid reminder that the nativity of Jesus did not occur in the peaceful surroundings of a stable society, but rather in the midst of tyranny and at the risk of life.

Herodium

Tekoa

About two miles south of Herodium, and 300 feet higher, is the hometown of Amos, Tekoa. Scattered over a large area on the summit are fallen building stones with the foundation of a wall along the north edge and the ruins of a Byzantine church that include a beautiful baptismal font. Nearby are ancient tombs dating to the Roman period. Today, farmers till their crops amidst the stones on the summit, illustrating a Biblical expression that sowing on a site is the ultimate evidence of its complete destruction. Tekoa is linked not only with Amos but also with Rehoboam, who fortified it (2 Chron. 2:6); it was also the home of the woman who assisted in the reconciliation between David and Absalom (2 Sam. 14).

Judean Wilderness

The vast desert to the east, visible from this hilltop, has been for centuries a place of refuge. David used it for this purpose, and he described himself as hunted like a partridge by Saul; here David lived so precariously that he could say "there is but a step between me and death" (1 Sam. 20:3). Later the Essenes found asylum here. They were Jewish recluses who fled, not for their lives, but from an environment which they felt was hostile to the cultivation of their personal sanctity. A few centuries later, Christian monks sought refuge here, likewise to escape from the world. To a modern visitor, the area seems to be "a God-forsaken place," but ascetics in impressive numbers have felt nearer to God here than anywhere else. Of the hundreds of monastic cells in the cliffs east of here, the monastery of Mar Saba is the only one remaining in use. In New Testament times a good military road led from Herodium to Masada by the Dead Sea. It took about eight hours by mule to travel from Herodium to Masada, the refuge to which Herod once fled with his family.

Among the other numerous monastic foundations and ruins in the wilderness area is the impressive summit of the Jebel El Muntar, about 1,200 feet in height, from which the Mount of Olives is discernible. It is traditionally associated with the Levitical scapegoat (Lev. 16:7-26) which was ceremonially released in the wilderness. On this summit Empress Eudoxia built a tower to confer with Saint Euthymius, by whose counsel she was reclaimed from monophysitism to orthodoxy.[16] In the excitement associated with the discovery of the Dead Sea Scrolls,

---

16. Eugene Hoade, *Guide to the Holy Land,* 4th ed. (Jerusalem: Franciscan Press, 1962), p. 554.

The baptismal font from the large Byzantine church at the site of Tekoa. One of the finest baptistries yet uncovered in Palestine, it is composed of a pinkish semi-metamorphosed limestone that has the appearance of marble.

Sheep and children on a barren, rocky hillside at Tekoa.

the local Bedouins conducted an unauthorized excavation of the site, making identification of the tombs and buildings very difficult.

Water has always been in short supply in this Judean hill country. Solomon is credited with bringing water to Jerusalem from the springs south of Bethlehem. Three reservoirs, now called "Solomon's Pools," were built here by the British during the Mandate period. Near the highway are the remains of the Turkish fort that formerly safeguarded these important springs. Herod the Great constructed an aqueduct that brought water from these springs to his fortress at Herodium and possibly to Jerusalem. Since the British Mandate, Bethlehem is supplied with water from this source. The valley to the east leads to the village and spring of Urtas (Artas), where women still come to draw water. Nearby is a beautiful convent honoring Mary, "Our Lady of the Garden," rebuilt in 1921.[17]

The hill or plateau gradually rises in elevation southward to the vicinity of Hebron. This has made possible the building of gravity aqueducts to convey water to Jerusalem, not only from Solomon's Pools but from still more copious sources of water at Arrub. From here, Pilate, after robbing the temple treasury, an act which infuriated the priests, built an aqueduct that supplied Jerusalem with needed water.[18]

The British installed a pumping station at Arrub in 1918, and in recent years a supplemental pipe has carried additional water to east Jerusalem. This area was strategic in the Maccabean War. To the west of Arrub is Beit Zeiten, probably the Beth-zaith from which Bacchides harassed the guerrillas under Judas Maccabeus. Nearby is Khirbet Kufin with a vast reservoir that perhaps once was the mass grave of the Jews killed by Bacchides in 162 B.C.; "he seized many of the men . . . and killed them, and threw them into the great pit" (1 Macc. 7:19).[19]

Farther south and west of the main highway are the extensive ruins of a twelfth-century tower of Beit Zur ((Beth Zur). The Canaanite city of Beth Zur (Josh. 15:18) was strengthened by Rehoboam (2 Chron. 11:7) and, during the time of the Maccabees, was a frontier between Judea and Idumea. Here in 165 B.C., Judas Maccabaeus with 10,000 soldiers defeated Lysias, who had an army of 65,000 (1 Macc. 5:26-35). Lysias and

17. Ibid., p. 406.
18. Jos. *Antiq.* XVIII. 3. 2.
19. Hoade, *Guide to the Holy Land,* p. 408.

the Syrians had come from the southwest by Maresha and approached the border fortress of Judea by a relatively easy route of access, thus avoiding the narrow passes farther north, scene of previous defeats (1 Macc. 4:28-61). The site was excavated by American archaeologists Albright and Sellers in 1931, and in 1957 the work was resumed under the same auspices, confirming the authenticity of the site. After this victory, Judas was able to occupy Jerusalem and rededicate the temple, thus instituting the Festival of Lights (Hanukkah), which survives to this day among the Jews. Three years later, however, not far from Beit Zur, Judas and his men faced another army under Lysias. This time the Syrians were successful, and after the success at Beth Zechariah (ten miles southwest of Jerusalem) they advanced and occupied Jerusalem (1 Macc. 6:28-63; 2 Macc. 13: 1-23). Later, Beit Zur, with Bethel, Beth-horon, Emmaus, Tekoa, and Jericho, was used by the Syrians as a series of fortresses to keep Judah in subjugation.[20]

Still later, Beit Zur and Jerusalem remained the only garrisons that the Syrians were able to occupy. Both, however, were captured by Simon in 145 B.C., thus facilitating the second golden age of Judean history, the period of Maccabean indpendence which lasted from 142 to 63 B.C. (1 Macc. 13:33; 14:7). Today there remain only the remnants of the Byzantine tower and a Crusader tower.

Opposite Beit Zur and at the east of the main highway is Ain Dirweh, an important spot for pilgrims known as "Philip's Fountain." According to tradition, including the map of Madaba, this was where Philip baptized the eunuch of Ethiopia (Acts 8:36-39). According to the Scriptures, however, it was a desert area near Gaza, far to the southwest. Until recent times, men and women came here to draw water, the women with earthenware jars or tin cans, the men with goatskins on mules. A church once stood east of here; the area also shows rock-cut tombs and traces of a Roman road. One of the highest places in this region is Halhul, with 2,000 inhabitants, at an elevation of 3,340 feet. It is a Canaanite town mentioned in Joshua 15:58 and believed by the rabbis to contain the tomb of Gad the prophet (2 Sam. 24:11).

Near Hebron and east of the main highway is the important enclosure of Haram Ramat el Khalil, Arabic for "the

20. Jos. *Antiq.* XIII. 5-8, 15.

Mamre

high place of the friend" (meaning Abraham). This marks the traditional site of the Oak of Mamre, Mamre being the name of an Amorite family (Gen. 14:13; 15:13). It was here that Abraham learned of the capture of Lot. Later, while resting under the oak tree, Abraham received three angels unawares and learned of the imminent fate of Sodom and Gomorrah (Gen. 18). The site where the tree once stood is surrounded by a vast enclosure including Herodian walls on the south and the west and the "well of Abraham" in the southwest corner where shepherds still water their flocks. The constructions, as discovered by archaeologists, are those by Herod the Great, by the emperor Hadrian, the basilica by Constantine, and the restoration by Modestus. Structures of Arab origin have also been discovered. Objects dating from the time of Abraham have been found here, and two towers attributed to the Israelite period have been identified. Mamre was a sacred place from prehistoric times, long before Abraham "built an altar to the Lord" (Gen. 13:18) here. Pagan rites, in addition to Jewish and Christian rites, were observed at this site until the Arab invasion. (A.D. 640).[21]

From a point near here, an impressive view of the southern end of the Dead Sea unfolds to the southeast, where Abraham is said to have witnessed the destruction of the cities rising like the smoke of a furnace (Gen. 19:28). The rival site is a living oak to the west of the highway surrounded by an iron fence and guarded by a convent occupied by White Russian monks. Mamre, however, without the tree, appears to be the authentic site. The other site has an ancient oak but not a clear claim to authenticity.

Hebron

The third most important city of the Judean hill country is Hebron, one of the oldest cities in the Bible, formerly known as Kiriath-arba and once inhabited by giants according to Numbers 13:33. It lies in a valley between two mountain ranges, the ancient site being on an adjacent hill, El Arbain, on the southwest. The site was recently excavated by an American expedition headed by Philip Hammond.

The modern city includes a population of nearly 40,000. In the riots of 1929 the synagogue was destroyed, and since then no Jews have lived here. Jews are now, however, reoccupying

21. V. R. Gold, "Mamre," *Interpreter's Dictionary of the Bible* (Nashville: Abingdon, 1962), vol. 2, p. 235.

some of the suburbs over the protests of the local residents. The chief Biblical interest lies in its ancient cave purchased by Abraham from the Hittites (Gen. 23). In selecting the first capital of his realm, David chose Hebron rather than Bethlehem because it was more centrally located. Its isolation gave it strength, and it was far enough removed from the Philistines on the west and the Amalekites on the south to be defensible. It lay athwart important trade routes: one led east to the oasis of En Gedi, another led southwest to Beer-sheba, another south to Arad, one west to Bet Guvrin and Maresha, and the other north to Bethlehem and Jerusalem.

Hebron marks the southern terminus of the hill country of Judea. From this height the land slopes down rapidly to the east, but gradually to the west and south. It is relatively fertile; the patches of rich soil lend themselves to the culture of grapes and small grain. To the south, grazing land is excellent. It was here that Nabal had extensive holdings. Here David and his brigands survived without pillaging the flocks of the

Sultan's Pool at Hebron.

local residents. Abner met his death here at the "well of Sirah" (Ain Sareh) a spring, now very difficult to find, on the northern suburbs of Hebron to the west of the highway (2 Sam. 3:26).

Hebron is known for its manufacture of glass and for the marketing of goatskins for water carriers and sheepskins for garments. It is a trade center serving the hinterland to the south and west. Hebron played no part in New Testament history, but because of the tomb of the patriarchs, it is one of the holiest cities both to Jews and to Moslems. The sacred cave is inaccessible, but it marks the resting place of Abraham and Sarah to which cenotaphs for Rebekah, Isaac, Leah, and Jacob later were added. One of the strangest buildings of this area is a windowless fortress, 193 feet by 112 feet, with huge drafted stones erected by Herod the Great and supplemented by Mameluke construction. In the southern part of this enclosure is a building originally Byzantine and later Crusader and now a mosque, with the cenotaphs of the patriarchs on the floor over the tomb, which is visible only through a hole in the floor. The Crusaders called Hebron "Saint Abraham," and it became a bishopric. Saladin recaptured it in 1187, Allenby occupied it on December 4, 1917, and the town surrendered to the Israelis on the evening of Wednesday, June 7, 1967.[22]

"THE NEGEB OF JUDAH" (Judg. 1:16)

South of Hebron is what the Bible calls the Negev (or Negeb) of Judah. It includes Tell Zif, three miles from Hebron to the southeast, and continues on to Carmel with its ruined churches, and to Maon, now a low hill with some collapsed caverns surrounded by tobacco and wheat fields. It was here that Abigal pacified an enraged David after he was insulted by the rancher, Nabal. Here, David acquired Abigal as his second wife. Her resourcefulness would seem to have qualified her better than Bathsheba to have been the mother of David's successors (1 Sam. 25:14-42). Directly east is the wilderness of Judea and En Gedi by the Dead Sea. The village of Samu (Eshtemoa) figured prominently in world headlines in November 1966, when the Israeli army allegedly destroyed 126 houses in the town in reprisal for border raids.

Ten miles farther south is the village of Arad (which was mentioned on national television September 13, 1971). Exca-

Arad

22. Randolph S. Churchill and Winston S. Churchill, *The Six Day War* (Boston: Houghton Mifflin Co., 1967), p. 146.

vations by Israeli archaeologists disclosed civilizations going back to the Bronze Age. Amid a desert virtually devoid of vegetation, it lies near the main road between Beer-sheba and the Dead Sea. Its value as an achaeological site is that its early history has not been covered by subsequent residences and structures. It is on the border of Judah and was the site of an important battle between the Israelites and the king of Arad, who blocked their attempt to enter Palestine from the south (Num. 14:44, 45; 21:1-3; 33:40; Deut. 1:41-44). After being repulsed at Arad and Hormah, they retreated to their base at Kadesh Barnea. Later, however, the tribe of Simeon was victorious here, as reported in Judges 1:16, 17. Excavation that has extended over seven seasons traces the city back to the Chalcolithic Age. After long nonoccupancy, it was occupied by Israel in the Iron Age, testified to by well-preserved artifacts and clearly stratified layers.[23]

There are now two Arads: the modern Arad is one of the faster-growing cities of modern Israel. Arad is important because hotel facilities make it a gateway for the Arabah, leading to the road to Elat, and a convenience for those visiting nearby Masada or Sedom at the Dead Sea. Thus it seems to be having another rejuvenation after a "rest period" of over a millennium.

Another important city of Judea is Beer-sheba, which was another border city of Judah. For centuries it was the gateway to the Negev. It is important because it is an oasis in a waterless region. The seven wells are linked with Abraham. More than any other city in the Holy Land, this one marks the division between the nomadic and the pastoral peoples. Along with Gaza, it was on the boundary between Canaan and Egypt. Today the waters of Galilee provide irrigation so that the desert is receding to the south. The deep loess soil of the area is very productive when given sufficient water. Around the ancient city, therefore, has grown up a modern city serving travelers to and from the Negev. Bedouin tribes nearby, however, continue to give it the flavor of a pastoral economy into which industry has intruded. It was here that Allenby's forces gained the initial advantage over Turkish defenders before returning to attack Gaza and moving up the coast toward Jaffa and Jerusalem.

Beer-sheba

23. Yohanan Aharoni, "Tell Arad," *Israel Exploration Journal* (1963): 334-337.

Avdat, in the Negev, as it appears from the air after excavation and restoration.

10

The Negev

The word *Negev* (Negeb) means "south" (cf. Gen. 12:9 KJV). It refers to the area south of the province of Judah (1 Sam. 27:10; Ps. 126:4). This is a vast area when compared to the rest of the Holy Land. On a modern map of Israel, the distance from Beer-sheba to the Mountain of Moses (Jebel Musa) is greater than from Beer-sheba to Dan at the base of Mount Hermon. In a larger sense, the entire area from Mount Hermon in Lebanon to the Mountain of Moses in Sinai is the Holy Land. Gebel Musa is linked not only with Moses but also with Elijah, whereas Mount Hermon is linked not only with the psalmist but also with Elijah and Jesus.

Another reason for including this extensive area in the geography of the Holy Land is the position it has recently acquired in the continuing Arab-Israeli conflict, especially in 1956 and since 1967. The armistice of 1948-49 defined the boundary between Israel and Egypt as a line from the Gulf of Aqaba to a point on the Mediterranean southwest of Khan Yunis. The area around Gaza had a unique status placed on it by the United Nations, making it separate from but under the control of Egypt and called the Gaza Strip.

It is 150 miles from Dan to Beer-sheba, and about 200 miles from Beer-sheba to Saint Catherine's monastery. Thus it is approximately 350 miles between these two sacred mountains— from the place where Moses is believed to have acknowledged that "the Lord our God is one Lord" (cf. Deut. 6:4; Exod. 20:4)

Beer-sheba

283

to the place where Peter said to Jesus, "Thou art the Christ, the Son of the living God" (Matt. 16:16 KJV). The greatest width of the Holy Land, however, is only 75 miles, from the southern end of the Dead Sea and the nearest place on the Mediterranean shore (at Raphia, scene of the defeat of the armies of Egypt by the Seleucids of Syria).

THE GATEWAY TO THE NEGEV

The gateway to the Negev is the old/new city of Beer-sheba with a population numbering nearly 75,000. It remains strategically located as the traffic center, tourist center, commercial center, and gateway to the Negev. Although the name *Beer-sheba* in Hebrew meant "the well of seven," it can also mean the "well of swearing," or "well of the oath," as the Greek (and the context) indicates, and as Eusebius states in his onomasticon (166: 20-21). Here Abraham and Abimelech, king of Gerar, swore an oath of mutual allegiance (Gen. 21:31), at which time Abraham gave to Abimelech seven lambs. "Therefore that place was called Beer-sheba because there both of them swore an oath" (Gen. 21:28-30). Later a dispute over the same issue arose between Abimelech and Isaac. Again an agreement was reached and an oath taken, whereupon Isaac learned that a new well had been dug by his servants. He named this new well, Shibah, "the well of the oath." "Therefore the name of the city is Beer-sheba to this day" (Gen. 26:31-35).

Biblical Beer-sheba has been identified with Tel Sheba, three miles northeast of today's city. It lies at the apex of a triangle, the base of which lies along the Mediterranean shore and extends eastward and upward to Beer-sheba at an elevation of about 500 feet. Another triangle extends southeasterly, its apex being at Beer-sheba and its base in the Arabah. In the geological age of the Miocene, and especially in the Pliocene, the sea penetrated this region and deposited chalk in much of the area.[1] As the sea receded toward the end of the Pliocene period, the region became covered with loess soil, which, in the Beer-sheba region is occasionally 100 feet in depth. This type of soil, transported by the winds, is often found at the edge of the desert areas; it is extensive in China. This soil is rich and productive when water is available. Beer-sheba usually marks the southern extremity of the agricultural area and the northern

---

1. Efraim Orni and Elisha Efrat, *Geography of Israel* (Jerusalem: Israel Program for Scientific Translations, 1964), p. 28.

Near Beer-sheba, a section of conduit nine feet in diameter is transported by truck. This pipe section is part of the waterline from Galilee to Beer-sheba to irrigate fields of the Negev.

edge of the grazing area to the south, which extends to the desert proper at Kadesh Barnea. The rainfall in Beer-sheba averages about fifteen inches per year, with about thirty-five rainy days per annum. By comparison, Jerusalem has a rainfall of twenty-two inches, whereas Eilat and Cairo have only about one inch each.

Long before this area entered Biblical history, the vicinity was inhabited by people of Chalcolithic culture, contemporary with that of Teleilat Ghassul, northeast of the Dead Sea.[2] On the sides of the Wadi Beer-sheba are numerous hillocks that contain underground dwellings in which there were silos and fireplaces, including houses built of brick on stone foundations. Here copper implements were produced, including maces and ornaments.

There is a notable absence of Middle and Late Bronze Age remains, which supports the Biblical evidence that when Abraham arrived, there was no settled population in that area. Thus, Hagar, after expulsion from Abraham's camp, wandered in the "wilderness of Beer-sheba" (Gen. 21:14). Abraham became recognized as a resident alien by an agreement with Abimelech, king of Gerar (Gen. 20:1; 21:22-32). Isaac remained in Beer-sheba, at least until his sons Jacob and Esau were grown (Gen.

2. Yohanan Aharoni, *The Land of the Bible: A Historical Geography*, trans. A. F. Rainey (London: Burns & Oates, 1967), p. 31.

28:10). Beer-sheba served as the southern boundary of the tribal territory during most of the Biblical period (Judg. 21:1; 1 Sam. 3:20; 2 Sam. 3:10). This continued during the reigns of David (1 Sam. 24:2, 15; 1 Chron. 21:2), Solomon (1 Kings 4:24, 25), and Hezekiah (2 Chron. 30:5). Beer-sheba also served as the boundary of Judah exclusive of Israel (2 Kings 23:8; Neh. 11: 30). Although originally assigned to the tribe of Simeon (Josh. 19:2), it later became recognized as the capital of the Negev of Judah (2 Sam. 24:7; cf. 1 Kings 4:24). Beer-sheba remained the administrative center under King Jehoshaphat (2 Chron. 19:4). During the New Testament period, it appears that the Edomites, or the Idumeans, occupied Beer-sheba most of the century. Later, under Roman administration, Beer-sheba became a major military center, with defense lines extending from the Dead Sea to Raphia.³ It served a similar function under the Ottoman administration.

In recent decades Beer-sheba's comeback has been phenomenal. When Edward Robinson and his party visited there on April 12, 1838, they found two deep wells, which he recognized as ancient Beer-sheba. The larger well he described as over twelve feet in diameter and sixty feet deep of which sixteen feet was water. The other well was five feet in diameter and forty-two feet in depth. Both were surrounded by stone drinking troughs. The place was deserted with no residents in the area. Only after searching were they able to find, on the adjacent hillsides north of the wells, the ruins of a small village. "Over these swelling hills, the flocks of the patriarchs once rolled by the thousands; where now were only a few camels, asses, and goats!"⁴

Toward the turn of the century, the Turks again made it a military garrison and administrative center. It had acquired a population of 2,000 when captured by Allenby's forces in 1917. Thirty-one years later, at the end of the British Mandate, its population numbered about 3,000. Its phenomenal growth to a count of 75,000 is due to Israel's advance into the Negev through this gateway. Today Beer-sheba remains the capital of the new Negev administrative district.

Southeast of Beer-sheba on the main road into the Negev, at the end of the modern railway, is Dimona. The population

---

3. Esuebius, *Das Onomastikon . . .* , trans. E. Klostermann (Hildescheim: G. Olms, 1966), p. 40.
4. Edward Robinson, *Biblical Researches in Palestine* (Boston: Crocker and Brewster, 1868), vol. 1, p. 205.

reaches a total of more than 20,000. Israelis have recently built an atomic reactor here, euphemistically labeled by some guides as a "synagogue." The highway continues east through a rocky area at an altitude of about 1,312 feet until it comes to the edge of the escarpment that plunges down into the valley of the Ghor. The road follows the pattern of the "ascent of the scorpions" *(Akrabbim)* mentioned so frequently in the Scriptures (cf. Josh. 15:3). At the bottom the road divides: one fork goes to the south, and the other to the north past the Dead Sea works where the mineral resources of the Dead Sea are being exploited. The buried cities of Sodom and Gomorrah are believed to be lying beneath the shallow sea south of the Lisan Peninsula. A new cafe here provides relief for visitors. One may enter the Salt Mountain nearby, in the interior of which is a cavity resembling a giant smokestack, extending straight up into the sky. The interior is black to look at but salty to the taste. The road continues north along the shore of the Dead Sea past Ein Gedi and, since 1971, past Ein Fashkah and Qumran to join the Jericho road.

EIN GEDI, MASADA, AND SOUTHWARD

Many travelers, including George Adam Smith, have described with enthusiasm the astonishment which greets the trav-

The wadi of Ein Gedi, the spring that feeds a refreshing oasis on the west shore of the Dead Sea.

The sheer east slope of Masada, the site of Herod's famed fortress by the Dead Sea.

A view from the top of Masada looking west over the twisted path on the siege ramp built by the Romans to gain access to the summit.

eler who has crossed miles of desert to find this exotic burst of vegetation, with a delightful series of waterfalls and pools in which one can take an exhilarating swim. Between the waterfalls of Ein Gedi and the seashore is the Israeli kibbutz where vegetables in profusion are being grown in defiance of the arid locale. Between Ein Gedi and Tekoa are spacious caves, the region where David and his men hid from Saul, and where, years later in Murabbaat Cave, Bar Kochba hid with his followers and conducted the administrative affairs of the second revolt, A.D. 132 to 134. Among the exciting finds by modern archaeologists are the letters and artifacts left by these fugitives nearly eighteen centuries ago. In the Wadi Hever, caves on opposite sides of the canyon were used. Elsewhere, forty-one fugitives died of thirst in the "Cave of Horror." For centuries therefore—from David to Bar Kochba and Byzantine monks—this desert has served as a place of refuge.

Ein Gedi

South of Ein Gedi and opposite the Lisan Peninsula is the awesome Herodian fortress of Masada. This can be approached from the west by a road or by foot from the east, up the so-called "snake path." Recently, a cable car with a capacity of forty people has been placed in operation on the east side. The western approach follows the white ramp erected by the Romans during the siege in A.D. 73. Entrance is gained through the gate on the west wall from whence is an amazing view of the scene below. The lines of the Roman wall of circumvallation are clearly evidenced, including the campsite of the Roman general, Silva, enclosed with a rectangular wall. Herod the Great earlier had found this a place of refuge when he fled from the Parthians. Later he hid Miriamne and his court here while he was in Rome. Subsequently he expended vast sums and resources to fortify it for a last ditch stand against his many enemies. Great cisterns were constructed to preserve the fall rains. Vegetable gardens provided food for the garrison. Herod's sumptuous palace was built on three levels at the extreme northeastern projection, on the plateau's crest. From here the view is exhilarating, the dawn can be welcomed, a breeze is most likely, and one can find shade from the sun. The modern steel stairway assures the visitor of safety as he climbs along the sheer side of the mountain to view the austere but lavishly decorated residence of the Idumean king. To the natural strength of the area, Herod added walls and took other precautions for a long

Masada

siege. Fortunately, he did not need to use it for himself, but Masada later stood in good stead to those Zealots (probably including a contingent of Essenes) who resisted the Romans until the mass suicide by 967 defenders. The Roman triumph was an empty one.[5]

It serves today as a symbol of heroism to the descendants of these Zealots. Memories of the recent attempts by Hitler's Nazis to liquidate Europe's Jews remind their survivors that there is no room for complacency, even in the twentieth century. Thus Masada represents for the modern Israelis what the Alamo does for the Texans, or Hiroshima for the Japanese, or Waterloo for the French, or Pearl Harbor for the Americans.

Far to the south, in the center of the Negev, is Avdat, a city whose importance only recently has come to be recognized. It lies directly south of Beer-sheba and beyond Sede Boqer in the area of the Wilderness of Zin. It is one of the best places yet

Avdat

found to display the three civilizations—Nabatean, Roman, and Byzantine. In terms of Middle East history, its life span is relatively short, namely about 1,000 years, ending with the Arab incursion of A.D. 640. This is Edomite country, but gradually Arabs infiltrated the area, and a mixture of inhabitants resulted that became known to history as the Nabateans. They were a people of great artistic talent and commercial strength, whose mysterious culture has just recently become known. Two centuries before Christ they reached the height of their influence; they were contemporary with the Maccabees, whom they admired and supported against the Greeks. The Nabatean king, Aretas, was a friend of the Christians (2 Cor. 11:32). The Nabateans for a time dominated the camel caravans that crossed the Negev, and Avdat became an important commercial center. The remains they left here, and at their capital, Petra, show that they were skilled traders, farmers, engineers, architects, and artists. The city lasted about a thousand years; it began during the third century B.C. The Nabateans were expert agriculturalists in this forbidding terrain, probably the farthest south that agriculture has been practiced for a millennia. By an ingenious system of dams and cisterns, they were able to conserve the winter rains and irrigate their small plantings. Since 1959, Israel has been seeking to duplicate their feat, using the same techniques of water conservation and irrigation.

---

5. Jos. *Wars* VII. 9. 1.

The name Avdat comes from one of their kings, called Obodas, who was the father of Aretas IV (99 B.C.—A.D. 40), and grandfather of a wife of Herod Antipas, tetrarch of Galilee. The Nabateans were later absorbed into the Roman Empire, with the annexation of their territory by Trajan in A.D. 106. When the Romans built the road linking Aqaba with Damascus, trade was diverted from Avdat and the city withered. However, when Diocletian (A.D. 284-305) constructed border fortresses in the area, Avdat was the site of one of the forts, and the city experienced a rebirth. A castle built by the Romans is still well preserved; its courtyard includes a cistern. From the watchtower, an impressive panorama unfolds, especially to the south. The remains of the Roman camp lie 1,000 feet east. Most of the existing remains date from Avdat's golden age, when the Byzantines were in the ascendancy. The Byzantines built a for-

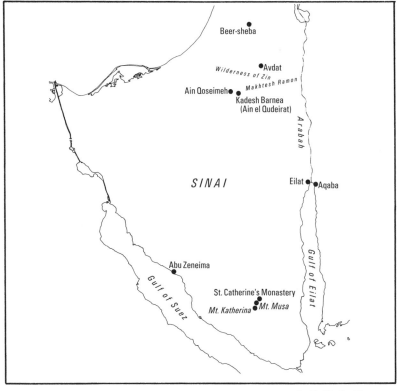

Sinai Peninsula

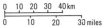

tress on the crescent of the hill, churches, a monastery, a baptistry, and many houses. The Byzantines constructed a north and south church, a potter's workshop, and other buildings necessary for a thriving community. Moslems came in A.D. 634, and the town slowly declined thereafter until it was abandoned during the tenth century. It was rediscovered by a British traveler named Palmer in 1871, and the Colt expedition of 1934-35 began its excavation. Further clearance and restoration was conducted by Israeli archaeologist Michael Avi Yonah. Today it is a major tourist attraction, largely because it displays three civilizations: Nabatean, Roman, and Christian (Byzantine).

Wilderness of Zin

Immediately to the south lies the inhospitable Wilderness of Zin. It is a waterless plateau draining in a northeasterly direction into the Arabah south of the Dead Sea. Here the Israelite nomads encountered another hardship: "The people of Israel . . . came into the wilderness of Zin . . . there was no water. . . . And the people contended with Moses . . . why have you brought the assembly of the LORD into this wilderness to die . . . ?" (Num. 20:1-5). Today's traveler, even though comfortably rushing through the area by auto, can sympathize with their plight.

A panorama of the area of Makhtesh Ramon near the main road from Beer-sheba to Eilat.

Farther south one encounters the largest of the three geological phenomena peculiar to the Negev. It is the Makhtesh
Ramon, or the "crater of Ramon." The two others to the north
and east are named Makhtesh Hagadol and Makhtesh Haqatan.
The main road from Beer-sheba to Eilat crosses the largest of the
craters, Makhtesh Ramon. Makhtesh Ramon begins at the mountain of Ramon at an elevation of 3,390 feet above sea level and
runs, like the other two, in a northeasterly direction toward
the Dead Sea. The crater is important for its numerous fossil
remains, including that of a giant lizard nine feet in length.
Remains of the extinct reptile group known as the Placodents,
not unlike sea turtles, have been found. Fossil frogs dating from
the Lower Cretaceous period are also found here.[6] Many varieties of rock, similar to the phenomenon in the Grand Canyon,
are exposed. Toward the bottom are layers of Triassic rock;
Jurassic rocks are found in the bottom toward the northeast
edge of the crater. Geologists believe that this phenomenon is
a result of aeons of erosion, started during the geological fault
and continued by rains, settling in the depression. The scanty

**Makhtesh
Ramon**

6. Zev Vilnay, *The New Israel Atlas: Bible to Present Day* (Jerusalem:
Israel University Press, 1968), p. 305.

rainfall means that it erodes vertically far faster than horizontally, with water escaping toward the northeast end.[7]

Very little rain falls in this entire region and it is virtually uninhabited. To the east lies the extensive wilderness of Paran, which is a broad shallow wadi draining into the Arabah, in the same southwest-northeast fault line from the Sinai watershed.

Rainfall in the Negev

Until recent years, it was widely believed that the northern Negev was unable to support anything but herdsmen, and that only precariously. Nelson Glueck, after many years of exploration in this area, has convinced many by demonstration that agricultural communities were scattered throughout the northern Negev, especially in the Middle Bronze Age, Iron Age II, the Nabatean Age, and the Byzantine Age.[8]

Not all agree with this assessment, however. Philip Meyerson, after noting the rainfall for a five-year period at Shivta and at Avdat, concludes that the region could not have supported the large number of inhabitants estimated to have been as many as 100,000 during the Byzantine period. Rainfall studies show that for a three-year period, from 1960 to 1962, rainfall was insufficient for the growing of crops, and that, whereas grain could be stored against dry years for a year or so, by the second or third year the residents would have to move. If this was true in the vicinity of Bethlehem in the time of Jacob and of Ruth and even of Saint Paul, it is understandable that the same would be true in this relatively arid region. By Saint Paul's time—perhaps as an innovation made by the earliest Christian communities—instead of people moving from areas of drought (and famine), supplies were sent from affluent areas to people in the stricken areas (Acts 11:27-30; 24:17; Rom. 15:25-27).

In the tests shown in the central Negev, rainfall varied in five years, from just over one inch to almost seven inches. It was only five inches at Avdat in 1962-63.[9] Meyerson concludes that in dry years the land simply was not sown and no harvest realized, whereas in rainy years, more than sufficient was raised for one year's needs. Upon this evidence, Meyerson believed that the numerous cisterns and terraces seen in the Negev

---

7. Orni and Efrat, *Geography*, pp. 26, 27.
8. Nelson Glueck, *Bulletin of the American Schools of Oriental Research* 138 (Apr., 1955): 11 ff.; 142 (Apr., 1956): 17 ff.; 145 (Feb., 1957): 11 ff.; 159 (Oct., 1960): 3 ff.; 149 (Feb., 1958): 8 ff.; 152 (Dec., 1958): 18 ff.
9. Meyerson, "Demography and Land Use in the Ancient Negeb," *Bulletin of the American Schools of Oriental Research* 185 (Feb. 1967): 40.

argue not for a dense population but rather for the necessity of compensating for a slight rainfall by elaborate precautions to preserve the rain that did fall. A clear indication, however, of the probable number of inhabitants is by the number of buildings that were left. Although the area has been explored but not excavated, Glueck has shown that frequently fortresses were built near agricultural villages. Also, the presence of extensive ruins of forts and churches, especially during the Nabatean and Byzantine periods, indicate a civilization relatively dense where now there is little but stone and sand.

KADESH BARNEA

By far the most important locality from a Biblical standpoint is an area of three oases lying about fifty miles southwest of Beer-sheba and thirty miles west of Makhtesh Ramon. Two geological factors make this a crossroads in the northern Sinai. The most important is the availability of water. Furthermore, it lies on a broad wadi extending north and south but bending westward toward the Suez. It is also near a road connecting the Gulf of Aqaba with the Mediterranean. The site was unknown until rather recently, and even now its accessibility is very difficult. Located on the expanse of a treeless limestone plateau between the Arabah and Gaza are three springs. They were discovered by the Reverend John Rowland in 1842, after being guided to the site by some Arabs from Gaza. One of the three springs is Ain Qedeis (Kadesh) which led Rowland and, later, Trumbull to identify it as the Kadesh Barnea of the Bible. The other two springs are Ain Qoseimeh and Ain el-Qudeirat. Of the three, only the latter supplies water continually through the year. Thus, in spite of the name Kadesh being associated with the first spring, the Kadesh Barnea of the Bible is linked by modern scholars with the largest of the three springs.[10]

Kadesh Barnea is mentioned first as the western edge of the area raided by Chedorlaomer (Gen. 14:4-9). It was in this area that Hagar was compelled to leave Abraham's tent (Gen. 16:14). To this spot, Moses led the Israelites, after receiving the decalogue at Mount Sinai, from across the wilderness of Paran to the country of the Amalekites (Deut. 1:19, 20). They remained here for many days (Num. 13:14). Miriam died here (Num. 20:1). It was here that Korah led his rebellion against the

Kadesh Barnea

10. S. Cohen, "Kadesh-Barnea," *Interpreter's Dictionary of the Bible* (Nashville: Abingdon Press, 1962), vol. 2, pp. 1, 2.

"establishment" (Num. 16 and 17). One problem is to explain how it was necessary to demand water in a place where water normally is to be found in abundance. It may be that the portion of the Israelites camped near one of the smaller springs, experienced drought, and complained to Moses rather than moving toward the larger spring, which was probably already overcrowded.

From here, spies were sent into Palestine. The majority report was accepted, and the punishment for their lack of faith was announced. Their determination to progress in spite of this curse led to their defeat at the battle of Arad (Num. 14:44-45; 21:1-3; 33:40; Deut. 1:41-44). After their defeat at Hormah, they retreated to Kadesh, and apparently spent most of their thirty-eight years in this area. This would be appropriate because it was relatively isolated and at the same time relatively well-supplied with water, not only for grazing but for raising some crops as well. Their existence here, however, would be in striking contrast to the fertile valley of the Nile, and their numerous complaints are understandable. The relative fertility of Palestine, in contrast to the Negev, seemed to be "a land flowing with milk and honey."

Prior to the coming of the Israelites under Moses, the patriarchs led by Abraham traversed this region. Glueck found numerous evidences of Middle Bronze civilization in this area. This would coincide roughly with the age of the Patriarchs and would lend additional credence to the Biblical account of life there by Abraham and Isaac. Indeed, Glueck's greatest contribution to Biblical history is said to be "his identification of the period of the early patriarchal narratives of Genesis, featuring Abraham with the Middle Bronze II (late 20th and 19th centuries B.C.)." Recently, additional material has confirmed Glueck's observations in a remarkable way.

Glueck's conclusion after exploring most of this area of central and northern Negev is that the periods of occupancy, in addition to the Middle Bronze I, are Iron Age II, Nabatean, and Byzantine. In several layers he actually found Chalcolithic remains.[11] He found evidence of farmers in the central Negev

---

11. Nelson Glueck, "Sixth Season of Archaeological Exploration in the Negev," *Bulletin of the American Schools of Oriental Research* 140 (Dec., 1955): 10.

12. Nelson Glueck, "Seventh Season . . . in the Negev," *Bulletin of the American Schools of Oriental Research* 162 (Apr., 1961): 20.

back in Abraham's time, especially in the area of Kadesh Barnea.[12] He found Chalcolithic settlements from the latter part of the fourth millennium B.C. as far south as the southern edge of the northern Negev. Abraham and his people were there according to the Biblical account, which synchronizes with the Middle Bronze I ending in the nineteenth century B.C. as attested by Glueck's surveys. Here Abraham and his pastoral companions would settle not far from agricultural settlements. After the nineteenth century, there was a civilization gap that lasted until Iron Age I, which Glueck links with the devastation by Chedor-laomer and his confederates as described in Genesis 14.[13]

The Jews settled here during their Kingdom period, did farming and initiated elaborate systems for preserving the rain-fall, a system which was later improved by the Nabateans and especially by the Byzantines. Glueck notes among other things that "this entire area fanning out east of Kadesh Barnea ... was an exceedingly important one in Middle Bronze I—Iron II, and

13. Ibid., p. 21.

A general view of the Negev south of Arad.

The Peak of Moses as viewed from the Rock Cave area.

must have been familiar to the Israelites of the Exodus during their periods of encampment at Kadesh Barnea."[14]

THE MOUNTAIN OF MOSES

No one who has crossed the desert of Sinai, either by an ancient taxi, a modern jeep, or a camel, will be surprised at the frequent murmurings voiced against the leadership of God and Moses by the Israelite escapees from Egypt. Nonetheless a trip to the traditional Mount of Moses (the Mount Horeb of the Elijah's stories) provides a most exhilarating experience. The usual route is to proceed along the Suez to the mining camp at Abu Zeneimeh in lower Sinai, then strike east across the desert following numerous broad water courses, often almost trackless, and climb from sea level to an altitude of 4,000 feet, approaching via the Wadi Feiran to the monastery gardens. Here a delightful oasis with vines, tropical vegetation, and water awaits weary travelers. Farther up the valley, nestled between towering granite peaks, is the monastery of Saint Catherine, which looks like, and for years was, a fortress, to which access was gained only by a rope windlass (still usable). Within is the traditional site of the burning bush, commemorated in a chapel of that name. This is the most famous monastery in the entire Near East, exceeding in importance even that of Mar Saba in the Judean "wilderness" or Mount Athos in Greece. It has one of the world's most important libraries, consisting mostly of manuscripts; the important ones have been photographed and are available in the Library of Congress. The monastery takes its name from Saint Catherine, who, according to Haggadic literature, was a martyr in Egypt and was carried by angels to Mount Sinai for burial. There are rival claims for the site of the giving of the Law. One of these is Mount Catherine, towering over 8,000 feet, the highest peak in Sinai. Jebel Musa however, though not as high, is more suitable for the story of the Exodus, for at its foot there is a plain large enough to accommodate a multitude and also provide an adequate water supply. Jebel Musa can be approached in two stages. Leaving the monastery at dawn, one may ride a camel for an hour and ascend the rest of the way on foot. From the top, an impressive panorama of peaks piled together stretches as far as eye can reach. The view to the south is the most spectacular because

14. Nelson Glueck in *Bulletin of the American Schools for Oriental Research* 159 (1960): 6, 7.

the peaks fall away in somewhat lower altitudes as they recede before the eye. To the west is the impressive valley where one may imagine the Israelites gathered while waiting for Moses to reappear but meanwhile concentrating on the golden calf, which Aaron obligingly supplied (Exod. 32:2-21). On the way down one notices a cleft in the rock, a reminder of the incident of Moses hiding himself until the Lord passed by (Exod. 33:21-23). The experiences of Sinai are not only presented with great impressiveness in the Book of Exodus (chapters 19 and 20), but this experience forms a "watershed" of the Book of Exodus, the Lord saying to Moses, "You have seen what I did," referring to His previous saving acts, and adding, "Now therefore, if you will obey my voice . . . you shall be my own possession," pointing to the future (Exod. 19:4, 5). Deliverance (the Exodus), therefore, is followed by the necessity for discipline (the Torah). Their new-found emancipation was to be accompanied by the regulation of conduct. The ancient tension between law and grace

Mount Sinai as seen from the plain of Sinai.

The rugged terrain in the area of Mount Sinai.

is nowhere more dramatically expressed than in this austere and awesome locale. Travelers have reported that storms in the area are especially alarming; though such storms are infrequent, they are sudden and slashing in intensity. This region forms the historical and poetical background for many passages in the Scriptures, referring to Sinai as the time when God appeared to give His people support and direction. It was here that eschatology was born, out of the confidence that in situations that look humanly impossible, God may be expected to intervene in response to the needs and prayers of His people. If the passage through the Suez was the baptism and birth of the nation, at Sinai it symbolically received its baptism of fire

Saint Catherine's Monastery, on the slopes of Mount Sinai.

when God manifested Himself both as the judge of sinners and the deliverer of believers.

Sinai again comes into the picture in the time of Elijah, at a period of another national crisis. After the great decision at Mount Carmel, Elijah was despondent and perplexed because of seeming failure. For reorientation, he took the long trip to the mountain of God, to Horeb, where revelation again came, not as at first—in thunder and lightning and earthquake—but rather in "a still small voice." The fiery prophet was commissioned to appoint his successor and through him designate the future ruler of Syria (1 Kings 19:9-18). Elijah, accompanied by Moses, appears again, 350 miles to the north, at the transfiguration of Jesus (Luke 9:30). Thus, representatives both of the law and the prophets experienced and expressed God's revelation at the southern and northern extremities of the Holy Land. Mount Sinai was not forgotten by the writers of the New Testament. There it is set in contrast to the spiritual Jerusalem and the new covenant (Gal. 4:24-26; Heb. 12:18-24); Sinai the symbol of the law, the new Jerusalem a symbol of grace; Sinai representative of judgment and the new Jerusalem of mercy.

This area leaped into history again in October 1956, when Israeli troops landed by air in the alluvial plain stretching to the south of Saint Catherine's monastery, and the monastery became the headquarters of the expedition during the brief Sinai campaign. The monks reported that the soldiers treated them with courtesy. The area has remained in world news since June 5, 1967, when Israeli forces were again on the move. Since then, as during the weeks of October 1956, archaeologists and scholars have been seeking to extract from the inhospitable desert the secrets it has held for centuries. The world today still looks with anxiety toward the Suez and the Sinai, wondering whether mankind will be confronted with another period of agony and attempted reconciliation. Today, Saint Catherine's monastery is accessible by air.

11

Jerusalem From the Moslem Conquest Through World War I

The vicissitudes of the city from the Moslem conquest through World War I and to the present comprise a complex but fascinating story. The recovery of Jerusalem under Byzantine rule in A.D. 629 was short-lived. In 636, the Moslems came to stay. This new and much more formidable foe emerged from the Arabian desert in one of the most remarkable and far-reaching political-religious crusades in history. Except for two relatively short periods—during the Middle Ages when the Crusaders ruled Jerusalem and the time of the British Mandate (1918-48) —the Holy City has been under Moslem rule, from A.D. 636 to 1967, a period of over 1,300 years, longer than the combined periods of Jewish and Christian dominance. Inspired partly by religious zeal and partly by dreams of conquest over the weakened Persian and Byzantine empires, Bedouins in hordes poured out of the Arabian Peninsula, conquering the Persians in 651 and defeating the Byzantine armies at the Yarmuk River August 20, 636, in one of the most decisive battles of history.[1]

MOSLEM CONQUEST

At the head of this army was the caliph Omar, the short, dark cousin of the prophet Mohammed. Surrounded by Arabians and cut off from Constantinople, the Jerusalem patriarch, Sophronius, watched the fall of Damascus and the humane treatment they had received from the Arabs. The patriarch, therefore, decided to negotiate with rather than to resist the Arab armies.

---

1. Michael Avi-Yonah, ed., *A History of the Holy Land* (New York: Macmillan Co., 1969), p. 196.

The Dome of the Ascension, in the temple area just northwest of the Dome of the Rock, marks the spot where according to Moslem tradition Mohammed prayed before ascending to heaven. 305

From the Mount of Olives the caliph Omar grieved that his armies were already being corrupted by the spoils of war in Jerusalem. In surprisingly easy terms, however, all Christians were permitted to remain secure in their homes and churches. The taxes previously paid to the Byzantines now would be collected by the Arabs. The patriarch conducted the Arab leader on a tour of the city. According to historians, Omar was taken first to the Holy Sepulchre. Although it was the hour of prayer, Omar refused to pray within the church, but performed his prayers to the east, explaining that if he prayed in the church his followers would have taken possession of it. The small Mosque of Omar, east of the Holy Sepulchre, commemorates this event. Omar was more interested in the site of the temple. After finally arriving at the temple area and finding it cluttered with debris, he prayed at the southern part of the enclosure facing Mecca and dramatically symbolized his intention of cleansing the site by throwing a handful of dirt into the Kidron Valley below. Jews were allowed to remain in their portion of Jerusalem, and the Christians as well, but both had to pay increasingly heavy taxes unless they embraced the faith of Islam. Therefore by a slow policy of economic and political attrition, the Jewish and Christian communities of the Holy Land gradually became Islamized.

The southeast corner of the Old City, including the temple area, as seen from the Jewish cemetery on the Mount of Olives.

Jerusalem, however, retained its prestige and sanctity, the Moslems calling it by the name Al-Quds, meaning "the sanctuary" or "the Holy City." The modest and temporary shrine that was built soon after the conquest of the city was replaced in 691 by the structure that people today see over the bare rock where the temple of Solomon once stood. This building was ordered by the Omayyad caliph in Damascus to reduce the inclination of his subjects to make pilgrimages to rival Mecca and Medina. He used Byzantine architects and artisans to create here the Dome of the Rock, which is still the most beautifully proportioned structure of the Arab world. Its impressiveness lies largely in its simplicity, in the wealth of its decorations, and the exposure of the bare rock, the place where it is believed Abraham prepared to sacrifice Isaac (Gen. 22). Its octagonal form recalls the structure of early Christian churches designed to facilitate inspection of the holy sites, such as the Church of the Holy Sepulchre, the church on Mount Gerizim, and the Chapel of the Ascension, each of which was circular in shape. The Dome of the Rock was possibly inspired by the dome of Saint Sophia in Constantinople, which had been built on Justinian's orders

Dome of the Rock

over a century earlier. The building, one of the oldest in Jerusalem, has three concentric rings, with a dome supported by ornate pillars and the interior of the dome inscribed with passages from the Koran as well as geometric designs for which Arab artists have become world famous.

Justinian's church, honoring Saint Mary, was transformed into the Aqsa Mosque, at the southern portion of the enclosure. As described by Muqaddasi in A.D. 987, it had been rebuilt several times but then contained 280 columns plus many splendid mosaics. The Aqsa Mosque, which has been recently strengthened and remodeled, today accommodates some 10,000 worshipers.

But the Dome of the Rock remains the chief pride and joy of the Moslems. It is venerated as a shrine rather than utilized primarily for gatherings of worshipers. In 1964, the Dome —repaired, redecorated, and illuminated for the first time—was rededicated. The cost of millions was borne largely by the oil-rich Moslems of the Middle East. According to Moslem tradition, it was from this rock that Mohammed made a miraculous journey to heaven. Here also, in Moslem tradition, Jesus will appear at the final Judgment to share with Mohammed the future determination of the souls of mankind, recalling the prophecy that, "I will gather all the nations and bring them down into the Valley of Jehoshaphat, and I will enter into judgment with them there" (Joel 3:2). This prophecy probably accounts for the vast cemeteries on both sides of the Kidron Valley, the Moslems on the west bank and the Jews on the east. They believe that those buried here will be the first to arise in the resurrection. For these reasons, Jerusalem is the third most holy place in Islam, following only Medina and Mecca.

The Jewish community, meanwhile, after having worked on rabbinical studies at Jamnia following the fall of Jerusalem, had moved their center to Tiberias. Although Tiberias remained as their center during the seventh and eighth centuries, some returned to Jerusalem after the Moslem conquest, living in the southern quarter near the "wailing wall." Later, as their numbers increased, they settled in the relatively unoccupied northeast portion near the Herod Gate.[2] During this time the Jerusalem Talmud was completed and much work was done on a series of commentaries known collectively as the Midrash. It was at

2. James Parkes, *A History of Palestine from 135 A.D. to Modern Times* (New York: Oxford University Press, 1949), p. 94.

The Dome of the Rock.

Interior view of the Dome of the Rock.

this time that the Biblical Hebrew text acquired a system of pointing and punctuation that we now know as the Masoretic Text. Gradually, however, as the Jewish community in Babylon decreased, Jerusalem became the center of world Jewry.

The rule of the Moslem Empire by the Omayyad Dynasty from Damascus lasted less than a century. In 678, a Christian tribe from Lebanon (Maronites) invaded Palestine as far as the walls of Jerusalem. The Moslems then became divided between the Omayyads of Damascus and the Abbasid Caliphs, who founded the city of Baghdad about A.D. 775. Jerusalem, threatened with civil strife, was prey to marauding Bedouins, as was the whole countryside. Many monasteries were plundered and monks murdered. The Moslems became increasingly rigorous, and the Christians developed increasing resistance. The Moslem Empire as a whole, however, was fairly prosperous, and the annual fair at Jerusalem continued to draw merchants from Europe. During the ninth century, the caliphs, who had become both rich and indolent, hired Turkish mercenaries. One of these Turkish generals, Ahmad ibn-Tulun, became governor of Egypt in 868 and conquered Palestine in 877. Jerusalem again became the scene of civil disorder. The Turks damaged the Church of the Holy Sepulchre in A.D. 937. A conqueror named Jawhar emerged from North Africa claiming descent from Fatima, daughter of Mohammed. The followers of the Fatimids built Cairo in the latter part of the tenth century.

The most infamous leader of this dynasty was Hakim, who ruled from A.D. 996-1021. He became insane and declared himself to be the Messiah. The sect of Druzes still revere him as an incarnate deity. In A.D. 1009, Hakim ordered the destruction of all churches in Palestine, except that of the Nativity at Bethlehem, and forbade all pilgrimages. This senseless destruction sparked the desire among European countries to form a crusade to rescue the Holy Land from her oppressors.

During this time of instability, the Christian community dwindled in size, as did the Jewish population, although Jerusalem regained its prestige during the transition of Jewish leadership from Babylon to the West. During this time, certain Jews called Karaites founded a brotherhood known as the Mourners of Zion, who spent their time, like monks, praying for the restoration of the temple.[3]

---

3. Ibid., p. 101.

By this time Jerusalem was largely Arabic-speaking, and the population of the countryside was mostly Moslem. On the whole, however, it was a period of sad decline for the Moslems as well as the Christians and Jews. A general deteriorating situation hastened the advent of the Crusades.

Few visitors and apparently few chroniclers appreciate the changes made in the Holy City and in the Holy Land by the Crusaders of the Middle Ages. In the relatively short time they were there, their building activities rivaled that of the ancient Romans, who were there much longer. The focal point of the Crusades was the city itself and particularly the Holy Sepulchre. Grave sites often draw pilgrims, and although the idea of pilgrimages as an act of devotion was largely unknown in the early Christian church, during the Middle Ages it had come to acquire an increasing degree of importance. The ignorance and superstition of the period aided the popularity of the pilgrimage, especially after the "invention" of sacred relics linked with the life of Jesus. Each church in Roman Catholicism

View to the east of the Old City, the temple area, and the Mount of Olives. The traditional site of Jesus' ascension is marked by the smaller of the two towers on the skyline.

needed a relic to enhance its sanctity; the law of supply and demand resulted in the production of "sacred" relics to meet the demand. Prominent among these were the bones and the hair of the saints, as well as the wood and the nails of the cross of Jesus.

THE CRUSADES

The idea of the Crusades began earlier among the Byzantines. The Byzantine emperor, Nicephorus Phocas (A.D. 963-69) and his successor, Johannes Tzimisces (A.D. 969-76), sought to reconquer Palestine from the Moslems, who had taken it 350 years earlier.[4] Meanwhile, merchants of southern Europe became interested in Palestine for commercial reasons. The city of Amalfi traded at Mediterranean coastal cities and built a convent in Jerusalem on the site of the Latin Church of Saint Mary. Jerusalem, then under the rule of the Fatimids of Egypt, was shocked by the invasion of the Seljuks, Turkish tribes from the northeast. They captured Aleppo in 1070 while another group captured Ramla and most other cities, except those on coastal area retained by the Fatimids. The Seljuk general, Atsiz, stormed Jerusalem in 1076 and its inhabitants were massacred. As the Turks weakened, the Fatimids recaptured Jerusalem and held it for three years until the arrival of the Crusaders.

The idea of the Crusade in Europe was born at Piacenza (March 1095) and proclaimed at Clermont in France (November 26, 1095). The drive was sustained mostly by the French, so much so that the Saracens referred to all Crusaders as "Franks."

There were eight Crusades, the first beginning in 1096, and the last ending in 1291. At one time, the kingdom of the Crusaders extended from Egypt to beyond the Euphrates, an area much larger than the territory controlled by Solomon.

Historians have detected many motives, all of which contributed to the Crusades, and which, incidentally, cannot be understood apart from a thorough knowledge of Europe in the Middle Ages. The most prominent motive of the Crusades was the repossession of the Holy Sepulchre. This motive can be explained by the fact that Charlemagne had been given the key to the city by the Orthodox Patriarch in A.D. 800, and additional privileges were granted by Caliph Harun al-Rashid in 807.[5] Therefore, Charlemagne sometimes is regarded as the "first"

---

4. Avi-Yonah, *History of the Holy Land*, p. 220.
5. R. Winston, *Charlemagne* (New York: Harper and Row, 1968), p. 122.

of the Crusaders. The destruction of the Church of the Holy Sepulchre by Caliph Hakim in A.D. 1010 was followed by the capture of Jerusalem by the Seljuk Turks in 1071. Christians were pained by the desecration of the holy place, and were annoyed also by the perils of the pilgrimage thereafter. Some volunteered to safeguard the journey of the pilgrims. Others were moved to respond to the plea of the eastern emperor. Others had the desire to reunite the Latin and Greek churches, following the schism of 1054. Another motive was the extension of the Christian offensive against Moslems, which had already begun in Western Europe. Also, church leaders had the desire to redirect and sanctify the pugnacity of the laymen. In addition, many feudal lords wanted to carve out a domain in the Near East. Italian merchants sought to acquire Eastern products more easily. Many laymen participated to acquire spiritual merit, a desire effectively exploited by the popes. Religious enthusiasm was created through the preaching of men like Peter the Hermit and Urban II. Furthermore, many serfs sought economic freedom in what appeared to them to be a new frontier. Others merely felt wanderlust, an instinct which appealed especially to the predatory Normans.

Jerusalem, prior to the coming of the Crusaders, remained structurally much the same as that left by Justinian and Heraclius, the last great Byzantine emperors. Most churches, however, especially the Holy Sepulchre, had been leveled to the ground by the mad Hakim. But many of the medieval buildings so familiar to the modern tourist were not in existence prior to the Crusades. These would include the Church of Saint Anne near Stephen's Gate, the facade of the Tomb of the Virgin in the Kidron Valley, the Dome of the Ascension on the Mount of Olives, and the Hall of the Coenaeculum, which commemorates the Last Supper and Pentecost. The Church of the Holy Sepulchre was missing, except for its foundations. These medieval structures, in addition to the modern structures, were erected after the Crusaders arrived. The surviving structures that were erected before the Crusades include the Dome of the Rock, the Aqsa Mosque, the so-called Tower of David on the west wall and the substructures of the present Damascus Gate. The part least changed is the entire temple area, including the southeast portion of the existing wall.

The first Crusade was the only one of the eight that was

The Dome of the Chain, an accessory building to the Dome of the Rock.

completely successful. Initiated in France (at the Synod of Piacenza) in March 1095, the disorganized peasants started in the spring of 1096, but reached only as far as Constantinople. The second and official phase of the first Crusade began in the spring of 1096, under the leadership of knights led by Godfrey of Bouillon and his brother Baldwin, Raymond of Toulouse, Bishop Adhemar, Bohemund, and his nephew Tancred. They assembled at Constantinople in the Spring of 1097 numbering some 50,000 men, including knights, infantry, and noncombatants.[6] They captured Nicaea from the Seljuks on June 18 after a difficult siege. Antioch was finally captured and secured by June 28 of the following year. By invitation they took possession of the Armenian city of Edessa (modern Urfa) which for half a century became part of the Latin Kingdom of Jerusalem.[7]

6. Steven Runciman, *A History of the Crusades* (Cambridge: At the University Press, 1951), vol. 1, pp. 335-341.
7. J. B. Segal, *Edessa: The Blessed City* (Oxford: Clarendon Press, 1970), p. 226.

After relaxation and further bickering among the leaders, the Crusaders finally left the vicinity of Antioch in May of 1099, arriving in Jerusalem a month later. During the month of their siege, the Crusaders, like their predecessors and successors, found the problem of water around Jerusalem very severe. A chronicler recorded the bringing of water in skins from a distance of six miles. The people inside the city depended upon cisterns. The Pool of Siloam, however, was available to the attackers because it was then outside the city walls, but this source was not sufficient to support an army of 12,000 warriors and their livestock. In addition to siege towers between Stephen's Gate and the tower on the corner, similar towers were located on Mount Zion, while Tancred had the tower on the northwest. The defenders set fire to the platforms and brought witches to make incantations against the strongest siege engines.[8]

On the morning of the fifteenth of May, all the Christians were ready to storm the city or die in the attempt. The battle lasted from dawn until dark. On the north, defenders were blinded by smoke. At the seventh hour, the Christians became discouraged, but on the Mount of Olives an unknown warrior appeared. This vision on Olivet cheered them. The bridge was lowered and attackers entered the city. The first Crusaders surmounted the wall between Herod's Gate and the so-called Stork's Tower on the northeast corner of the old city, opposite where the Rockefeller Archaeological Museum now stands. Godfrey's army was the first, and Raymond's, the last to enter. Scaling ladders were used at several places. After Stephen's Gate was opened, people poured in and killed everyone within reach. Everywhere lay heaps of severed heads.[9]

The Count of Toulouse, on the south opposite Zion Gate, was not aware of the entrance on the north. Defenders retreated to the citadel because it was close at hand. Tancred pursued defenders into the temple "after a terrible carnage." The chronicler noted, "It was indeed the righteous judgment of God that profaners of His sanctuary should expiate their sin by death and by pouring out their own blood purify the sacred precincts."[10] In the temple area alone, 10,000 people were reported to

8. William of Tyre, *Chronicles of the Crusades* (New York: Columbia University Press, 1943), vol. 1, p. 366.
9. Ibid., p. 370.
10. Ibid., p. 372.

have perished. After a month's siege, the weak Fatimid garrison in the citadel was overcome. Moslems and Jews were mercilessly slaughtered. With Jerusalem secured, the Crusade had achieved its stated objective four years after its start.

After this victory, most of the Crusaders, having accomplished their vow, returned to Europe. Those that remained were insufficient in number and were constantly on the defensive. They successfully met the Egyptian counterattack at Ashkelon and proceeded thereafter to capture cities along the Mediterranean. This accomplished, they pressed their conquest eastward across the Jordan as far as the Gulf of Aqaba, building the important fortress of Montreal (Shaubak), and the large one at Kerak, to control the caravan traffic and to prevent their enemies in Egypt and in Syria from joining in a counterattack. After four and one-half centuries of Moslem control, Jerusalem was now predominantly a Christian city. On Christmas Day of A.D. 1100, the Latin Kingdom of Jerusalem was founded, with Godfrey of Bouillon as the "advocate [defender] of the Holy Sepulchre." In the rivalry between Antioch and Jerusalem, the latter prevailed thanks largely to Italian galleys and the inflow of pilgrims. The Crusaders rapidly divided Palestine into feudal states. The Latin Kingdom of Jerusalem had titular control over the entire area of conquest, including the separate provinces, or "counties," of Edessa, Tripoli, and Antioch. Eastern Christians, however, who had lived for centuries with the Moslems, came to resent the overbearing Franks, and rivalry between the East and West Christians became even more bitter than that between many of the Moslem residents and their Christian neighbors. The Crusaders were concerned more with administration than with colonization. Their cause later was greatly strengthened by the creation of the Knight's Templar and the Knight's Hospitalers (later Knights of Saint John). These religious orders brought stability, wealth, and expertise to the control of the Kingdom of Jerusalem.

One of the first concerns of the conquerors was the repair of the Church of the Holy Sepulchre. Although repaired in 1048, extensive reconstruction was now imperative. Exactly fifty years after their conquest, the rebuilt church was rededicated. Left intact was the circular rotunda around the sepulchre itself. The small cubicle over the sepulchre was rebuilt. The building was now enlarged to include Calvary in a two-story chapel in which the first four Crusader rulers of Jerusalem were later buried.[11]

At this time, an unknown architect built a chancel and a large transept in a Romanesque style with rounded arches. The present entrance is on the south transit and still shows the arch of the Crusader period. The Armenian patriarchate, descendants of the Armenians of Edessa, the country that first accepted Christianity, fared well under the Latin Kingdom of Jerusalem. At this time they built their patriarchal Church of Saint James the Great, south of the Holy Sepulchre. Nearby was the Church of Saint John of the Hospitalers. Gradually this order, which had its headquarters there, gave more attention to military matters and less to hospital service. They enlarged their quarters to form the present Muristan. Nearby, the Benedictine friars built a small chapel, called Saint Mary the Latin, now part of the Lutheran Church of the Redeemer. At that time the northeastern section of the city was inhabited by Christians from Syria. Here, in addition to the striking Church of Saint Anne near the Pool of Bethesda, churches were built honoring Saint Agnes, Saint

11. The four kings—Godfrey, Baldwin I, Baldwin II, and Fulk—are honored in the heraldic "Jerusalem Cross."

The Church of the Holy Sepulchre.

Chapel of the Ascension on the Mount of Olives. The bottom section of this structure is of Crusader architecture, which is capped by an Islamic dome.

Elia, and Saint Margaret.[12] The Church of Saint Anne, though simple and austere, is the best example of Crusader construction surviving to the present day. Its northwest corner was damaged during the fighting in 1967, but since then it has been repaired.

The Crusaders, better warriors than historians, wrongly assumed that the Dome of the Rock was the Temple built by Solomon! They made it into a place of Christian worship and provided the iron railing surrounding the bare rock that gives the building its name. They also called it the Temple of the Lord (Templi Domini). The Knight's Templar acquired the Aqsa Mosque in 1124. The eastern aisle of the great mosque was converted into a chapel, as evidenced by the Frankish rose window. On the western side they erected a large building to serve as a school, now used as a museum. The extensive space

---

12. Michael Join-Lambert, *Jerusalem*, trans. Charlotte Haldane (London: Elek Books, 1958), p. 216.

underneath this pavement, dating from Byzantine times, was called Solomon's stables; here they stabled their 2,000 horses.

The Crusaders were not archaeologists. Faith was strong but uncritical. Scores of relics were "invented," or "discovered," most of which found their way to Europe. Pilgrimages greatly increased during this period, and from this time on many structures were erected for the convenience of pilgrims. Instead of public hotels or inns, pilgrims from different nations or communions would go to the hospice or inn built especially for them. Many of these buildings remain in Jerusalem to this day, including a hospice for pilgrims from India (near Herod's Gate) and others for Russians, Italians, and Germans. The main streets as laid out by the Romans remain largely unaltered to this day. The Cordo Maximus going south from the Damascus Gate contained markets, or *souks,* then as now. The same is true of David's Street, which leads from the Jaffa Gate to the temple area.

At the site of the Ascension on the slope of the Mount of Olives, the Crusaders also built the circular walls on the base created by Helena in the fourth century. What is now the Dung Gate was then the Postern of the Tannery. Stephen's Gate was called the Gate of Jehoshaphat, taking its name from the valley of that name. The facade of the church in the Kidron honoring Mary was erected at that time. The Church of Saint Stephen was built north of Stephen's Gate, the gate now called the Damascus Gate but which at other times was called the Nablus Gate. This preserves the (probably correct) tradition that the site of Stephen's stoning was north of the city walls rather than east of the city. Supporting the position are those adherents of the Garden Tomb, who say that Jesus' crucifixion was in this area rather than farther south at the site of the Holy Sepulchre.

What is now the New Gate was then called the Postern of Saint Lazarus. The northwest corner of the Old City, now dominated by the French hospice, was then called Tancred's Tower. Herod's Gate was then called the Postern of Saint Magdalene. What is now the Via Dolorosa was then the Street of Jehoshaphat, taking its name from the adjacent gate. The southeast gate ("Nebi David") then was known as the Zion Gate, and gave its name to the street leading from there straight north to the Damascus Gate where it became known as Stephen's Street. The street that still goes from the Damascus Gate to the

Dung Gate through what was the Tyropoeon Valley was then called the Spanish Street on the north, and the Street of the Furriers on the south.[13]

In the fifteenth century, Jaffa Gate was called Pisan's Gate to honor the people of Pisa, Italy, who participated in the Crusades and later settled in that section. The palace of the Crusader kings was near the site of Herod's palace and the Tower of David, or the Citadel. This gave them command of the most important part of the city, the approach from the sea.

THE TESTIMONY OF PILGRIMS

For centuries thereafter, it was customary for pilgrims arriving in Jerusalem by way of Joppa to be housed near the western edge of the city in a convent and to be led at the earliest possible time to the Holy Sepulchre. Pilgrims usually desired to spend the night in this holy place, and many reported a memorable spiritual experience in spite of their weariness and the distraction from other pilgrims.

Instructive and often inspiring is the testimony of pilgrims both before and after the Crusades. Sylvia of Aquatania, arriving about A.D. 385, described in detail the worship services in Jerusalem. Of the daily services, she wrote,

> "Every day before cock crow all the doors of the Anastasis (Holy Sepulchre) are opened and all the monks and virgins . . . descend, . . . also the laity . . . who desire to have an early vigil. From that hour to daybreak hymns are sung and songs of antiphons sung in response. And after each hymn, prayer is offered."[14]

She continued by noting that priests and deacons took turns saying prayers after each hymn. When the bishop arrived "and forthwith enters the cave, and within the rails he first says a prayer for all and . . . blesses the catechumens." As the bishop departed, they all approached to kiss his hands, and at dawn the service was dismissed. The services were resumed at the sixth hour, when again psalms and antiphons were sung until the bishop arrived; he addressed the people and blessed them.

---

13. See map, "Palestine of the Crusaders," in F. J. Salmon, *Survey of Palestine* (Jaffa: 1937).

14. Sylvia of Aquatania, "Pilgrimage . . . to the Holy Places," *The Churches of Constantine at Jerusalem,* trans. J. H. Bernard (London: Palestine Pilgrims' Text Society, 1887-1897; New York: A.M.S. Press, 1971), vol. 1, p. 45.

Looking eastward from the YMCA tower toward the city wall and the Jaffa Gate with the Mount of Olives in the background.

As he left, they again would kiss his hands. The same service was repeated at the ninth hour, and at the tenth hour there was a service of lights, at which candles were lit in abundance. Prayers and songs and greetings continued until long after dark. Such was the daily ritual, which included at least four distinct services during each of the weekdays. The hour of the morning service would naturally vary considerably, since the cockcrow to start the new service and to complete the previous service varied with the seasons of the year. The services were performed with great ardor and enthusiasm, and pilgrims both from the West and the Near East were numerous. After the Crusades, the number of pilgrims increased but their enthusiasm for worship apparently waned. Most of the pilgrim reports of this later period were content to merely enumerate or identify the various holy places, with little description of daily life. An anonymous pilgrim from the early eleventh century reported:

"In Jerusalem there is a chamber covered with one single stone, wherein Solomon wrote his book of wisdom. There, too, the blood of Zacharias was shed between the temple and the altar. Not far from this place is the stone to which the Jews come every year, anoint it, lament, and so go wailing away. There is the house of Hezekiah, king of Judah, to whom the Lord granted thrice five years of life. There is also the house of Caiaphas and the pillar to which Christ was bound, and was scourged and buffeted. Near the Gate of Neapolis is Pilate's Judgment hall, where Christ was judged by the chief priests. Not far from thence is Golgotha, or the place of Calvary, where Christ the Son of God was crucified, where the first man Adam was buried, and where Abraham offered sacrifice to God."[15]

The author continued by noting that a stone's throw to the west of this site was the church built by Emperor Constantine, where Joseph of Arimathea buried Jesus; and that, "from Mount Calvary it is thirteen feet toward the west of the middle of the world."[16]

This pilgrim also noted a Latin monastery, dedicated to Mary, where her house once stood with an altar where the three Marys grieved over the crucifixion. Later pilgrims repeated essentially the same description. A twelfth-century pilgrim, for example, noted that "two bow shots from that place is the Lord's Temple built by Solomon having four entrances and twelve doors."[17] Many of these itineraries are content to identify places much as a guide would do along a walking tour. Apparently it was sufficient for most of the pilgrims (then as now) to identify the places without lingering or inquiring about their origin or age. The emphasis was upon the sites rather than the history of the sites. Most pilgrims were uncritical and primarily interested in the religious merit that would reward their visit.

Shortly after this pilgrim's visit to Jerusalem, the Christian Knights were defeated by Saladin and his Saracens in Galilee (July 4, 1187). Soon after Saladin captured Jerusalem after a twelve-day siege (October 4, 1187). Of its 60,000 defenders, 15,000 were sold as slaves.[18]

This political change did not affect to any degree the build-

15. Palestine Pilgrims' Text Society, *Eleventh and Twelfth Centuries,* trans. Aubrey Stewart, Library of the Palestine Pilgrims' Text Society, vol. 6 (New York: AMS Press, 1971), p. 1.
16. Ibid., p. 2.
17. Ibid., p. 71.
18. Will Durant, *The Age of Faith* (New York: Simon and Schuster, 1950), p. 598.

ings of the city. The pilgrims continued to come. A tract in French, dating after the time of the Saladin conquest (c. A.D. 1220), entitled "Citez de Jherusalem," noted that David Street leads from the Tower of David to the Golden Gate and that "on the left of the Tower of David is a place where they sell corn." The tract continued to point out that farther east, Patriarch [now Christian] Street gave access to the Holy Sepulchre and the House of the Hospital. Nearby was Trinity Chapel, "where all the women of the city were married. And there is the font where they baptized all the children of the city."[19] David Street intersects with Mount Zion Street, which is "a covered street, vaulted over, called the Street of Herbs, where they sell all the herbs, and all the fruits of the city, and spices. At the top of this street is the place where they sell fish. . . . On the right hand of this Market are the shops of the Syrian gold-workers; and here they sell the palms which the Pilgrims bring from the seas."[20]

This pilgrim tract gives evidence that a large Christian community remained after the Moslem reconquest and that much of the old city had changed little since the period of the Latin Kingdom of Jerusalem. The Crusaders apparently made little change in the walls of the city. Excavations by Dr. J. B. Hennessy in 1965, however, revealed an ecclesiastical building of the Crusader period located outside of the north wall and west of the Damascus Gate. In addition, remains of a massive structure was found about sixty-six feet north of the Damascus Gate. The structures in this area have been identified as the Church of Saint Abraham. This church, in the Jerusalem of the twelfth century, was located inside the north wall and west of the Damascus Gate, then called Stephen's Gate.

The walls of the the old city took their present form under the rule of Suleiman the Magnificent. He rebuilt the walls in A.D. 1538-1541. Although the upper levels are of later construction, "his masonry can be seen in the lower courses for almost the entire circuit; Damascus Gate today looks much as it did in the sixteenth century. We know now that, at least at key points on the north and south, Suleiman's wall follows the line of the walls of Aelia Capitolina."[21]

19. Palestine Pilgrims' Text Society, *Eleventh and Twelfth Centuries*, pp. 6-8.
20. Ibid.
21. Kathleen M. Kenyon, *Jerusalem: Excavating 3000 Years of History* (Toronto: McGraw-Hill Book Co., 1967), p. 197.

Next in the series of Jerusalem's vicissitudes was a ten-year reoccupancy by Christians following a treaty between Fredrick II and the Moslem leader Al-Kamil, the sultan of Egypt, in A.D. 1229. Fifteen years later, while Crusader leaders were quarreling, Turks from Central Asia, hired by the sultan of Egypt, captured Jerusalem and massacred the inhabitants. Five years later, in 1249, Egyptian slaves called Mamelukes, overthrew the government of Egypt and seized control of Palestine. They rebuilt the walls of Jerusalem to exclude "Mount Zion." They restored the Citadel on the site of Herod's palace in much the form that it is today.[22] In addition, they repaired the aqueduct that brought water from the springs north of Hebron. The Mamelukes built four important schools of learning (madrasahs). They also adorned the temple area by adding fountains, arcades, prayer chapels, and minarets. They furnished the beautiful arches at the top of the steps between the Dome of the Rock and the Aqsa Mosque. The Church of Saint Anne, meanwhile, was converted into a mosque. The Mameluke rule was relatively tolerant; Jews and Christians were given a large

22. Teddy Kollek and Moshe Pearlman, *Jerusalem: A History of Forty Centuries* (New York: Random House, 1968), p. 191.

The children's hospital above the cliff and a section of the north wall is the site from which General Charles G. Gordon spotted in a nearby hill a skull-like rock formation suggesting the scene of Golgotha.

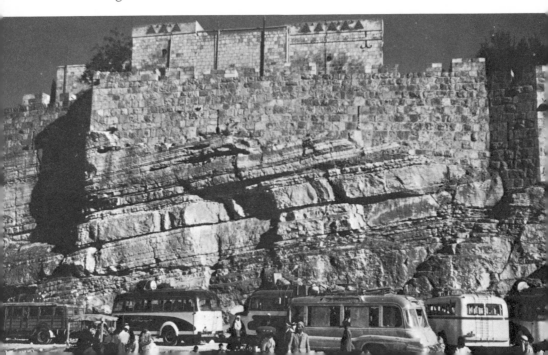

measure of freedom, although they definitely remained second-class citizens. By the fourteenth century, the Jewish community in Jerusalem had become quite numerous and considerably cosmopolitan. Most of them had come from France. The Jews were specialists in such handicrafts as dyeing, tailoring, and shoemaking. Even earlier, Benjamin of Tudela recorded that most Jews were in the dyeing and tanning business.[23]

In the following century, another Jewish pilgrim from Italy counted nearly 300 Jewish families in Jerusalem. The Jewish community appears to have been devout but impoverished.

Pilgrims continued to visit Jerusalem during the seventeenth century. In 1697, for example, Henry Maundrell reported that on Easter Sunday morning, March 28, the Lamentations having been ended, the pilgrims joyously gathered, "this being the day in which their Lenten discipline expired, and they were come to a full belly again."[24] After the celebration of mass outside the Holy Sepulchre, they dined with the friars and visited among other places "a large grotto, a little without the Damascus Gate, said to have been some time the residence of Jeremiah. On the left side of it is shown the prophet's bed, being a shelf on the rock, about eight feet from the ground; and not far from this is the place where they say he wrote his Lamentations."[25] This cavern is still accessible today, but it is now occupied by fruit vendors who appreciate the relative coolness of the cave. It lies underneath the hill now called "Gordon's Calvary." Maundrell includes a careful description of the so-called Tombs of the Kings, now known to be those of Queen Helena. He marveled at the enormous stone doors, six inches thick, which "turned upon two hinges in the nature of axles." Maundrell reported that on the day following Easter, a group of the pilgrims went under armed convoy to the Jordan for baptism. The fee each pilgrim paid for the armed escort for protection against the Arabs was "twelve dollars." What he saw then as an old ruin in Bethany called Lazarus' Castle is pointed out today as the House of Simon. A Jewish pilgrim of this period noted innumerable graves, which today can be seen covering the

23. Benjamin of Tudela, "Travels (A.D. 1100-1173)," *Early Travels in Palestine,* ed. Thomas W. Wright (New York: KTAV Publishing House, 1968), p. 83.
24. Henry Maundrell, "The Journey from Aleppo to Jerusalem," ibid., p. 446.
25. Ibid.

Kidron Valley east of the old walled city. He reported that in early times they chose a site as close as possible to the temple, "at the foot of the slope of the temple mount."[26] He continued, "the new ones are at the foot of the Mount of Olives and the Valley of Kidron runs between the graveyards." These "newer graves" continued to "climb" the Mount of Olives until they formed a vast area of stone slabs through which, in recent years, a modern highway has been cut, desecrating many of the graves. During the latter portion of the Mameluke rule, Jerusalem and its environs were largely neglected. The population became demoralized and impoverished, and it shrank. When the Ottoman Turks took over the city in 1516, the population probably numbered little more than 10,000.[27]

OTTOMAN RULE

The Ottoman Empire was founded by Sultan Osman I in the latter part of the thirteenth century. They conquered Constantinople in 1453 and they occupied Syria and Egypt by 1517. The greatest of the Ottoman sultans was Suleiman the First ("the Magnificent"), who reigned from 1520 to 1566. Although far from the center of his domain, Suleiman thought Jerusalem worth rehabilitating. He rebuilt the walls as we see them today. The southern wall followed the line of Hadrian's city, and thus excluded the southwest portion often called "Mount Zion." In his rebuilding, special care was taken of the Damascus Gate. The builders sought to make it ornamental as well as useful. The graceful pointed arch in the center and the pinnacled battlement contribute to its beauty and grace. The passage through it follows a right-angled path to facilitate defense. In this respect, it is like each of the other gates of the city except Stephen's Gate and the Golden Gate on the east, the Dung Gate on the south, and the New Gate on the northwest. Entrance through the others—Jaffa, Herod's and David's—are also at right angles, hence, useful only for pedestrians. After three years of construction, the wall was completed about 1540. In addition to rebuilding the walls, Suleiman rebuilt aqueducts that brought water into the city from Solomon's Pools near Bethlehem. The low-level aqueduct brought water to the temple area, and the upper-level brought it to the upper city on the west. Jerusalem was relatively prosperous after this, though Christians and Jew-

26. Kollek and Pearlman, *Jerusalem,* p. 196.
27. Ibid.

Stephen's Gate (or the Sheep Gate), which is located along the east wall of the Old City.

ish residents had to pay a special tax. Many Jews who had been persecuted in many countries of Europe and expelled from Spain and Portugal in 1492 found relative freedom here under the Ottoman rule. These settled mostly in Safad, Tiberias, and Jerusalem.

The last three centuries of Ottoman rule found Palestine decadent, neglected, impoverished, and lawless. Bribery throughout the empire became prevalent. Taxes were high and administration was almost nonexistent. The land was often taxed in accordance to the number of trees on it, and the way to reduce taxes was to cut down the trees. This in turn facilitated erosion, a condition worsened by hungry goats that kept young trees from growing. The result was catastrophe. Erosion left the limestone hills denuded of soil, as they remain to this day. Meanwhile, bitter rivalries arose among the Christians, especially between the Greeks and the Latins. The Crusades had placed the Latins in ascendency, but as the Crusaders receded, the Orthodox churches sought to reassert their prior rights. At length, keys of the Holy Sepulchre were entrusted to a Moslem family because the Christians were so quarrelsome. Thus, it has remained for centuries. European countries, which the Ottomans wanted to avoid offending, defended the Latin churches against the Greeks. By the end of the eighteenth century, the Russian czars joined with the Greeks in defending the holy places. After a clash in the middle of the eighteenth century between the Greek Orthodox and the Franciscans at the Church of the Holy Sepulchre, the Ottoman sultan sought to settle the quarrel by giving portions of the Holy Sepulchre to the Latins and other portions to the Greeks. Even this did not solve the tensions because each foot of the sanctuary was disputed. The Franciscans could clean the steps of the Golgotha Chapel, for instance, but not the courtyard. Pilgrims, however, continued to come, but they lamented the impoverished condition of the

The Golden Gate as seen from inside the Old City.

country and the quarrels of the rival Christian sects, especially at the Holy Sepulchre. Maundrell noted that sometimes the Christians "proceeded to blows and wounds even at the very door of the sepulchre, mingling their own blood with their sacrifices." The various Christian sects continually complained to the Turkish authorities about infractions of the rules by another sect and vied with each other for obtaining special favors from the governors. Today, various portions of the Holy Sepulchre are assigned to the Orthodox, to the Roman Catholics, to the Armenians, to the Copts, whereas the Ethiopians possess only the roof, where they have built a small monastery.

As a pilgrim walks through the streets of Jerusalem today, guides point out the various places where Jesus suffered a succession of humiliations. (It is noteworthy that the Roman Catholics stress the sufferings of Jesus whereas the Greeks stress His resurrection.) As a result, largely through the influence of the Franciscans who were given custody of the holy places in the fourteenth century, fourteen "stations of the cross" were designated along the presumed path of Jesus on His way from Pilate's Praetorium to Calvary and the tomb. Of the fourteen, nine are events referred to in the Gospels, such as the flagellation and of Simon being commandeered to bear the cross. Five have been derived from ecclesiastical traditions, including Veronica's veil. Two of these are in the Fortress of Antonia, seven are along the street, and the last five within the Church of the Holy Sepulchre. These "stations" have been duplicated by the Roman Catholics in many parts of the world; one of the most impressive are the sculptures on the mountain overlooking Bogota, Colombia.

During the centuries of Turkish misrule, the Jews fared even worse than the Christians. The Christians had influential protectors: the Greeks in Constantinople and Moscow, the Latins in Western Europe. The exception to this was a brief period, from 1620-1625, under the leadership of Mohammed Pasha, when the Holy City contained more Jews than at any time since their banishment in the second century.[28]

The Jewish communities in the Holy Land included the Sephardim from the Iberian Peninsula and North Africa and the Ashkenazi from central and eastern Europe. Each class of Jews wore a distinctive garb. The Ashkenazi of eastern

---

28. Ibid., p. 217.

The view southeast over the Old City from the Lutheran Tower. The Aqsa Mosque is visible at the extreme left in the background.

Europe, then as now, were characterized by ringlets hanging from the temples of the men, long black garments and a fur-trimmed turban, such as now worn by ultra-Orthodox in the Mea Shearim section of west Jerusalem. The Sephardi Jews from western and southern Europe were treated with greater tolerance by the Ottomans than were the Ashkenazi, because of the political tensions between Russia and Constantinople. The latter group, however, finally reestablished itself in Jerusalem in the second decade of the nineteenth century and began building synagogues and schools. Their chief pride and glory was the synagogue completed in 1864 in the southeast corner of the old city, a building which was destroyed during the conflict of 1948. It is now being restored.

During the nineteenth century, the influence of Western powers continuously increased in the Middle East, largely be-

cause of European colonies farther south and east. This made
it easier for both Christian and Jewish communities in the Holy
Land. From that period an important chapter in Jerusalem's
history occurred when Mohammed Ali, a Moslem of Egypt but
who was born in Kavalla, Greece, rebelled against the sultan
in 1831 and sent his son Ibrahim Pasha to occupy Palestine.
Jerusalem was governed by Ibrahim for ten years, until the
Ottoman rule was reestablished with help from Great Britain.
This decade of rule by the Egyptians was beneficial to non-
Moslems in Jerusalem. The first consulate was opened here in
1838—the Consul of Great Britain. Later, France, Prussia, Aus-
tria, Spain, and eventually Russia, had consuls in Jerusalem.
This gave Christian and Western Jews the opportunity to appeal
for protection by their national representatives residing in Jeru-
salem. The British Consul from 1845 to 1864, was especially

helpful to the Jewish community.[29] In fact, the concept of Zionism was active among a group of English leaders long before Zionism became an avowed policy among European Jews. During most of these times, however, Jews and Christians were not permitted to visit such Moslem shrines as Hebron and the temple mount. The Jews did the next best thing, they prayed and wept at the western wall.

Rivalry among Western powers over the control of Christian sanctuaries and the protection of pilgrims was a contributing cause of the Crimean War (1854-56) between Russia and Western allies. As a result the Ottoman government defined more precisely the religious and political privileges of the various communities in the Holy City.

Another important chapter in Jerusalem's history occurred in the middle of the nineteenth century, when the Jewish philanthropist Moses Montefiore received from the sultan in Constantinople the right to purchase land outside the walls of Jerusalem for a Jewish colony. In addition to repairing the Tomb of

29. Ibid., p. 224.

The Wailing Wall. This is part of the western wall of the temple area enclosure and includes stretches of masonry erected by Herod the Great.

Rachel near Bethlehem, he built a windmill west of the Old City and constructed nearby a series of low rental apartments for immigrants. Up to this time it was considered extremely dangerous to live outside the protection of the walls. The first Jewish settlement outside the walls began in 1869 on the northwest edge of the Old City, called Nachlat Shiva. The second Jewish settlement was the Mea Shearim, called the "city of a hundred gates," into which the ultra-Orthodox from eastern Europe moved and where they still reside today. Meanwhile, persecution of Jews in eastern Europe accentuated the immigration, and the Jewish community both inside the wall and outside increased significantly toward the end of the nineteenth century and the beginning of the twentieth. Political Zionism came into being then, and Jewish immigration became more firmly established.

Although Russia was defeated in the Crimean War, the influence of the Russian Orthodox Church greatly increased in the latter part of the nineteenth century. At this time the large Russian compound was erected outside the city walls, which included a cathedral, a hospital for the sick, and hostels for the accommodations of the pilgrims. Crowning the Mount of Olives and still its most conspicuous feature is the beautiful Chapel of the Ascension with its Russian bell tower 214 steps above the level of the street.

England and France became increasingly influential in Palestine at the same time. Germany's entrance into the political and religious picture was signalized by the visit of Kaiser Wilhelm II, who made a state visit to the Near East in 1898. At that time he authorized the building of a new tomb for Saladin in Damascus, the Lutheran Church of the Redeemer opposite the Holy Sepulchre, the Roman Catholic Church of the Dormition on so-called Mount Zion at the southwest corner of the city area, and the Augusta Victoria hospice with its tower on Mount Scopus. This was linked with the Prussian leader's "drive to the east" and German plans for the Berlin-to-Baghdad railroad. Under the Ottomans, the first railroad to be built in Palestine in 1892, connected Jerusalem with Jaffa. Eventually one could go by rail from Jerusalem to Cairo, Jaffa, Haifa, Beirut, and Damascus.[30]

---

30. George Olaf Matson, *The Palestine Guide,* 5th ed. (Jerusalem: Joshua Simon, 1946), p. 97.

The Tower of the Dormition in Jerusalem, battle-scarred from the fighting in 1948.

12

Jerusalem From
World War I
to the Present

Jerusalem was involved in World War I. In 1914, Turkey, along with the Central Powers, declared war on the Allies. The Turkish desert campaign swept across the Sinai Peninsula with the view of controlling the Suez Canal and invading Egypt, which was then held by the British. An epidemic of typhus spread from the Turkish armies. This and a visitation of locusts in the spring of 1916 were serious problems for Jerusalem and the cities of central Palestine. In the summer of 1917, the British undertook to drive the Turks out of Palestine. Beginning from Egypt, the column pushed up along the Mediterranean through the Sinai Desert, while Lawrence of Arabia with Bedouin troops harassed Turkish garrisons and their communications east of the Jordan with significant success. Arab nationalists saw that it was to their advantage to eject the Ottoman rulers in view of promised assistance from the British in helping them achieve independence. Allenby's forces broke through on the Beer-sheba-Gaza line in October, and pushed up along the coast, arriving on the outskirts of Jerusalem on the south, west, and north. There was no fighting inside the city, for as the Turks realized their position was untenable, they hastily withdrew on the eighth of December after borrowing a bedsheet from Mrs. Bertha Vester of the American colony, to use as a flag of surrender. The surrender was negotiated between the Arab mayor of Jerusalem and a representative of General Allenby. In contrast to the ostentatious entry of Kaiser Wilhelm II in 1898, which necessitated the removal of a portion of the west wall to accommodate his carriage, General Allenby simply dismounted, walked through the Joppa Gate, and issued his proclamation on the eastern steps of the Citadel. British authorities assured the inhabitants of protection and the repair of damages. Many on this historic occasion wept for joy that four centuries of Turkish "rule" was ended and, for the first time since the Crusaders left, Jerusalem was governed by Christian leaders. The supply of food and water and fuel was promised, and access to all holy places guaranteed.

JERUSALEM UNDER THE BRITISH (1918-1948)

The American colony was formed by a devout group of Christian immigrants from America led by Henry Spafford of Chicago. With him gathered a group of Christians who ardently expected the second coming of Christ and wanted to be in the Holy City when the Messiah returned. They established a "home" north of the Damascus Gate, between the tombs of the kings and near the Sheik Jarrah Quarter on the Nablus Road. This served as a hospice for pilgrims, especially for Americans, but the community took deep roots in the city and initiated a series of social services such as a hospital, an orphanage, and an eye hospital that still flourishes. The hospital is located just inside the northern wall east of the Damascus Gate, at the highest point of the ridge. From the roof of this hospital General ("Chinese") Gordon looked across the road to the continuation of the ridge, where a Moslem cemetery is now located, and saw openings in the cliff suggesting a human skull (Golgotha"—Mark 15:22). Since then this cliff has been called "Gordon's Calvary." The Garden Tomb Association resulted from the discovery of an ancient tomb near this hill in 1875. The garden now serves as a place of meditation and worship.

Before the establishment of the Mandate, English influence already was reflected in the construction of Saint Charles Anglican Church, inside the Old City opposite the citadel. The archbishop resided on the Nablus Road north of the city, where Saint George Cathedral and Saint George Academy were built. It still remains as the main religious institution for English-speaking Protestants in the Jerusalem area. The Rockefeller Museum was built at this time opposite the so-called Stork's Tower northeast of Herod's Gate. It is a repository of a priceless collection of Palestine antiquities, which includes the remains of the Omayyad Palace near Jericho and fragments from the Qumran Caves. In the late nineteenth century, the American Schools of Oriental Research was established on Saladin Street north of Herod's Gate, surrounded by an iron fence, containing facilities for archaeological research. Nearby is the world-famous Ecole Biblique, founded by the Dominicans, which possesses one of the best libraries on Palestine to be found anywhere. Other Christian buildings include the YMCA building, opposite the King David Hotel in west Jerusalem, believed to be the most expensive YMCA building in the world. From its Jesus Tower Christmas carols are played, and it continues to perform effective service, predominantly to the Jewish community. The YMCA building in east Jerusalem, near the Saint George Church, was seriously damaged in the war of June 1967, but has since been repaired. This building and the Augusta Victoria Hospital on Mount Scopus were the two most heavily damaged buildings of the Six-Day War.

Even before the period of the Mandate, British interest in the Holy City was reflected by the creation of the Palestine Exploration Fund, which sponsored excavations of Jerusalem by Captain Warren, who by the use of tunneling operations ascertained the nature and extent of the walls of the temple area. This pioneer work still remains as the most accurate, detailed description of the Herodian walls. During this period the Jews developed Mount Scopus, building there their Hadassah Hospital and a Hebrew University that was inaugurated in 1925. During the Mandate period occurred the largest increase of Jewish inhabitants; they numbered 34,000 in 1922, but when the British departed in 1947, their numbers had increased to 97,000.[1]

Simultaneously, Arabs moved outside the city to the north where hotels, schools, and churches are to be found in a relatively uncrowded area, extending from the old walls to the western edge of Mount Scopus. During this period, the British maintained the religious status quo, which permitted Christians but not Jews to enter the temple area. As the Jewish residents increased, not only in Jerusalem but throughout Palestine, by the efforts of the international Jewish community through its National Fund, Arab apprehensions increased. Hostility deepened, and in 1929,

---

1. Teddy Kollek and Moshe Pearlman, *Jerusalem: A History of Forty Centuries* (New York: Random House, 1968), p. 239.

Arabs clashed with Jews in Jerusalem, Hebron, and elsewhere. Resentment continued to increase, and disturbances also occurred in 1933, in 1936, and again in 1939. The British Royal Commission recommended partition of the country between Jewish and Arab sectors, but this proposal was shelved during World War II.[2]

After the war was over in 1945, Arab-Jewish tension greatly increased. Jewish immigration was drastically curtailed, and the British government informed the United Nations that it was ready to terminate Mandate on the expiration of its thirty-year period.

The United Nations, meeting in November of 1947 at Lake Success, New York, voted for a partition of Palestine between the Jews and the Arabs. The plan of partition was drawn in such a way that mutual coexistence would be imperative if these proposed boundary lines were respected, because neither Jews nor Arabs could survive without some dealing with the other. The Arabs needed access to the sea, the Jews depended on access to food-producing regions of the hinterland. The Jews accepted but the Arabs rejected this United Nations partition plan. Nevertheless, the British proceeded with their announced plans of terminating their thirty-year Mandate, and the time of withdrawal was fixed at May 1948. The United Nations also recommended that Jerusalem be made an international community, the only city in the world to be designated as such. Arab-Jewish hostility increased immediately, however, and fighting between the Arab Nationalists and Jewish Zionists escalated during the closing months of the British Mandate. The Laborite government in Britain was opposed to further Jewish immigration, which resulted in Jewish forces (the Haganah, the Irgun, and the Stern Gang) fighting both the Arabs and the British. The Arabs possessed in the Arab Legion the best fighting force in the Moslem world, trained and led by British officers. This advantage they used effectively to defend the Old City and the adjacent territory north, south, and east. The Jewish holdings on Mount Scopus, the hospital and university, were deep within the Arab zone and therefore cut off from their compatriots in west Jerusalem. Also, the large Jewish community in the so-called Jewish Quarter in the southeast portion of the Old City

---

2. The period is objectively and succinctly treated in James Parkes, *A History of Palestine from 135 A.D. to Modern Times* (New York: Oxford University Press, 1949), pp. 318 ff.

was isolated from west Jerusalem. Water was cut off from New (west) Jerusalem, and the Jewish populace, numbering 100,000 were forced to depend on cisterns for their water supply. Several armed convoys from Tel Aviv reached Jerusalem during this period, but by April 1948, the Arab Legion possessed the heights at Latrun dominating the highway, and west Jerusalem was completely isolated.[3]

On the day the British troops left, David Ben Gurion in Tel Aviv read the Declaration of Jewish Independence, and the state of Israel was formally recognized, first by the United States and later by other nations. On May 14, 1948, Jerusalem became the main battle area as the British-trained Arab Legion sought to drive the Jews from Jerusalem, but the defenders stubbornly resisted. The Arabs had the advantage of many of the so-called Taggart Forts, which the British built through the length and breadth of the land during their Mandate. In addition to the

3. John Gray, *A History of Jerusalem* (London: Robert Hale, 1969), p. 306.

A bombed building in the section of Jerusalem designated "no-man's land" before the six-day war of June, 1967.

Arab Legion, military forces from Egypt and Iraq joined in the effort to resist the Zionists. In the three weeks following, Arab artillery dropped more than 10,000 shells into New Jerusalem. Only in the Jewish quarter of the Old City, however, were the Arab attacks effective. House-to-house fighting resulted in extensive civilian casualties and in the destruction of houses and over fifty synagogues and schools.[4]

The Jewish quarter fell on May 28, two weeks after the Declaration of Independence. Elsewhere, the Jewish defenders remained intact or took the offensive and regained some territory. This led to a United Nations truce on June 11. The fighting resumed, however, with Jews gaining still more territory until an armistice agreement was effected in the spring of 1949. Armistice agreements with the Jews included Egypt, Lebanon, Trans-Jordan, and Syria. The result was the infamous no-man's land, which divided Jerusalem north and south running along Saint George Road to the Damascus Gate, thence around the west wall to the Hinnom Valley near David's Gate.

JERUSALEM FROM 1948 TO 1967

The house of the British high-commissioner on the hill south of Jerusalem became the headquarters of the United Nations Truce Commission. The only communication between the two halves of the city was through diplomatic corps and pilgrims who were permitted to pass from the east side to the west through the so-called Mandelbaum Gate near the American Consulate. The exception to this was at Christmas and Easter, when the families from the Jewish sector were permitted to visit their relatives in the east. The enclave on Mount Scopus was limited to a custodial force, which was exchanged every two weeks under armed convoy. This situation continued until June 1967.

Compared with their military efforts the Arab economic boycott of Israel was relatively effective. Travelers who had their passports checked at the Mandelbaum Gate by Jordanian officials as they entered Israel, risked having subsequent access to Arab lands denied because of visiting Israel. The Mandelbaum Gate, therefore, was the only place where visitors in Arab countries were permitted entrance into Israel. Electric service, water service, mail service on each side of the no-man's land was separate, with no possibility of communication by phone or by letter.

---

4. Kollek and Pearlman, *Jerusalem,* p. 250.

The nations that recognized the state of Israel had their consulates in Tel Aviv. The Israelis, however, decided to make Jerusalem their capital, over the protests of the United Nations, with the result that the Israeli Parliament building, the Knesset, is in west Jerusalem today, but foreign embassies are still at Tel Aviv.

Since the Hebrew University campus was not accessible, a new campus, which is now the main campus, was started in west Jerusalem. Jewish immigration greatly increased during this period, and west Jerusalem expanded rapidly, especially to the north and to the west. A new road from Jerusalem to Tel Aviv was constructed to bypass the Arab Legion fortress at Latrun. The Jordanians, meanwhile, built another road from Jerusalem to Bethlehem, some thirteen miles in length, because the Israeli forces had cut off the main six-mile road from Jerusalem to Bethlehem.

Tension continued until it climaxed in the latter days of May 1967, when President Nasser declared the closing of the Tiron Straits to Israeli shipping and demanded a withdrawal of the United Nations troops on the border between Israel and Egypt. On Monday morning, June 5, Israeli planes left before dawn for the airfields of their Arab neighbors in Egypt, Jordan, Syria, and Iraq. At 11:25 A.M., after King Hussein had ignored the Israeli plea for calm, an Arab Legion gun from the Mount of Olives hit the portion of the Dormition Church where a Jewish garrison was stationed.[5]

Shortly thereafter, a contingent of the Arab Legion moved across no-man's land and occupied the headquarters of the United Nations (The Government House) and the world heard the voice of Secretary General of the United Nations appealing to the Jordanians to withdraw. This plea went unheeded, but Jewish armed forces, moving from West Jerusalem, dislodged the Jordanians and occupied the premises while United Nations personnel found refuge in the American Consulate and the American School of Oriental Research. The American Consulate itself was in the midst of heavy fighting as was the East Jordanian YMCA building, both of which were near the armistice line. Heavy shelling continued through the afternoon and night, but by Tuesday, the Jewish counterattack had partially encircled

---

5. W. A. Dever, "Archaeology and the Six Day War," *Biblical Archaeologist* 30 (September 1967): 103.

Two scenes of the expanding modern campus of the Hebrew University in Jerusalem.

the city. On Wednesday morning Israelis occupied the Mount of Olives, forced their way into the Old City through Stephen's Gate, and after reaching the Wailing Wall, held a thanksgiving service.[6]

Both Arab and Jewish forces sought to avoid destruction of the Old City, with its innumerable shrines. Some shells, however, fell in the Haram area, and Saint Anne's Church was slightly damaged. The Golden Gate, along the east wall of the Old City, showed the marks of shell fire, but elsewhere there was relatively minor damage, far less than in the conflict of 1948.

Civilian casualties were remarkably few considering the intensity of the fighting. Among the best-known victims of the fighting was Warden Mattar, of the Garden Tomb, who was accidentally killed by Israeli gunfire as he ran from the shelter of the Garden Tomb to his residence. Three days later his burial was conducted in the Garden Tomb, nextdoor to his neighbors at the École Biblique.

Two families of the American consulate were housed in the building of the American Schools of Oriental Research during the hostilities, and Dr. Nelson Glueck, who arrived on June 12, was able to coordinate the continuing roles of the American Schools of Oriental Research and the Hebrew Union College in east and west Jerusalem.[7] The British School of Archaeology, as reported by Director Hennessy, was only slightly damaged. The Palestine Archaeological Museum was involved in the fighting, from the tower and within, but its exhibits were quickly restored by Israeli archaeologists.[8]

From the Jewish standpoint, the rejoicing at the western wall, or Wailing Wall, by Israeli soldiers and the senior chaplain of Israeli armed forces was particularly memorable, the chaplain declaring: "We have taken the city of God. We are entering the Messianic era for the Jewish people."[9] An "irreligious" Israeli said recently that he shook with uncontrolled emotion as he stood by the wall on that occasion. That the Holy City was spared more destruction was due to disciplined restraint in the Old City and the strategy of a circling movement

---

6. Sifriat Maariv, *Jerusalem the Eternal* (Tel Aviv: Otpaz, 1968), pp. 108-160.
7. Dever, "Six Day War," p. 103.
8. Ibid., p. 104.
9. Robert J. Donovan, *Israel's Fight for Survival: Six Days in June* (New York: New American Library, a Signet Book, 1967), p. 120.

to the south from the Government House and to the north from Mount Scopus.[10]

The attacking force west of Jerusalem finally captured the Arab strongpoint at Latrun, and by Tuesday morning, they had also captured the northern suburb of Shufat and the adjacent French Hill. At midday they met survivors of the paratroop battalion who had fought their way through the northern suburbs of Jerusalem in spite of heavy casualties. After the battle ceased, Israeli authorities quickly removed the barriers that had separated the two halves of the city for two decades. Bulldozers removed Arab houses built against the western wall of the temple area, and on June 14, one week after the battle for Jerusalem had ended, the Jewish festival Feast of Weeks occurred with a quarter million Jews converging in the cleared space at the western wall.[11]

On June 23, Moslems who had been living in Israel worshiped at the Dome of the Rock for the first time in nineteen years, and on June 25, Arab Christians both from the West Bank and from Israel worshiped together at the Church of the Holy Sepulchre.

JERUSALEM AFTER 1967

The annexation of Jerusalem was made official by the Knesset over the protest of most Arabs and of the United Nations. Although at first suspicious of each other, the Arab and Jewish civilians were soon fraternizing in spite of years of deepest distrust and hostility. Israeli medical facilities, parks, and cinemas in west Jerusalem were patronized by Arabs of east Jerusalem. Arab stores in the Old City were soon depleted of wares by Israeli shoppers, but the Arab merchants soon were complaining because they had to pay taxes equal to that of Jewish merchants, which was twice as much as they had been paying before. At the same time, sources of their wares from Arab countries became no longer available. East Jerusalem's main source of income had been the tourist business, and tourist agencies in east Jerusalem were among the businesses most adversely affected. Gradually, Israeli tourist agents began to use the excellent east Jerusalem hotel facilities and also the Arab guides, especially in the area of the West Bank. (The "West

10. Kollek and Pearlman, *Jerusalem,* p. 261.
11. Ibid., p. 270.

The Shrine of the Book museum in Jerusalem, where Dead Sea Scrolls are preserved. The white cupola and the black basalt wall represent the War of the Sons of Light against the Sons of Darkness as depicted in Qumran literature.

Bank" designates the territory west of the Jordan annexed by the Hashemite Kingdom of Jordan in 1952).

Jews were allowed to visit the spacious temple area to gaze upon their ancestors' graves in the valley of the Kidron. With tourists from all parts of the world they now could gaze upon the Holy City from the Mount of Olives, for many the most impressive sight on the globe. The city planners immediately began to work on the restoration and reactivation of the hospital on Mount Scopus, the university, and more recently the Harry Truman Art Center overlooking the Wilderness of Judea has been completed and dedicated. It is an ultra-modern building and includes the picturesque amphitheater, which was begun in the 1920s, built into the hillside and facing the wilderness.

Student housing has sprung up north of the British War Cemetery on the northern approaches to Mount Scopus, over the protests of many who lament the appearance of modern structures in this unique environment. Even greater protests, not only within Israel but from the world community, have been voiced against the extensive apartment buildings erected north of the Old City, leading its sponsors to consider a revision of the program. In this connection it has been noted that "more than a hundred Arabs had applied for 23 apartment units . . . in Wadi Joz," a suburb in northeast Jerusalem.[12]

In recent months, archaeologists have conducted excavations at the south and west corners of the Haram area. They have dug down to Herodian levels and exposed the lower sections of the west wall. Today, Jews from Mea Shearim and elsewhere may be seen winding their way for prayers at the open-air synagogue against the western wall. Of particular interest is the recent accessibility of the area under and around "Wilson's Arch." Portions of the west wall at this point have been exposed to a depth of about seventy feet, revealing the superb Herodian masonry in near-perfect condition.

One of the most drastic changes is the "urban renewal" going on in the former Jewish quarter (the southeast quarter) of the Old City. Many of the old buildings are being demolished. Some are being reconstructed. Only construction from stone

12. *The Jerusalem Post*, 2 February 1971, p. 4.

View of west Jerusalem, looking north from the YMCA tower.

was permitted within Jerusalem during the Mandate period, and the city planners have continued this precedent. In the fall of 1969, excavations in the northwest portion of this quarter disclosed some frescoes of "an elaborate building" from the time of Herod "of high artistic standard."[13]

Of particular interest is the Menorah (seven-branched candelabra) incised on plaster, the oldest detailed representation known. Portions of an Iron Age II wall, discovered east of this site, provide evidence that "the western hill of Jerusalem was well occupied at the end of the Judean monarchy."[14]

The second season (1970) revealed a city wall of the kingdom (preexilic) period, a residence from Herodian times, a bath house, and a Byzantine church.[15] Excavations and rebuilding are continuing and new finds are awaited with great interest.

Elsewhere, life in the Old City goes on as it has for decades. Virtually all the holy places and sites are intact. To the problem of the internationalization of Jerusalem, directed by the United Nations in 1947 and reaffirmed several times since, has been added the ecological problem caused by sprawling suburbs near the scenic and historic areas to the north and south. It is hard to avoid the conclusion that plans for the enlargement of east and north Jerusalem are, for the most part, politically motivated —to present the world with a *fait accompli* before political decisions have been finalized, rather than to meet a need for luxury housing in this particular area. It is true that east Jerusalem and the West Bank of the Jordan were annexed by Trans-Jordan without the sanction of the world community, but does this justify the acquisitions by the Israeli government? At the same time, few would deny that a united Jerusalem is a great convenience to both tourists and residents.

Thus, the Holy Land in general and the city of Jerusalem in particular remains a continuing problem for the world community. Current issues involve the opening of the Suez Canal, the withdrawal of Israel occupation forces from Sinai, the status of the Gaza Strip, the rehabilitation of refugees, and the political and economic future of the West Bank. Today, as in most centuries previously, the issues are not likely to be settled on Pal-

---

13. N. Avigad, "Excavations in the Jewish Quarter of the Old City of Jerusalem," 1969/1970," *Israel Exploration Journal* 20, nos. 1 and 2 (1970): 3.
14. Ibid., p. 8.
15. Ibid., nos. 3 and 4, p. 140.

estinian soil, but by decisions made outside the territory. At very few times in her checkered history have the residents of the area been able to settle their own affairs independent of their neighbors. The land is too limited in area and in resources to permit it becoming other than dependent on world powers outside her borders. Few West Bank residents would welcome a return to the situation prior to 1967; they have fared better than anticipated under Jewish rule. In March 1972, however, King Hussein announced the formation of the "United Arab Kingdom" in which "the Israeli-occupied West Bank—with Jerusalem as its capital—and perhaps eventually the Gaza Strip" would be united with Trans-Jordan.[16]

Since Israel claims Jerusalem shall never again be divided, and since Gaza belonged to Egypt, this is no more than a plan. But the possibility remains that Palestinians of the West Bank, never claimed by Israel, would prefer a federation with Jordan as the least objectionable option. This would be especially desirable if the refugees who fled across the Jordan in 1948 and in 1967 were permitted to return.

Relations between the more sophisticated West Bank residents with Trans-Jordan have never been cordial, even though refugees, until recently, found Jordan the most friendly of the host countries. Only in Jordan have they been given citizenship privileges.

By 1972, Israeli army units had driven Palestinian commandos back from the Israel-Lebanon border. The commandos were replaced by elements of the regular Lebanese army. Thus in Lebanon in 1972 as in Jordan in 1970, the commandos found themselves opposed not by Israel alone but also by the regular army of the host country.

Clashes on the Israel-Syria frontier appear unlikely to produce any long-range effect.

Meanwhile the world can only hope and pray and work to the end that the peace of Jerusalem, for which the devout are exhorted to pray (Ps. 122:6), will be one that is both just and lasting.

---

16. *Newsweek*, 27 March 1972, p. 41.

Bibliography

Abel, F. M. *Geographie de le Palestine*. 2 vols. Paris: Gibalda, 1933-38.

Abel, F. M. and Vincent, L. H. *Jerusalem: Recherches de Topographies, d'Archeologie et Histoire*. Paris: 1912-22.

Adams, J. McKee. *Biblical Backgrounds: A Geographical Survey of Bible Lands in the Light of the Scriptures and Recent Research*. Nashville: Broadman Press, 1934.

Adrichem, Christiaan Van. *Jerusalem, 1584 (Jerusalem et suburbia eius ... per Christianum Adrichom Delphum, 1584)*. Ithaca, N.Y.: Historic Urban Plans, 1965.

Aharoni, Yohanan. *The Land of the Bible: A Historical Geography*. Translated by A. F. Rainey. London: Burns & Oates, 1967.

Aharoni, Yohanan and Avi-Yonah, Michael. *The Macmillan Bible Atlas*. Prepared by Carta, Jerusalem. New York: Macmillan Co., 1968.

Albright, William F. "Danish Excavation at Shiloh." *Bulletin of the American Schools of Oriental Research* 9 (1923).

Allenby, E. H. H. *The Advance of the Egyptian Expeditionary Force, July, 1917 to October, 1918*. London: His Majesty's Stationery Office, 1919.

Amiran, David H. K.; Elster, Joseph; Gilead, Mordeha; Rosenan, Naftali; Kadmon, Naftali; and Paran, Uzi, eds. *Atlas of Israel*. Jerusalem: Survey of Israel, Ministry of Labour; Amsterdam: Elsevier Publishing Co., 1970.

Anati, Emmanuel. *Palestine Before the Hebrews: A History from the Earliest Arrival of Man to the Conquest of Canaan*. New York: Alfred A. Knopf, 1963.

Archer, T. A. *The Crusades*. New York: G. P. Putnam's Sons, 1894.

Ashbed, C. R., ed. *Jerusalem*. London: John Murray, 1920, 1924.

Avi-Yonah, Michael. *The Holy Land*. Grand Rapids: Baker Book House, 1966.

——. *The Madeba Mosaic Map.* Jerusalem: Israel Exploration Society, 1954.

——. *Roman Palestine.* 2d Ed. New York: Oxford University Press, 1940.

Baly, Denis. *The Geography of the Bible: A Study in Historical Geography.* New York: Harper & Row, Publishers, 1957.

Baly, Denis and Tushingham, A. D. *Atlas of the Biblical World.* New York: World Publishing Co., 1971.

Biran, A. "A Mycenean Character Vase from Tel Dan." *Israel Exploration Journal* 20, nos. 1 and 2 (1970).

Blaiklock, E. M. *Cities of the New Testament.* Old Tappan, N.J.: Fleming H. Revell Co., 1965.

——., ed. *The Zondervan Pictorial Bible Atlas.* Grand Rapids: Zondervan Publishing House, 1969.

Boulanger, Robert. *Hatchette World Guides: The Middle East, Lebanon, Syria, Jordan, Iraq, Iran.* Translated by J. S. Hardman. Paris: Hatchette, 1966.

Casola, Pietro (1427-1507). *Canon P. Casola's Pilgrimage to Jerusalem.* Translated by M. M. Newett. Manchester, Eng.: University Press, 1907.

Ceram, C. W. *The March of Archaeology.* New York: Alfred A. Knopf, 1970.

Churchill, Randolph S. and Churchill, Winston S. *The Six Day War.* Boston: Houghton Mifflin Co., 1967.

Conder, C. R. *Palestine.* New York: Dodd, Mead & Co., n.d.

Conner, C. R. and Kitchener, H. H. *The Survey of Western Palestine.* 8 vols. London: Palestine Exploratory Fund, 1883.

Couriet, A. *La Prise De Jerusalem Par Les Perses en 614 A.D.* Orleans, 1896.

Cross, Frank Moore, Jr. *The Ancient Library of Qumran and Modern Biblical Studies.* Garden City, N.Y.: Doubleday & Co., 1958.

Dalman, Gustaf. *Sacred Sites and Ways: Studies in the Topography of the Gospels.* Translated by Paul P. Levertoff. London: Society for Promotion of Christian Knowledge; New York: Macmillan Co., 1935.

De Joinville, Lord John, comp. *Chronicles of the Crusades: Contemporary Narratives of the Crusade of Richard Coeur de Lion, by Richard of Devizes and Geoffrey de Vinsauf, and of the Crusade of Saint Louis.* London: Bell and Daldy, 1870.

Donovan, Robert J. *Israel's Fight for Survival: Six Days in June.* New York: The New American Library; London: The New English Library, A Signet Book, 1967.

Douglas, J. D., ed. *The New Bible Dictionary.* Grand Rapids: Eerdmans Publishing Co., 1962.

Epp, Frank H. *Whose Land Is Palestine? The Middle East Problem in Historical Perspective.* Grand Rapids: Eerdmans Publishing Co., 1970.

Eusebius. *The Ecclesiastical History.* 2 vols. Translated by J. E. L. Oulton. London: William Heinemann; New York: G. P. Putnam's Sons, 1932.

———. *Das Onomastikon.* Translated by E. Klostermann. Hildesheim: 1966.

Fodor, Eugene and Foder, William, eds. *Fodor's Modern Guides: Israel 1967-68.* New York: David McKay Co., 1967.

Forster, Arnold. *Report from Israel.* New York: Anti-Defamation League of B'nai B'rith, n.d.

Fulcher of Chartres. *A History of the Expedition to Jerusalem, 1095–1127.* Translated by Frances Rita Ryan (Sisters of Saint Joseph). Edited with an introduction by Harold S. Fink. Knoxville: University of Tennessee Press, 1969.

Glueck, Nelson. *The Other Side of the Jordan.* New Haven, Conn.: American Schools of Oriental Research, 1940.

———. *The River Jordan.* New York: McGraw-Hill Book Co., 1968.

Grant, Michael. *The Climax of Rome.* London: Weidenfeld & Nicolson, 1968.

Gray, John. *A History of Jerusalem.* London: Robert Hale, 1969.

Harrison, R. K. *Old Testament Times.* Grand Rapids: Eerdmans Publishing Co., 1970.

Hindson, Edward E. *The Philistines and the Old Testament.* Grand Rapids: Baker Book House, 1971.

Hoade, Eugene. *Guide to the Holy Land.* 4th ed., rev. Jerusalem: Franciscan Press, 1962.

Jeremias, Joachim. *Jerusalem in the Time of Jesus.* Translated by F. H. Cave and C. H. Cave. London: SCM Press, 1962, 1967.

Jirku, Anton. *The World of the Bible.* Translated by Ann E. Kepp. London: Weidenfeld and Nicholson, 1967.

Johns, C. N. *Palestine of the Crusades.* Historical introduction and map. Jaffa: 1938.

Join-Lambert, Michael. *Jerusalem.* Translated by Charlotte Haldane. London: Elek Books, 1958.

Josephus. *Josephus: Complete Works.* Translated by William Whiston. Grand Rapids: Kregel Publications, 1964.

Kenyon, Kathleen M. *Archaeology in the Holy Land.* New York: Praeger, Publishers, 1960.

———. *Jerusalem: Excavating 3000 Years of History.* New York: McGraw-Hill Book Co.; London: Thames & Hudson, 1967.

Kitchen, J. Howard. *Holy Fields: An Introduction to the Historical Geography of the Holy Land.* Grand Rapids: Eerdmans Publishing Co., 1955.

Kollek, Teddy and Pearlman, Moshe. *Jerusalem: A History of Forty Centuries*. New York: Random House, 1968.

Kopp, Clemens. *The Holy Places of the Gospels*. New York: Herder & Herder, 1963.

Kraeling, Emil G., ed. *Rand McNally Historical Atlas of the Holy Land*. Chicago: Rand McNally & Co., 1959.

Landau, Eli. *Jerusalem the Eternal: The Paratroopers' Battle for the City of David*. Translated by R. Lev. Edited by Murray Roston. Tel-Aviv: Otpaz, 1968.

Lawrence, T. E. *Crusader Castles*. London: Golden Cockerel Press, 1936.

Louvish, Misha, ed. *Facts About Israel, 1970*. Jerusalem: Keter Books, 1970.

Library of the Palestine Pilgrims' Text Society. 12 vols. New York: AMS Press, 1971.

Matson, G. Olaf. *The Palestinian Guide, Including Trans-Jordan*. Jerusalem: Joshua Simon, 1946.

Mazzolani, L. S. *The Idea of the City in Roman Thought (from walled city to spiritual commonwealth)*. Translated by S. O'Donnell. Toronto: Hollis & Carter, 1967, 1970.

Meistermann, P. Barnabe. *Guide de Terre Sainte*. Paris: Editions Franciscaines; Librarie Letouzey & Ané, 1936.

Meysels, Theodor F. *Israeli in Your Pocket*. Tel Aviv: Ben-Dor Israel Publishing Co., 1956.

Michaud, Joseph Francis. *History of the Crusades*. Translated by W. Robson, New York: Redfield, 1853.

Migne, J. P. *Sancti Eusebii Hieronymi Patrologiae Latinae*. Liber de Situ et Nominibus Locurum Hebraicorum, vol. 23. Turnholti, Belgium: n.d.

Moore, Elinor, A. *The Ancient Churches of Jerusalem: The Evidence of the Pilgrims*. London: Constable, 1961.

Munro, T. C. "The Speech of Pope Urban II at Clermont." *American Historical Review* 11 (1906).

Napoleon. *Guerre de l'Orient: Campagnes d'Egypte et de Syrie par General Bertrand*. Paris: 1847.

Needler, Winifred. *Palestine Ancient and Modern*. Toronto: Royal Ontario Museum of Archaeology, 1949.

Newton, A. P., ed. *Travel and Travellers in the Middle Ages*. London: 1930; Freeport, N.Y.: Brooklyn Libraries Press, 1967.

Noth, Martin. *The History of Israel*. New York: Harper & Row, 1958.

Oldenbourg, Zoe. *The Crusades*. Translated by Anne Carter. London: Weidenfeld and Nicolson, 1966.

Oman, W. W. C. *A History of the Art of War in the Middle Ages*. 2d. ed., rev. 2 vols. London: 1934.

Orni, Efriam and Efrat, Elisha. *Geography of Israel*. Jerusalem: Israel Program for Scientific Translations, 1964.

Orsheofsky, Milton. "The Bulldozers Carve Out Israel's New Frontiers." *Life*, 12 March 1971, pp. 32-34.

Palestine Pilgrims' Text Society. John H. Bernard. *The Churches of Constantine at Jerusalem*. Library of the Palestine Pilgrims' Text Society, vol. 1. New York: AMS Press, 1971.

———. *The Epitome of S. Eucherius About Certain Holy Places* (circ. A.D. 449 and the *Breviary* or *Short Description of Jerusalem* (circ. A.D. 530). Translated by Aubrey Stewart. Library of the Palestine Pilgrims' Text Society, vol. 2. New York: AMS Press, 1971.

———. *The Pilgrimage of Arculfus in the Holy Land*. Translated by James Rose Macpherson. Library of the Palestine Pilgrims' Text Society, vol. 3. London: 24 Hanover Square, W., 1895.

———. Nasir-I-Khusrau. *Diary of a Journey Through Syria and Palestine*. Translated by Guy Le Strange. Library of the Palestine Pilgrims' Text Society, vol. 4. London: 24 Hanover Square, W., 1895.

———. *Fetellus*. Translated by James Rose Macpherson. Library of the Palestine Pilgrims' Text Society, vol. 5. London: 24 Hanover Square, W., 1896.

———. *Eleventh and Twelfth Centuries*. Translated by Aubrey Stewart. Library of the Palestine Pilgrims' Text Society, vol. 6. London: 24 Hanover Square, W., 1894.

———. *The Wanderings of Felix Fabri*. Library of the Palestine Pilgrims' Text Society, vols. 7 and 8. New York: AMS Press, 1971.

———. *Felix Fabri*. Translated by Aubrey Stewart. Library of the Palestine Pilgrims' Text Society, vols. 9 and 10. London: 24 Hanover Square, W., 1893.

———. *Extracts from Aristeas, Hecataeus, Origen and Other Early Writers*. Translated by Aubrey Stewart. Library of the Palestine Pilgrims' Text Society, vol. 11. London: 24 Hanover Square, W., 1895.

———. *Burchard of Mount Sion*. Translated by Aubrey Stewart. Library of the Palestine Pilgrims' Text Society, vol. 12. London: 24 Hanover Square, W., 1896.

Paris, M. P. *Guillaume de Tyr et ses Continuateurs*. Paris: 1879.

Parkes, James. *A History of Palestine from 135 A.D. to Modern Times*. New York: Oxford University Press, 1949.

Paz, Ury. *The Shortest War: Israel Fights for Survival*. Israel: Ramdor Publishing Co., 1967.

Pearlman, Moshe and Yannai, Yaacov. *Historical Sites in Israel*. New York: Vanguard Press, 1964.

Perowne, Stewart. *Jerusalem—Bethlehem*. South Brunswick, N.Y.: A. S. Barnes Co., 1965.

———. *The Life and Times of Herod the Great*. Nashville: Abingdon Press, 1959.

———. *The Later Herods*. Nashville: Abingdon Press, 1959.

Pfeiffer, Charles F. *Baker's Bible Atlas*. Grand Rapids: Baker Book House, 1961.

——. ed. *The Biblical World: A Dictionary of Biblical Archaeology* Grand Rapids: Baker Book House, 1966.

Pfeiffer, Charles F. and Vos, Howard F. *The Wycliffe Historical Geography of the Holy Lands*. Chicago: Moody Press, 1967.

Pfeiffer, Robert H. *History of the New Testament Times, with an Introduction to the Apocrypha*. New York: Harper & Bros., 1949.

Philipson, David, ed. *Hebrew Union Jubilee Volume: 1875-1925*. New York: KTAV Publishing House, 1968.

Pritchard, James B., ed. *The Ancient Near East: An Anthology of Texts and Pictures*. Princeton: Princeton University Press; London: Oxford University Press, 1958.

Robinson, Edward. *Biblical Researches in Palestine and in the Adjacent Regions*. Boston: Crocker and Brewster, 1868.

——. *Later Biblical Researches in Palestine and in the Adjacent Regions*. Boston: Crocker and Brewster, 1856.

Romanoff, Paul. *Onomasticon of Palestine*. New York: American Academy of Jewish Research, 1937.

Roth, Cecil. *The Casale Pilgrim*. London: Soncino Press, 1919.

Runciman, Steven. *A History of the Crusades*. Cambridge: At the University Press, 1951.

Salmon, F. J. *Palestine of the Crusades*. A booklet to accompany map of the same name, drawn by the author and assisted by Pere Abel of the École Biblique in Jerusalem. Jaffa: 1937.

Sanday, William. *Sacred Sites of the Gospels*. Oxford: Oxford University Press, 1903.

Sandmel, Samuel. *Herod: Profile of a Tyrant*. Philadelphia: J. B. Lippincott Co., 1967.

Schubert, Kurt. *The Dead Sea Community: Its Origin and Teachings*. Translated by J. W. Doberstein. London: Adam & Charles Black, 1959.

Segal, J. B. *Edessa: The Blessed City*. Oxford: Clarendon Press, 1970.

Serao, Matilde. *In the Company of Jesus*. Translated by Richard Davey. London: Thomas Nelson & Sons, n.d.

Simons, J. *Jerusalem in the Old Testament*. Leiden: E. J. Brill, 1952.

Smail, R. *Crusading Warfare, 1097 and 1193*. Cambridge: At the University Press, 1956.

Smith, George Adam. *The Historical Geography of the Holy Land*. 15th ed. New York: A. C. Armstrong & Son, 1909.

——. *Jerusalem: The Topography, Economics and History from the Earliest Times to A.D. 70*. 2 vols. New York: A. C. Armstrong & Son, 1908.

Tenney, Merrill C., ed. *The Zondervan Pictorial Bible Dictionary*. Grand Rapids: Zondervan Publishing House, 1963.

Thomson, William M. *Central Palestine and Phoenicia*. The Land and the Book, vol. 2. Hartford, Conn.: S. S. Scranton Co., 1908.

Thompson, Edward. *Crusaders Coast*. London: Ernest Benn, 1929.

Toynbee, Arnold, ed. *The Crucible of Christianity: Judaism, Hellenism and the Historical Background to the Christian Faith*. London: Thames and Hudson, 1969.

Tristram, H. B. *The Land of Israel: A Journal of Travels in Palestine*. London: Society for Promoting Christian Knowledge, 1865.

Turnowsky, W., ed. *Tour Guide to Israel*. Tel Aviv: Litour, 1952.

Vilnay, Zev. *The Guide to Israel*. Jerusalem: Ahiever, 1968.

———. *The New Israel Atlas: Bible to Present Day*. Jerusalem: Israel University Press, 1968.

Vincent, L. H. *Jerusalem de L'Ancien Testament: Recherches d'Archeologie et d'Histoire*. Paris: Librarie Lecoffre, 1954.

Warren, C. and Conder, C. R. *Survey of Western Palestine and Jerusalem*. London: Palestine Exploration Fund, 1884.

Wiener, Harold M. "The Rama of Samuel." *Journal of the Palestine Oriental Society* (1927).

William, Archbishop of Tyre. *A History of Deeds Beyond the Sea*, vol. 2. Translated by E. A. Babcock and A. C. Krey. New York: Columbia University Press, 1943.

Wilson, Capt. Warren. *The Recovery of Jerusalem: A Narrative of Exploration and Discovery in the City and the Holy Land*. Edited by Walter Morrison. New York: D. Appleton & Co., 1871.

Wittek, P. *The Rise of the Ottoman Empire*. London: 1938.

Wilson, Edmund. *The Scrolls from the Dead Sea*. New York: Oxford University Press, 1955.

Wright, George Ernest and Filson, Floyd Vivian, eds. *The Westminster Historical Atlas to the Bible*. Philadelpha: Westminster Press, 1945.

Wright, Thomas, ed. *Early Travels in Palestine*. New York: KTAV Publishing House, 1948, 1968.

Index of Persons and Places

Index of Scripture References

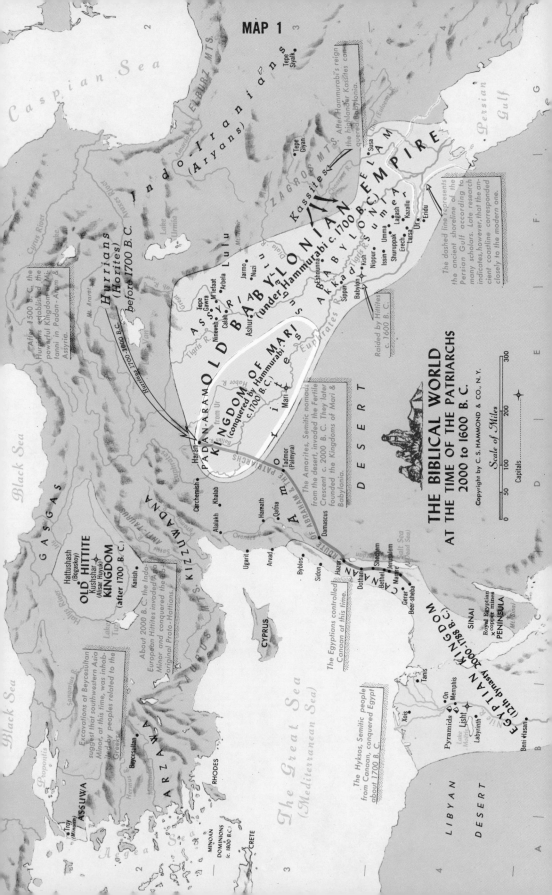

MAP 1

Caspian Sea

ELBURZ MTS.

Tepe Siyalk

Indo-Iranian (Aryans)

After 1500 B.C. the Hurrians established the powerful Kingdom of Mitanni in Padan-Aram & Assyria.

Hurrians (Horites)
before 1700 B.C.

Mt. Ararat

ZAGROS MTS.

Kassites

After Hammurabi's reign the highlander Kassites conquered Babylonia.

PERSIAN EMPIRE

Tepe Giyan

Susa

ELAM

Lulu

Eridu

The dashed line represents the ancient shoreline of the Persian Gulf according to many scholars. Late research indicates, however, that the ancient coastline corresponded closely to the modern one.

Persian Gulf

OLD BABYLONIAN (under Hammurabi c. 1700 B.C.)

SUMER

Tepe Gawra
Nineveh
M'lefaat
Jarmo
Nuzi
Arbela
Calah
Ashur
Tigris
ASSYRIA
Ur
 Eshnunna c. 1700 B.C.
AKKAD
Sippar
Babylon c. 1700 B.C.
Nippur
Issin
Umma
Shuruppak
Lagash
Erech
Larsa
Kazallu
Kish

Harran
PADAN-ARAM
KINGDOM OF MARI (conquered by Hammurabi c. 1700 B.C.)

from Ur

Habor R.

Mari

Amorites

The Amorites, Semitic nomads from the desert, invaded the Fertile Crescent c. 2000 B.C. They later founded the Kingdoms of Mari & Babylonia.

Hurrians 1700-1600 B.C.

Carchemish

Khalab

Alalakh

Qatna

Hamath

Tadmor (Palmyra)

DESERT

Damascus

ROUTE OF ABRAHAM

Ugarit

Arvad

Byblos

Sidon

Hazor

CANAAN

Shechem

Dothan

Bethel

Jerusalem

Mamre

Gerar

Beer-sheba

Salt Sea (Dead Sea)

The Egyptians controlled Canaan at this time.

**THE BIBLICAL WORLD
AT THE TIME OF THE PATRIARCHS
2000 to 1600 B.C.**

Copyright by C. S. HAMMOND & CO., N.Y.

Scale of Miles

0   50   100   200   300

Capitals ....

GASGAS

Hattushash (Bogaskoy)

OLD HITTITE KINGDOM
Kushshar (Alisar Huyuk) (after 1700 B.C.)

Kanish

Excavations at Beycesultan suggest that southwestern Asia Minor, at this time, was inhabited by peoples related to the Greeks.

About 2000 B.C. the Indo-European Hittites invaded Asia Minor and conquered the original Proto-Hatttians.

KIZZUWADNA

ANTI-TAURUS MTS.

TAURUS MTS.

ARZAWA

Beycesultan

ASSUWA

Troy (Minoan)

RHODES

CYPRUS

The Great Sea (Mediterranean Sea)

Aegean Sea

MINOAN DOMINIONS (c. 1600 B.C.)

CRETE

Black Sea

SINAI PENINSULA

Royal Egyptian copper mines x

Mt. Sinai

EGYPTIAN KINGDOM (12th dynasty 2000-1788 B.C.)

The Hyksos, Semitic people from Canaan, conquered Egypt about 1700 B.C.

Tanis

Xois

On

Memphis

Pyramids

Lisht

Lake Moeris

Labyrinth

Beni Hasan

LIBYAN DESERT

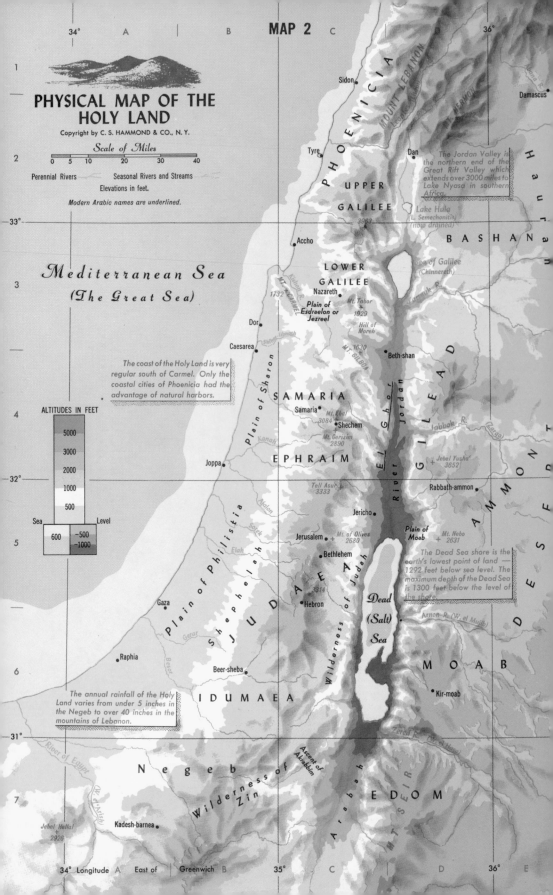

MAP 2

PHYSICAL MAP OF THE HOLY LAND

Copyright by C. S. HAMMOND & CO., N. Y.

Scale of Miles

0 5 10   20   30   40

Perennial Rivers   Seasonal Rivers and Streams
Elevations in feet.

Modern Arabic names are underlined.

ALTITUDES IN FEET

5000	
3000	
2000	
1000	
500	
Sea	Level
600	−500
	−1000

Mediterranean Sea
(The Great Sea)

The coast of the Holy Land is very
regular south of Carmel. Only the
coastal cities of Phoenicia had the
advantage of natural harbors.

The Jordan Valley is
the northern end of the
Great Rift Valley which
extends over 3000 miles to
Lake Nyasa in southern
Africa.

The Dead Sea shore is the
earth's lowest point of land —
1292 feet below sea level. The
maximum depth of the Dead Sea
is 1300 feet below the level of
the shore.

The annual rainfall of the Holy
Land varies from under 5 inches in
the Negeb to over 40 inches in the
mountains of Lebanon.

PHOENICIA

MOUNT LEBANON

Hauran

UPPER
GALILEE

Lake Hula
(L. Semechonitis)
(now drained)

BASHAN

LOWER
GALILEE

Sea of Galilee
(Chinnereth)

Plain of
Esdraelon or
Jezreel

Hill of
Moreh

GILEAD

SAMARIA

Plain of Sharon

EPHRAIM

El Ghor

River Jordan

AMMON

Plain of
Moab

JUDAEA

Plain of Philistia

Shephelah

Wilderness of Judah

Dead
(Salt)
Sea

DESERT

MOAB

IDUMAEA

Negeb

Wilderness of
Zin

Ascent of
Akrabbim

Arabah

EDOM

MT. SEIR

River of Egypt

Sidon

Tyre

Damascus

Dan

Accho

Nazareth
1732
Mt. Tabor
1929

Dor

1630
MT. GILBOA

Beth-shan

Caesarea

Samaria
Mt. Ebal
3084
Shechem
Mt. Gerizim
2890

Jebel Yusha'
3652

Joppa

Tell Asur
3333

Rabbath-ammon

Jericho

Mt. of Olives
2680

Mt. Nebo
2631

Jerusalem
Bethlehem

3314

Gaza

Hebron

Kir-moab

Raphia

Beer-sheba

Jebel Helal
2926
Kadesh-barnea

Arnon R. (W. el Mujib)

Zered R. (W. el Hesa)

34°   A   B   MAP 2   C   36°

34° Longitude   A   East of   Greenwich   B   35°   C   D   36°   E

MAP 3

THE NATIONS ACCORDING
TO GENESIS 10

Copyright by C. S. HAMMOND & CO., N.Y.

Scale of Miles

0   100   200   400   600

GOMER Descendents of Japheth   OPHIR Descendents of Shem
LUBIM Descendents of Ham

Descendents of Magog later inhabited this area.

Descendents of Gomer and Javan later inhabited this area.

Isles of the Gentiles

Descendents of Ham later inhabited this area.

Caspian Sea

Black Sea

Great Mediterranean Sea

Persian Gulf

Arabian Gulf (Red Sea)

PARTHIA

MADAI

MEDIA

ELAM

PERSIS

ASHKENAZ

CAUCASUS

MESHECH

TUBAL

TOGARMAH

ASHKENAZ

RIPHATH

GOMER

ASHKENAZ

ASIA MINOR

LYDIA

LUD

CILICIA

TARSHISH

KITTIM

CYPRUS

ASSHUR

ASSYRIA

MESOPOTAMIA

Tigris

Euphrates R.

NIMROD

SHINAR

BABYLONIA

ARPHAXAD

CHALDEA

MASH

HAVILAH

DEDAN

SEBA

SHEBA

RAAMAH

OPHIR

HAZARMAVETH

HAVILAH

UZAL

SHEBA

OPHIR

JOKTAN

ARABIA

ARABIAN DESERT

ARABIA DESERT

DEDAN

DEDAN

CANAAN

PHILISTINE PALESTINE

HETH

ARAM

SYRIA

TIRAS

THRACE

CRETE

CAPHTORIM

JAVAN

ELISHAH

THE

GREECE

TARSHISH

MIZRAIM

EGYPT

PATHRUSIM

PATHROS

Nile

Nile

LEHABIM

LUBIM

LIBYA

PHUT

CUSH

ETHIOPIA

AFRICA

EUROPE

MAP 4

CANAAN BEFORE THE CONQUEST

Copyright by C. S. HAMMOND & CO., N. Y.

Scale of Miles

0 5 10 20 30 40

Perennial Rivers ——
Seasonal Rivers & Streams — — —
Capitals .... ✛

Phoenicians from the cities of Sidon and Tyre traded throughout the Mediterranean.

Canaan at this time was an Egyptian province organized on a city-state system. The local kings were only required to pay tribute and to furnish labor for Egyptian royal projects.

The 13th and 12th century kingdoms of Bashan, Ammon, Moab and Edom displaced the Rephaim, Zuzim, Emim and Horites respectively.

The destroyed cities of Sodom and Gomorrah are believed to be beneath the shallow waters of the Dead Sea which now cover the Vale of Siddim (shaded portion).

The Great Sea

(Mediterranean Sea)

HITTITE EMPIRE
Ubi
Damascus

MOUNT LEBANON
Sidonians (Phoenicians)
MT. HERMON

Sidon
Zarephath
Tyre
Kanah
Misrephoth-maim
Achzib
Accho
Achshaph

Kedesh
Laish (Dan)
Hazor
Merom
Chinnereth
Madon

BASHAN (KINGDOM OF OG)
Karnaim
Ashtaroth

Sea of Chinnereth

MT. CARMEL
Shimron
Mt. Tabor
Jokneam
Dor
Megiddo
Taanach
Ibleam
Dothan
Sochoh

Canaanites

Yarmuk R.
Edrei
Ham
Ramoth-gilead

Beth-shan
Pella
Jabesh-gilead
Mahanaim

Tirzah
Shechem
Jacob's Well
Mt. Ebal
Mt. Gerizim

Succoth
Penuel (Peniel)
Adam

Jordan River
Jabbok R.

Aphek
Tappuah
Joppa
Ono
Lod

Bethel
Ai
Beeroth
Gibeon
Jericho
Gilgal

Gezer
Ekron
Chephirah
Kirjath-jearim
Jerusalem (Jebus, Salem)
Bethlehem

Jazer
Rabbath-ammon
Heshbon
Mt. Nebo (Pisgah)
Medeba

Ashdod
Ashkelon
Beth-shemesh
Makkedah
Libnah
Jarmuth
Adullam
Gath
Lachish
Eglon
Mamre
Kirjath-arba (Hebron)
Kirjath-sepher (Debir)
Hazeon-tamar (En-gedi)

Gaza (Azzah)

Gerar
Raphia
Sharuhen

Beer-sheba
Hormah
Arad

Salt Sea (Dead Sea)

Kiriathaim
Jahaz
Dibon
Aroer

AMMON

KINGDOM OF SIHON
Amorites

Plains of Moab

Arnon R.

Kir-moab (Kir-hareseth)
Ar

M O A B

Amalekites
Kenites
Hittites
Hivites
Jebusites

Rehoboth
Zoar

Ascent of Akrabbim

Wilderness of Zin

River of Egypt
Gerar
Besor

Bozrah
Oboth

E D O M

Kadesh-barnea (En-mishpat)
Punon

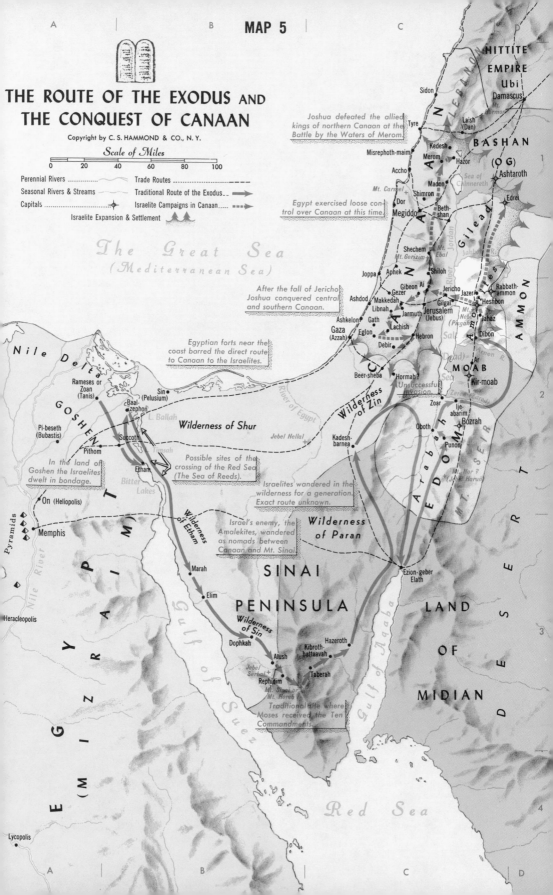

MAP 5

THE ROUTE OF THE EXODUS AND THE CONQUEST OF CANAAN

Copyright by C. S. HAMMOND & CO., N. Y.

Scale of Miles

0   20   40   60   80   100

Perennial Rivers ....
Seasonal Rivers & Streams ......
Capitals ....
Israelite Expansion & Settlement

Trade Routes ....
Traditional Route of the Exodus....
Israelite Campaigns in Canaan.....

The Great Sea
(Mediterranean Sea)

Joshua defeated the allied kings of northern Canaan at the Battle by the Waters of Merom.

Egypt exercised loose control over Canaan at this time.

After the fall of Jericho Joshua conquered central and southern Canaan.

Egyptian forts near the coast barred the direct route to Canaan to the Israelites.

In the land of Goshen the Israelites dwelt in bondage.

Possible sites of the crossing of the Red Sea (The Sea of Reeds).

Israelites wandered in the wilderness for a generation. Exact route unknown.

Israel's enemy, the Amalekites, wandered as nomads between Canaan and Mt. Sinai.

Unsuccessful invasion.

Traditional site where Moses received the Ten Commandments.

HITTITE EMPIRE
Ubi
Damascus

Sidon
Tyre
Laish (Dan)
BASHAN (OG)
Ashtaroth
Edrei

Kedesh
Merom
Hazor
Misrephoth-maim
Accho
Madon
Mt. Carmel
Shimron
Dor
Megiddo
Beth-shan
Gilead

Sea of Chinnereth

Shechem
Mt. Ebal
Mt. Gerizim
Shiloh

Joppa
Aphek
Gezer
Gibeon Ai
Jericho
Jazer
Rabbath-ammon
Gilgal
Heshbon
Ashdod
Makkedah
Libnah
Jarmuth
Jerusalem (Jebus)
Mt. Nebo (Pisgah)
Jahaz
Ashkelon
Gath
Lachish
Dibon
Gaza (Azzah)
Eglon
Hebron
Debir
AMMON

Beer-sheba
Hormah?
MOAB
Kir-moab
Wilderness of Zin
Zoar
Ije-abarim
Bozrah

Nile Delta
Rameses or Zoan (Tanis)
Sin (Pelusium)
Baal-zephon
L. Ballah
GOSHEN
Pi-beseth (Bubastis)
Succoth
Pithom
River of Egypt
Jebel Hellal
Wilderness of Shur
Kadesh-barnea
Oboth
Punon
On (Heliopolis)
Etham
Timsah
Bitter Lakes
Memphis
Pyramids
Nile River

EDOM
Mt. Hor? (Jebel Harun)
Wilderness of Etham
Marah
Elim
Wilderness of Paran
Ezion-geber Elath

Heracleopolis

SINAI PENINSULA

Wilderness of Sin
Dophkah
Alush
Kibroth-hattaavah
Hazeroth
Taberah
Jebel Serbal
Rephidim
Mt. Sinai or Mt. Horeb

LAND OF MIDIAN

Gulf of Suez
Gulf of Aqaba

Red Sea

Lycopolis

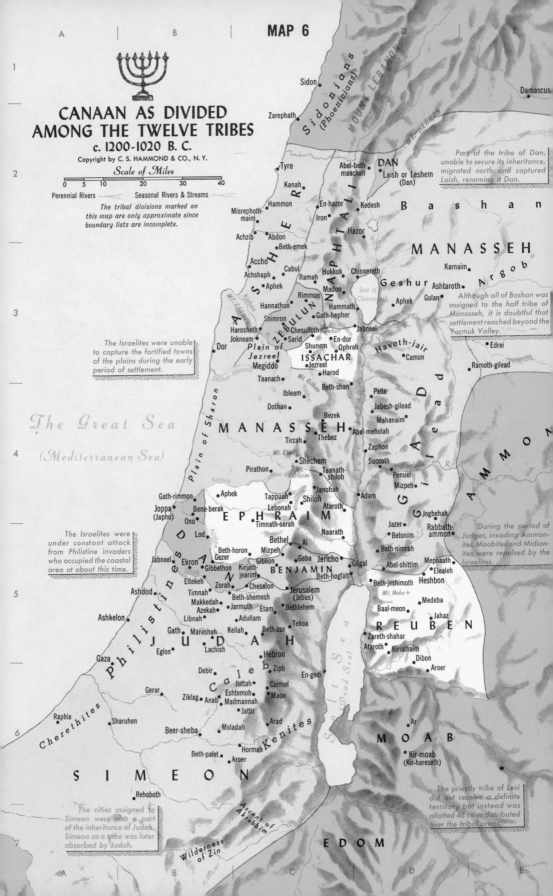

MAP 6

CANAAN AS DIVIDED AMONG THE TWELVE TRIBES
c. 1200-1020 B.C.

Copyright by C. S. HAMMOND & CO., N.Y.

Scale of Miles

0 5 10 20 30 40

Perennial Rivers   Seasonal Rivers & Streams

The tribal divisions marked on this map are only approximate since boundary lists are incomplete.

Part of the tribe of Dan, unable to secure its inheritance, migrated north and captured Laish, renaming it Dan.

The Israelites were unable to capture the fortified towns of the plains during the early period of settlement.

Although all of Bashan was assigned to the half tribe of Manasseh, it is doubtful that settlement reached beyond the Yarmuk Valley.

The Israelites were under constant attack from Philistine invaders who occupied the coastal area at about this time.

During the period of Judges, invading Ammonites, Moabites and Midianites were repulsed by the Israelites.

The cities assigned to Simeon were also a part of the inheritance of Judah. Simeon as a tribe was later absorbed by Judah.

The priestly tribe of Levi did not receive a definite territory but instead was allotted 48 cities distributed over the tribal areas.

The Great Sea
(Mediterranean Sea)

Damascus

Sidon
Zarephath
Tyre
Kanah
Hammon
Misrephoth-maim
Achzib
Accho
Achshaph
Aphek
Cabul
Ramah
Rimmon
Hannathon
Shimron
Harosheth
Jokneam
Dor
Megiddo
Taanach
Ibleam
Dothan

Abel-beth-maachah
En-hazor
Iron
Abdon
Beth-emek
Hukkok
Madon
Chesulloth
Sarid
Shunem
Jezreel
Harod
Beth-shan

DAN
Laish or Leshem (Dan)
Kedesh
Hazor
Chinnereth
Gath-hepher
Hammath
Tabor
En-dor
Ophrah

Bashan
MANASSEH
Karnaim
Geshur
Ashtaroth
Aphek
Golan
Havoth-jair
Camon
Edrei
Ramoth-gilead

Pella
Jabesh-gilead
Mahanaim
Abel-meholah
Zaphon
Succoth
Penuel
Mizpeh

ASHER
NAPHTALI
ZEBULUN
ISSACHAR
MANASSEH
GILEAD
Plain of Jezreel
Bezek
Thebez
Tirzah
Mt. Ebal
Shechem
Pirathon
Mt. Gerizim
Taanath-shiloh
Janohah
Adam

AMMON

Plain of Sharon

Aphek
Tappuah
Lebonah
Shiloh
Ataroth
Joppa (Japho)
Bene-berak
Ono
Timnath-serah
EPHRAIM
Lod
Bethel
Ai
Naarath
Jabneel
Ekron
Beth-horon
Gezer
Mizpeh
Geba
Jericho
Gilgal
Gibbethon
Gibeon
Kirjath-jearim
BENJAMIN
Beth-hoglah
Eltekeh
Zorah
Chesalon
Jerusalem (Jebus)
Ashdod
Timnah
Makkedah
Beth-shemesh
Jarmuth
Bethlehem
Azekah
Libnah
Adullam
Beth-zur
Tekoa
Ashkelon
Gath
Mareshah
Keilah
Gaza
Eglon
Lachish
Hebron
Ziph
En-gedi
Debir
Juttah
Carmel
Gerar
Eshtemoh
Maon
Ziklag
Anab
Madmannah
Jattir
Arad
Raphia
Sharuhen
Moladah
Beer-sheba
Beth-palet
Hormah
Aroer
Rehoboth

Jazer
Betonim
Beth-nimrah
Jogbehah
Rabbath-ammon
Abel-shittim
Mephaath
Elealeh
Heshbon
Beth-jeshimoth
Mt. Nebo
Medeba
Baal-meon
Jahaz
REUBEN
Zareth-shahar
Ataroth
Kiriathaim
Dibon
Aroer
Ar
MOAB
Kir-moab (Kir-haresheth)

Sea of Chinnereth

Salt Sea (Dead Sea)

Sidonians (Phoenicians)
MOUNT LEBANON
MT. HERMON

Mt. Carmel
Mt. Gilboa
Mt. Nebo

Yarmuk R.
Jabbok R.
Arnon R.

Philistines
Cherethites
JUDAH
Caleb
Kenites
SIMEON
EDOM
Wilderness of Zin
Ascent of Akrabbim

A   B   C   D   E

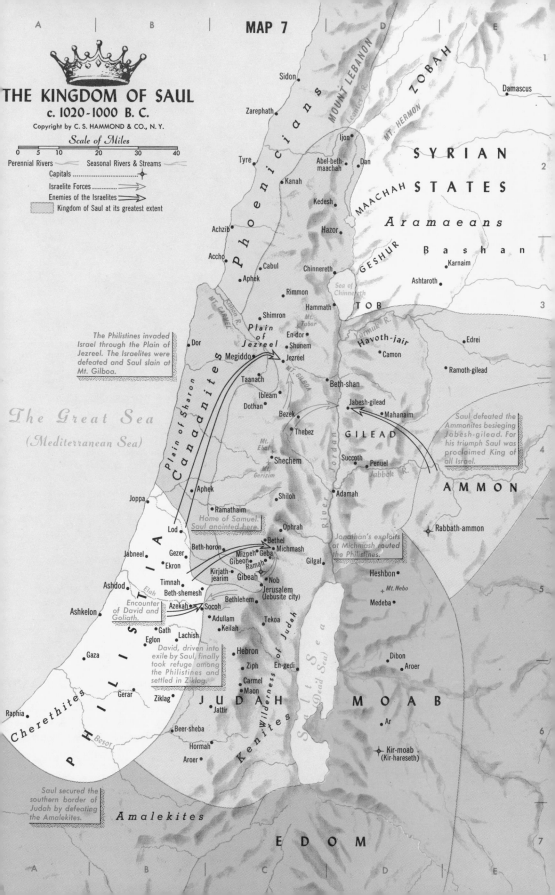

MAP 7

THE KINGDOM OF SAUL
c. 1020-1000 B.C.

Copyright by C. S. HAMMOND & CO., N. Y.

Scale of Miles

0 5 10 20 30 40

Perennial Rivers
Seasonal Rivers & Streams
Capitals ....
Israelite Forces ....
Enemies of the Israelites ——▶
Kingdom of Saul at its greatest extent

The Philistines invaded Israel through the Plain of Jezreel. The Israelites were defeated and Saul slain at Mt. Gilboa.

Saul defeated the Ammonites besieging Jabesh-gilead. For his triumph Saul was proclaimed King of all Israel.

Home of Samuel. Saul anointed here.

Jonathan's exploits at Michmash routed the Philistines.

Encounter of David and Goliath.

David, driven into exile by Saul, finally took refuge among the Philistines and settled in Ziklag.

Saul secured the southern border of Judah by defeating the Amalekites.

The Great Sea
(Mediterranean Sea)

ZOBAH
Damascus
SYRIAN STATES
Aramaeans
MOUNT LEBANON
MT. HERMON
MAACHAH
GESHUR
Bashan
TOB
GILEAD
Havoth-jair
AMMON
Rabbath-ammon
MOAB
EDOM
Amalekites
Cherethites
PHILISTIA
Canaanites
Plain of Sharon
Wilderness of Judah
Kenites
Salt Sea (Dead Sea)
JUDAH
Plain of Jezreel

Sidon
Zarephath
Tyre
Kanah
Achzib
Accho
Cabul
Aphek
Rimmon
Shimron
Dor
Megiddo
Taanach
Ibleam
Dothan
Bezek
Thebez
Aphek
Joppa
Ramathaim
Lod
Gezer
Beth-horon
Jabneel
Ekron
Timnah
Beth-shemesh
Ashdod
Azekah
Socoh
Ashkelon
Gath
Eglon
Lachish
Gaza
Gerar
Raphia
Ziklag
Jattir
Beer-sheba
Hormah
Aroer
Hebron
Ziph
Carmel
Maon
En-gedi
Adullam
Keilah
Tekoa
Bethlehem
Jerusalem (Jebusite city)
Nob
Gibeah
Kirjath-jearim
Ramah
Gibeon
Mizpeh
Geba
Michmash
Bethel
Ophrah
Gilgal
Adamah
Shiloh
Shechem
Mt. Ebal
Mt. Gerizim
Mt. Gilboa
Mt. Tabor
En-dor
Shunem
Jezreel
Beth-shan
Jabesh-gilead
Mahanaim
Succoth
Penuel
Heshbon
Mt. Nebo
Medeba
Dibon
Aroer
Ar
Kir-moab (Kir-haresheth)
Ijon
Abel-beth-maachah
Dan
Kedesh
Hazor
Chinnereth
Hammath
Sea of Chinnereth
Karnaim
Ashtaroth
Edrei
Ramoth-gilead
Camon
Jordan River
Jabbok R.
Yarmuk R.
Leontes R.
Besor
Elah
Kishon R.
Mt. Carmel
Phoenicians

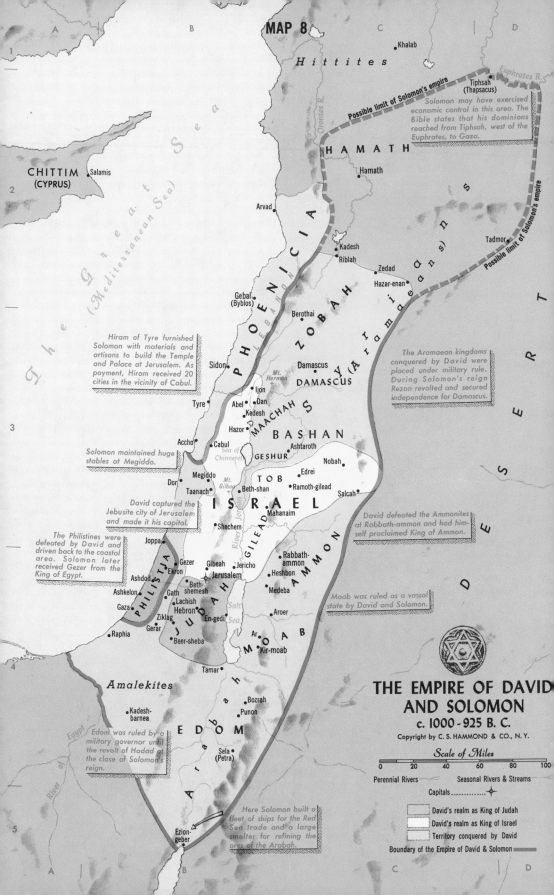

MAP 8

Hittites

• Khalab

Euphrates R.

Possible limit of Solomon's empire

Tiphsah
(Thapsacus)

Solomon may have exercised
economic control in this area. The
Bible states that his dominions
reached from Tiphsah, west of the
Euphrates, to Gaza.

HAMATH

• Hamath

CHITTIM
(CYPRUS)

• Salamis

The Great Mediterranean Sea

• Arvad

Possible limit of Solomon's empire

• Tadmor

• Kadesh
• Riblah
• Zedad

Hazar-enan

Gebal
(Byblos)

• Berothai

Z
O
B
A
H

Y
(A
r
a
m
a
e
a
n
s
)

The Aramaean kingdoms
conquered by David were
placed under military rule.
During Solomon's reign
Rezon revolted and secured
independence for Damascus.

PHOENICIA

Hiram of Tyre furnished
Solomon with materials and
artisans to build the Temple
and Palace at Jerusalem. As
payment, Hiram received 20
cities in the vicinity of Cabul.

• Sidon

• Damascus

DAMASCUS

Mt.
Hermon

D
E
S
E
R
T

• Tyre

• Ijon

Abel • • Dan

• Kedesh

M
A
A
C
H
A
H

BASHAN

• Hazor

• Ashtaroth

Solomon maintained huge
stables at Megiddo.

• Accho

• Cabul

Sea of
Chinnereth

GESHUR

• Nobah

T
O
B

• Edrei

• Megiddo

Mt.
Gilboa

• Beth-shan

• Ramoth-gilead

• Salcah

Dor • • Taanach

I S R A E L

G
I
L
E
A
D

David captured the
Jebusite city of Jerusalem
and made it his capital.

• Mahanaim

• Shechem

David defeated the Ammonites
at Rabbath-ammon and had himself proclaimed King of Ammon.

The Philistines were
defeated by David and
driven back to the coastal
area. Solomon later
received Gezer from the
King of Egypt.

• Joppa

• Gezer

• Rabbath-
ammon

A
M
M
O
N

• Ashdod

• Gibeah • Jericho

• Heshbon

• Ekron

Jerusalem

Beth-
shemesh

• Medeba

Moab was ruled as a vassal
state by David and Solomon.

• Ashkelon

PHILISTIA

Gath •

• Lachish

• Aroer

• Gaza

Hebron •

Salt
Sea

• Ziklag

En-gedi •

• Gerar

J
U
D
A
H

M
O
A
B

• Raphia

• Beer-sheba

• Ar

• Kir-moab

• Tamar

Amalekites

A
r
a
b
a
h

• Bozrah

THE EMPIRE OF DAVID
AND SOLOMON
c. 1000 - 925 B. C.

Copyright by C. S. HAMMOND & CO., N. Y.

• Punon

• Kadesh-
barnea

E
D
O
M

Edom was ruled by a
military governor until
the revolt of Hadad at
the close of Solomon's
reign.

River of Egypt

• Sela
(Petra)

Here Solomon built a
fleet of ships for the Red
Sea trade and a large
smelter for refining the
ores of the Arabah.

• Ezion-
geber

Scale of Miles

0   20   40   60   80   100

Perennial Rivers

Seasonal Rivers & Streams

Capitals ⸱⸱⸱⸱⸱⸱⸱⸱⸱⸱⸱⸱⸱ ✦

David's realm as King of Judah

David's realm as King of Israel

Territory conquered by David

Boundary of the Empire of David & Solomon ▬▬▬

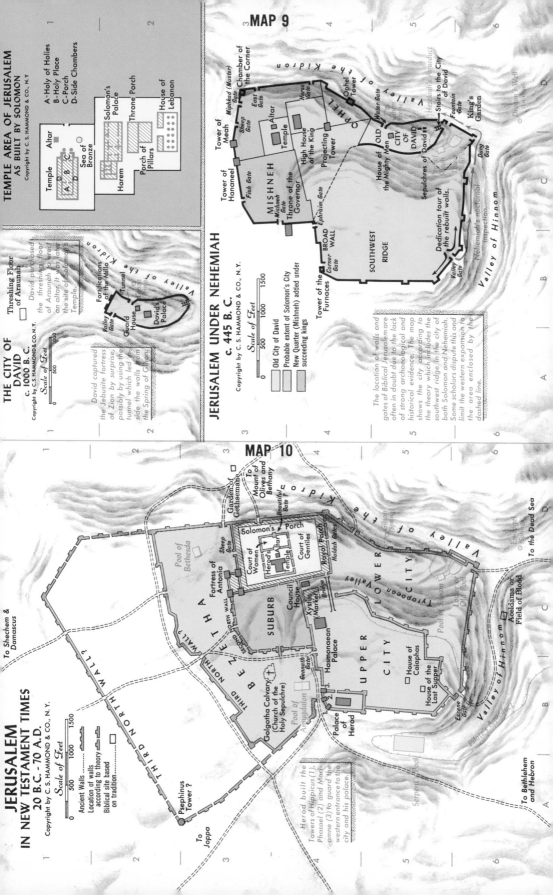

TEMPLE AREA OF JERUSALEM
AS BUILT BY SOLOMON

Copyright by C. S. HAMMOND & CO., N.Y.

A - Holy of Holies
B - Holy Place
C - Porch
D - Side Chambers

Temple
Altar

Sea of Bronze

Solomon's Palace

Throne Porch

House of Lebanon

Harem

Porch of Pillars

Threshing Floor of Araunah

David purchased the threshing floor of Araunah to erect an altar. It was later the site of Solomon's Temple.

THE CITY OF DAVID
c. 1000 B.C.

Copyright by C. S. HAMMOND & CO., N.Y.

Scale of Feet
0   500   1000

Valley of the Kidron

Fortifications of the Millo

Tunnel

Valley Gate

Guard House

David's Palace

David captured the Jebusite fortress of Zion by surprise, possibly by using the tunnel which led inside the walls from the Spring of Gihon.

MAP 9

Valley of the Kidron

Miphkad (Muster) Gate

Chamber of the Corner

Miphkad Gate

Horse Gate

Ophel Tower

East Gate

Water Gate

Hezekiah Aqueduct to the City of David

Tower of Meah

Sheep Gate

Altar

Temple

High House of the King

OPHEL

Stairs to the City of David

Tower of Hananeel

Fish Gate

MISHNEH

Mishneh Gate

Throne of the Governor

Projecting Tower

House of the Mighty Men

OLD CITY OF DAVID

Fountain Gate

King's Garden

Ephraim Gate

Sepulchres of David

Dragon's Well

Dung Gate

Broad Wall

BROAD WALL

Dedication tour of the rebuilt walls.

Nehemiah's nocturnal inspection.

Corner Gate

SOUTHWEST RIDGE

Valley Gate

Valley of Hinnom

Tower of the Furnaces

JERUSALEM UNDER NEHEMIAH
c. 445 B.C.

Copyright by C. S. HAMMOND & CO., N.Y.

Scale of Feet
0   500   1000   1500

Old City of David

Probable extent of Solomon's City

New Quarter (Mishneh) added under succeeding kings

The location of walls and gates of Biblical Jerusalem are often in doubt due to the lack of strong archaeological and historical evidence. The map shows the city according to the theory which includes the southwest ridge in the city of both Solomon and Nehemiah. Some scholars dispute this and limit the western expansion to the area enclosed by the dashed line.

MAP 10

To Shechem & Damascus

Garden of Gethsemane

To Mount of Olives and Bethany

Beautiful Gate ?

Solomon's Porch

Pool of Bethesda

Sheep Gate

Court of Women

Herod's Temple

Altar

Court of Gentiles

Valley of the Kidron

Gihon Spring

Fortress of Antonia

SECOND NORTH WALL

Royal Porch

Huldah Gates

BEZETHA

THIRD NORTH WALL

SUBURB

Council House

Xystus (Market)

Bridge

En-rogel

Lower or Old Pool

Tyropoeon Valley

UPPER CITY

LOWER CITY

To the Dead Sea

Golgotha Calvary (Church of the Holy Sepulchre)

Pool of Amygdalon

Genath Gate

Hasmonaean Palace

Serpent's Pool

House of Caiaphas

House of the Last Supper

Aceldama or Field of Blood

Palace of Herod

Essene Gate

Valley of Hinnom

Pilate's Aqueduct

JERUSALEM
IN NEW TESTAMENT TIMES
20 B.C. - 70 A.D.

Copyright by C. S. HAMMOND & CO., N.Y.

Scale of Feet
0   500   1000   1500

Ancient Walls

Location of walls according to theory

Biblical site based on tradition

Psephinus Tower ?

To Joppa

To Bethlehem and Hebron

Herod built the Towers of Hippicus (1), Phasael (2) and Mariamne (3) to guard the western entrance to the city and his palace.

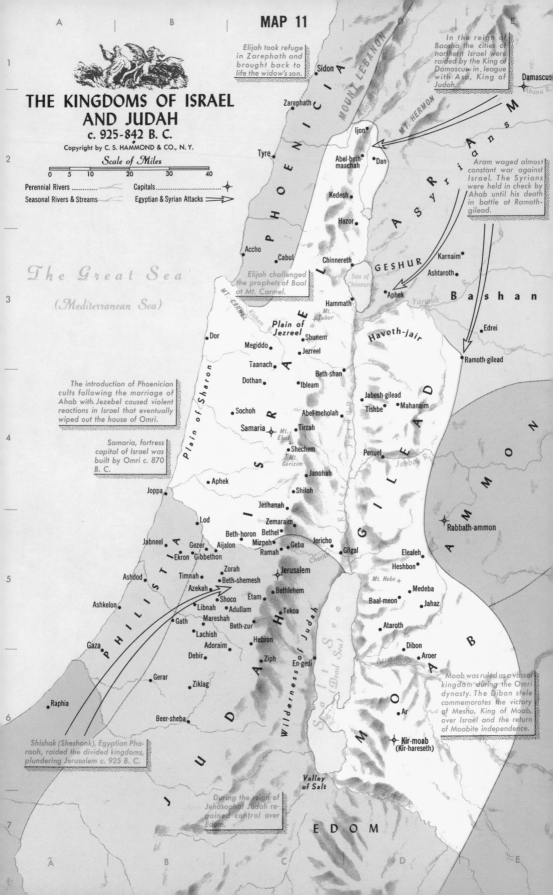

MAP 11

THE KINGDOMS OF ISRAEL AND JUDAH
c. 925-842 B.C.

Copyright by C. S. HAMMOND & CO., N.Y.

Scale of Miles

0   5   10   20   30   40

Perennial Rivers ....
Seasonal Rivers & Streams
Capitals ....
Egyptian & Syrian Attacks

Elijah took refuge in Zarephath and brought back to life the widow's son.

In the reign of Baasha the cities of northern Israel were raided by the King of Damascus in league with Asa, King of Judah.

Aram waged almost constant war against Israel. The Syrians were held in check by Ahab until his death in battle at Ramoth-gilead.

The introduction of Phoenician cults following the marriage of Ahab with Jezebel caused violent reactions in Israel that eventually wiped out the house of Omri.

Elijah challenged the prophets of Baal at Mt. Carmel.

Samaria, fortress capital of Israel was built by Omri c. 870 B.C.

Moab was ruled as a vassal kingdom during the Omri dynasty. The Dibon stele commemorates the victory of Mesha, King of Moab, over Israel and the return of Moabite independence.

Shishak (Sheshonk), Egyptian Pharaoh, raided the divided kingdoms, plundering Jerusalem c. 925 B.C.

During the reign of Jehoshaphat Judah regained control over Edom.

The Great Sea
(Mediterranean Sea)

MOUNT LEBANON
MT. HERMON
PHOENICIA
A S S Y R I A N S
GESHUR
Bashan
Havoth-jair
GILEAD
ISRAEL
Plain of Sharon
Plain of Jezreel
MT. CARMEL
PHILISTIA
JUDAH
Wilderness of Judah
Salt Sea (Dead Sea)
AMMON
MOAB
EDOM
Valley of Salt

Sidon
Zarephath
Tyre
Accho
Cabul
Dor
Megiddo
Taanach
Dothan
Sochoh
Samaria
Joppa
Aphek
Lod
Jabneel
Gezer
Aijalon
Ekron
Gibbethon
Ashdod
Timnah
Zorah
Ashkelon
Azekah
Beth-shemesh
Shoco
Gath
Libnah
Adullam
Mareshah
Beth-zur
Lachish
Hebron
Adoraim
Debir
Ziph
Gaza
Gerar
Ziklag
Raphia
Beer-sheba

Damascus
Ijon
Abel-beth-maachah
Dan
Kedesh
Hazor
Chinnereth
Sea of Chinnereth
Aphek
Karnaim
Ashtaroth
Edrei
Ramoth-gilead
Hammath
Mt. Tabor
Shunem
Jezreel
Beth-shan
Ibleam
Jabesh-gilead
Tishbe
Mahanaim
Abel-meholah
Tirzah
Shechem
Mt. Ebal
Mt. Gerizim
Penuel
Janohah
Shiloh
Jeshanah
Zemaraim
Beth-horon
Bethel
Mizpeh
Geba
Ramah
Jericho
Gilgal
Jerusalem
Bethlehem
Etam
Tekoa
En-gedi
Rabbath-ammon
Elealeh
Heshbon
Mt. Nebo
Medeba
Baal-meon
Jahaz
Ataroth
Dibon
Aroer
Ar
Kir-moab (Kir-haresheth)

Kishon
Yarmuk
Jabbok R.
River Jordan
Cherith
Arnon R.

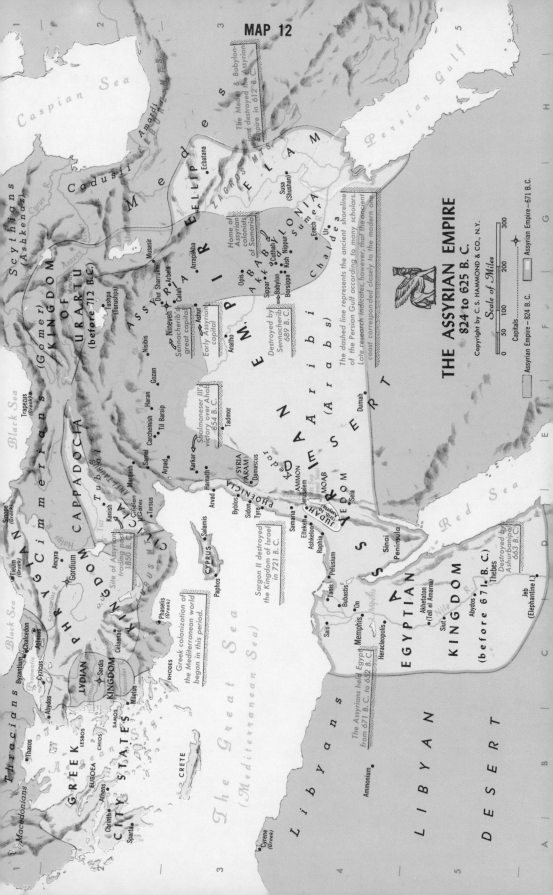

MAP 12

THE ASSYRIAN EMPIRE
824 to 625 B.C.

Copyright by C. S. HAMMOND & CO., N.Y.

The dashed line represents the ancient shoreline of the Persian Gulf according to many scholars. Late research indicates, however, that the ancient coast corresponded closely to the modern one.

Scale of Miles

0   50   100   200   300

Capitals.

Assyrian Empire – 824 B. C.   Assyrian Empire – 671 B.C.

Caspian Sea

Black Sea

Persian Gulf

The Great Sea
(Mediterranean Sea)

Red Sea

Scythians
(Ashkenaz)

Cadusii

M e d e s

The Medes & Babylonians destroyed the Assyrian Empire in 612 B.C.

Amardi

Ecbatana

E L L I P I

E L A M

Susa
(Shushan)

KINGDOM OF URARTU
(before 712 B.C.)

Tushpa
(Turushpa)

Musasir

Home of the Assyrian colonists of Samaria

B A B Y L O N I A

S u m e r

Erech

Ur

Nippur

Kish

Cuthah

Babylon

Borsippa

Sippar

Opis

Arrapakha

Arrapha

Calah

Arbela

Dur Sharrukin

Nineveh
Sennacherib's
great capital

Ashur
Early Assyrian
capital

Anatho

Destroyed by
Sennacherib
689 B. C.

A S S Y R I A N   E M P I R E

C h a l d e a

Nisibis

Gozan

Haran

Carchemish

Til Barsip

(Gomer) Cimmerians

CAPPADOCIA

Kanish

Site of an Assyrian
trading post
1850 B.C.

CILICIAN GATES
Cilician Gates

Tarsus

ANTI-TAURUS MTS.

Margash

Samal

Arpad

Shalmaneser III's
victory over Ahab
854 B. C.

Karkar

Hamath

Arvad

Tadmor

K e d a r

M E S O P O T A M I A

A r i b i   (Arabs)

Dumah

D E S E R T

SYRIA
(ARAM)

Damascus

PHOENICIA

Byblos

Sidon

Tyre

Samaria

Jerusalem

JUDAH

AMMON

MOAB

EDOM

Sela

Dead Sea

Red Sea

Sargon II destroyed
the Kingdom of Israel
in 721 B. C.

Eltekeh

Ashkelon

Raphia

Pelusium

Tanis

Bubastis

On

Memphis

EGYPTIAN
KINGDOM
(before 671 B.C.)

The Assyrians held Egypt
from 671 B.C. to 652 B.C.

Sais

Heracleopolis

Akhetaton
(Tell el Amarna)

Siut

Abydos

Thebes

Destroyed by
Ashurbanipal
663 B.C.

Jeb
(Elephantine I.)

LIBYAN
KINGDOM
(before 671 B.C.)

L I B Y A N S

Ammonium

Cyrene
(Greek)

CRETE

RHODES

Greek colonization of
the Mediterranean world
began in this period.

CYPRUS

Paphos

Salamis

Phaselis
(Greek)

Celaenae

Miletus

Samos

CHIOS

LESBOS

SAMOS

EUBOEA

Athens

Corinth

Sparta

GREEK
CITY STATES

GREEK STATES

Thasos

Abydos

Thracians

Macedonians

Byzantium

Chalcedon

Astacus

Cyzicus

Sinope
(Greek)

Trapezus
(Greek)

Teium
(Greek)

Ancyra

Gordium

PHRYGIAN KINGDOM

LYDIAN KINGDOM

Sardis

Sippylus

TAURUS MTS.

Tubal

ZAGROS MTS.

ARMENIAN HIGHLANDS

Caspian Gates

Halys R.

Sangarius R.

Cyrus R.

Araxes R.

Propontis

D E S E R T

MAP 13

Assyrian power in Syria at this time was limited, allowing minor states to flourish unmolested until the coming of Tiglath Pileser III.

A S S Y R I A N

E M P I R E

HAMATH

•Khalab

Euphrates R.

Orontes R.

•Karkar

Hamath•

•Tadmor
(Palmyra)

CHITTIM
(CYPRUS)

•Salamis

•Kition
(Phoenician
colony)

S Y R I A

•Arvad

•Kadesh

Zedad•

Hazar-enan•

Jeroboam restored the borders of Israel from the entry to Hamath to the Dead Sea as prophesied by Jonah.

The
Great
Sea
(Mediterranean Sea)

P H O E N I C I A

Gebal
(Byblos)•

•Berothai

KINGDOM
OF
DAMASCUS

Berytus•

L E B A N O N

Sidon•

Mt. Hermon

•Damascus

Damascus, weak from the Assyrian invasion of 805 B. C., was defeated by Joash of Israel and his son Jeroboam II.

Tyre•

•Ijon

Abel• •Dan

Kedesh•

Accho•

Hazor•

•Karnaim

•Aphek

B A S H A N

D E S E R T

Gath-hepher•

Dor• •Megiddo

I S R A E L

Taanach• •Ibleam

•Edrei

•Ramoth-gilead

Israel enjoyed outward prosperity and success but, as Amos depicted, was inwardly corrupt and wicked.

Samaria•

•Shechem

G I L E A D

A M M O N

Joppa•

Bethel•

•Gilgal

Rabbath-
ammon•

The Philistines were conquered by Azariah (Uzziah) King of Judah.

Jabneh• •Ekron

Ashdod•

•Gath

Ashkelon•

Jerusalem•

Tekoa•

Heshbon•

•Medeba

Gaza•

Lachish•

Hebron•

Dead
Sea

P H I L I S T I A

Gerar•

•Beer-sheba

J U D A H

•Ar

M O A B

Raphia•

Kir-moab•
(Kir-hareseth)

EGYPTIAN

•Bozrah

•Kadesh-
barnea

•Punon

KINGDOM

E D O M

A r a b a h

River of Egypt

•Sela

Azariah regained control of the Arabah and fortified Elath.

•Elath

ISRAEL AND JUDAH
AT THE TIME OF
JEROBOAM II
c. 785-745 B.C.

Copyright by C. S. HAMMOND & CO., N.Y.

Scale of Miles

0 20 40 60 80 100

Perennial Rivers   Seasonal Rivers & Streams
Capitals..........
Israel and areas   Judah and areas
governed by Israel   governed by Judah
Limits of territory under political
or economic control of Jeroboam II

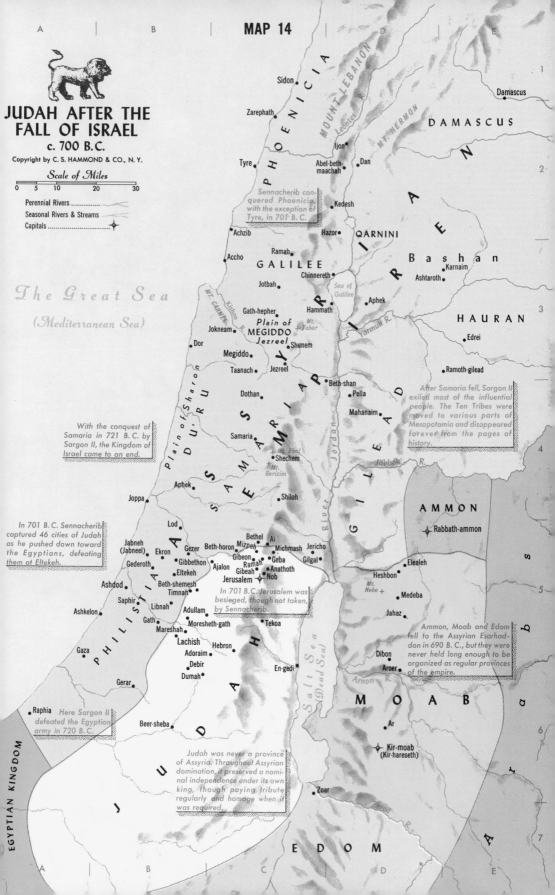

MAP 14

JUDAH AFTER THE FALL OF ISRAEL
c. 700 B.C.

Copyright by C. S. HAMMOND & CO., N. Y.

Scale of Miles

0 5 10 20 30

Perennial Rivers ....
Seasonal Rivers & Streams ....
Capitals ....

A   B   C   D   E

1
2
3
4
5
6
7

The Great Sea

(Mediterranean Sea)

PHOENICIA

MOUNT LEBANON

Leontes R.

MT. HERMON

DAMASCUS

Damascus

Sidon

Zarephath

Tyre

Ijon

Abel-beth-maachah

Dan

Kedesh

Achzib

Hazor

QARNINI

Bashan

Karnaim

Ashtaroth

Accho

Ramah

GALILEE

Chinnereth

Sea of Galilee

Aphek

HAURAN

Jotbah

Edrei

MT. CARMEL

Kishon R.

Gath-hepher

Hammath

Mt. Tabor

Plain of MEGIDDO

Jezreel

Shunem

Yarmuk R.

Ramoth-gilead

Jokneam

Dor

Megiddo

Taanach

Jezreel

Beth-shan

Pella

Plain of Sharon

DU-RU

Dothan

Mahanaim

River Jordan

GILEAD

Samaria

Mt. Ebal

Shechem

Mt. Gerizim

Jabbok R.

Aphek

Shiloh

AMMON

Rabbath-ammon

Joppa

Lod

Bethel

Ai

Michmash

Jericho

Elealeh

Jabneh (Jabneel)

Ekron

Gezer

Beth-horon

Mizpeh

Gibeon

Geba

Gilgal

Heshbon

Gederoth

Gibbethon

Eltekeh

Ajalon

Raman

Anathoth

Mt. Nebo

Medeba

Ashdod

Beth-shemesh

Gibeah

Jerusalem

Nob

Saphir

Timnah

Jahaz

Ashkelon

Libnah

Adullam

Moresheth-gath

Tekoa

Dibon

Gath

Mareshah

Salt Sea (Dead Sea)

Aroer

Gaza

Lachish

Hebron

Arnon R.

Adoraim

Debir

En-gedi

MOAB

Gerar

Dumah

JUDAH

Ar

Raphia

Kir-moab (Kir-hareseth)

Beer-sheba

Zoar

PHILISTIA

SAMARIA

EGYPTIAN KINGDOM

EDOM

Sennacherib conquered Phoenicia, with the exception of Tyre, in 701 B. C.

After Samaria fell, Sargon II exiled most of the influential people. The Ten Tribes were moved to various parts of Mesopotamia and disappeared forever from the pages of history.

With the conquest of Samaria in 721 B.C. by Sargon II, the Kingdom of Israel came to an end.

In 701 B.C. Sennacherib captured 46 cities of Judah as he pushed down toward the Egyptians, defeating them at Eltekeh.

In 701 B.C. Jerusalem was besieged, though not taken, by Sennacherib.

Ammon, Moab and Edom fell to the Assyrian Esarhaddon in 690 B. C., but they were never held long enough to be organized as regular provinces of the empire.

Here Sargon II defeated the Egyptian army in 720 B.C.

Judah was never a province of Assyria. Throughout Assyrian domination, it preserved a nominal independence under its own king, though paying tribute regularly and homage when it was required.

MAP 15

GREAT EMPIRES OF THE SIXTH CENTURY B.C.

Copyright by C. S. HAMMOND & CO., N.Y.

Scale of Miles

0 100 200 300 400 500

Capitals •

Limits of the Persian Empire c. 500 B.C.

Persian Royal Road

Red Sea-Nile Canal Built by Darius I

The Persians under Cyrus the Great overthrew the Medes, conquered Lydia and Babylonia to fulfill the prophecy of Daniel.

Darius I extended the Persian Empire into Europe. Attempts to subjugate Greece by Darius and Xerxes I failed as the Greeks won at Marathon and Salamis.

The Edict of Cyrus (538 B.C.) allowed the Jews to return to their homeland.

The rise of the New Babylonian (Chaldean) Empire brought an end to the kingdom of Judah and exile to her people.

Pharaoh Necho defeated Josiah but was later driven out of Palestine after being defeated at Carchemish (605 B.C.).

Egypt came under Persian rule after Cambyses defeated Psamtik III at Pelusium in 525 B.C.

A L A N S

S c y t h i a n s

ILLYRIA

EPIRUS

MACEDONIA

THRACE

Apollonia

Byzantium

Chalcedon

Bithynia

PAPHLAGONIA

Sinope

COLCHIS

Phasis

Trapezus

Panticapaeum

Chersonesus

Olbia

Black Sea (Pontus Euxinus)

Ister R. (Danube)

Thermopylae

GREECE

Marathon

Athens

Salamis

Sparta

CRETE

RHODES

Ephesus

Miletus

Sardis

KINGDOM OF LYDIA (670-546 B.C.)

PHRYGIA

PISIDIA

Ancyra

Pteria

CAPPADOCIA

Tarsus

CILICIA

CYPRUS

Mediterranean Sea

Halys R.

Carchemish

Haran

Thapsacus

Arvad

Byblos

Sidon

Tyre

Damascus

Tadmor

Megiddo

Jerusalem

JUDAH

Gaza

Pelusium

Tahpanhes

Sais

On

Memphis (Noph)

Naucratis

Ammonium

KINGDOM OF EGYPT (26th DYNASTY 663-525 B.C.)

Libyans

Cyrene

Barca

Elath

Syene (Elephantine)

Pathros

Thebes (No)

Red Sea

E T H I O P I A (CUSH)

Nile River

Mediterranean Sea

ARABIA

NEW BABYLONIAN EMPIRE (625-539 B.C.)

Sippar

Babylon

Nippur

Erech

Opis

ELAM

Susa (Shushan) (SUSIANA)

Erech

Persian Gulf

PERSIS

Persepolis

Pasargadae

Aspadana

Utians

CARMANIA

GEDROSIA (MAKA)

Paricanians

Pactyans

ARACHOSIA

Drangiana

Sagartians

Sarangians

PARTHIA

ARIA

Rhagae

Amardi

Rhage

Behistun

Arbela

Ecbatana (Achmetha)

Urmia L.

Tigris R.

Euphrates R.

ASSYRIA

Cadusii

MEDIA (625-550 B.C.)

ARMENIA

Caucasus Mts.

Caspian Sea (Mare Hyrcanium)

HYRCANIA

Dahae

MARGIANA

CHORASMIA

Aral Sea

Jaxartes R.

Oxus R.

Massagetae (Scythians)

Saka

SOGDIANA

Maracanda (Samarkand)

Bagae

Bactra

BACTRIA

Hindu Kush

GANDARA

Taxila

Indus R.

Probable old course of Indus R.

Pattala

Present shoreline

Arabian Sea

I N D I A

M E D I A N   E M P I R E

P E R S I A N   E M P I R E

MAP 16

THE RESTORATION OF JUDAH
c. 445 B.C.

Copyright by C. S. HAMMOND & CO., N. Y.

Scale of Miles

0 5 10 20 30 40

Perennial Rivers ———
Seasonal Rivers & Streams ———
Route of the Returning Exiles ⟶

After Cyrus the Persian issued a decree permitting the exiles to return to their homeland in 538 B. C., many exiles took the long journey back to Judah.

In 458 B. C. (398 B. C.?) Ezra led a group of the exiles back to Judah to reform conditions there according to the laws of God.

Judah was a small province in the Fifth Persian Satrapy which extended from the borders of Syria and Cilicia to the borders of Egypt, including all Phoenicia, Palestine, Syria and Cyprus.

In 445 B. C. Nehemiah led a group of exiles to Judah to rebuild the walls and gates of Jerusalem.

Lod, Ono and Hadid were Jewish cities outside the province of Judah.

After the reformation in Judah, the priests became the dominating power and influence among the Jews. They kept the Jews a distinct race by forbidding marriage with other tribes and peoples.

Sheshbazzar, who brought with him from Babylon the sacred vessels carried away by Nebuchadnezzar, started the rebuilding of the Temple in Jerusalem. The Temple was completed by Zerubbabel in 515 B. C.

The Edomites were driven north from their land into the southern half of the old territory of Judah by the Arabs.

The Great Sea
(Mediterranean Sea)

PHOENICIANS
MOUNT LEBANON
MT. HERMON
From Babylonia
Aramaeans

Sidon
Damascus
Tyre
Leontes R.
Dan
Kedesh
Hazor
Accho
GALILEE
Bashan
KARNAIM
Karnaim
MT. CARMEL
Kishon R.
Sea of Galilee
Mt. Tabor
Yarmuk R.
Dor
Megiddo
Megiddo
Edrei
Jezreel
Beth-shan
Ramoth-gilead
Pella
Plain of Sharon
DOR
SAMARIA
GILEAD
River Jordan
Samaria
Shechem
Mt. Gerizim
Jabbok R.
Joppa
Ono
Neballat
Lod
Hadid
Mizpeh
Bethel
Ai
Michmash
Jericho
Rabbath-ammon
Ekron
Gezer
Beth-horon
Gibeon
Geba
Gilgal
AMMON
Emmaus
Ramah
Anathoth
Chephirah
Nob
Zareah
Kirjath-jearim
Jerusalem
Heshbon
Zanoah
Beth-haccherem
JUDAH
Azekah
Jarmuth
Bethlehem
Medeba
Adullam
Tekoa
Keilah
Lachish
Beth-zur
Ashdod
PHILISTINES
ASHDOD
Ashkelon
Hebron
Gaza
En-gedi
Dibon
Arnon R.
Gerar
Ziklag
En-rimmon
Raphia
Jeshua
IDUMAEA
Edomites
MOAB
Moladah
Beer-sheba
Kir-moab
(Kir-hareseth)
Beth-phelet
Salt Sea (Dead Sea)
Arabs
Zered R.
Arabs

MAP 17

THE EMPIRE OF
ALEXANDER THE GREAT
323 B.C.
AND THE KINGDOMS OF
ALEXANDER'S SUCCESSORS
c. 305 B.C.

Scale of Miles
0   100 200 300 400 500

Alexander's Route
Nearchus' Voyage
Major Battles Fought by Alexander

Prior to the Battle
of Ipsus 301 B.C.

Kingdom of Antigonus Cyclops
Kingdom of Seleucus
Kingdom of Ptolemy
Kingdom of Lysimachus

Alexander after succeeding
his murdered father, strengthened
his kingdom in Macedonia and in
334 B.C. crossed the Hellespont
with an army of about 35,000 men.

Alexander defeated the western satraps
of Darius III at the Granicus R. near Zeleia.

At Gaugamela in 331 B.C. Alexander
defeated the reorganized Persian army.
Darius fled to Media and was later
slain by his own men.

After defeating Darius III at
Issus Alexander occupied Phoenicia, Judaea and Egypt.

Alexander founded
the city of Alexandria
in 332 B.C. He visited
the oracle of Ammon
and was told of his
divine origin.

Alexander died
at Babylon, June 13,
323 B.C., after a
short illness.

Persepolis
was looted
and burned
by Alexander
in 331 B.C.

Alexander subdued
the eastern
Persian satrapies after a long and
difficult campaign. At Maracanda
Alexander killed his friend Cleitus.

Alexander
gave up the
advance beyond the
Hyphasis R.

Seleucus ceded
Alexander's east-
ern provinces
to Sandrapottus
for 500
war elephants
(307 B.C.)

While Nearchus
explored the Arabian
Sea, Alexander made
the difficult overland
march to return to
Babylon.

ILLYRIA
EPIRUS
MACEDONIA
Pella
THESSALONICA
Thessalonica
THRACE
Getae
Olbia
SCYTHIANS
Panticapaeum
Tanais R. (Don)
Borysthenes R.
Dnieper R.
Black Sea
Byzantium
BITHYNIA
Heraclea
PONTUS
Sinope
Trapezus
COLCHIS
ARMENIA
PAPHLA-
GONIA
Ancyra
CAPPADOCIA
Mazaea
PHRYGIA
Zelea
Ilium
MYSIA
Sardis
LYDIA
Ephesus
CARIA
Miletus
RHODES
CRETE
Athens
Sparta
HELLAS
Aegean Sea
Mediterranean Sea
CYPRUS
PISIDIA
LYCIA
CILICIA
Tarsus
Issus
Antioch (300 B.C.)
PHOENICIA
Tyre
Damascus
SYRIA
Thapsacus
Euphrates R.
MESOPOTAMIA
Nisibis
Arbela
Gaugamela
Ninus
Seleucia (Opis)
Tigris R.
Babylon
BABYLONIA
Susa
SUSIANA
MEDIA
Ecbatana
Rhagae
Caspian Gates
PARTHIA
HYRCANIA
Hecatompylus
Caspian Sea
(Mare Hyrcanium)
Chorasmii
Aral Sea
CAUCASUS
Cyrus R.
Jerusalem
Petra
Nabataeans
JUDAEA
Gaza
Pelusium
Memphis
EGYPT
Alexandria
Ammonium
LIBYAN
DESERT
Cyrene
CYRENAICA
LIBYA
Red Sea
Nile River
Syene
Thebes
Ptolemais
Persian Gulf
PERSIS
Persepolis
PERSIA
331
324
Carmania
CARMANIA
Harmozia
Pura
GEDROSIA
DRANGIANA
Prophthasia
ARIA
Alexandria Ariorum (Herat)
BACTRIA
Bactra
Bagae
Oxus R.
SOGDIANA
Maracanda (Samarkand)
Alexandria Eschate
Jaxartes R.
Dahae
Massagetae
Sakas
INDIA
Alexandria
ARACHOSIA
Alexandria Arachosiorum
Taxila
Bucephala
Nicaea
Hydaspes R.
Acesines R.
Hydraotes R.
Hyphasis R.
Indus R.
Pattala
Present shoreline
Arabian Sea

ILLUSTRATION

MAP 18

PALESTINE UNDER THE MACCABEES
166 TO 63 B.C.

Copyright by C. S. Hammond & Co., N.Y.

Scale of Miles

| 0 | 5 | 10 | 20 | 30 | 40 |

Perennial Rivers
Seasonal Rivers & Streams
Capitals ....

GROWTH OF MACCABEAN JUDAEA

Judaea at the start of the revolt, 166 B.C.
Acquisitions under Jonathan, 161-142 B.C.
Acquisitions under Simon, 142-134 B.C.
Acquisitions under John Hyrcanus, 134-104 B.C.
Acquisitions under Aristobulus I, 104-103 B.C.
Acquisitions under Alexander Jannaeus, 103-76 B.C.

Maximum extent of the Maccabean dominions ———

Territorial expansion under the Maccabees was not a steady process. Internal strife and the nature of guerrilla warfare limited Maccabean control.

The Great Sea
(Mediterranean Sea)

SELEUCID EMPIRE

The Maccabaean revolt arose from the attempt of the Seleucid monarch, Antiochus IV (Epiphanes) to force Hellenization upon the Jews.

Sidon
Damascus

MOUNT LEBANON
COELE SYRIA
I T U R A E A

Tyre
Panias
MT. HERMON

Ladder of Tyre
Cades (Kedesh)

Mageth
Raphon

PHOENICIA

Hazor
Carnaim
Bosor

Ptolemaïs (Accho)
Site of Tryphon's treacherous seizure of Jonathan.

Magdala
Arbela
Water of Genesar (Sea of Galilee)
Gamala

GALILEE
Mt. Tabor
Hippos
Dion

Philoteria
Abila
G I L E A D

Dora (Dor)
Gadara
Edrei

Plain of Esdraelon
Ephron

Strato's Tower
Scythopolis (Beth-shan)
Pella
Mizpeh
Gerasa

Besieged and razed by John Hyrcanus.
SAMARIA
John Hyrcanus destroyed the Samaritan Temple on Mt. Gerizim.
Asophon
Ragaba

Apollonia
Samaria
Amathus
Death place of Alexander Jannaeus.

Capharsaba
Shechem
Mt. Gerizim

Pharathon
Alexandrium
A M M O N

Original home of the Maccabees or "Hasmonaeans."
Jazer
Philadelphia (Rabbath-ammon)

Joppa
Ramathaim
Gophna
Ephraim
Dok

Beth-dagon
Adida (Hadid)
Mt. Azotus
Modin
Beeroth
Bethel
Michmash
Jericho

Lydda (Lod)
Gazara (Gezer)
Elasa
Mizpeh
Jamnia (Jabneh)
Beth-horon
Adasa
Heshbon
Samaga

Ekron
Capharsalama
Medeba

Cedron
Emmaus (Nicopolis)
Khirbet Qumran
JUDAEA

In 63 B.C. Jerusalem fell before the forces of Pompey and Judaea came under Roman control.
Jerusalem

Azotus (Ashdod)
Timnah
Bethlehem
Beth-zacharias
Tekoa

Ascalon (Ashkelon)
Free City State
Adullam
Machaerus

Anthedon
PHILISTIA
Marisa (Mareshah)
Beth-zur
En-gedi
Dibon

Gaza
Adora
Hebron
Arnon R.

I D U M A E A
Gerar
Masada
Kir-moab (Kir-haresheth)

Raphia
Arad

Salt Sea (Dead Sea)

Machaerus

Feast of Hanukkah is celebrated by the Jews in memory of the cleansing of the Temple by Judas Maccabaeus.

N A B A T

ACRABATHANE

MAP 19

THE ROMAN WORLD
IN THE TIME OF CAESAR
60 TO 44 B.C.

Copyright by C. S. HAMMOND & CO., N.Y.

Scale of Miles

0   100 200   400   600

Roman territory at the beginning
of the 1st Triumvirate—60 B.C.

Dependencies and client kingdoms

Limits of Roman control at

Territory acquired under the
Triumvirate and Caesar

Major battles fought by Caesar

MAP 20

PALESTINE IN THE TIME OF CHRIST

Copyright by C. S. HAMMOND & CO., N.Y.

Scale of Miles

0 5 10   20   30   40

Perennial Rivers ....
Seasonal Rivers & Streams ......
Capitals ....
Roads & Trade Routes _____

- Tetrarchy of Lysanias
- Tetrarchy of Philip
- Tetrarchy of Herod Antipas
- Territory under Roman procurator
- Areas tributary to Salome
- Decapolis *
- Independent *
- Roman province of Syria

Cities of the Decapolis........

* The Decapolis and Ascalon retained
their independence under the Roman
governor of the province of Syria.

Archelaus, upon Herod's death, became ruler of Judaea, Samaria and Idumaea. His reign lasted until 6 A.D. when he was removed and exiled. His territory then was placed under a Roman procurator.

Salome, Herod's sister, was given Jamnia, Azotus and Phasaelis. They, in turn, passed to Livia, wife of Augustus and then to Emperor Tiberius.

The Great Sea

(Mediterranean Sea)

ABILENE
Abila

Sidon

PHOENICIA

MOUNT LEBANON

Sarepta
(Zarephath)

MT. HERMON

Damascus

ITURAEA

Tyre

PANIAS

Dan · Caesarea Philippi

TRACHONITIS

Ladder
of Tyre

Cadasa
(Kedesh)

ULATHA

Lake
Semechonitis

GAULANITIS

BATANAEA

BASHAN

Gischala

Raphana

Ptolemais
(Accho)

Horns of Hattin
(Kurûn Hattin) is a
possible site of the
Sermon on the Mount.

Chorazin

Bethsaida
(Julias)

Seleucia

Jotapata
Cana

Sepphoris

GALILEE

Magdala
(Dalmanutha)

Capernaum

Tabigha

Gergesa

Gamala

Dion

AURANITIS

Edrei

Hippos

Nazareth

Tiberias

Philoteria

Abila

Gadara

Capitolias

Mt. Tabor

Plain of
Esdraelon

Nain

Bethabara

DECAPOLIS

Dora

En-gannim
(Ginaea)

Scythopolis
(Beth-shan)

Pella

Gerasa

GILEAD

Caesarea
Residence of
Roman procurators.

SAMARIA

Samaria
(Sebaste)
Mt. Ebal

Amathus

Shechem
Mt. Gerizim

Sychar
Jacob's Well

Apollonia

Plain of Sharon

Antipatris

PERAEA

Joppa

Phasaelis

Archelais
Ephraim

Beth-nimrah

Philadelphia
(Rabbath-ammon)

Lydda
(Diospolis)

Arimathaea
(Ramathaim)

Gophna

Gezer
(Gazara)

Bethel

Jericho

Julias
(Livias, Beth-haram)

Heshbon

Jamnia

Ramah

Emmaus

Mt. of Olives

The Dead Sea Scrolls
were found in a cave
here; also the ruins of
an Essene monastery.

Ekron

Nicopolis
(Emmaus)

Emmaus

Jerusalem

Bethany

Khirbet
Qumran

Azotus (Ashdod)

Bethlehem

Herodium

Callirhoe

Ascalon

JUDAEA

Mareshah
(Marisa)

Hebron

Wilderness of Judah

Salt Sea

Machaerus

Here John the Baptist
was imprisoned and
beheaded by order
of Herod Antipas.

Gaza

Ziph

En-gedi

Dibon

Juttah

Carmel

Gerar

Masada

Rabbath Moab
(Areopolis, Rabba)

Raphia

Beersheba

IDUMAEA

Kir-moab
(Kir-haresheth)

NABATAEANS

ARABIA

MAP 23

ILLYRICUM (DALMATIA)

MOESIA

THRACE

Pontus Euxinus (Black Sea)

Rome • Ortona
Three Taverns •
Appii • Beneventum
Forum • Neapolis
Puteoli • Buxentum
Tarentum
Anxa

ITALY

Brundisium

Scodra

Dyrrhachium

MACEDONIA

Philippi
Amphipolis • Neapolis
Berea • Apollonia
Thessalonica

EPIRUS

Corcyra

Larisa

Mesembria

Byzantium
Nicomedia
Nicaea

Heraclea
Pontica

Amastris

Germanico-
polis

Sinope

Amisus

PONTUS

Paphlagonia

BITHYNIA

Ancyra

Amasia

Zela

Sebastia

Tavium

GALATIA

Caesarea
Mazaca

CAPPADOCIA

Troas
Assos
Adramyttium
LESBOS
Mitylene
Pergamum
Mysia
Thyatira
Sardis
Smyrna Philadelphia
CHIOS Ephesus Hierapolis
Laodicea
Miletus Colossae
SAMOS Caria
Trogyllium
CYCLADES
Cnidus
COOS

Dorylaeum

ASIA

Lydia

Pessinus

Antioch

Lycaonia
Iconium
Lystra
Derbe

Pisidia
Phrygia

Tyana

Starting point
of 1st & 2nd
journeys

Nicopolis
ACHAIA
Athens
Corinth
Cenchrea
(GREECE)
Sparta

Tyrrhenian
Sea

SICILY
Agrigentum
Syracuse

Messana •
Rhegium •
Croton

MELITA
(MALTA)

RHODES

Perga
Attalia
PAMPHYLIA
LYCIA
Xanthus Myra
Selinus
Patara

CILICIA
Tarsus

Seleucia

Antioch

SYRIA

CYPRUS
Salamis
Paphos

Phenice
CRETE
CLAUDA
Cydonia
Cnossus
Lasea
C. Salmone

Fair Havens

The Great Sea

(Mediterranean Sea)

In the past it was believed that
Paul visited the Galatian cities of
Pessinus, Ancyra and Tavium.
Modern scholars doubt this.

Damascus
Phoenicia • Sidon
Tyre
Ptolemais • Galilee

Caesarea
Joppa •
Jerusalem
Gaza • Judaea

Limit of Roman Empire

ST. PAUL'S FIRST AND SECOND JOURNEYS

Copyright by C. S. HAMMOND & CO., N.Y.

Scale of Miles

0 50 100   200   300

First Journey   Second Journey

Catabathmus

Marmarica
Paraetonium

Libya

PHAROS

Alexandria

EGYPT

Pelusium

ARABIA

Memphis
Heliopolis

Nile R.

MAP 24

ILLYRICUM (DALMATIA)

MOESIA

THRACE

Pontus Euxinus (Black Sea)

Rome • Ortona
Three Taverns •
Appii • Beneventum
Forum • Neapolis
Puteoli • Buxentum
Tarentum
Anxa

ITALY

Brundisium

Scodra

Dyrrhachium

MACEDONIA

Philippi • Neapolis
Amphipolis
Berea • Apollonia
Thessalonica

EPIRUS

Corcyra

Larisa

Mesembria

Byzantium
Nicomedia
Nicaea

Heraclea
Pontica

Amastris

Germanico-
polis

Sinope

Amisus

PONTUS

Paphlagonia

BITHYNIA

Ancyra

Amasia

Zela

Sebastia

Tavium

GALATIA

Caesarea
Mazaca

CAPPADOCIA

Troas
Assos
Adramyttium
LESBOS
Mitylene
Pergamum
Mysia
Thyatira
Sardis
Smyrna Lydia Philadelphia
CHIOS Ephesus Hierapolis
Laodicea
Miletus Colossae
SAMOS Caria
Trogyllium
CYCLADES Cnidus
COOS

Dorylaeum

ASIA

Pessinus

Antioch

Lycaonia
Iconium
Lystra
Derbe

Pisidia
Phrygia

Tyana

Starting
point of
3rd journey

Nicopolis
ACHAIA
Athens
Corinth
Cenchrea
(GREECE)
Sparta

Tyrrhenian
Sea

SICILY
Agrigentum
Syracuse

Messana •
Rhegium •
Croton

MELITA
(MALTA)

RHODES

Perga
PAMPHYLIA
Attalia
LYCIA
Xanthus Myra
Selinus
Patara

CILICIA
Tarsus

Seleucia
Antioch

SYRIA

CYPRUS
Salamis
Paphos

Phenice
CRETE
CLAUDA
Cydonia
Cnossus
Lasea
C. Salmone

Fair Havens

The Great Sea

(Mediterranean Sea)

An ancient tradition states that
Paul traveled extensively throughout the Mediterranean world after
his journey to Rome.

Damascus
Phoenicia • Sidon
Tyre
Ptolemais • Galilee

Caesarea
Joppa •
Jerusalem
Gaza • Judaea

Starting point of
journey to Rome

Limit of Roman Empire

ST. PAUL'S THIRD JOURNEY AND HIS JOURNEY TO ROME

Copyright by C. S. HAMMOND & CO., N.Y.

Scale of Miles

0 50 100   200   300

Third Journey   Journey to Rome

Catabathmus

Marmarica
Paraetonium

Libya

PHAROS

Alexandria

EGYPT

Pelusium

ARABIA

Memphis
Heliopolis

MAP 25

During in the 7th cent. the Christian Church introduced Nestorian Christianity into Central Asia.

The Christian Coptic Church was introduced on the Upper Nile and in Ethiopia in the 4th cent.

Christianity in Roman Britain was wiped out by the Anglo-Saxon invasion. The faith was reestablished in the 7th cent. by Irish missionaries.

THE SPREAD OF CHRISTIANITY

Copyright by C. S. HAMMOND & CO., N.Y.

Scale of Miles

0   100   200   300   400   500

INTRODUCTION OF CHRISTIANITY

Areas known to contain Christians at the time of Irenaeus, c. 185

185-325 (by the time of Constantine)

325-600 (by the time of Gregory I)

600-800 (by the time of Charlemagne)

800-1300

Northern limit of area permanently lost to Mohammedanism. --------

Russians (989-1015)

Lithuanians (13th Cent.)

Prussians (13th Cent.)

Pomeranians (1122-1130)

Poles (962-1025)

Czechs (c. 1000)

Magyars (950-1050)

Saxons (785-805)

Thuringians (8th Cent.)

Alemanni (7th Cent.)

IRELAND

BRITAIN

GAUL

SPAIN

ITALY

ARMENIA

EGYPT

CRETE

CYPRUS

RHODES

SICILY

SARDINIA

CORSICA

BALEARIC IS.

Clonard
York
Lincoln
London
Canterbury
Cadbury
Utrecht
Bremen
Magdeburg
Marienburg
Gnesen
Riga
Cologne
Fulda
Mainz
Trier
Reims
Rouen
Paris
Nantes
Tours
Bourges
Lyons
Vienne
Marseille
Arles
Narbonne
Toulouse
Bordeaux
Tarragona
Saragossa
Leon
Astorga
Merida
Evora
Faro
Cadiz
Toledo
Cordova
Seville
Malaca
Cartagena
Valencia
Lixus
Caesarea
Cirta
Madaura
Lambaesis
Hippo Regius
Carthage
Hadrumetum
Leptis Magna
Milan
Augsburg
Regensburg
Genga
Pisa
Florence
Verona
Aquileia
Ravenna
Ancona
Rome
Puteoli
Naples
Beneventum
Messina
Syracuse
Salona
Siscia
Sirmium
Singidunum
Esztergom
Preslav
Sardica
Philippi
Thessalonica
Beroea
Larissa
Nicopolis
Athens
Corinth
Sparta
Gortyna
Cnossus
Durazzo
Tomi
Chersonesus
Anchialus
Develtum
Constantinople
Nicaea
Nicomedia
Chalcedon
Amastris
Sinope
Pityus
Pergamum
Troas
Thyatira
Sardis
Smyrna
Ephesus
Laodicea
Myra
Paphos
Salamis
Paga
Iconium
Ancyra
Antioch
Vagarshapat
Melitene
Nisibis
Arbela
Ctesiphon
Seleucia
Ephesa
Tarsus
Caesarea
Tyre
Damascus
Palmyra
Jerusalem
Alexandria
Memphis
Hermopolis
Oxyrhynchus
Ptolemais
Thebes
Cyrene
Berenice
Kiev

Caspian Sea
Black Sea
Mediterranean Sea
Red Sea
North Sea
Baltic Sea
Atlantic Ocean
Sea of Azov
Don R.
Volga R.
Dnieper
Danube
Tigris R.
Euphrates
Meander

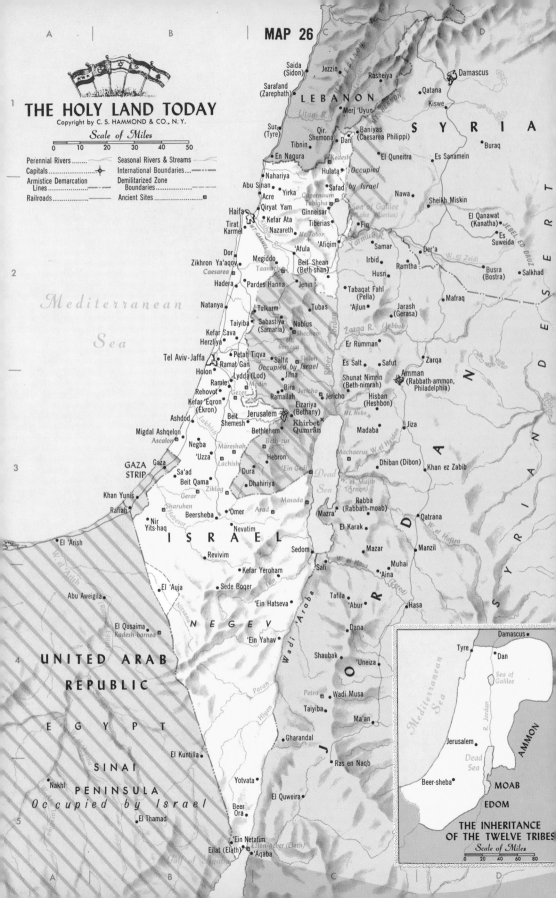

MAP 26

THE HOLY LAND TODAY

Copyright by C. S. HAMMOND & CO., N.Y.

Scale of Miles

0   10   20   30   40   50

Perennial Rivers ....
Capitals ....
Armistice Demarcation
 Lines ....
Railroads ....

Seasonal Rivers & Streams
International Boundaries...
Demilitarized Zone
 Boundaries ....
Ancient Sites ....

Mediterranean Sea

LEBANON

S Y R I A

Saida (Sidon)
Jezzin
Rasheiya
Damascus
Qatana
Kiswe
Sarafand (Zarephath)
Merj 'Uyun
Qir. Shemona
Baniyas (Caesarea Philippi)
Buraq
Sur (Tyre)
Tibnin
Dan
El Quneitra
Es Sanamein
En Nagura
Kedesh
Hulata
Occupied by Israel
Nawa
Sheikh Miskin
El Qanawat (Kanatha)
Nahariya
Abu Sinan
Yirka
Capernaum Tabgha
Safad
Fig
Es Suweida
Acre
Qiryat Yam
Ginneisar
Sea of Galilee (Lake Tiberias)
Haifa
Kefar Ata
Tiberias
Der'a
JEBEL ED DRUZ
Tirat Karmel
Nazareth
Mt. Tabor
'Afiqim
Samar
Busra (Bostra)
Salkhad
Dor
'Afula
Irbid
Ramtha
Mafraq
Zikhron Ya'aqov
Megiddo
Beit Shean (Beth-shan)
Husn
Caesarea
Taanach
Jenin
Tabaqat Fahl (Pella)
Hadera
Pardes Hanna
'Ajlun
Jarash (Gerasa)
Natanya
Tulkarm
Tubas
Taiyiba
Sabastiya (Samaria)
Nablus
Er Rumman
Kefar Sava
Herzliya
Shechem
Mt. Gerizim
Es Salt
Safut
Zarqa
Tel Aviv-Jaffa
Ramat Gan
Salfit
Shiloh
Shunat Nimrin (Beth-nimrah)
Amman (Rabbath-ammon, Philadelphia)
Holon
Petah Tiqva
Jifna
Occupied by Israel
Lydda (Lod)
Modin
Bira
Jericho
Hisban (Heshbon)
Ramle
Gezer
Ramallah
Eizariya (Bethany)
Jiza
Rehovot
Kefar 'Eqron (Ekron)
Beit Shemesh
Jerusalem
Khirbet Qumran
Madaba
Mt. Nebo
Ashdod
Bethlehem
Migdal Ashqelon
Ascalon
Mareshah
Beth-zur
Machaerus
W. el Heidan
Dhiban (Dibon)
Khan ez Zabib
Negba
'Uzza
Lachish
Hebron
'Ein Gedi
Gaza
GAZA STRIP
Sa'ad
Dura
Dhahiriya
Dead Sea
W. el Mujib (Arnon)
Khan Yunis
Beit Qama
Ziklag
Masada
Rabba (Rabbath-moab)
Rafiah
Gerar
Sharuhen
Habesor
Beersheba
'Omer
Arad
Mazra'
El Karak
Qatrana
Nir Yits-haq
Nevatim
Sedom
Mazar
Manzil
I S R A E L
Revivim
Safi
Aina
Muhai
El 'Arish
W. el Hasa
W. el Hafira
Kefar Yeroham
Tafila
'Abur
Hasa
Abu Aweigila
Sede Boqer
'Ein Hatseva
Dana
El Qusaima
Kadesh-barnea
N E G E V
'Ein Yahav
Shaubak
'Uneiza
UNITED ARAB
REPUBLIC
Petra
Wadi Musa
Taiyiba
Ma'an
E G Y P T
Gharandal
S I N A I
El Kuntilla
Ras en Naqb
Nakhl
P E N I N S U L A
Occupied by Israel
Yotvata
El Quweira
Beer Ora
'Ein Netafim
Eilat (Elath)
Ezion-geber (Elath)
'Aqaba

THE INHERITANCE OF THE TWELVE TRIBES

Scale of Miles

0   20   40   60   80

Damascus
Tyre
Dan
Sea of Galilee
Mediterranean Sea
R. Jordan
Jerusalem
AMMON
Dead Sea
Beer-sheba
MOAB
EDOM